for Peter,
with best birthday
wishes, and affection,
from Brian

Terence Rattigan

you could always
Fungus it!

TERENCE RATTIGAN
The Man and His Work

Michael Darlow and Gillian Hodson

QUARTET BOOKS
LONDON MELBOURNE NEW YORK

First published by Quartet Books Limited, 1979
A member of the Namara Group
27 Goodge Street, London W1P 1FD

Copyright © 1979 by Michael Darlow and Gillian Hodson

ISBN 0 7043 2160 2

Printed in Great Britain by Billing & Sons Limited,
Guildford, London and Worcester

FOR SCOTT

Contents

Acknowledgements

We wish particularly to acknowledge the help of the late Sir Terence Rattigan, who gave us permission to write his life story and without whose help it would have been impossible to complete this book. Although mortally ill and in continuous pain he gave generously of his time, telling us many things we did not know and advising us about the best people to contact for the truth behind many events in his life.

We would also like to thank Sir Terence's agent, Michael Imison, who throughout the almost two years that we have been working on this project has given us unstinting help and encouragement, providing us with information and documents and never failing to respond with good humour to the demands we have repeatedly made on his time and patience.

We acknowledge the help of the British Broadcasting Corporation, who gave permission to quote from broadcasts made by Sir Terence and others. This book came about as the result of a BBC Television programme, and we owe a special debt of gratitude to James Cellan Jones and Graham Benson—Head of Plays and the producer responsible for the programme—not only for starting us on the road that led to this book, but for continuing to encourage and help us long after the television programme was completed. Others in the BBC to whom we owe special thanks are

9

Kathy Sykes, Judy Shears and the unfailingly helpful staffs of the BBC's book, newspaper cuttings, record and script libraries.

We are grateful for the generous permission from authors and publishers to quote from works listed in the bibliography and specifically acknowledged in the text. In particular we are grateful to Hamish Hamilton and Dr Jan van Loewen Ltd for permission to quote from his published plays and prefaces. In addition, we would like to thank the following institutions for help during our research: the British Library, Islington Public Library, New York Public Library Theatre Collection, the Registrar of Births, Marriages and Deaths at Somerset House, the Imperial War Museum, the British Film Institute, Harrow School, Sandroyd School, Thames Television, ATV and *The Spotlight*. Raymond Mander and Jo Mitchenson have been tireless in answering our many queries.

We would like to pay special tribute to Miss Holly Hill, the young American critic and champion of Terence Rattigan's work. During her researches for a doctoral dissertation for the City University of New York between 1974 and 1977 she had access to certain papers of Sir Terence's which have since become dispersed and so were not available to us. With Sir Terence's permission she generously turned over to us her original research notes, plus records of conversations with Sir Terence. These proved invaluable. She also allowed us to draw on ideas contained in her dissertation. Sir Terence's work has been even more undervalued in the United States than in Britain, and Miss Hill has almost single-handedly blazed a trail in that country for a proper re-evaluation of his work. Her dissertation, 'A Critical Analysis of the Plays of Sir Terence Rattigan' (1977), can be obtained through University Microfilms International; and while our views do not necessarily always coincide, it is our hope that the insights contained in her work may reach a wider audience.

It is perhaps invidious to single out any names from the legion of Sir Terence's many friends and professional colleagues who have given unstintingly of their time and memories. However, we cannot fail to mention just four who have been especially helpful to us: Adrian Brown, Peter Glenville, John Perry and David Heimann (son of the co-author of Rattigan's first performed play, *First Episode*, with whose permission we have quoted from the unpublished text of this play).

We owe continuing thanks to David Wilson for reading, improving, pruning and making many helpful suggestions to our manuscript, and to Sophie Darlow for typing much of our first draft. To both we owe thanks for their patience in putting up with us in our single-minded pursuit of the project through the long months of its gestation. We would also like to thank Liz Beecham for typing our final manuscript.

Last, but by no means least, we would like to thank Naim Attallah, without whose prompting we would never have started this book and without whose continuing infectious enthusiasm we would never have completed it.

Michael Darlow, Gillian Hodson
London, February 1979

Introduction

Late in 1976, we were asked by the BBC to make a television programme about Sir Terence Rattigan. It was known that Sir Terence was seriously ill with cancer and was not expected to live long. Our first move was to ask the efficient BBC Library service to furnish us with all the books and serious articles about him and his work. It was then that we discovered, to our amazement, that there was no book about him. There were very few articles either, and most of those had been written at least fifteen years previously. We soon realized that the dearth of serious assessments of the life and work of the playwright who for so many years had dominated the British theatre, for good or ill, was symptomatic of the quite unreasonable critical disdain with which he was treated for almost the whole of his career.

We discovered, too, that those who had attempted to take Rattigan's work seriously in the last few years were themselves treated with the same derisive dismissal as had so often been experienced by Rattigan himself. We will give just two examples from many; one from each side of the Atlantic.

In 1973, Frank Dunlop, Artistic Director of the Young Vic, suggested that his company should revive Rattigan's first successful comedy, *French Without Tears*. He described the reaction to this proposal:

They thought I must be mad. I put it to the Arts Council, who had hysterics. They said, 'You've got to be mad. This is just trash.'

But I remembered seeing a production of *French Without Tears* and finding it very entertaining. Then I read it, and found it absolutely smashing—wonderfully constructed, very funny, and very moving because all of the characters are very, very true. In it you see people behaving the way you did when you were young and felt desperate about a lot of things ...

I thought the play just as relevant in 1973 as when Rattigan had written it almost forty years before. The hero is fighting to write and get out of his social class and into contact with other people. That is still very relevant in England—breaking out of one's class, doing some sort of job, making connections between people from different strata of society. Rattigan does it very delicately and implicitly, rather than with some big message.

Dunlop told that story to Holly Hill, an American who was preparing a dissertation on the plays of Terence Rattigan for her PhD at Columbia University. She had suffered similar rebuffs. When, in 1969, she suggested Rattigan as the subject of her master's thesis and PhD dissertation to her professor, who was, incidentally, British, she was curtly dismissed: 'Nobody takes Rattigan seriously.'

Our growing irritation at what, during the course of our work for the BBC, we had come to believe was an injustice to Rattigan's reputation prompted us to talk to a publisher, the chairman of Quartet Books, Naim Attallah. He, being in our view more enlightened than either Miss Hill's professor or the officials of the Arts Council with whom Frank Dunlop had dealt, shared our surprise and outrage, and that is how this book came to be written.

From what we have said it might be supposed that we have set out to write a critical book about Rattigan's work, aimed at promoting a re-assessment. In fact, that is only a part of our intention. There are others far better qualified than ourselves for that task, and, in any case, Holly Hill has now made a useful start in filling the critical breach. We hope others, who may enjoy wider publication than she has yet received, will follow.

On starting work at the BBC, we had re-read all of Rattigan's

14

plays, published and unpublished, and viewed all his films and television plays that we could lay our hands on. From the evidence of his work alone we began to suspect a striking and perhaps distinctive relationship between his life and his writing. Investigation, especially of the less well-known aspects of his life which did not fit the public image of the unruffled, establishment-minded English gentleman, tended to confirm this. Rattigan himself had said that if a playwright was honest he had to admit that he was 'compelled' to write the same play over and over again. That did not sound like the cool craftsman of conventional opinion, but it did accord with the evidence of the plays themselves.

We knew too of the reflections of another playwright, David Rudkin, quoted by Anthony Curtis in a radio programme on Rattigan.[1] Rudkin had written:

> I detect in his plays a deep personal, surely sexual pain, which he manages at the same time to express and disguise. The craftsmanship of which we hear so much loose talk seems to me to arise from deep psychological necessity, a drive to organize the energy that arises out of his own pain. Not to batten it down but to invest it with some expressive clarity that speaks immediately to people, yet keeps himself hidden. I really think the Aunt Edna business and the ethic of the well-made play are but the most outward social manifestations of this and because it is possible if one is very innocent, inattentive or self-dishonest, to sit right through a Rattigan play and not have the ghost of an idea what is going on ... I think Rattigan is not at all the commercial middlebrow dramatist his image suggests but someone peculiarly haunting and oblique who certainly speaks to me with resonance of existential bleakness and irresoluble carnal solitude.

Early in our work Anthony Curtis told us that Rattigan had confirmed the truth of what Rudkin had detected.

We became convinced that not only was there a special relationship between Rattigan's life and its visible reflection in his work, but that understanding more about his life would aid a full appreciation of his plays. Although this conviction informed the way in which we shaped our television programme, it was not an idea that could be adequately developed within the confines of a one-hour programme which was almost certain to be Rattigan's obituary. For that we needed the freedom and space of a book.

We recognize that, even in a book, by invading some areas of Rattigan's private life that afforded him great pain we may be airing a subject which many of his most sincere admirers may think better concealed. We believe, however, that these matters have to be brought out, not only in the interests of honest biography and the appreciation of a major dramatist whose principal subject was the difficulty and pain of love and sex, but also for the sake of that very understanding and tolerance which Rattigan devoted his talents to advocating. The private misery of Rattigan's own life, as much as his plays, is an indictment of the prejudice and repression that still pervade so much of our society. Rattigan's recurring theme is the need for an end to concealment and emotional repression, and the substitution of self-awareness and the opportunity for self-expression. We are therefore in no doubt that in our attempt to honour and promote Rattigan's own ideals we have a duty to try to understand him as he really was, even if some people may think that thereby we bring to light things that they might prefer left unsaid.

Note:

1   Rattigan's Theatre. Radio Three, 30 March 1976.

I
Entrances

Saturday, 10 June 1911 was wet and blustery. A long spell of sweltering heat had ended abruptly the day before. A rain storm had settled the eye-pricking dust of London's pavements and soaked those taking part in the full-scale rehearsal of the Coronation. George the Fifth was to be crowned in twelve days' time.

Most of the visitors who already thronged the capital were relieved at the sudden drop in temperature, but not Frank Rattigan, home on leave from North Africa, nor the royal guest who had been put in his charge for the duration of the celebrations—Sid Menebhi, ex-Grand Vizier of Morocco. Frank Rattigan was thirty, on his own admission an unconventional diplomat, with a brilliant career before him. For four years he had been on the staff of the British Legation in Tangier; an important position because Morocco had recently been the focus of international tension between the French and the Germans.

It was typical of Frank Rattigan that in taking leave with his beautiful young wife Vera in May 1911 he should combine professional advantage with domestic convenience. Many other British colonial administrators, diplomats and officers serving overseas arranged their annual leave that year to coincide with the Coronation. Unlike Frank Rattigan, however, few of them managed to get themselves a role in the ceremony itself. Escorting

17

his Arab charge to meet Lord Derby, the Duke of Rutland and senior officials at the Foreign Office was good for Frank Rattigan's career; accompanying him to the ball at Derby House, playing tennis with him at Belvoir Castle, with Lady Anglesey and the seventeen-year-old Lady Diana Duff-Cooper, helped his social standing; arranging the provision of amenable young ladies for the Grand Vizier's off-duty hours (the demands of visiting Arab potentates have not altered) provided him with the opportunity to indulge his own taste for fluffy blondes.

Frank and Vera Rattigan had been married for five and a half years. She was only seventeen at the time of the wedding, which took place while Frank was on the staff of the British Embassy in the Hague. At first Vera had been nervous of the social duties entailed in being a diplomat's wife, but being a girl of energy and character, she entered easily into her husband's hectic life. With the help and guidance of other wives in the diplomatic circle in the Hague, she soon mastered the complex etiquette and rules governing the round of functions and entertaining that made up diplomatic existence in the capitals of Europe. Frank was lax in these matters almost to the point of eccentricity. While on the embassy staff in Vienna he had sent other dancers flying at a court ball in honour of the Prince of Wales by a wild performance of the polka when partnering Princess Mary. On another occasion he had been rebuked by the court Chamberlain for dancing a Boston with the daughter of an Ambassador when the orchestra had been playing a waltz. In breach of every rule of etiquette Frank Rattigan had sneaked away from the ballroom on yet another state occasion because he was bored by the slow rigidity of the dancing. In the refreshment room he was joined by an Austrian, resplendent in a General's uniform, who asked him why he was not dancing. He replied, with undiplomatic honesty, that he was bored. The General, whom Rattigan did not recognize, laughed and suggested an inspection of the palace's collection of sporting trophies might be more amusing. The identity of the General, who was by then showing Frank Rattigan round the gun rooms, was only revealed when an aide-de-camp clicked his heels and approached them saying: 'Your Imperial Highness, some of the important guests are about to leave!' The 'General' had been Frank Rattigan's host, the Archduke himself.[1]

Vera provided a steadying influence on Frank. She was also an

18

asset in her own right. A striking beauty, blonde and vivacious, she was well able to hold her own in the most exalted company. She was an instant favourite with the royal families of each of the countries to which they were posted.

Both Vera and Frank came from distinguished families of Irish lawyers. Frank's grandfather, Bartholomew Rattigan, seems to have moved from County Kildare in the 1840s to practise as an advocate in India. His son William in turn practised at the bar in India, becoming the greatest authority of his day on Indian law and publishing numerous books on the subject. He also produced a short book entitled *Events to be Remembered in the History of India From the Invasion of Alexander to the Latest Times*. In his first chapter, he said he was trying to rescue the story of Alexander from 'the enveloping dark and filmy haze of mythological story', an enterprise to be undertaken later by his grandson Terence, in his own, rather different, way. At the time of Frank's birth, William Rattigan was Chief Justice of the Punjab. When he retired with a knighthood and returned to Britain, Sir William became member of parliament for North-East Lanarkshire. Another Rattigan, Sir Henry Adolphus Rattigan, followed in his footsteps and became Chief Justice of the Punjab.

In spite of the social position they had achieved, the Rattigans were not wealthy. Frank's father, Sir William, believed in the virtues of self-reliance. When he was six, Frank, who spent his early childhood in India, was presented by his father with a saloon rifle and a daily ration of six cartridges and told to roam about and fend for himself. Later, as a young man studying for the Diplomatic entry exam at a crammer in France, Frank was short of money, and kept himself in funds by winning a weekly sweepstake on a pigeon-shooting competition at the local country club. Frank, who undoubtedly loved and respected his father, would in his turn expect the same self-reliance and ingenuity from his sons Brian and Terence.

There was nothing in either Frank's or Vera's family background that would have led anyone to expect that their second child would turn out to be a dramatist. The only evidence of an interest in the theatre was on Vera's side of the family, and that was tenuous. Her family, the Houstons, included a professor of political economy at Trinity College, Dublin—Arthur H. Houston. He was a noted authority on English drama and in 1863 gave a public lecture, which was subsequently published, entitled 'The English Drama—Its Past History and Probable Future'. The lecture contained one sentiment which his descendant Terence Rattigan would endorse a century later: 'The highest type of dramatic composition is that which supplies us with studies of character, skilfully worked out, in a plot not deficient in probability and by means of incidents not wanting in interest.' However, Arthur Houston's prognosis for the future of drama was not encouraging—he predicted that the drama would 'languish as a literary production' and that 'whatever power of depicting character and describing incidents as exists today ... will be diverted into novel-making.'

The Rattigans' first child, Brian, had arrived after three years of marriage. He had been born with a deformity in one leg. A major reason for the Rattigans' return to England on leave in 1911 was that Vera was due to be delivered of a second child that summer. It seems improbable that Frank Rattigan was present when his second son, Terence Mervyn Rattigan, was born on that wet Saturday, 10 June, as he was much taken up with his official duties and preparations for his minor role in the Coronation. He did not register the birth until over a month later, and then he got the date wrong, recording it as 9 June. His attitude can be gauged from the fact that in an autobiography he wrote a few years later he records the official visits he made in those weeks in the company of his Arab guest, the balls he attended and even the results of the tennis matches he played with his visitor, but he does not so much as mention the birth of his son. In the same book, covering his life until 1920, Frank Rattigan includes such minutiae as his school cricket scores and the number of birds he bagged on various hunting expeditions, but alludes to his children only once, and then not by name.

The address recorded by Frank Rattigan on Terence's birth certificate was 'Lanarkslea', Cornwall Gardens; that is to say, just off Gloucester Road, in Kensington. Although Frank Rattigan stated that 'Lanarkslea' was his 'residence', it seems that it was actually the house of his mother, Lady Rattigan, where Frank and Vera were staying for their leave. Lady Rattigan was now a widow; Sir William had been killed in a motor accident in 1904. This formidable Victorian lady started to play a large part in Terence Rattigan's life from the moment of his birth. Although

Vera was not sufficiently recovered from the confinement to attend the Coronation ceremony itself on 22 June, she was soon up and about again, taking her place at the diplomatic receptions and magnificent balls that continued to be given in the weeks after the Coronation itself was over. As a result, baby Terence was left in the care of Lady Rattigan and the family servants.

Dennis Potter once referred to 'the lost but dangerous land from which every writer is in exile: Childhood'. Over the years, as we shall see, many people were to remark on the direct influence Vera Rattigan exerted on what her son wrote, but missed the less immediately obvious, but equally important, presence of his father in almost all his work. Many of his most deeply-felt plays are about relationships between fathers and sons. They are, at only a slight remove, about his relationship with his own father.

The first few months of Terence Rattigan's life are of particular interest not only because of their presumed sub-conscious psychological effect on him, but because in his writing he would return over and over again to events that occurred during these first weeks.

In a general sense all Rattigan's writing can be seen as probing the uneasy translation of his class and generation out of the comfortable certainties of the days immediately before the First World War into the uncertainties and self-doubts of the period after the end of the Second War—the years of Rattigan's most consistent strength and maturity as a writer. The reason that the years before 1914 are generally seen as a golden sunset age may, in part at least, be that it was the period of the greatest advance and influence of the middle class. Rattigan's writing is exclusively concerned with the lives of the middle class—their loves and laughter, problems and disillusionments. The values he inherited, and reacted against, were those of the successful middle class whose apotheosis came in the years immediately before the First World War.

Frank had been educated at Harrow and expected his children to be so too; in addition to the family house in Kensington, he had acquired a rambling Tudor house in the country. He spent his annual leave on the Continent or at shooting parties. His father had received a knighthood; Frank and other members of the family were well placed to be similarly honoured.

Serving abroad, Frank and Vera Rattigan may have been cut

21

off from the true nature of affairs back in England, but a look at the newspapers on the day of Terence Rattigan's birth reveals that public events were just as threatening as the storms which had swept away the recent spell of fine weather. In Germany yet another battleship was launched on that day. The naval armaments race between Britain and Germany had been unconcealed for almost five years. The news from the East on 10 June 1911 was of the barbarous way in which the Sultan of Turkey had put down a rebellion in Albania. This was just one in a succession of revolts against the Ottoman Empire. A major European conflict was creeping inexorably nearer.

At home the Seamen's Union announced its intention that day to call an all-out strike. In Birmingham, on 10 June, Lloyd George made a stirring speech in support of his new National Insurance Bill, by which he proposed a super-tax on high incomes to pay for sickness and unemployment benefits as well as old-age pensions for the needy. That year there were national strikes not only of seamen, but on the railways and in the docks. The women's movement erupted into violence. 1911 was probably the worst year of civil and industrial unrest the nation had ever known. For those members of the middle and upper classes who did not like the Liberal government, there was at least one notable victory to celebrate that summer. In July 1911, the government finally paid compensation of £3,000 to Colonel Archer Shee for the wrongful expulsion of his son from Osborn Naval College for the alleged theft of a five-shilling postal order. This seemingly trivial case had become inflated into a public trial of strength between the government and those who proclaimed that they were defending the rights of the individual against the growing and unbridled power of the state.

Nevertheless, the news which dominated the week of Terence Rattigan's birth was the preparation for the Coronation of George the Fifth and Queen Mary (who had once been his father's partner in the wild polka in Vienna). Capital and Empire were set for an interlude of complacent rejoicing.

The Rattigans' leave in London ended with the departure of their official Arab visitor. Frank Rattigan uprooted his family and returned to his post in Morocco. The journey marked the start for Terence Rattigan of what was to become a lifetime of travelling and removals from one home to another.

Hardly had the Rattigans begun to settle back into Legation routine at Tangier than a message arrived from the Foreign Office in London informing them that Frank had been appointed Second Secretary in Cairo. As they packed their household possessions for the P & O steamer voyage that would take them dog-legging across the Mediterranean via Gibraltar, Marseilles and Malta to Egypt, Frank and Vera were sorry to be leaving Morocco. They would look back on their years in Tangier as the best, the most carefree and harmonious, of their married life. But the posting to the British Agency in Cairo was a golden opportunity for an aspiring diplomat. Not only did it represent an advance in Frank Rattigan's career, it meant serving under the legendary Lord Kitchener, hero of Omdurman and Commander-in-Chief in the Boer War.

The Rattigans arrived in Cairo in November 1911. For some weeks, while they looked for a flat, the family lived close to the British Agency in the Semiramis Hotel, overlooking the Nile. Kitchener had a reputation for being cold, hard and inhumanly efficient. Frank was dumbfounded when, the morning after his arrival, he was summoned by his new chief and told he was to write the annual report on the Sudan, a massive document detailing the work of every branch of that country's administration. Kitchener asked sharply, 'Have you any comment to make?' Rattigan replied, 'No, sir, except that for the moment I know nothing about the Sudan.' 'Then you are in luck,' retorted Kitchener, 'for when you have finished you should know everything that can be known about it. I can give you exactly a fortnight to finish the draft report!'

Frank Rattigan accomplished the task and the two men subsequently became friends, Kitchener being a frequent and welcome guest in the Rattigan household. Frank's hours in Egypt were long and the work arduous. He had little time to spend with his wife and children, but in his few free hours Kitchener fostered Frank's interest in antiques by taking him on forays into the bazaars of Cairo. He also encouraged Frank's interest in excavating archaeological sites. The Rattigans' flat soon became fairly encrusted with small statuettes, bronze cats and other priceless objects of ancient Egyptian origin. By the time he could crawl, these objects had started to exercise an irresistible

23

fascination over young Terence who would hurl them to the floor with excited cries.

Frank Rattigan's greatest friend in Cairo was Ronald Storrs, the Oriental Secretary at the Agency, later described by T. E. Lawrence in *Seven Pillars of Wisdom* as the most brilliant Englishman in the Near East, 'always first and great man among us'. Storrs, as much as anyone else, was to be the instigator of the Arab Revolt, and Lawrence's foremost champion and advocate. Although young Terence Rattigan cannot then have been aware of the identity of the public figures around him, and can hardly have remembered Ronald Storrs when he came to portray him as a character in *Ross,* such 'famous characters' were to bulk large in family reminiscences in later years. By the time Terence was an adolescent, Frank Rattigan's own career had come to an abrupt end, but the 'great days' and characters of his successful diplomatic past remained a part of the family consciousness. Frank, by then denied the opportunity to consort with the famous or be personally involved in momentous events, would endeavour to sustain his own self-respect by keeping alive in his family memories of former times. Many families develop what could be called a family myth—memories of hard or successful, happy or anxious times shared which, through being repeatedly recalled over the years, take on a legendary character. The Rattigan family myth covered the time from just before Terence's birth until he was about ten.

At the end of 1913 Frank Rattigan was posted from Egypt to Berlin; as a result young Terence, now two and a half years old, was separated from his parents for the first six months of 1914. This was probably because Frank and Vera were uncertain as to where they would live in Berlin. They must also have known that there would be a heavy load of work and formal engagements for both of them. Terence's elder brother Brian was now old enough to go to school and, although one cannot be absolutely certain, it seems very probable that both boys were once again left in the care of Lady Rattigan in Kensington.

The children were not reunited with their parents until late July 1914, when Vera and Frank returned to England to take a family seaside holiday. However, hardly had their holiday begun, than the confrontation between Austria and Serbia, following the assassination of the Archduke Franz Ferdinand at Sarajevo, erupted, threatening a European war. Reading the news, Frank Rattigan realized he was needed back at his post. He telephoned the Embassy in Berlin direct from the seaside resort and offered to return.

On 31 July, leaving his family to continue their holiday, he succeeded in boarding the last boat and train through to Berlin, which was packed with Germans returning in response to their government's Order of General Mobilization. When he arrived the next day it was only to find that Germany had already declared war on Russia.

On 9 August, Vera and Lady Rattigan, who were still holidaying by the sea, were startled to receive a telegram from Frank summoning them and the children to London. He had already returned home again, although he had been forced to abandon their collection of furniture and antiques to the mercies of an angry anti-British mob raging through the streets of Berlin. He had applied in person to his old mentor and friend Lord Kitchener, now Secretary for War, for a post in the army, and was leaving next day for France.

When the women and children arrived back in Kensington they were dismayed to find Frank already kitted out in khaki, wearing the uniform of a captain which he had bought ready-made from a military tailor that morning. He was full of enthusiasm for his new role. He tried to allay their fears by assuring them that he had a post on the staff which would not entail the slightest danger. Next morning he left for France and a series of characteristically eccentric adventures. Terence and Brian were again in the care of their mother and grandmother.

Owing to staff shortage, Frank Rattigan was recalled from France at the end of 1914 to work night shifts at the Foreign Office. Then, in March 1915, coinciding with the disastrous British campaign in Gallipoli, he was posted as Second Secretary to the British Legation in Romania. Vera, as usual, accompanied him. Although Romania was still neutral, it was likely to be engulfed in the war at any moment and was not therefore a safe place to take the children.

This posting marked the beginning of a separation between Terence Rattigan and his parents which was to last for almost three years. Now nearly four, he had already seen little enough of his father because of his absences from home caused by work or sporting activities. Already much under the influence of the powerful personalities of his mother and grandmother, he would now be almost totally bereft of adult male company for three more formative years. During these years he was brought up by a grandmother whom he increasingly grew to dislike, and by various well-intentioned aunts and friends. Rattigan claimed later that while his grandmother spoilt her other grandchildren, especially his elder brother Brian, she was hard on him.

But he was not short of companionship during these years. His grandmother's household seems to have been constantly full of a changing assortment of relatives' children deposited on Lady Rattigan whenever their parents became victims of the chaos and separation of war. On 1 July 1916, Frank Rattigan's younger brother was killed during the first day of the Battle of the Somme—one of 60,000 British soldiers who died that day. This younger brother had caused a family scandal some years earlier by marrying a Gaiety Girl—Barbara. Their three young children now came to live with Lady Rattigan, and seem to have spent the rest of their childhood in her care. It is not clear why Barbara Rattigan should have consented to allow Lady Rattigan to become entirely responsible for the upbringing of her children after her husband's death, but it was probably because of the combination of comparative poverty and Lady Rattigan's continuing disapproval of the marriage. Rattigan would later recall a mysterious and much-disapproved-of Aunt Barbara lurking in the family background. He also mentions in his Prefaces an indulgent Kensington aunt who fostered his interest in play-making by taking him to London theatres. Aunt Barbara seems to have been the only person in the family directly connected with the theatre, and it would be nice to think that Barbara Rattigan was that 'indulgent aunt'. Most of the details now seem irrecoverably lost, but what is certain is that when, towards the end of his own life, Rattigan discovered that his Aunt Barbara was still alive and living in straitened circumstances in Penzance, he took immediate steps to help her.

By December 1916, further worrying news from the battle-fields was reaching Lady Rattigan's household. Frank Rattigan's task in Bucharest had been to further the British policy of persuading the Romanians to enter the war on the Allied side. In August, encouraged by a powerful Russian offensive, they had done so. But the Germans inflicted a massive defeat on the Russians and swept the small Romanian army from the field. Bucharest fell, and for some time the fate of Frank and Vera was uncertain.

Frank and Vera did not complete their escape from Eastern Europe until November 1917. By the time they arrived back in London, having survived starvation after the collapse of Romania and a spell in hospital in revolutionary Petrograd, Frank was so ill that he was unfit for service during most of 1918. Vera had cared devotedly for her injured husband throughout their hair-raising adventures in Romania and their protracted and dangerous journey home across Russia, then in the throes of the Revolution. Yet on their arrival home there was an unmistakable change in the relations between them—a change which Terence undoubtedly detected and which in turn affected his own relations with each of them. It subsequently loomed large in his writing.

It is hard at this distance to pin down the precise details of what had happened, but it seems that Frank Rattigan had had an affair with a Romanian countess (it is even alleged she was a member of the Romanian royal family). Whether she was the first of a succession of ladies with whom Frank would enjoy himself or simply the first that Vera found out about it is impossible now to say. At all events rumour had it that the affair became so public as to threaten a diplomatic scandal, and that there was talk of recalling Frank Rattigan to London. In Frank Rattigan's book there is a photograph of the wife of a Romanian cabinet minister, Vera Rattigan and a third lady described only as 'Countess'. There is no reference anywhere else in the text to this 'countess'. Whether or not this is the lady with whom Frank Rattigan had the affair we do not know, but she bears a striking similarity to the succession of bubbly blondes with whom he later did have affairs.

Throughout the rest of his childhood Terence Rattigan was aware of 'atmospheres' between his parents, half-concealed rows and outbursts, often suppressed into 'not-in-front-of-the-children' whispers or conducted in diplomatic French. His mother recalled that one morning during the last year of the war, when his parents were both at home, Rattigan, then aged seven, wandered into his mother's bedroom and announced that he would never marry—'Wives can be an awful handicap to writers. They are constantly telling their husbands to do this, fetch that, and ordering them from the house.'

From his earliest schooldays Terence Rattigan's contemporaries remarked on his lonely, self-possessed air. It was not that Terry, as he was known, was unpopular or did not join in whatever games and activities were going on. Far from it. But behind the pretty blue eyes, fair hair and perfect manners, children and adults alike sensed a premature reserve. Even as quite a little boy, he was possessed of exceptional charm and gentleness. When asked, in later life, what made him a playwright, he would reply that it was a misguided question and ask in return, 'What makes a man start doing anything—building bridges or making candlesticks?' He repeated many times that he could not remember a time when he did not want to be a writer. Certainly by 1918, before Rattigan's seventh birthday, the idea was fixed and would never change.

By November 1918 Frank Rattigan was fit enough to be sent to Scandinavia as King's Messenger with dispatches. He returned in time for Christmas and then, early in 1919, he and Vera set out again for war-ravaged Bucharest. He was now British Chargé d'Affaires in Romania, responsible for developing a lasting understanding between the new Romanian administration and the Allies. The result for Terence was a further two years of separation from his parents.

In September 1920 Rattigan was enrolled at Mr W. M. Hornbye's preparatory boarding school 'Sandroyd', near Cobham in Surrey. Sandroyd was a very grand school which prepared the sons of the richest and most distinguished families for entry to Harrow, Eton and Winchester. It was, of course, assumed that Terence and Brian would follow their father by going to Harrow.

Terence Rattigan distinguished himself early at Sandroyd. Because his elder brother Brian was already there, he was automatically known when he arrived as Rattigan Minor. But, even at the age of nine, surnames were not Rattigan's style. He told everyone his name was 'Terry' and insisted on calling everyone else by their Christian names—in those days a virtually unheard-of thing at a private preparatory school. Contemporaries remember him as a rather inky little boy, with two consuming interests—the theatre and cricket.

Rattigan next saw his parents in the Christmas holidays of

1920. That holiday he regularly pestered one or the other of them to take him to the theatre. His mother later commented, 'If he had had his way he would have got there long before the dust sheets were removed from seats.' But no sooner were the holidays over than Frank Rattigan was posted abroad again, this time as Assistant High Commissioner in Constantinople.

Meanwhile Terence's passion for the theatre continued to grow. When he accepted a part in a school play, his work fell off so badly that the headmaster offered him the choice of abandoning the part or taking a beating.[2] Rattigan chose the beating. At school and home alike he rapidly became accepted as the resident theatre expert, entertaining everyone with names, dates and places connected with the most obscure productions. He devoted all his pocket money to play-going—taking gallery seats at a shilling or one-and-sixpence a time. He kept the extent of his compulsive play-going a secret from the family and school authorities alike, sneaking out of the house, and sometimes out of school also, it seems, without telling anyone. In middle age he recalled the excitement of those stolen afternoons and evenings in the theatre:

> By the age of eleven I was already a confirmed and resolute playgoer ... If my neighbours gasped with fear for the heroine when she was confronted with a fate worse than death, I gasped with them, although I suppose I could have had but the haziest idea of the exact nature of the lady's peril; when my neighbours laughed at the witty and immoral paradoxes of the hero's bachelor friend, I laughed at them too, although I could have appreciated neither their wit nor their immorality; when my neighbours cheered the return of some favourite actor I cheered with them, even though at the time of his last appearance in London I had, quite possibly, not been born.
>
> All of which, no doubt, sounds very foolish—seemingly no more than an expression, in a rather absurd form, of the ordinary child's urge to ape the grown-ups. Yet I don't think it was only that. Up in my galleries (or, as my pocket money increased proportionately with my snobbishness, down in my pits), I was experiencing emotions which, though no doubt insincere of origin in that they were induced and coloured by the adult emotions around me, were none the less most deeply felt.[3]

29

One is struck by the similarity of Rattigan's experience to that of other artists who have felt neglected by their parents during childhood. Charles Dickens recalled that as a boy he would sneak upstairs to a room and shut himself up for hours—'keeping alive my fancy and my hope something beyond that place and time ... reading as if for life!' As a boy François Truffaut would sneak out of the house to go to the cinema, and still ascribes his sense of delinquent excitement about every aspect of film-making to the thrill associated with those clandestine visits to local cinemas. Rattigan's lifelong obsession with the theatre, the way in which everything else in his life was subordinated to it, echoes the experience of Dickens and Truffaut.

In the summer of 1922 two events occurred which affected Rattigan for the rest of his life. The first was the abrupt end of his father's career in the Diplomatic Service. As we have seen, Frank Rattigan was in many ways an unconventional diplomat, accustomed to speaking his mind without regard to the status or authority of those with whom he was dealing. But in 1922 he crossed swords with Lord Curzon, the Foreign Secretary, a fatal error. The occasion was the Chanak crisis, the post-First World War equivalent of the Suez Crisis. While serving in Romania, Frank Rattigan had become a staunch champion of Balkan nationalism. When a long-simmering dispute between Turkey and Greece boiled up around the British occupied zone in the Dardanelles at Chanak, Frank Rattigan was one of those who advocated British armed intervention on the side of the Greeks. The British Cabinet was itself hopelessly split over the issue but, unfortunately for Frank Rattigan, Curzon was the chief proponent of non-intervention and was in no mood to countenance opinionated opposition from his number two man in the crisis centre itself—Constantinople. If Assistant High Commissioner Frank Rattigan could not keep his opinions to himself he would have to go. Rattigan seems to have decided that he could not conscientiously carry out Curzon's policy, and he resigned. It is only fair to point out that if Frank Rattigan had not gone of his own free will he would probably have been pushed. The unconventional diplomat had overstepped the mark once too often, a fatal mistake and one that his son would be careful not to repeat.

During the long school holidays in August and September

1922, Frank Rattigan's future was still in doubt. Although still on the Foreign Office pay-roll, he was suspended from active service. Vera Rattigan took the boys away on holiday alone to a country cottage owned by a drama critic called Hubert Griffiths. Rattigan said that this summer holiday was the turning point in his progress towards becoming a playwright. The only books in the cottage were plays, and for three weeks he read nothing else. He found himself fascinated by how they were written, how character and situation were established and how stories were told through dialogue. At the age of eleven he was becoming immersed in the techniques of playwriting.[4]

At the end of 1922 Frank Rattigan's connection with the Diplomatic Service was finally severed, and he was retired on a small pension. This was nothing like enough for him to maintain his family in the style to which they had become accustomed. While they did not have to endure anything that approximated to poverty—Frank Rattigan had some investments and was able to play the stock market, though often with catastrophic results—they all had to make adjustments. Frank tried to increase the family income by developing his interest in antiques into a business, and he also settled down to write an autobiographical account of his adventures in the Diplomatic Service. Neither venture seems to have been particularly successful, and Rattigan himself estimated that the total family income never rose above £1,000 a year before that time when he himself was able to supplement it from his own earnings.

Although Terence Rattigan was kept on at Sandroyd, he was not immune to the pressures of his father's changed circumstances. From now on, he knew that if he was to take his place at Harrow he would have to earn it by winning a scholarship. For the next fifteen years he was never as well off as his friends at school or university. His social position was never as secure. Everything that he coveted had to be won.

The family now lived in a rather poky flat at the top of a terrace house in Stanhope Gardens, Kensington, on the other side of Gloucester Road from Lady Rattigan's home in Cornwall Gardens. Rattigan's school friends who lived near by noticed that although he was always invited to their birthday parties, they were never invited to his home. One who did manage to get himself invited in after a visit to the cinema was intrigued to discover how small the flat was when they reached it after climbing to the fourth floor.

Later, people could not understand how Rattigan, who had apparently come from such a comfortable background and had always appeared to possess such social poise, could write with such sympathy and precision about the feelings of social misfits and emotional failures. For many years he took steps to conceal the difficulties of his own childhood. His plays abound in characters who hide their insecurity and feelings of inadequacy behind a veneer of extrovert confidence and bluff social conformity.

The drop in the family's income was not the only aspect of his father's resignation from the Diplomatic Service which affected Rattigan. It must be reckoned that once the first flush of self-righteousness had evaporated from his gesture of resignation, his father increasingly came to see himself as a failure. He found himself entering what should have been the prime of life at a loose end—a middle-aged man with a brilliant future behind him. Perhaps to bolster his self-esteem he styled himself 'Major', the rank to which he was entitled as a result of his brief war service in France, and took to reminiscing about his great days shooting with European royalty or adventuring in the mysterious East. His one remaining hope was his sons. Poor Brian, with his club foot, could never hope to emulate his father's schoolboy prowess at games, so Frank Rattigan concentrated all his own frustrated ambitions on Terence. He was determined that his son should follow in his footsteps and become a diplomat and a sportsman. The previously absent father became a pressurizing father.

Despite the fact that he was now at home, Frank Rattigan's casual affairs with unsuitable young blondes continued, and even increased in number. Relations between Frank and Vera continued to deteriorate and there are grounds for supposing that the possibility of divorce arose more than once during the years that followed.

Vera Rattigan put her own rather different kind of pressure on her son. Her demands were emotional. 'That poor lost boy, Terry Rattigan' was how at least one family of friends referred to him in his early teens: gentle, polite but sad, the second son of what those close to the family knew to be an unhappy marriage. Vera was still a beautiful woman and not a few men were attracted to her, but she was not the sort of person to permit herself to enter into an affair. Hurt and disappointed in her relationship with her husband, she turned, like so many mothers before and since, to her children for emotional compensation. It was perhaps inevitable that her prime target should be her younger son. She was, as we already know, a strong personality and must have fairly smothered Terence with possessive emotion. She did more than show a consuming interest in all he did: she demanded an exclusive filial affection. Whether she could help herself or not, she vilified Frank Rattigan to his sons and tried to focus all their love on to herself, building up the impression of how unfairly and unfeelingly he had treated her. From this, plus occasional explosive outbursts and an all-pervading 'atmosphere', Rattigan grew up to side with his mother against his father.

Rattigan had been saying he wanted to be a playwright since he was seven, but when the time came for him to leave Sandroyd and sit the scholarship examination for Harrow, his parents were becoming seriously alarmed that he might really mean it. They warned him that no one could make a career by simply writing plays—which prompted him to try writing novels as well. One attempt, started when he was about ten but abandoned halfway down page three, and called '*Self Sacrifice*—An Enthralling Novelette by the Famous Playwright and Author T. M. Rattigan', survived among his papers into adult life.

His earliest completed play to survive was probably begun in his last term at Sandroyd and finished during his first year at Harrow. Inspired by reading Raphael Sabatini, it was a blood-curdling story about the Borgias called *The Parchment*. It had two acts and a playing time of about ten minutes. It opened with a Prologue set in a contemporary English drawing room and then flashed back to the Palace of the Borgias in Rome in 1549. The finished work was carefully put into covers, which were then decorated with a variety of coloured inks. On the front, in green ink, 'The Author' made it clear that he wished to apologize for any historical inaccuracies. He continued: 'He wishes it known that the following cast would be eminently suitable for a presentation of this work.' The names that followed included Godfrey Tearle, Gladys Cooper, Marie Tempest, Matheson Lang, Isobel Elsom, Henry Ainley—the most famous stars of the day. Rattigan later claimed he had actually sent it to Marie

Tempest, whose part consisted of just one line, 'Milk *and* sugar Mr Fortesque', with the accent firmly on the 'and'. She does not seem to have replied. Another innovative piece of casting was the selection of Noël Coward, then a rising young star, for the part of a velvet-jacketed poet. At about the time of the play's composition Rattigan's parents had prevented him from seeing Coward's *The Vortex* because they considered it 'unsuitable'.

Rattigan once described himself at this period lying on his hard school bed, his soul split between rival dreams of making witty first-night speeches to wildly cheering houses (after being kissed by Marie Tempest and Gladys Cooper simultaneously) and of bowling out the entire Australian eleven for thirteen—'eight of which I usually conceded to my hero, Macartney, the rest being byes'.[5]

Rattigan entered Harrow in 1925, having won a scholarship with credits in Latin and French. The parents of most boys who won scholarships to Harrow did not accept the money. Rattigan's did. During his first year an incident occurred which Rattigan later recalled as evidence that by the age of fourteen he had two of the essentials for a playwright—a sense of theatre and a compulsion to keep writing plays. Mr Laborde, the French master, set Rattigan's form to compose a one-act playlet during prep. While the others composed uneventful little dramas whose dialogue was within the scope of their severely limited French, Rattigan plunged straight into the climax of a full-blown tragedy, without regard for his total inability to render the words of his emotion-torn characters into correct French. The Comte de Boulogne, driven mad by his wife's passion for a handsome young gendarme, rushes into the countess's boudoir where she sits at her dressing-table having her hair done by three maids (Rattigan commented that he had not yet become as economical with the small parts as he would later) and announces that her gendarme (who is all along hidden in a cupboard) is none other than her long-lost brother, Armand. The heroine faints—or, as T. M. Rattigan put it, 'mesure son longueur'. Curtain! Mr Laborde awarded Rattigan only two marks out of ten, commenting in angry red ink—'French execrable: theatre-sense first class'.[6]

In his first two years at Harrow, one master had a particular fascination for Rattigan—his ageing, dry-as-dust Greek teacher, Mr Coke Norris. A rigid disciplinarian who never showed a lighter side, he was very unpopular with the boys. During Rattigan's second year Coke Norris retired, probably because of ill health. It seems that one of the boys gave him a leaving present (it may have been Rattigan himself, but fifty years later Rattigan was not sure). Coke Norris received this small gift, almost certainly a book, with hard words rather than any apparent pleasure. Rattigan could not understand how anyone could return kindness with unkindness. Knowing nothing about Coke Norris's personal life, not even whether he was married, he invented a number of different life stories and family backgrounds for him. These imaginary broodings produced nothing, but Rattigan put them into what he came to call his 'writer's cupboard'. One of the things that had provoked Rattigan's brooding about Coke Norris was the boredom of his classes. One of the set Greek texts Coke Norris used was the *Agamemnon* of Aeschylus. Somewhere beneath the repetitious parsing, scansion and insistence on grammatical exactitude of Coke Norris' Greek lessons Rattigan detected that they were being made to read, fragment by dead fragment, a living play. His Greek was not good, but the theatre enthusiast in him recognized a good scene when he saw one. Frustrated, he went to the school library and read the play in translation. He found that indeed this was no dead text, but an exciting, emotion-packed drama. He was furious. Why did Coke Norris, who must presumably once have loved Aeschylus, use the *Agamemnon* as a Greek translation excercise, but pay no attention to the fact that it was a play? Spurred on by this realization, Rattigan read more plays in the library. First the 'dangerous' modern playwrights who were represented on the shelves—Pinero, Barrie, Galsworthy. Shaw he found disappointing because he was not moved by his plays. These playwrights influenced him before the English classical dramatists. He at first ignored Shakespeare and only came back to him later. By the time he left Harrow he had read all the plays in the library and many more acquired from outside.

As he progressed through school he continued to write plays of his own, even though there seems to have been no intention of having them performed, even by his friends. He himself described the progress of his theatre craft by the time he came to leave school:

... my heroines had ceased to measure their lengths at moments of crisis. I had found other ways of bringing down the second-act curtain. My heroes and my villains had stopped glaring at each other, boldly on one side and malevolently on the other. They had merged gradually into one and had become much the same person. Impossibly happy endings and convenient last-act suicides had been, or at least were in process of being, eliminated. Now self-discipline began to tighten even more, and those grandly built-up entrances for the star, together with those comic or dramatic exit lines to take them off to applause ... were sadly but ruthlessly included in the list. Curtains no longer fell slowly. They simply fell.[7]

Evidence of the manner of that progress is to be found in a schoolboy play which has survived in two copies. The original, written in black ink on the ruled sheets of a school exercise book and bound with a dark blue ribbon, was called *Integer Vitae*. Among Rattigan's papers there is also a later, typed copy, on which someone has written 'age 15'. It has a new title. *Integer Vitae* has been inked out and *The Pure in Heart* written in. It is in two acts and the credit is, 'By T. M. Rattigan, author of *The Consul's Wife, King's Evidence*'. It is set in a suburban house and deals with relationships under stress in a family where the parents have used their savings to send their son to a public school in the hope that he will make a good career and keep them in their old age. He has disappointed them by becoming a wastrel.

The themes of this little drama are already strikingly close to those Rattigan was to explore as an adult playwright. Although the plot involves a murder, the play's central preoccupation is deception—suppressing awkward truths about oneself in the all-important pursuit of keeping up social appearances.

Rattigan first saw his name in print in the school magazine—*The Harrovian*. In an article on modern drama which appeared in 1929, his theme was 'The ceaseless conflict being waged in the drama today, "Entertainment versus Instruction".' This theme too foreshadowed much that he would write and say later. In the same article he prophesied 'a mechanized drama of the future', which might replace the theatre. In another edition of the magazine he had a short story published—'The Laughter of the Gods'. The story's theme is archetypal Rattigan. It concerns a circus trapeze act and the vengeful emotions provoked in the catcher, David, when a powerful impresario entices his beloved, but more talented, youthful partner, Luigi, away from him with offers of money and fame. When he hears Luigi accept the impresario's offer and say that he has no scruples about deserting his partner, David's world crashes—'He had not known what misery was until that moment.' Climbing up to the trapeze to begin their act, David finds himself elated by the idea of paying Luigi back. As he looks down at the crowd of white faces below him, 'he wondered were they all as vile as this boy whom he had loved, who had been a part of himself?' He determines to kill him. He will let his grip slip in one of the catches. He will be the agent of divine retribution. At the last moment he changes his mind, but there is a real accident and the boy slips, falling to his death.

Writing was not Rattigan's only concern at Harrow. He had entered a fiercely masculine and competitive world, and public schools were harsh places at the time. To win the approval of the masters was not enough; a boy had to win the acceptance of his fellows. Academic ability alone, which Rattigan had in abundance, counted for little with the other boys. They demanded conformity, toughness, a British stiff upper lip. Those who excelled at sport were worshipped as heroes. Those who did not conform, or were regarded as cissies, were bullied—in ways which we would now find incredible and would almost certainly consider criminal. It is true that most of the worst nineteenth-century excesses had disappeared, but public schools in the 1920s were still brutal and intolerant by today's standards. They were breeding grounds of the worst kind of male chauvinism.

Rattigan, although very sophisticated for his age, was, as we have seen, by nature a gentle boy, not muscular or hard. He had no inclination towards athletics, football, boxing or the games of contact. His reserve could have made him a misfit, but he compensated through his wit, his charm and, above all, his natural eye for games like cricket, racquets and squash. It was lucky for Rattigan too that Harrow allowed a good deal more privacy and independence than some other public schools. The boys did not sleep in communal dormitories. Even as juniors they were given rooms which they shared with one other boy. The more senior boys had a room of their own. Rattigan never seemed to do any work, but his academic brilliance got him moved into higher forms ahead of his contemporaries.

His impoverished family circumstances, his own sense of not really belonging, but perhaps above all the need to live up to his father's expectations, sharpened Rattigan's competitive streak at Harrow and at the same time caused him to disguise it under a cloak of elegant detachment.

Rattigan's father boasted that he had been a member of the strongest cricket team the school had ever fielded, playing in the First Eleven for four out of his five years at the school. Although his son did not do as well as that, he was well pleased that by the 1929 season he had become established as an opening bat and regularly laid the foundations of the First Eleven's score. He was a graceful stroke-maker whose timing rather than strength enabled him to hit many boundaries that season. His trademark was a sliced off-drive to the left of cover. He was selected for the team to meet Eton at Lord's, the highlight of the school's sporting and social year, though Harrow had not won since 1908. (While Rattigan's father had been in the team, in the 1890s, Harrow were never defeated.) Rattigan's father and mother were among the fashionably dressed crowd at Lord's on Friday, 12 July 1929, a grillingly hot day, when he took his place in the slips at the start of the Eton innings. It was to prove an historic match.

Before lunch he took a very good slip catch to dismiss one of Eton's top batsmen, but during the afternoon he dropped an easier ball. By late afternoon Eton were all out for a formidable 347 and it fell to Rattigan to open the Harrow innings with N. M. V. Rothschild. By then the heat had abated and a wind had got up. Rattigan seemed a little shaky and snicked one to the wicket-keeper. Luckily for him the catch was missed and went on to the boundary. Having taken the first shine off the ball, Rothschild started to hit out, while Rattigan was content to play more cautiously, keeping the bowling at bay while his partner made the runs. The score was 67 for no wicket, of which Rothschild had scored 43, when an event occurred that went down in the annals of cricket. It was the last ball of the over and Rattigan was facing the Eton medium-fast bowler Franks. He played the ball to extra cover, who was fielding deep. After some hesitation he called for a single. The ball was thrown in hard and chanced to hit one of Rothschild's pads. Deflected out of the wicket-keeper's reach it ran all the way to the boundary: five runs to Rattigan! But the umpires were not satisfied and halted play while they consulted together. They decided to disallow the four extra runs and in the confusion sent the batsmen back to the ends they had been occupying when Rattigan had faced the last ball of the over. They were now technically at the wrong ends, but the new over commenced with Rothschild facing the bowling. Rothschild mistimed his stroke and played the ball on to his wicket. By rights it should have been Rattigan who faced that ball; but the umpires had made a mistake and they could not go back on it. Rothschild was given out. It was now up to Rattigan to justify himself by making a good score, but after keeping his end for a while he was out for a disappointing 29. Rattigan's, and his father's, disappointment was sharpened next day when he was out for only one run in the second innings, and Harrow had to struggle for a draw.

Despite this disappointment Rattigan often looked back on 1929 as the happiest year of his life. As well as being in the cricket eleven he was in the school racquets and squash teams. He was more than just another member of the school hierarchy; because of his gentleness and wit he was a hero to many of the junior boys. He had grown into a tall and strikingly handsome boy, with wavy, light brown hair, smooth skin and regular features. That summer, although he still had a full year to go in the Sixth Form, he won the Bourchier History Prize and second place in the St Helier English Literature Prize. For most people who are successful at school their last year is the happiest, because it is the one that brings the greatest rewards and the most freedom. That it was not so for Rattigan was due to a number of factors that all came to a head in 1929-30. The gap between the generations was unusually large in the 1920s. To Rattigan and his friends, people of his father's generation, those who had fought in the Great War, with their ideas of patriotism and their moral and political conservatism, seemed not so much out of touch with the post-war world as relics of a bygone age who had been preserved by some accident of time; comic-opera figures, good only for laughter. 'Major' Frank Rattigan, with his ramrod back, moustaches and reminiscences, seemed a particularly ripe example. Rattigan's antagonism to him and all he stood for, fostered by his unhappy mother, was increased by Frank Rattigan's habit of turning up at Harrow to visit his son, complete with sharp-cut suit and red carnation in his buttonhole, with his latest mistress on his arm. Frank Rattigan would invent elaborate covers for this string of improbable young ladies, who typically came from dress shops and had names like Cora, claiming they were cousins or nieces he had brought down to meet his son. Behind his father's back Rattigan laughed and told his friends the embarrassing truth.

To Rattigan and his friends, the ideals proclaimed by his father's generation were so much humbug. In 1929 the head-master of Harrow, Dr Cyril Norwood, brought out a book on public school education:

> What has happened in the course of the last hundred years is that the old ideals have been recaptured, the ideal of chivalry which inspired the knighthood of medieval days, the ideal of service to the community which inspired the greatest of the men who founded schools for their day and for posterity, have been combined in the tradition of English education which holds the field today. It is based upon religion, it relies largely upon games and open-air prowess, where these involve corporate effort ...[8]

Rattigan's attitude to that sort of sentiment can be gauged by the fact that he clandestinely passed round the works of Bertrand Russell and the Huxleys, which were banned at Harrow. He and his friends were inspired by Marx and Freud rather than by the ideals of medieval chivalry. Before he left Harrow he had adopted a philosophy that was broadly rational and socialist, liberal and humanist. To these principles was added a youthful delight in anything that shocked the older generation.

For example, it became fashionable among rebellious-minded public schoolboys, not just at Harrow, to proclaim their genuine or affected homosexuality. As a senior boy, Rattigan quite openly eyed juniors entering his house at Harrow, pointing out the ones he found attractive to his friends. Many boys pass through a homosexual phase in adolescence, but for Rattigan to advertise it so openly was a piece of deliberately unconventional behaviour. Dr Norwood's housemasters regularly called their boys together to lecture them on the evils of unnatural habits, admonishing them to take 'a cold tub and a brisk trot' whenever they felt the onset of 'urges'. Rattigan admitted that the sub-plot of his last play, *Cause*

Célèbre, was largely autobiographical. In it two seventeen-year-old public schoolboys, Tony and Randolph, discuss their feeling of being forced to relieve their sexual frustrations with other boys, not because they want to, but because of the attitude of their parents and teachers:

TONY: I wonder what our parents think we *do* between thirteen and twenty-one.

RANDOLPH: What we do, I imagine ... solo ... they hope of course, but if it's the other—better than with some nasty woman.

TONY: It's such damn humbug. No female of our age will look at us, and any female older than us isn't allowed to have us.

Homosexuality was something that Rattigan confidently expected to grow out of. Even if his publicly flaunted homosexuality was passed over by other boys as defiance of adult authority, his slightly fey and detached manner, his graceful movements, feminine gentleness and rather nasal voice could, in the exaggeratedly masculine atmosphere of Harrow, have made him a target for the more conventional bully-boys but for his prowess at games. That he was liable to such attacks became apparent in his last year at school.

A strand of Rattigan's radical beliefs that particularly shocked his parents' generation and his more conformist contemporaries was his anti-militarism. Between 1927 and 1930 appeared a spate of books and a play, *Journey's End*, about life in the trenches during the Great War. The work of Blunden, Sassoon, Graves and R. C. Sherriff affected Rattigan and his friends deeply. By portraying the futility and horror of war, those authors confirmed the new generation's determination that it should not happen again. They embraced the ideals of the Kellogg Pact, whereby the nations of the world had renounced war as an instrument of policy, and placed internationalism and pacifism above what they regarded as short-sighted nationalism. For this the conventionally-minded branded them as unpatriotic.

An obvious target for their pacifism was the compulsory Officer Training Corps parades at Harrow. These were normally held twice weekly. One, held at lunchtime on Fridays, was particularly irksome, so Rattigan and a group of protestors tried to get it stopped. One of them, possibly Rattigan himself, wrote a letter signed 'Sufferer' to *The Harrovian*, asking by what right boys could be compelled to join the Corps. The letter declared that it was an out-of-date institution and that compulsion was illegal. This provoked sneering replies about the writer's effeminacy, suggesting that if he did not accept what happened at Harrow he could always leave. The issue took on some of the character of a national scandal when Rattigan wrote a letter to *The Times* which was noticed by the Prime Minister, Baldwin, who was an old Harrovian, and who brought it to the attention of the House of Commons. The protest had no effect and compulsory OTC parades continued. Michael Denison, a junior boy at the time and Rattigan's fag, remembers mistakenly applying far too much polish to Rattigan's Sam Browne in the belief that the more applied the greater the shine. When Rattigan appeared on Corps parade with his belt a sticky mess he was reprimanded. Later he called Denison to his study. 'Look, old boy, I don't care about the OTC, but I *do* care about getting ticked off for something you are supposed to have done. So just learn how to do it, will you?'[9]

Rattigan was in further trouble over his relationship with a local bookie and the horse-racing correspondent of a national newspaper called Gilbey. Rattigan and a friend, John Bayliss, were in the habit of betting, and Bayliss's expertise with the form book ensured that they won regularly. This in itself would not have caused trouble, but the fact that the bookie and Gilbey seemed always to be hanging round Rattigan became the subject of gossip and then scandal, which looked as though it might escalate to the point where he might be expelled. Rattigan claimed the bookie was collecting his debts and the journalist giving him tips. His detractors suggested that, in view of his sexual proclivities, there was more to his relationship with the two men than an interest in gambling.

All these things clearly upset Frank Rattigan, as indeed they were meant to. But the greatest bone of contention between father and son was his choice of career. Trouble had been brewing for some time over this, but now that he was entering his last year at school his father wanted a clear decision. Frank Rattigan was as determined as ever that his son should follow him into the Diplomatic Service; Rattigan was just as determined to be a playwright. There were endless rows over the next few years:

father insisting that no one could support himself by playwriting and that Terence should get himself into 'the Diplomatic' and do his playwriting in his spare time; the son insisting that he wanted playwriting to be his life, not his hobby. They remained at an impasse, except that Rattigan conceded that, if need be, he would be a journalist until such time as he could support himself from his plays alone.

The hardest blow of Rattigan's final year at Harrow fell only weeks before he was due to leave. He was now nineteen. He had already won a string of academic prizes and been recommended for the School Leaving Scholarship Examination. But this meant less to him, and to his father, than that he should do well in the Eton and Harrow cricket match at Lord's. It was his third season in the eleven and everyone expected him to open the Harrow batting. He had begun the season well, being top scorer in the matches played in May. However, in the trial match in mid-June against Harlequins, he had made a surprisingly sleepy stroke to a half-volley and was out for a duck. In the final trial before the match itself, against an Old Harrovian eleven which contained many of his old team-mates from the previous two seasons, he was moved down the batting order. But he was out of form; in neither innings did he reach double figures. To the joy of those who had jeered at him, the captain decided to drop him and replace him with a younger boy from the same house.

He seems to have been broken-hearted by the decision. He went up to his room and wrote a telegram for his father, who was naturally planning to be at Lord's, to warn him of what had happened. After that he could control his tears no longer and sat with his head on his desk, sobbing. A few doors away in the same corridor a friend, Dorian Williams, heard sobs coming from Rattigan's room and then his name being called. Williams went in, and through his tears Rattigan asked if he would go to the post office and send a telegram for him. Williams agreed, but when he was at the door Rattigan stopped him: 'You'd better read it first.' That was the first Williams knew of what had happened. Rattigan's humiliation was complete when his father, having received the telegram, rushed down to Harrow and started to lobby all and sundry to have him reinstated.

Although Rattigan would look back on his days at Harrow as among the best of his life, they had also given him the taste of humiliation and the realization that his own popularity was superficial, something cultivated to cover inner insecurity and a feeling of not belonging.

Notes

1   Much of the information on Frank and Vera Rattigan's early life is taken from Frank Rattigan's autobiography—*Diversions of a Diplomat*, Chapman and Hall, London, 1924.

2   Told to Rattigan by Kenneth Tynan and reproduced in an article in the London *Evening Standard*, 1 July 1953.

3   Preface to *Collected Plays of Terence Rattigan*, Volume II, Hamish Hamilton, London, 1953.

4   Rattigan interviewed by Sheridan Morley for BBC Radio *Kaleidoscope*, July 1977.

5   Preface to *Collected Plays*, Volume II.

6   Preface to *Collected Plays*, Volume II.

7   Preface to *Collected Plays*, Volume II.

8   *The English Tradition in Education*, by Dr Cyril Norwood, John Murray, London, 1929.

9   *Overture and Beginners*, by Michael Denison, Gollancz, London, 1973.

2

First Episode

On 10 October 1930, Rattigan entered Trinity College, Oxford. He had won a minor scholarship to read history, thus relieving his father of some of the strain of supporting him through university.

Rattigan was not the sort of person to push himself forward, yet he was one of those in his generation who, his contemporaries agree, made an impression while still at Oxford. This was not through any particular achievement as an undergraduate, but through a combination of immaculate good looks, perfect manners, sophistication, elegant wit and the declared and unswerving determination to become a playwright. Rattigan was distinguished too through his circle of friends, who included many of the most colourful characters in the literary and theatrical life of the university during the early 1930s. Paul Dehn, Angus Wilson and Peter Glenville went on to become famous; others disappeared or were killed in the war. Tony Goldschmidt, who had been at Harrow with Rattigan, was widely considered one of the most brilliant young men of his generation. Another outstanding Harrovian friend who went up to Oxford at the same time was John Bayliss.

The university was divided, as it had been through much of the 1920s, into two, often mutually hostile, camps—Aesthetes and Hearties. Rattigan was unusual in that he managed to keep a foot in each. He shared the enthusiasm of the Aesthetes for writing, the arts, acting, the theatre; he went to their parties and enjoyed their company; yet he was quieter, more reserved. He did not show off, talk too much and too loud. He stayed in the background at their gatherings, a quietly amused observer who made witty asides, but did not push himself to the centre of the stage. Despite prejudice to the contrary, being an Aesthete did not necessarily mean being a homosexual. Often it went little further than a rather outrageous affectation of homosexual manners, part of the familiar juvenile attempt to shock their elders. Questioned about homosexuality at Oxford at this time, one of Rattigan's friends said, 'We might have worn a purple hat or a green cloak, but as far as doing anything—really—almost nothing. It wouldn't have occurred to most of us.'

The other group, the Hearties, were the sporting, beer-drinking upholders of unchanging undergraduate convention: the players of team games and their supporters. They were also raggers and practical jokers, although their idea of a joke often seemed perilously close to vandalism or bullying. One of their favourite diversions was to corner some unsuspecting Aesthete who was out on his own and taunt him, finally attacking him and stealing some part of his clothing, usually his trousers, and running off whooping with joy. Rattigan, although identified with the Aesthetes, won acceptance among the Hearties because of his excellence at games, his conventional dress, good manners and modesty.

During his first year at Oxford, Rattigan lived in college at Trinity. He said he was not going to make the mistake of working. He was determined to be a writer and did not want to be 'marked out for life by getting a degree'.

Then, as now, Oxford could be used as a stepping stone to the professional theatre. The Oxford University Dramatic Society put on an important annual production attended by the London critics. Many who later went on to successful theatrical careers first made their mark in OUDS. The 'star' members when Rattigan joined included George Devine, Hugh Hunt and Giles Playfair. The Society's club rooms, where members could read, eat and drink, were a convivial meeting place for kindred spirits, and Rattigan was soon enjoying the long lazy Sunday breakfasts.

Rattigan first made his mark in OUDS through his contributions to their 'smokers'. The smoker was a revue performed in the club room for members and their guests. The sketches were often risqué, even lewd by the standards of the day. They usually abounded in in-jokes about events and characters in OUDS and the university. Many famous wits had first drawn blood and felt the intoxication of provoking laughter at smokers. Rattigan developed a celebrated turn for these occasions, delivering a stream of catty comments on his contemporaries in the guise of an outrageous female character he created for himself.

Rattigan's father was still determined that his son should go into the Diplomatic Service and had decided that he would spend his long summer vacations at crammers in France and Germany, getting his languages up to the required standard. He accordingly arranged for him to stay in the house of Monsieur Martin at Wimereux, near Boulogne, for the long vacation of 1931.

Monsieur Martin had written to Frank Rattigan saying that he would meet his son off the steamer at Boulogne. He would, he said, 'be extremely distinguishable' from all the others on the quay by having a white handkerchief which he would be holding in his right hand. As the steamer drew alongside on the afternoon of 17 July 1931 Rattigan, now twenty years old, spotted among the small crowd on the quay a man with a high domed forehead, grey hair, jutting beard and ferocious expression, holding a far from clean white handkerchief rigidly above his head. On shore, Rattigan advanced to meet his new French tutor and host. Holding out his hand and smiling, he asked politely, 'Monsieur Martin?' The reply was a grim nod. Rattigan continued in his best undergraduate French: 'Comment allez-vous?' There was a long pause while Monsieur Martin stuffed the off-white handkerchief back into his pocket. Then he took Rattigan's hand in a vice-like grip and, speaking very slowly and loudly, with exaggeratedly perfect pronunciation, said: 'Enchanté de faire votre connaissance, Monsieur.' Rattigan smiled politely, but Monsieur Martin did not release his hand. Instead he repeated very slowly 'Enchanté de faire votre connaissance, Monsieur.' Rattigan was confused—why, he wondered, should Monsieur Martin keep on saying 'How do you do?' By now they had been shaking hands for some time and were attracting the attention of others in the crowd on the quayside. As Monsieur Martin was about to go into the routine for a third time, Rattigan realized that he was trying to tell him what *he* should have said. Nervously, he tried out the formula for himself. 'Accent abominable,' Monsieur Martin growled, but after a moment let go of his hand and turned to look for a porter. Rattigan had had his introduction to Monsieur Martin's teaching method.[1]

Monsieur Martin's house turned out to be a rambling villa where six or seven other young men were spending the summer polishing their French. Each had a bedroom to himself for private study. The only language permitted in the house was French. Meals were taken together in the company of Monsieur Martin, and each had a daily tutorial with him, in addition to having to write French essays, stories and letters. Despite a good deal of high-spirited horseplay, Rattigan did not enjoy himself much that summer. He was the youngest there and everyone else seemed far more proficient in French than he was. He squirmed under Monsieur Martin's daily cries of 'Ah, Mon Dieu! Entendez, Messieurs, cette nouvelle abomination de Monsieur Rottingham!'

He was lonely, in spite of being with young men of his own age. The others were essentially conformist, working to better their chances in the very career he had decided to reject. He saw himself as a rebel, and these young men were in no way kindred spirits. While everyone else worked diligently at French exercises, Rattigan brooded in his room about the plays he would write, including the soul-searing tragedy that was taking shape in his head, based on the glum experience he was living through at that moment.

When he returned to Oxford in October, he stopped living in at Trinity and moved into digs. 'Canters', Canterbury House in King Edward Street, was a fashionable address among undergraduates and Rattigan did well to get rooms there. Another who moved in at the same time was a fair-haired, athletic-looking South African, Philip Heimann. A year older than Rattigan, Heimann had already taken a general degree at Witwatersrand University and was at Oxford to read law. Like Rattigan, he was in revolt against his father over the choice of his career. Heimann's father owned a business in South Africa, but Heimann had refused to go into it and intended to practise at the bar instead. The two young men rapidly became very close friends.

Another undergraduate who followed Rattigan into 'Canters' was Peter Glenville. He came from a theatrical background, and he and Rattigan quickly established a reputation for throwing

48

elegant, often hilarious, parties in their rooms. Rattigan's scholarship and the allowance from his father did not stretch very far, so he had to pay his share of the costs of these sometimes wild and invariably alcoholic functions from winnings on the horses. John Bayliss was still his tipster, devising ever more ingenious ways of laying out a few shillings against the possibility of bringing in pounds. His schemes came good with surprising frequency and he managed to pick two Derby winners, April the Fifth and Windsor Lad.

To those who did not know what he was doing, Rattigan seemed studious, spending much of his time alone working in his room, but he was writing plays rather than history essays. One of these, a one-acter which Rattigan described as 'a highly experimental piece rather in the vein of Constantin's effort in *The Seagull*', Rattigan submitted for production to the OUDS President, George Devine. Devine turned it down, telling him that some of it was absolutely smashing 'but it goes too far'.

From the Autumn of 1931 he wrote cinema and theatre reviews for one of Oxford's leading university papers. His friend Tony Goldschmidt had become co-editor of *Cherwell*. Rattigan's first piece as a critic appeared on 31 October 1931 and was headed 'George Street Cinema'. It did not mention the title of the film, a western, probably because Rattigan did not know it. He had arrived towards the end in time to see only the final shoot-out: 'a most glorious battle in which every one of the twenty or so combatants were wiped out except the hero. Even he must have been pretty badly wounded, seeing that he seemed to have been shot through the heart. However, these heroes (I could not make out if he was a bandit or a ranger) are notoriously tough.' He must also have seen the final clinch because he devoted most of his two-hundred-word article to praising Mary Pickford.

A week later *Cherwell* dispatched him to London to cover Noël Coward's *Cavalcade*, which had just opened at Drury Lane. Before he left, Tony Goldschmidt took him on one side and pointed out that as the rival undergraduate paper *Isis* had just printed an article headed 'Noël Coward; Genius and Prophet' the policy of their paper demanded that he be not over-generous in his praise. *Cherwell* paid for his return rail fare and an upper circle seat. On his return from the matinée performance he began his review with the heading: 'No, No, Noël'. This, it seems, was too racy even for *Cherwell* and they did not use it. However, they did print the long article that followed. Rattigan argued that whereas Coward's early plays had led serious students of drama to believe that a young revolutionary dramatist of immense promise had emerged, he had now, alas, succumbed to the lure of commercial success and sold his soul to the devils of Shaftesbury Avenue. *Cavalcade* was merely a parade of sentimentalized popular emotion. It eulogized the generation that fought the Great War in order to damn the current gutless generation. T.M.R., as Rattigan signed himself, compared Coward unfavourably with Bernard Shaw, and castigated those who had recently hailed him as a genius. Coward was merely a skilful follower of the public mood—'He has the happy knack of feeling strongly what other people are feeling at the same time. If he has the ability to transform this knack into money and success, we should not begrudge them to him. But such cannot be the qualities of genius.' The irony of Rattigan's attack on Coward is that it was identical to the one that would one day be launched against him.

The OUDS major production of the 1931-2 season was to be *Romeo and Juliet*. George Devine, the President of the Society, invited John Gielgud to direct. Although Gielgud was the rising poetic actor of his generation, this was to be his first production as a director. OUDS did not have women members, and the Society therefore persuaded professional actresses to appear in their major productions. Devine managed to get Peggy Ashcroft to play Juliet.

The allocation of the male parts among the students in OUDS, as in all amateur dramatic societies, was traditionally based on the status and seniority of the members and a consensus view of their acting ability. Gielgud, however, took a more professional approach and held readings to determine the casting. As a result, Christopher Hassall was selected to play Romeo, George Devine Mercutio, William Devlin Tybalt and Giles Playfair was awarded the part of Friar Laurence. Rattigan got one line as one of the musicians who discover Juliet's body at the end of Act IV. In the text this musician has nine lines, but either Gielgud did not trust Rattigan to deliver them all adequately or the Society wanted to share the lines out equally because of the number of aspirants for a place in this prestigious production. With only fourteen days to go before the production opened, Gielgud managed to persuade

Edith Evans, who had just returned from America in low spirits after a Broadway flop, to play the Nurse.

Meantime, trouble had broken out among the student members of the cast. George Devine and Giles Playfair had recently contested an acrimonious election for the presidency of OUDS. Rehearsals began in an atmosphere of chaos and high excitement. Gielgud, full of bounding enthusiasm and nervousness, was too preoccupied with the problems of the production to take any notice of the partisan rivalries which obsessed his young cast off-stage. Playfair withdrew, and his part was taken over by Hugh Hunt. After rehearsal each day, when Gielgud had gone back to London, rival factions were locked in fierce argument over drinks in the club room. Sometimes Edith Evans, who, like the other ladies in the production, was staying in Oxford, would burst into the smoke-filled room crying in Lady Bracknell-like tones, 'All this frousting about!' She would then lead one faction out on a bracing walk along the Oxford Canal, while Peggy Ashcroft would soothe another party over an omelette at 'The George'. Awed though the boys were by Gielgud, Edith Evans and Peggy Ashcroft, there was great competition for their attention. They inundated them with invitations to parties, dinners and tête-à-têtes. Rattigan watched all these rivalries, manoeuvrings, politickings, romances and theatrical affectations with amusement. He took no very active part himself but as usual noted everything and stored it away in his 'writer's cupboard'.

The first night itself was a splendid undergraduate occasion. The large and excited audience at Oxford's New Theatre included critics from most of the London papers. Gielgud had been given the night off from the production in which he was appearing in London and sat shaking with nerves in the pit. It was a free-flowing production without breaks and all went well until towards the end, when Rattigan produced a roar of quite the wrong sort of laughter by the way he played his single line: 'Faith, we may put up our pipes, and be gone.' In spite of Gielgud's patient help, he had struggled with the line throughout rehearsals. The roar of laughter on the first night was mortifying. His embarrassment became still worse when he thought he detected in Edith Evans' playing of her next line an extra edge aimed at him: 'Honest good fellows, ah, put up, put up; For well you know, this is a pitiful case.'

The last phrase in particular could have been designed as a comment on his performance. In this hypersensitive moment he imagined he saw a look of disapproval on Peggy Ashcroft's face too, although in reality she was concentrating so hard on keeping still as the dead Juliet that she was oblivious to Rattigan's contortions. At each succeeding performance Rattigan tried a different inflection of the line in order to try to kill the laugh, but to steadily worsening effect. He did not manage to stop the audience from laughing at him until the last performance, when he spoke his line so softly that no one heard it.

The production had lasting results for Rattigan. It checked a sneaking, but strengthening, desire to become an actor. It also introduced him to Gielgud and to John Perry, the two people to whom he attributed his eventual success in the theatre. Perry, an actor and writer, was only a little older than Rattigan, and had recently taken a house with Gielgud in the hills above Henley-on-Thames. He visited Oxford with Gielgud during the rehearsals and performances and continued to visit Rattigan once the production was over. Rattigan regarded Gielgud as 'the greatest man alive'. He was far too much in awe of him to approach him directly. A brasher young man, fired with Rattigan's single-minded ambition, might have turned his failings as an actor to his advantage, using them as an excuse to approach Gielgud under the guise of asking for correction and advice. However much he might have wanted to, Rattigan could not have brought himself to do this. Meeting John Perry presented an alternative way of getting closer to Gielgud and being introduced into theatrical circles.

Even though Rattigan's friendship with Perry may have been tinged with opportunism at the outset, it quickly developed into something more important. Their mutual admiration and respect lasted for the rest of Rattigan's life. Rattigan became a regular visitor in the Gielgud/Perry household. There were frequent high-spirited house parties. Perry and Rattigan shared a boyish enthusiasm for poker schools and exuberant ping-pong. Both were addicted to betting, and Rattigan would take days off from Oxford to go to race meetings with him. Rattigan remained too overawed to get very close to Gielgud. He was coltishly, unashamedly, star struck. So grown-up and sophisticated among his undergraduate friends, he was almost gauche when faced by Gielgud, Perry and their friends. Perry, although nothing like so well known as Gielgud, was to him a dazzling figure—'He was God!' He had almost everything Rattigan dreamed of—he moved among a glittering circle of actors who seemed able to choose their own productions and parts, to control their own careers and destinies. This was, of course, largely illusory, but Rattigan did not realize this. He was particularly impressed one day when Perry, having lost about a hundred pounds in their poker school, wrote a cheque for the full amount. Rattigan and his undergraduate friends rarely paid their debts.

Rattigan was moving into circles many of which were frankly homosexual. To these people, homosexuality was not a game or an affectation as it was among many Oxford Aesthetes. The theatre is one of the few professions in which it has almost never been a disadvantage to be homosexual. But it must not be supposed that this homosexuality was in any sense public knowledge. It had to remain the darkest of secrets, acknowledged only among close friends. Public admission of their sexual preferences would have ruined the careers of many theatre stars. Taboos against being 'queer' or 'degenerate' were absolute. The liberalizing influence of Edward Carpenter and Havelock Ellis had so far produced no effect on public or legal attitudes. E. M. Forster could not publish even the most discreet stories in which one man loved another. The Lord Chamberlain would not license any play which contained a tacit, let alone explicit, homosexual relationship. Noël Coward's 1926 play *Semi-Monde* remained unperformed until 1977. In many countries, the 1920s had seen an intellectual association of socialism with pacifism, free thinking, and liberal sexual attitudes which included homosexuality. In Germany in particular a more liberal attitude prevailed briefly, at least in large cities and among the political and creative avant-garde.

But these liberal views had never won general public acceptance, and by 1930 a massive reaction had set in. Public toleration of homosexuality was widely associated with national degeneration. A feature of fascist movements in all countries was their 'queer-bashing' mentality. Fascists promised to end national decline by, among other things, restoring moral discipline and ending sexual chaos. In Britain, homosexual acts, even between consenting adults in private, were illegal.

Outside hostility led inevitably to mutually protective homosexual in-groups. The accusation was made, and has been made at regular intervals ever since, that such groups controlled the theatre, or at least had a disproportionate influence over which plays and authors were encouraged, which actors, directors and designers were used in the most prestigious productions; that no man could make a successful career in the theatre unless he was 'bent', prepared to humour the powerful homosexuals with whom he came into contact. This was wild exaggeration in the early 1930s. The truth is that the theatre was more tolerant than society at large, and theatre people more liberal in their attitudes than people in other professions.

Rattigan was now almost twenty-one. As we have seen, he had expected his homosexual escapades at Harrow to be simply a passing phase 'until something better comes along'. He had been brought up to believe in the inevitability of marriage and children—even if his father's example suggested there might be a succession of 'right girls' rather than just one. While his friends were busy competing for the attentions of the limited number of girls at Oxford, he was still not really at ease with women and found men, rather than women, sexually attractive. 'Coming out' as a homosexual is almost never easy, even in the most sympathetic circumstances. One only has to consider Rattigan's background and the public attitude of the period to appreciate how difficult he must have found it to come to terms with the growing realization that he was a homosexual. It was obviously a subject that could never be broached at home. Although his friends at Oxford were tolerant, he did not like the sense of being different. Increasingly he tried to keep the knowledge secret from all but his closest friends and began to be careful not to do anything that might give him away. He still hoped that his homosexuality might not be final and might in some way be averted. The sense of guilt about his sexual feelings was never to leave him.

His visits to John Perry and his circle of theatrical friends were a relief. It was no secret that they found him attractive—'He was wonderfully good-looking. Very much the school cricket captain, you know. Very attractive', says one of them. Weekends away from Oxford lengthened and grew in number.

During this period, although he never specified the exact date,

Rattigan contracted venereal disease. He later claimed that this finally put him off women. A psychologist might interpret this as a rationalization frequently heard from homosexuals to justify the homosexuality they are reluctant to accept. In *Cause Célèbre*, Rattigan's last play, the boy Tony contracts a venereal disease from a prostitute and great play is made of the 'filthy, disgusting cure' he has to undergo as a result of this 'filthy, disgusting disease'. Rattigan claimed that he himself contracted VD as a result of an experiment with a prostitute. However, the radio and stage versions of *Cause Célèbre* are contradictory over this episode. In the earlier, and probably more autobiographically reliable, radio version, Tony tries but fails to make it with a prostitute. He leaves, ashamed and disillusioned. Whichever is closer to the true version of what happened, it is clear from what Rattigan said about the play that he had felt driven to try a sexual experiment with a woman, while attempting to come to terms with his sexual inclination. *Cause Célèbre* conjures up a picture of youthful desperation. The real-life consequences were disastrous, confirming feelings about himself which he wanted to avoid. In the long summer vacation of 1932, Rattigan had again been sent to a French crammer, this time at La Baule in Brittany. There is some evidence to suggest that the episode with the prostitute occurred while he was there.

As we have seen, even at Harrow Rattigan was interested in politics and the ideal of world peace. At university, his socialist leanings broadened. A hunger march passed through Oxford and made a profound impression on all thoughtful undergraduates. Like many of his friends, the nearest he had come to slums or factories was probably the view of smoking chimneys and rows of tiled roofs seen from the window of the train from Paddington to Oxford or on journeys to stay with friends near Liverpool. This lack of personal experience of real poverty did not mean that he lacked feeling for the suffering of others. Nevertheless it was inevitable that his concerns remained essentially middle class, and his most passionate political feelings were directed mainly towards international affairs.

In January 1933, Hitler came to power in Germany. Although with hindsight we may judge Rattigan's generation as naïve because they did not grasp the nature of Hitler's military intentions, the Nazi take-over strengthened their belief in the necessity for pacifism. World peace was a higher loyalty than narrow patriotism. Pacifism and disarmament were the best policy for Britain because they were the only hope for the world. Such was the reasoning behind a motion that came up for debate in the Oxford Union in February 1933: 'That this House will in no circumstances fight for its King and Country'. Its supporters, who included Rattigan and his friends Tony Goldschmidt and Philip Heimann, did not see themselves as disloyal, but as more far-sighted than their blinkered opponents.

To Rattigan and the 450 or so others who attended the debate it did not seem a particularly notable occasion. C. E. M. Joad, as the main speaker for the motion, made a brilliantly emotive pacifist speech, and Tony Goldschmidt spoke in his support in the general debate that followed. Rattigan was one of 275 who voted in favour of the motion, which was carried by 122 votes. But those who supported the motion had reckoned without the campaigning zeal of the *Daily Telegraph* and the Beaverbrook press. A few days later these newspapers orchestrated an outcry which reverberated around the world. Those who had voted for the motion were branded as 'woolly-minded Communists, practical jokers and sexual indeterminates'. They were indecent and decadent; they had proved that Britain had 'gone soft'.

As early as 1931 Philip Heimann had himself proposed a motion in the Oxford Union, which had been carried, but which had caused no stir at all. It had claimed that 'Pacifism is the only true form of Patriotism'. The importance of Rattigan's closeness to both Goldschmidt and Heimann at this period cannot be overstated. It was his involvement with Heimann that provoked his first mature play. For over a year Heimann had been embroiled in a romance with a woman undergraduate called Va-Va Basilewich. There were five Basilewich sisters. John Bayliss had fallen for another sister, Lydia. In 1933 the eldest of the five, Irina, who had married an Indian Army officer at the age of sixteen, left her husband and returned to England. She was twenty-six. In Oxford she met Philip Heimann and, despite recriminations and complications with the other sisters, they had fallen in love.

Rattigan was attracted to Heimann himself. He watched his friend, as he saw it, making a fool of himself over a woman who seemed far older than he was. He asked himself why Heimann and his other friends made their lives so difficult for themselves over women. At least one of his companions had been sent down for being found with a woman in his room. In spite of the prejudice and penalties imposed by the outside world, in his experience sex was easier between men. They did not make the mistake of confusing physical need with love.

He and Heimann spent hours discussing the possible consequences of Heimann's involvement with Irina. As he watched the development of his friend's relationship and monitored his own reactions to the feeling that she was coming between them, he began to conceive the idea for a play. As Heimann was so deeply involved in its conception, it was only logical that they should work on it together. The plot of *Embryo*, as they provisionally called it, was hammered out on spring morning walks in Christ Church Meadow. They decided to set it in an undergraduate lodging house in a university town thinly disguised from Oxford. It concerned four young men during a production of *Antony and Cleopatra* by the University Dramatic Society. Their lives are upset by the introduction into their midst of two very attractive professional actresses, one of whom is a star and quite a lot older than themselves. A love affair develops between her and one of the boys. A triangle situation is created when she finds she is competing for her young lover's affections with his closest friend—another of the boys living in the digs.

Some months previously Rattigan had been left £1,000 by his grandmother. He and Heimann had decided to invest it in putting on plays. They had advertised in the *Morning Post* for scripts and had received one they liked from a successful author. However, when they met him they were unimpressed and decided that they themselves must be able to do better than this 'uneducated second-rater'.[2]

They had a lot of fun satirizing the antics of their friends—they packed their play with betting, casual bedding, parties and in-jokes. Their animated conversations, interrupted by shrieks of laughter as they walked round the Meadow, were followed by more intense bursts of writing back at Canterbury House, but their play was still not complete by the end of the 1933 summer term.

Although Rattigan still had another year to do at Oxford, Heimann completed his law degree that summer and was due to return to South Africa. Rattigan's father had arranged for him to spend that summer polishing up his German at a crammer in a village in the Black Forest, so Heimann decided to go to Germany with Rattigan so that they could complete their play. In July 1933 Heimann left Irina Basilewich behind in England, and the two young men set off alone for a small village in the hills above Karlsruhe.

The weeks in Germany were happy. There seemed little compulsion to study German seriously and Heimann was allowed to put up in the house itself, sharing Rattigan's room. Everyone in the village soon knew about the two fair-haired young Englishmen who were writing a play. From the screams of laughter, they guessed it must be a comedy. One day Rattigan was delighted to hear the Germans speaking of their 'lustige Schauspiel'. Thinking 'lustige' meant 'lusty' rather than 'merry' he ran out into the garden, throwing sheets of manuscript into the air.

The two young men found a good deal to laugh at about the Germans, and planned to include in their play a skit on Hitler. Their German hosts were not amused—the *Hausfrau* was herself a Nazi. A few nights later Philip woke up in the middle of the night to find a member of the Hitler Youth in their bedroom. He had found the manuscript of *Embryo* and was about to steal and destroy the blasphemous document. They managed to retrieve the precious manuscript and bundle the zealous youth out of the room. The skit on Hitler did not appear in their finished manuscript, but Rattigan, as always, stored away his impressions of Germany during the first months of Nazi rule.

When the play was at last finished they parcelled it up and sent it to a manager with a reputation for putting on new work. Heimann returned to South Africa.

The loss of one friend was soon made good by the appearance of another. John Perry travelled out from England and took over Heimann's vacant place. The two friends were much amused by the antics of the other students. The small party of young men had been cooped up together for some weeks and must by now have been getting on each other's nerves. In the evenings Rattigan and Perry were also entertained by frantic arguments between the Nazi *Hausfrau* and her non-Nazi spouse. Hitler had consolidated the seizure of power that summer by removing his political opponents and was now opening a new phase—the psychological mobilization of the German masses. One night there was a massive torchlight rally in Karlsruhe, which Rattigan and Perry travelled down from their remote mountain village to see. 'Very pretty', was their reaction. Despite his deepening involvement with the Left, Hitler and the Nazis still seemed to Rattigan mainly a joke, something to be laughed into oblivion.

After five days away from the crammer, playing truant together in Salzburg, Rattigan and Perry returned to the Black Forest to find a message from Mr Rose, the theatre manager, suggesting an immediate production of *Embryo*. Borrowing the money for the air fare from Perry, Rattigan set out for Croydon. He described the excitement of that flight, with its free champagne and his first sight of London from the air, in the radio version of *Cause Célèbre*. In an unusually long stage direction, he begged the producer to select background sounds for the arrival at Croydon Aerodrome which would 'point up the extreme contrast between the leisurely sounds of Croydon in 1933 and Heathrow in 1975, when passengers have been transformed into so many cubic centimetres of idiot animal but insensate matter, to be mistreated, mishandled and misdirected at electronic will'. Travelling to Croydon in the 1930s, he added, was 'gentle and as comfortable a process as can never now be imagined'.

Back in London, he put up £200 towards the production, which was to open at a small experimental theatre near Kew Bridge—the Q—on 11 September. The play was retitled *First Episode*. Although the play is in places not fully realized, it is a truly remarkable first effort, especially when one considers that Rattigan was barely twenty-two at the time of its composition. With the benefit of hindsight, one can read in it an announcement of the themes that Rattigan would return to over and over again in his work. He shows a touching concern for incompatible lovers, in this case the actress Margot who falls victim to an uncontrollable passion, but finds the youthful object of that passion unable to make an adequate or enduring response. Inequality between lovers and the betrayal or humiliation fostered by such situations are an enduring motif in Rattigan's work. With Margot, too, we encounter the first of a series of portraits, seen largely from the perspective of the awestruck male, of predatory and intimidating females. Among the students in *First Episode* we meet prototypes of characters who will be repeated and developed in later plays: the guileless hearty, who seems impregnable to the envious, troubled and emotional intellectual; the apparently confident, but inexperienced, younger man who finds it difficult to articulate his emotions but who nevertheless triggers off a passion he cannot fully return and finds himself trapped thereby.

The young American critic and champion of Rattigan, Holly Hill, has defined what she calls 'the mind-body dichotomy' as a major theme running through Rattigan's work. This she describes as 'the assumption that man's spiritual and physical natures are irreconcilable and that one can only be satisfied at the expense of the other'. *First Episode* is the first of a long line of plays in which the characters are caught up in a conflict between physical desire and the dictates of reason. Repeatedly Rattigan's characters find themselves driven by bodily craving—normally sex—to act in ways which they know are against their own best interests, ways which are contrary to the prompting of their reason, and which defeat the power of their own wills. Even if some of the clumsier lines in the scenes in which the undergraduates in *First Episode* philosophize about the difference between mind and body are not Rattigan's but Heimann's, as suggested by John Barber, the critic and Oxford contemporary of Rattigan, the conflict between reason and desire which Margot, Tony and his best friend David each experience in their own ways is mainstream Rattigan.

In the relationship between Tony and David, we touch the element in the play which not only put it ahead of its time for a 1930s audience, but made it premature in Rattigan's development. Rattigan would portray many rewarding and sustaining friendships between men, but he steered away from openly depicting homosexual characters or relationships for almost thirty years after *First Episode*. In the intervening plays, as we shall see, he did sometimes covertly depict homosexual relationships, but under the guise of heterosexual ones. He was unwilling to risk either a clash with the Lord Chamberlain or too much self-revelation. Even in this play, the homosexual implications of the relationship between Tony and David are oblique rather than explicit. Their relationship can be played as an extension of the wholesome *Boy's Own* tradition of friendship between pure-minded men which dominated the Edwardian fiction of Rattigan's youth. But we know that, even at Harrow, Rattigan and his friends were scornful of that tradition and rejected the ideals it stood for. The necessary ambiguity in David and Tony's relationship is one of the unfolding strengths of the play; Rattigan portrays the two men becoming aware of the underlying nature of their feelings in a way that befits the early 1930s and his own post-Freudian generation.

The other Rattigan trademark which is already clearly in evidence is the economy of the dialogue. At first sight, Rattigan's dialogue is guilessly realistic, simply a reproduction of everyday speech. Closer examination reveals the layers of unspoken meaning behind even quite simple exchanges. With no apparent skill or contrivance, Rattigan achieves extraordinary condensation. *First Episode* is uneven compared to later work, but there are already some dialogue sequences of surgical economy. In the second act Tony tries to persuade Margot to go away with him, and Rattigan conveys a host of meanings, which would take many dramatists a full emotional outburst or a torrent of explanatory dialogue, in just three lines. Margot says that she is 'so very much more in love with you than you are with me'. Tony objects: 'That's not true, Margot; I do love you passionately.' And Margot replies: 'That's just it, and it may only be passion.' The last line in particular is not just the simple retort which at first it seems. It opens up a whole range of possibilities about both Tony's feelings and Margot's previous experience.

Again, early in the play Margot says to David: 'The friendship of young men can be very selfish.' David replies in three words: 'But so impregnable.' This looks effortless and in David's mouth simply glib, yet those two lines act like a depth charge whose shock waves spread out through the play until in the last Act the full explosive impact is realized by the reiteration of almost exactly the same words just as Margot is about to make her final exit, humiliated and defeated by a friendship between the boys, the depth of which the rest of the play has slowly revealed.

When analysed, his economy of dialogue can be seen as a skilful device, but Rattigan seems to have used it, at least in his most important scenes, almost unconsciously. It is a measure of his remarkable natural talent for theatre. What had interested Rattigan from his boyhood beginnings as a playwright was the drama of the implicit. In *First Episode*, as in so many of the plays that were to follow, he goes to tortuous lengths to set up a situation where there is a confrontation redolent with meanings and emotions which gain their full power from not being directly expressed. This central dramatic device in Rattigan's work is very closely bound up in his own rather elusive personality, and it is striking when reading his manuscripts to see how confidently written are these central, multi-layered scenes, with hardly a change between first draft and final text. The crossings out and changes of mind occur in the more consciously manipulated establishing scenes. Having arrived at his play's emotional centre, he writes with unwavering confidence dialogue which conveys depths of unspoken meaning.

Another similarly economic device was to become a characteristic of Rattigan's comedy writing, but in *First Episode* it is absent to such an extent that one is forced to the conclusion that most of the comedy either is Philip Heimann's or is an uneasy afterthought inserted to meet the demands of the play's commercial producer. *First Episode*'s greatest weakness to the modern reader is the obviousness of the comedy characters and situations.

The extent to which *First Episode* is drawn directly from Rattigan's and Heimann's own experience of Oxford is obvious. When they portray and explore their own emotional experiences, their escapades with bookies, proctors, parties and girls, the Gielgud production of *Romeo and Juliet*, they are not behaving so very differently from other writers. But the extent to which Rattigan would follow this format throughout his career is unusual. The core of *First Episode* is the adjustment of two young men to an essentially homosexual, if ambiguous, relationship: the effect on them of coming to terms with adult emotions and the fact that they do not reciprocate those emotions in equal measure. Rattigan's plots almost never exactly parallel the events of his own life. However, the fulcrum of the plot, the essential underlying issues, will always be close to his deepest concerns; and his plays' themes can usually be seen as working out or coming to terms with an emotion, a problem, a piece of self-revelation. In the same way, no one character can be said to stand for Rattigan, but the central characters may each contain aspects of his own personality, and the plot will contain elements of his own experience.

In a passage which we quoted in the Introduction, David Rudkin spoke of Rattigan's writing arising from a 'deep psychological necessity, a drive to organize the energy that arises out of his own pain', to express his own inmost feelings, yet keep himself hidden. The unique feature of *First Episode* is that Rattigan does not disguise what he is doing. Later in his life Rattigan more or less disowned the play and claimed to have burned his own copy. It had revealed with touching, but to him embarrassing, clarity his dawning homosexuality and the inner struggle connected with it.

Notes

1   Rattigan in an introduction to a season of his plays on BBC Radio in 1957.

2   In addition to the recollections of Rattigan himself, John Perry and the stories later told by Philip Heimann to his son David, our description of the composition of *First Episode*, as it came to be called, is taken from an article by John Barber in the *Daily Telegraph*, 18 July 1977.

3
French Without Tears

First Episode opened at the Q Theatre, near Kew Bridge, for a one-week run on 11 September 1933. It was directed for laughs, and the more serious side of the play, especially the homosexuality, was cut and toned down drastically. Even so, local reviewers found it a disturbing picture of university life, which would have been impossible to stage even as recently as the 1920s. The betting, the drinking, above all the casual sex, all came in for comment. It was perhaps lucky for Rattigan that news of the play did not reach the Oxford proctors. However, the small storm helped to make the play seem like a viable proposition for commercial transfer to the West End.

For the West End opening, the play was thrust even more firmly, by producer Muriel Pratt, in the direction of comedy than it had been at the Q and the cast was strengthened, again with comedy in mind.

The little Comedy Theatre in Panton Street was packed on Friday 26 January 1934. Philip Heimann had returned from South Africa to be present at the West End first night, and in addition to many Oxford friends there was a full turn-out of critics from the national and provincial press, including the most revered and hated critic of the day, James Agate. Also in the ranks of critics that night was Rattigan's undergraduate friend John Bayliss, who had got himself a commission to review the play from the magazine *Everyman*. He sat with pencil sharpened, intending to tear it apart.

In the event the first night was a success. For most of the play's duration, the audience roared with laughter. While most of them appeared to find the play shocking, they felt able to forgive it because of the production's infectious youthfulness.

Rattigan and Heimann took a shy curtain-call together, one wearing a white rose in his button-hole, and the other a red. After the first-night party, they went down to Fleet Street to buy the first editions. To their excitement, most of the critics were backing *First Episode* to run. The *Daily Telegraph* headlined the 'Success of *First Episode*' and their critic, W. A. Darlington, called it 'an exceedingly cheerful entertainment full of youthful high spirits'. Most of the reviewers saw it purely as a comedy, and where they detected a more serious side to the play either congratulated the authors on not dwelling on it or regretted that they had dragged it in at all. Even James Agate predicted that the play would run if its title was altered to '*When Children Wake*'. He told his readers that the play was 'remarkable for the avenues which it declines to explore'—he was not to know that all the authors' excursions down more serious avenues had been ruthlessly cut out. John Bayliss, in his piece in *Everyman*, confessed himself to have been completely won over. Admitting that the authors were his friends and that he was reluctant to believe that they were capable of anything, he said their first play demonstrated that they had 'all the talents necessary to the dramatist; their wit, their construction and their characterization are all of the highest class ...'[1] Over one thing the reviews were unanimous—the play was shocking, dirty, naughty; most identified the unnamed university as Oxford. The *News Chronicle* carried the headline 'STAGE SHOCK FOR OXFORD. Lurid picture in New Play'. In *First Episode*, Oxford had once again lived up to the 'degenerate' label attached to it after the 'King and Country' debate.

In Oxford itself the Proctors took a perhaps understandably dim view. As well as press enquiries they received letters from all over the country complaining about this 'disgusting new play about Oxford life'. Just how seriously they took the sensation that had been caused was gauged when they summoned Paul Dehn, the editor of *Cherwell* and one of Rattigan's friends, and issued an edict forbidding the paper from printing any review of the play.

By early March, *First Episode* had notched up fifty performances. Philip Heimann had decided to stay on in London and
moved into a flat on the corner of Half Moon Street to be near
Irina, who lived just across Green Park in Catherine Place. He
announced to the world that he and Rattigan were planning a
series of plays.

In fact he and Rattigan were getting no money from *First
Episode.* They had discovered that under the terms of the contract
they had signed the play had to take an impossibly high figure at
the box office before they were entitled to any royalty payments.
In spite of the encouraging reviews, *First Episode* was limping
rather than running at the Comedy. In its best week it had taken
barely £1,500. Rattigan and Heimann had received £100 advance
between them before the transfer to the West End, but nothing
more—not even repayment of the £200 Rattigan had put into the
original production.

Rattigan did not notice, however, that he was receiving no
money. He was too intoxicated with the excitement of simply
having a play running in the West End. He began to believe the
eulogizing quotes from the press posted up outside the theatre.
His fate was sealed when the management put up a notice
announcing '50th performance. Great success!' Oxford was tame
after this. He had known all along that he wanted to be a writer.
He would not take his finals or the Diplomatic entry exam, both
of which were drawing ominously close. He would embark upon
his career as a playwright at once.

With great dramatic flourish he wrote to his father from
Oxford. The great divide had been reached; he was going to be a
playwright, not a diplomat; he was going to live on his own and
his father would not know where to find him. Next, he went to
the Proctors and told them peremptorily that he was leaving.
They pointed out the consequences of such a step, but Rattigan
was unmoved. He then returned to London and moved in with
Philip Heimann in Half Moon Street—in those days an area
much favoured by impecunious but aspiring young men.

It was a riotous life while it lasted, despite their lack of money.
Wild schemes for plays, restaurants and parties every evening,
betting on account and praying a winner would come in at good
odds before Friday. In the mornings, a glass of tonic at Perkin's

the chemist on the corner of Piccadilly to chase the hangovers away.[2]

Rattigan felt he would be happy to live with Heimann in this way for ever; but in real life, unlike the theatre, Irina's claims on Heimann outweighed his. Before long Heimann returned to the family business in South Africa, taking Irina with him as his wife. There he wrote an unpublished novel about the triangular relationship between Irina, Rattigan and himself and then stopped writing. Although he and Rattigan remained friends, they did not complete another successful play together.

After receiving his son's letter from Oxford, Frank Rattigan very quickly found out where he had gone to live. He telephoned Heimann's flat and told his son that if he had absolutely decided to leave Oxford it might be wiser to live at home where he would at least have to pay no rent. But even if Rattigan did not like that argument, he was left with little alternative when *First Episode* closed at the beginning of April and left him without even the hope of an income. He was now completely broke and could not expect to go on living indefinitely off gambling and the hospitality of his friends. He returned home to face his father.

It seems probable that a number of people had approached Frank Rattigan and pointed out that his son did have real potential as a playwright. Vera almost certainly sympathized with her son's ambitions, and Frank cannot have been wholly unimpressed with the fact that his son had succeeded in getting his first play produced in London. The reviews had been generally favourable, the play had staggered on for three months, and everyone conceded that he had promise. For whatever reasons, and they may have been no more than paternal affection, Rattigan found his father much more understanding than he might have expected. He offered him an allowance of £200 a year for two years, during which time he could stay at home and write. If, after that time, he had not succeeded to the point where he could support himself, he would be directed into whatever safe job his father could find, for by then he would be too old to enter the Diplomatic Service.

A worldly twenty-three-year-old, Rattigan felt humiliated at the prospect of having to live at home, supported by his parents, yet it was a generous offer and not one he could afford to refuse. Thus began a desperate race against time for success. A desk was moved into his upstairs room at the back of his parents' flat at 19 Stanhope Gardens, and every morning, with the regularity of a junior clerk in an office, he sat down to confront the blank pages of an exercise book. Looking back on it, he found it incredible that he should have embarked on his career in this way—the daily confrontation with the blank sheet and more often than not no idea what he was going to write about. As a student he had always been so full of ideas. Now, faced with two clear years and the need to produce work that would succeed, they seemed to evaporate. Yet despite distractions he persisted. There was no turning back—'I just kept on writing until somehow I had finished a play. Then I started the next one.' Each one he parcelled up and posted in the pillar box at the corner to a theatrical manager; but they all came back, some with polite notes of rejection, some with no note at all. Out they went again to another management and back again. Round and round until each play had been to all the managements he could find in the telephone directory.

During that two-year period he wrote, and then re-wrote, six plays in all. Comedies, plays aping the style of favourite dramatists—O'Neill and Chekhov. Most have disappeared without trace, but two at least survived. One, *Black Forest*, was probably completed in the autumn of 1935 in Denmark, where he went for a holiday after receiving a nominal fee of £50 from Bronson Albery for his part in making an adaptation of *A Tale of Two Cities* and from an unsuccessful New York production of *First Episode*.[3]

Black Forest was a gloomy tale which grew from Rattigan's days at the crammer in Nazi Germany.[4] The play explores the rivalry of two young men over two girls. It contains a number of extremely intolerant allusions to Germans by a middle-aged Englishman—'The place is always so full of Germans it must smell terribly'. The play also contains Rattigan's first portrait of an energetic schoolboy trying with little success to fathom the standards of the adults around him. When his family are indignant about an unmarried couple who are living together, he asks: 'You mean if a clergyman came along and married them today, they'd suddenly change from nasty people to nice people?' Holly Hill's judgement is that *Black Forest* 'founders in its serious intentions: in the tangled inability of an assortment of

68

young people to recognize and reconcile their emotional and physical needs'. Rattigan himself called it 'a ghastly item ... a turgid drama about tangled emotions'.

He also wrote a play based directly on his experiences at both the French and German crammers. This failed to produce any favourable response from the managements and he completely re-wrote it early in 1935. It had been called *Joie de Vivre*, but he retitled it first *French Chalk* and then *Gone Away*. It was a comedy based on life at a French crammer very similar to the one he had been to in 1931 in Wimereux. The proprietor was firmly based on Monsieur Martin, and the plot grew out of imagining what would happen if a good-looking, man-hunting blonde with similarities to Philip Heimann's fiancée Irina was introduced into the circle of sex-starved young men incarcerated at the crammer.

Cooped up at home with his parents, surrounded by manuscripts and rejection slips, and generally rather ashamed of himself, Rattigan was glad to escape for weekends with friends. He went as often as he could to John Perry, who now had a house with John Gielgud at Fowlslow, near Finchingfield, in Essex. There he could be himself, free of the constraints and pretence of life in Stanhope Gardens. He was among friends, theatre people who shared his tastes and enthusiasms.

Fowlslow became a refuge also from the company of a detested collaborator, Hector Bolitho. Bolitho was a middle-aged New Zealander who wrote rather old-womanish travel books and novels. He was, however, successful, with a series of royal biographies to his name. When he invited Rattigan to collaborate on a stage adaptation of one of his novels, it was not the sort of opportunity Rattigan could afford to turn down. The introduction to Bolitho and the suggested collaboration very probably came about through Rattigan's father. Bolitho and the Rattigans had a number of friends in common and Frank seems to have been diligent in his efforts to find his son commissions. The story to be adapted was a turgid melodrama set in a Cambridgeshire farm. A possessive father goes steadily mad because his nineteen-year-old son has fallen in love with a girl undergraduate. In a fit of manic rage at what he sees as rejection by his son, the father strangles the maid and then goes upstairs to blow his own brains out. Bolitho and Rattigan no doubt thought that the father would provide a fine show part for a dramatic actor, and their main theatrical device was to have him stare broodingly at his upturned and flexing thumbs at regular intervals throughout the three acts, building up to a climactic outburst of mania and strangulation.

At the outset there was a certain kudos for Rattigan in being associated with Hector Bolitho, although it was not long before he discovered that his lack of enthusiasm for the plot of their play was more than matched by his growing dislike for his co-author. But there was no getting out of it, and he had to keep his feelings to himself. The best he could do was to move out of Bolitho's Tudor country house at Hempstead whenever he was not actually working with him and concentrate on his own writing in a near-by inn on the banks of the Cam. Better still, he could escape to Perry and Gielgud's house which was only eight miles away. This resulted in another, still more important, commission. Gielgud was under contract for a number of productions to Bronson Albery, and had conceived the idea of adapting Dickens' *A Tale of Two Cities* in such a way that he could play both Sidney Carton and the wicked Marquis de St Evremonde. Gielgud too was looking for a collaborator, and it was almost certainly John Perry who suggested asking Rattigan. Years afterwards, Rattigan recalled Gielgud saying to him vaguely: 'I can't find anyone to do this *Tale of Two Cities*. You're not doing anything—I'm sure you're not doing anything. Would you like to do it?' and then wondering out loud, 'I wonder if it's all right to have anyone without any experience?' It was a great opportunity for Rattigan and he accepted with alacrity.

For most of the summer of 1935 they worked together, Gielgud shaping the scenario and Rattigan writing the dialogue. When the first two acts were complete, they showed it to Albery, who promised that if the third act was equally good he would stage it in the autumn. They rushed back to the country and completed the script in a little over a week. Albery liked it and plans for the production went ahead. It was to be staged at Drury Lane, and a trio of young lady designers, the Motleys, who had first worked with Gielgud on the Oxford *Romeo and Juliet*, were brought in to design a composite set on which the complex succession of short scenes could alternate from one side of the stage to the other, using an upper stage that was reached by a central stairway for some of the intermediate episodes. Casting began immediately.

Gielgud and Rattigan's *Tale of Two Cities* is inevitably a

simplification of the original. It concentrates on the adventure-story aspects of the novel, omitting much of Dickens' richness and density of texture. A 1930s English jokiness is introduced, and some of the lines are so un-Dickensian that one is tempted to believe that they strayed in unnoticed while Rattigan's mind was on his comedy about the French crammer. The brooding quality of the novel and the depth of the characters are diminished thereby. Rattigan and Gielgud appeared to be using their adaptation as a liberal defence—inside a popular theatrical entertainment—of British democratic values set against the dictatorship and tyranny to be found abroad. In 1935 that was a valuable thing to attempt. Yet a closer adherence to Dickens' original might have served that purpose even better. Dickens' emotional power and ability to plumb the depths of human drudgery was outside Rattigan's range and would always be so. But if this version of *A Tale of Two Cities* was short on spirituality, it was strong on sweep and gusto. With the pro-duction that was being lined up it seemed certain to succeed and to establish Rattigan's reputation.

One can imagine Rattigan's shock when in September 1935, only two weeks before *A Tale of Two Cities* was to go into rehearsal, Gielgud said to him, as if he already knew what had happened, 'It's a pity about Martin Harvey, isn't it? But it's lucky that the design works for *Romeo and Juliet*, so we can do that instead. Larry says he'll do Mercutio. Isn't it marvellous?' Thus, without so much as an apology, Rattigan discovered that the production of *A Tale of Two Cities* had been dropped.[5] Gielgud had received an emotional letter from the ageing actor-manager Sir John Martin Harvey begging him not to put the play on since it was a part he was still playing successfully in numerous farewell performances in an adaptation entitled *The Only Way*. To put on a rival production would be disgraceful, he said, like putting on *The Bells* while Irving was still alive. Gielgud had taken the letter to Albery and together they met the veteran actor at the Garrick Club. Then, after consulting some critics, including James Agate, they decided reluctantly to drop the production. Albery and Gielgud needed an alternative production quickly. As he had wanted to have another go at *Romeo and Juliet* ever since the Oxford production, and realizing that he already had the services of a powerful cast, Gielgud proposed this instead.

The set the Motleys had designed for *A Tale of Two Cities* would, with a minimum of modification, serve perfectly for *Romeo and Juliet*. The crowning stroke was discovering that Laurence Olivier was prepared to drop a production he was planning to come into Gielgud's, so that the two of them could alternate the roles of Romeo and Mercutio. Gielgud was not deliberately unfeeling towards Rattigan; he simply did not see it from his point of view and was delighted that it had been possible to salvage a potentially disastrous situation. To Gielgud, 'what was good for the theatre was good, full stop!' Rattigan managed to conceal his feelings during the interview with Gielgud, but he went away and, alone in his room, he wept.[6]

The Gielgud-Olivier *Romeo and Juliet*, which opened on 17 October 1935, was of course one of the theatrical landmarks of the inter-war years. But Gielgud did not forget Rattigan. He persuaded Bronson Albery to send him a cheque for £50 in appreciation of his work on the adaptation of *A Tale of Two Cities*. With the cheque arrived a letter saying that Albery would be interested to read any other play he might have written. After eighteen months of frustration and rejection slips, at last a manager had asked him to submit a script. Rattigan debated long and earnestly which of his scripts to send. Albery had already received a number of Rattigan scripts, so the choice was limited to those he had not already rejected. This left two possibilities: one which Rattigan described as 'a rather turgid and ultra-serious psychological drama after Eugene O'Neill, an extremely long way after, I'm afraid'—this was probably *Black Forest*—or the comedy *Gone Away*. Albery's reputation was for serious plays rather than comedies, and Rattigan decided to send him the pseudo-O'Neill. At this point his mother intervened. 'Terence,' she said, 'better let him read a good farce than a bad drama!' Despite his protestations that eight other managements had already turned it down, she put the copy of *Gone Away* into an envelope and grimly sealed it.

Despite his new circle of friends and the areas of his life which he had kept carefully concealed, Rattigan and his mother had grown ever closer. Vera Rattigan was very interested in everything her son wrote. He had always enjoyed reading aloud what he wrote, and while he lived at home he had taken to trying out on her each new scene or important section of a play as he finished it. He found her reactions useful and increasingly he acted on her advice and criticism. For more than twenty years she would be the first audience for almost every play he wrote.

Bronson Albery read *Gone Away* on a train journey, laughing out loud at some of the lines. For a few pounds he bought a nine-month option. Gielgud also read a copy and he, too, liked it. He urged Albery to produce it quickly and suggested putting it on at the Embassy Theatre in Swiss Cottage with Jessie Matthews as the girl. However, Albery did not like the play so much that he was prepared to give it precedence over other more ambitious productions he had in the pipeline. *Gone Away* was put to one side.

1936 opened with Rattigan not really much further forward. The two years during which, according to his agreement with his father, he was to prove himself were almost up. Despite being asked to collaborate with Gielgud and Bolitho, he was no nearer being able to support himself. Apart from *Gone Away*, all the other plays he had completed had gone the rounds of the managements and had all been rejected, eight or nine times in most cases. His confidence was beginning to flag, yet he doggedly continued to write and rewrite. Another young writer, Emlyn Williams, told him, 'You just have to get over your disappointment and sit down and get on with it. Pick yourself up like we all have to do.'

During the summer of 1935, a sensational trial had caught his attention, the Rattenbury murder case, in which a middle-aged woman and her young lover, who was the family chauffeur, were accused of murdering her husband. Rattigan followed the case in the newspapers day by day as it unfolded. Alma Rattenbury had taken her young lover, Stoner, because of her husband's failure as a sex partner, but had soon found herself sexually and emotionally dependent on him. When Mr Rattenbury was found brutally beaten to death with a mallet, Mrs Rattenbury and young Stoner were jointly charged with the murder. Popular prejudice held that the boy must have been under Mrs Rattenbury's influence because she was so much older, and there was a public outcry when the jury found only Stoner guilty. On 5 June 1935, a few days after the end of the trial, Rattigan was on a London bus when he saw an evening newspaper headline—'Mrs Rattenbury: Suicide'. He jumped off the bus and bought the paper. Despite being acquitted, she had stabbed herself to death, leaving a note which implied that everything beautiful in her life had been destroyed. Even as he read it, he thought—there's a play there! For months he brooded, but a full year later he had still not managed to organize the story into a play.

As 1936 drew on Rattigan became steadily more discouraged. He wondered if he should give up the idea of being a playwright and find some other way of making his living in the theatre. He wrote to St John Ervine, who was both a critic and a playwright, telling him that he had written several plays but they had all been rejected, and asking if he should give up playwriting. He wondered if he should try turning his hand to criticism. St John Ervine replied that he must press on. Although he had not read any of his plays and expected that they were pretty awful, it was better to be a creative writer than a critic.

That summer Albery's option on *Gone Away* ran out and he had still not produced it. Dispirited, Rattigan showed the script to a friend, Norman Hast. 'Don't worry,' Hast told him after reading it. 'Within three years you will have a successful play running.' But Rattigan's two years were up. He now had to accept whatever job his father could find him.

The problem of his son's career had never been far from Frank Rattigan's mind. Although his son had disappointed all his hopes and seemed to be turning out to be the sort of young man he most disapproved of, he still did not desert him. He turned to a film producer he had met to see if he might find him some sort of job in a film studio. Through the producer's influence, and on the strength of *First Episode*, Rattigan was eventually given a job by Warner Brothers as a scriptwriter at their Teddington Studios. It was a seven-year contract with yearly options on the management side but none on his. At the end of that time the studio had the option to renew for an indefinite period. They could loan him out to other studios as they saw fit. In the unlikely event of their wanting to send him to Hollywood, they could do so for only a fifteen-per-cent increase in his salary. The salary was £15 per week, going up to £20 at the end of two years and thereafter increasing at yearly intervals until it reached £45 per week in the seventh year—not a bad living wage by the standards of the time.

At this time each of the major studios had a number of writers on their payroll. These writers were expected to clock on and off each day even when there was nothing for them to do. They sat in the Writers' Room waiting for a scenario to be assigned to them or for a scene that needed knocking into shape for whatever picture was on the floor. After he had been at Teddington a little while, Rattigan approached the head of the studio, Irving Asher, with a proposition. He would be prepared to sell Warner Brothers the rights to *Gone Away* for a single lump-sum payment. Asked how much he wanted, Rattigan did a rapid calculation: 'You can have the whole thing—world rights, everything, all for £200. I need the money.' Asher agreed to read it. Later, Rattigan got a message, passed down through his head of department—Asher was sorry but his script was no good, either as a film or a play.

His first major assignment at the studio came in the autumn of 1936. He was given two weeks to prepare a script from Eleanor Smith's novel of gipsy life, *Tzigane*. He sweated away and by the end of the fortnight congratulated himself that he had done a pretty good job. He sent it to Irving Asher and sat back confidently. Next day Asher summoned him. Crossing the pile carpet towards the vast desk, Rattigan was dismayed to see his boss pick up the script by one corner like a dirty handkerchief. 'Did you write *this*?' Asher asked. 'Well, yes, as a matter of fact I did,' replied Rattigan, still believing that if there was any justice in the world congratulations should follow. 'I thought so,' said Asher. Then he took the script firmly in both hands, tore it in two and dropped it in the waste-paper basket. Next he rang the bell and asked his secretary to send in another scriptwriter who had been with the company for some time. This character speedily appeared and Asher told him, 'I want you to take this young man Terence Rattigan away, and show him how to write scripts *properly*.'

In later years Rattigan conceded that the soulless regime of the studio was of value to him. It taught him a still more ruthless economy: 'There was no time for frills. The plot had to be told in three lines.' The experience purged him of any lingering pretensions towards fine writing acquired at Oxford. How his work read was unimportant; it was how it played that mattered. Nevertheless, his true feelings about work in the studio were graphically revealed shortly after he left. A fellow writer who inherited his desk in the Writers' Room found a studio list of Do's and Don't's for scriptwriters in one of the drawers. At the bottom Rattigan had scrawled, 'Look behind radiator'. The newcomer did. He found a large sheet of cardboard. Scrawled boldly across it was a single word: 'Balls'.

Unknown to Rattigan, while he was undergoing the humiliations of being a studio writer, things were moving in his favour. Bronson Albery's autumn schedule of productions had run into trouble. A major production had unexpectedly flopped, and in late September the play he had put into the Criterion, *The Lady of La Paz* starring Lilian Braithwaite, started to lose money. Albery desperately needed a cheap production to put in as a six-week stop-gap until his next big production was ready. The play that had made him laugh on the train journey was remembered. *Gone Away* called for only one set and a young cast—it would be cheap to put on.

Casting began at once. As a new young author, Rattigan found he was not consulted, but it did not matter—having the play produced was excitement enough. During the next two weeks Albery and his director rapidly assembled a cast. Kay Hammond, Rex Harrison and Roland Culver were the only actors that anyone outside the theatre had heard of—and none of them was a big enough name to be a draw. Albery fixed the top salary at £25 a week. Harrison asked for £30, but did not get it. No one could be found to play the youngest of the students. At the last moment Rattigan's agent, A. D. Peters, who had demonstrated his faith in his client by putting £500 of his own money into the production, suggested a lad called Trevor Howard.

The first reading of *Gone Away* was in Bronson Albery's office at the New Theatre on the evening of 15 October 1936. These readings are always dry-mouthed occasions. No one quite knows how much is expected of him, and yet there is a feeling of being watched and judged. Even the most struttingly confident actors can be reduced to the edge of incoherence. For the author it is worst of all. When Rattigan entered Albery's office high above St Martin's Lane just before 7.30 that Wednesday evening, he had not so much as been introduced to the director, Harold French. Over-loud and rather too enunciated voices, the trademark by which any group of actors is immediately recognizable in a crowd, filled the room. Actors and actresses were catching up on each other's gossip. No one noticed Rattigan, a conventionally dressed young man hovering in a corner outside the animated group.

The stage manager called everyone to order. The cast took their places on chairs arranged in a semi-circle facing a small table, where Harold French sat with Albery and the stage manager. Rattigan found a chair in a corner.

The reading began. Harrison mumbled, Culver put in an 'er' before almost every line and Kay Hammond kept losing her place. However, there was an occasional chuckle from the cast and Rattigan himself could not help smiling at some of the lines. At the end of the second act there was a break while coffee was served. He was too shy to push himself forward and get a cup, so he hovered empty-handed on the edge of the group discussing the play. Then Kay Hammond spotted him, realized who he was, and approached with the director. French apologized for having ignored him and produced a cup of coffee. The reading resumed, and when it was over there was fuller discussion of the play. Then French asked Rattigan if he would care to join him for a drink at the Green Room Club. His eyes lit up—at the time Harold French thought it was the prospect of a drink that appealed to him—but on the way there Rattigan shyly confessed that he had always wanted to enter that theatrical holy-of-holies, ever since he had heard of its existence as a stage-struck schoolboy.

It was an evening Rattigan would never forget. Harold French was a rising director and to Rattigan appeared some kind of king. This impression grew as he plied Rattigan with dry Martinis, and club members—most of them household names—strolled past. Rattigan tried hard not to stare but to keep his mind on the suggestions that French was making about the play. Even so, from time to time he could not help interrupting to ask if that wasn't this or that famous star? Always the answer was 'Yes'. It was a dream come true. French could have asked him to change anything in the play and he would have agreed. Here he was, with a distinguished director treating him as an equal, asking his opinion on possible changes with charming deference, calling him 'old fellow', 'dear chap' and on one occasion even 'my dearest darling boy'. He feared that such endearments between men in a public place might get them thrown out, but no moustache bristled, no irate eyebrow was raised. From time to time, one of the passing gods stopped to exchange a word with French and

Rattigan was introduced—'The author of the new play I'm directing at the Criterion. Brilliant work—I only hope I don't let it down.'

After the third Martini, French broached the serious topic he wanted to discuss: the play's title. *Gone Away* suggested a hunting background, pink coats, horses and hounds. Rattigan saw what he meant; as a title, it raised false expectations: 'Would you mind awfully if I gave it some thought?' One more drink and he left.

Back at home, through a haze of drink and excitement, he racked his brains for a new title. Then he remembered a popular little French primer by Lady Bell—*French Without Tears*. It was 1.30 in the morning but he telephoned Harold French. 'This is Terry Rattigan here. I'm terribly sorry to disturb you, but I've been thinking, and you're quite right ... er ... This is only an idea. Kick it out if you don't like it ... but would *French Without Tears* be any good?' French liked it at once. The new title was fixed.

The first dress rehearsal at the Criterion Theatre was on Wednesday, 4 November. Apart from the usual problems with missed lighting cues, some ill-fitting costumes and the unfamiliarity of the cast with the set and furniture, it was not too bad. Rattigan lurked unobtrusively in the Dress Circle, but as the play neared its end he realized that the final twist he had given to his light plot did not produce quite the effect he had intended. Having been rejected by all the other young men at the crammer, the man-hunting girl, played by Kay Hammond, waits expectantly for the arrival of a new student, the titled heir to a fortune, Lord Heybrook. When he appears, he is an effeminate young man trailing a Borzoi dog. The man-hunter is confounded. Rattigan found this left a bad taste in the mouth, and felt it would send the audience out of the theatre in the wrong mood.

French asked him to go round with him while he gave 'notes' to the cast. Backstage the mood was good, morale was high, yet Rattigan was uneasy. That ending was not right. He asked French to have dinner with him at the Public Schools Club. Over the meal they talked about the play and one or two small cuts French wanted to make before the next day's final dress rehearsal, but Rattigan was not really listening. French could see something was wrong. Rattigan was reluctant to reveal such last-minute misgivings, but finally blurted out in a voice that made him sound angry, 'You know, Harold, I don't like the end of the play.' French started to protest, but he hurried on, 'What I don't like is that blond, swishy queer coming in with his dog and that fatuous dragged-in line, "Come along, Alcibiades." It's sort of … out of character with the rest of the play. Do you see what I'm getting at?' French was silent. Rattigan continued: 'It might easily kill Kay's and Rex's lines afterwards … or am I being a bloody fool?'

There was a silence. Eventually French asked, 'Have you any alternative in mind?' Rattigan had to confess that he hadn't. They sat in silence. Then an idea began to form in Rattigan's mind. A title can be inherited at any age. Why couldn't Lord Heybrook be a little boy of thirteen or fourteen? Then, enthusiasm growing, he hurried on: 'It would be just as big a smack in the eye for Kay; the twist to the play would be there, without the unpleasant taste. What do you think?'

French obviously liked the idea, but the play was due to open in less than forty-eight hours. Albery would have to be told, a boy would have to be found and a loyal actor fired. Even if all that were possible, the new ending would have to be rehearsed before the next evening's final dress rehearsal. A last-minute dislocation of this sort could upset the cast, who were building themselves up for Friday's opening. But Harold French agreed. It would make a much better ending to the play.

Next morning, Albery was bearded in his office. He finally dropped his objections when French pointed out that not only would a boy's salary be smaller than a grown actor's, but that he would not have to pay for the hire of the Borzoi dog. Rattigan kept out of the way for the rest of the day while French and his stage manager auditioned boys from stage schools and made all the other arrangements. That evening Rattigan telephoned him and asked if he could bring his mother to the final dress rehearsal. He promised she would not get in the way.

At 6.15 the final dress rehearsal began. There were a dozen or so people dotted about the box-like, plush and gilt theatre. Apart from Harold French, Rattigan and his mother, there were the people who had put up the £1,500 for the production, A. D. Peters and Alban Limpus, the man who had put on many of Noël Coward's successes. Among the few friends and other interested parties present were Ralph Lynn, the famous farceur, and Rattigan's film-studio boss, Irving Asher. Sitting far apart in a dark auditorium, this handful of people felt isolated and constrained. They were in no mood to laugh. The result, added to uncertainty about the new ending, was disastrous. The actors were slow, and 'dried'. Someone had had a row with Kay Hammond and it showed. Harrison was forced and Culver put in even more 'ers' than he had at the first read-through. There was not so much as a titter from 'the house'.

The moment the final curtain came down Albery and Alban Limpus hurried out. Albery telephoned his office and made immediate arrangements to bring in another show which he had in the provinces, as soon as it could be moved. He gave *French Without Tears* a week. Limpus made a series of phone calls and off-loaded his share of the production to a big theatrical agency called O'Brien, Linnett and Dunfee.

While Harold French still sat frozen with misery in the stalls, A. D. Peters had gone backstage and was offering his share in the production to any of the actors for £100. No one would take it. Ralph Lynn was also talking to the cast: 'Don't open! It's simply dreadful. Don't open!' he told them. Rattigan packed his mother off home and waited miserably by the stage-door to see what would happen. There Irving Asher found him: 'Don't worry too much, Terry,' he said gently, 'everyone has these flops!' Rattigan knew he was trying to comfort him in preparation for the bashing he was going to get from the critics.

Suddenly Harold French appeared backstage, galvanized into action. He called the disconsolate cast together and gave them the most terrible dressing down: 'That was the most disgusting performance I have ever seen from actors who call themselves professionals. How bloody dare you!' One or two started to protest, saying they could not open. But French would have none of it: 'I don't want any excuses.' He ordered them to go back to their dressing-rooms to get ready for another dress rehearsal immediately. The curtain would go up in fifteen minutes. He ordered that the set, which was a nasty dark green, was to be repainted before the next day's opening. The only member of the cast who remained at all confident was Roland Culver. He told Jessica Tandy to stop worrying—the play would be a great success.

Fifteen minutes later, French and the Front of House Manager found Rattigan in the foyer, head down, apparently studying the pattern in the carpet. French said, 'Terry, I don't know if anyone has told you, but we are having another full rehearsal right away.' Rattigan looked up and then said slowly, 'I don't think I could stand it again.' 'Balls,' said French, grabbing his arm, and the three men went down the stairs into the stalls. French sat near the front while Rattigan and the Front of House Manager sat further back. This time the run went smoothly. Afterwards the Front of House Manager reassured Rattigan and French: 'The show's fine, Bronnie Albery must be potty, and I'm going to tell him so first thing in the morning.'

It was now ten o'clock and Rattigan decided to go to the Savoy for supper. Perhaps he hoped to cheer himself up. He was still convinced his career as a playwright was finished. Entering the restaurant, he spotted Irving Asher and told him he could still buy the play. Asher politely declined. Another diner at the Savoy that evening was one of his friends from Oxford, Peter Glenville, who was now embarked on a successful theatrical career and had just returned from playing Romeo, Petruchio and Mark Antony at Stratford. They exchanged gossip, Rattigan bemoaning the fact that fame and fortune had eluded him. Later they drove home together. Turning into Piccadilly, Rattigan pointed to the Criterion and said casually, almost as an afterthought, 'They're doing a play of mine there tomorrow night. Don't congratulate me. They're only running it as a stop-gap because another play has folded.' That was the first mention he had made to Glenville of the production of *French Without Tears*.

Friday, 6 November, was a wet and gloomy day. Finding himself with nothing that he could usefully do and desperate to keep his mind off what was going to happen that evening, Rattigan went out and walked round London. Then he turned into a barber's shop and had his hair cut.

That evening, before the performance, he and his parents went out to dinner. They had a bottle of champagne in an attempt to celebrate, but it was a glum meal. Although they were too polite to say so, they all privately felt that it was going to be a disastrous evening. After the meal, Vera slipped the champagne cork into her purse as a souvenir. When they reached the theatre, their spirits sank still lower. It was still raining and there were two other first nights in London that evening: opera at Covent Garden and the première of a Marlene Dietrich film. The West End was choked with traffic and the audience was coming into the theatre soaked and bad tempered.

The curtain went up to reveal Trevor Howard, as the youngest of a group of students at a French crammer, eating his breakfast and trying to finish his French composition in time for a tutorial. He was joined immediately by another student, played by Guy Middleton, whose first lines consisted of ordering bacon and eggs in loud but appalling French. The sublime over-confidence with which he did it produced a peal of infectious laughter from Cicely Courtneidge, the musical-comedy star, who was sitting a few rows back in the stalls. That set the tone for the rest of the audience and, a few lines later, when Middleton translated, 'She has ideas above her station' as 'Elle a des idées au-dessus de sa gare', the audience gave a full-throated roar of delight. Only a page into the play and they were off to a good start.

The cast did not seem able to believe their ears. Still tense and nervous, they hurried on, without waiting for the laughs, or timing their lines so as to build them. Hovering at the back of his box, Harold French was uneasy. If the cast did not calm down and play the audience accurately they would lose their sympathy. The rush continued for fifteen or twenty minutes, until Roland Culver came on. A few seconds after his entrance, he played a line he knew should get a laugh; it came. Then with the self-assurance built of experience and his faith in the play, he waited. The laugh grew. There was applause. Only then, with perfect timing, did he complete the line. He had steadied the anxious cast and now they all started to play with that confidence and touch which is the greatest joy of an actor's craft. The evening developed into one of the most magical first nights of all time.

As the final curtain rattled down, there was a storm of applause and people rose in their seats calling 'Author, Author!' Harold French dived backstage looking for Rattigan, who had vanished from his place at the back of the Dress Circle. When he found him, in white tie and tails, he was green-faced and leaning for support against the back wall of the theatre. French virtually threw him on to the stage. The cheering grew louder. The success of the play was so unexpected that no one had arranged for the customary first night speeches. As Rattigan stepped forward to thank the audience the curtain unceremoniously came down on his head.[7]

In the small hours of the next morning, Rattigan lay, with the rest of the cast, on the floor of Kay Hammond's sitting room reading the first editions of the morning newspapers. With the exception of the *Daily Herald* ('It has no conceivable relation to British Drama, and is a depressing commentary on the West End Theatre'), they were falling over themselves with praise. 'This brilliant little comedy'—'Full marks'—'Joyous jest'. In the *Daily Telegraph*, W. A. Darlington hailed Rattigan as a young author with the rare gift of lightness, while the *Morning Post* said his play was 'gay, witty, thoroughly contemporary without being unpleasantly "modern", brisk without blather and with a touch of lovable truth behind all its satire'. As the first light of dawn crept into the sky and the other guests started to tiptoe away, Rattigan was still stretched out on the floor, the papers strewn round him. He turned on his back and, staring up at Kay Hammond, whispered in blank and awestruck amazement: 'But I don't believe it. Even *The Times* likes it.'

When Harold French had first read *French Without Tears*, the thing that appealed to him particularly was a quality of tenderness which showed through the humour. It is this survival from the play's serious beginnings in Rattigan's own, at times painful, experience which gives the play its ultimate durability. Since the initial idea for the play, five years previously, Rattigan had rewritten and refined his material many times, but the essential core of feeling, which is necessary for any comedy to be other than merely empty and transient, remained. Although everything in the play was now seen for its humour, and each comic permutation was exploited to the full, both situation and characters were still rooted in real experience. People who knew the background to the story thought the characters too life-like. Rattigan's mother was concerned right up to the first night that the real people on whom the characters were based would recognize themselves and sue. Indeed, after that first night Irina Basilewich's sister cornered Rattigan and accused him of modelling Kay Hammond's character, the man-hunting girl, on Irina. 'That was a bit near the bone,' she said. 'The nearer the bone the sweeter the meat,' he replied gracefully.

The action of *French Without Tears* is set in the living room of Monsieur Maingot's French cramming establishment in a small seaside town on the west coast of France. There are five students in residence, and the plot traces the comic results of the man-hunting activities of a beautiful young woman, Diana, who contrives in turn to hook each of the young men incarcerated in the crammer, and then unscrupulously attempts to play them all simultaneously.

French Without Tears is an advance on *First Episode*, primarily because of its delicacy and wit. Where the humour in *First Episode* is often crass and juvenile, with most of its ideas borrowed from the repertory of stock comedy and grafted rather uneasily on to a play to which they do not really belong, *French Without Tears* is a comedy in which the humour and the emotion are inseparably blended, each arising naturally from the other. Such serious ideas as there are in the play seem for the most part to belong to it. *French Without Tears* can lay claim to being the best, as well as the best-known, comedy of the 1930s, and the representative British play of that decade. Noël Coward wrote nothing to compare with *French Without Tears* between 1930 and the war; Shaw wrote nothing of importance for the theatre during the decade; the work of Auden and Isherwood was not in the mainstream of popular theatre; and it is arguable that, although it only deals with the antics of a few privileged young people, *French Without Tears* touches more precisely on the central concerns of the generation that was rising to confront the onset of the Second World War than any of Auden and Isherwood's more obviously committed plays. J. B. Priestley produced four good plays in the 1930s: *Dangerous Corner*, *Laburnum Grove*, *When We Are Married* and *Johnson Over Jordan*; but none of them has the combination of tenderness and humour which pervades *French Without Tears*.

Rattigan himself said that his model while writing *French Without Tears* was Chekhov. He cited the succession of short scenes between different groups of characters, and the way the central situation is built up almost imperceptibly through an accumulation of small events and revelations. The characters are all fully developed and of almost equal importance. There is another sense in which, with the benefit of hindsight, the play can be seen as belonging in the Chekhov tradition. Where Chekhov conveys the mood of uneasiness and underlying tension in middle-class Russian society in the years leading up to the Revolution, Rattigan seems to achieve something of the same effect in *French Without Tears*. Today, one cannot fail to be aware that, behind the apparently empty-headed exuberance of his young people, their love affairs and petty squabbles, lurks a sense of futility, of being at the mercy of outside events. Beyond the set there lies a world of political violence which is not subject to reason or argument.

The most obviously political passage in the play is a long section in the second act where Alan, a student who is at the crammer at the insistence of his father but who really wants to be a novelist, not a diplomat, describes a novel he has just had rejected by yet another publisher. The plot of his novel concerns two pacifists who desert their country rather than fight in a new war. In exile they, like the boys in the play, come to blows over a woman. Nevertheless, Alan tells the vehemently patriotic Commander, their saving grace is that they have the honesty to accept that the instinct to fight, either each other or a war, is something to be ashamed of; they do not rationalize it as patriotism or manliness. They go back to fight for their country only because they admit that their reason is not strong enough to stand up against this ignoble instinct. The Commander says triumphantly that they were proved wrong in the end, but Alan tells him that because they were unable to live up to their ideal, that does not prove it was wrong. Another student asks, 'What's the use of an ideal, if you can't live up to it?' Alan replies, 'In a hundred years' time men may be able to live up to our ideals even if they can't live up to their own.' This belief in the eventual painful triumph of reason over instinct is one of the consistent hopes of Rattigan's life and work.

The conflict between emotion and reason which is a motif in all Rattigan's plays surfaces repeatedly through *French Without Tears*. In one scene the Commander and a younger student, Kit, are struggling to subdue their urge to fight over Diana. Kit asks, 'I wonder why it's such a comfort to get away from reason.'

COMMANDER: Because in this case reason tells us something our vanity won't let us accept.

KIT: It tells us that Diana's a bitch. (*The Commander's belligerent instincts rise again.*) Reason!

COMMANDER: You're right.

In Rattigan's plays the consequence of giving way to overpowering emotions is almost always shame. The tension lies in the struggle of his characters to resist the demands of such emotions. The most envied of the students is Brian. He manages to remain detached while the others suffer and squabble over the beautiful Diana. He relieves his frustrations by saving up to purchase the favours of a local prostitute. His fellow students concede that he has solved the problem of living better than any of them by the simple expedient of paying for sex rather than feeling love. It is Brian who finally opens their eyes to the way to deal with Diana by making them see that all they have to do is to ask her directly for sex. When she refuses they are free from her.

Even in this lightest of comedies Rattigan is preoccupied with the results of unequal love and love which goes unspoken, with painful consequences for the lovers. Kit and the Commander both love Diana, but she does not really love them—and the result is hilarious. Diana secretly loves Alan, but in vain. She dare not risk the humiliation of letting him know her feelings. When she does, it is hilariously too late. Again the results are disastrous. Jacqueline, the long-suffering daughter of the proprietor of the crammer, loves Kit but won't tell him, and so is unhappy because he does not notice her. Once someone else has told Kit how Jacqueline feels, the way is open for them to come happily together. In *French Without Tears*, the inequalities of love and the failure to express hidden feelings are worked out lightly. In the plays which followed, they are worked out in steadily more passionate earnest.

Notes

1   One Sunday newspaper, the *Sunday Express*, recalled that in 1920 another professional actress, Cathleen Nesbitt, had gone to Oxford to play Cleopatra and had actually married her undergraduate Antony. Miss Nesbitt herself believed that Heimann and Rattigan must have based their play on her case, but in fact neither of them knew of that episode until after their play had been produced and it was pointed out to them.

2   It was not until years later that it was discovered that the contents of Perkin's 'tonic' were sixty per cent medical alcohol, when a habitual customer was convicted for drunken driving. No wonder successive generations of West End party goers found that a call on the way to work for a glass of tonic drunk at the shop counter was the only way they could face the day.

3   Writing of the New York production of *First Episode*, Brooks Atkinson called the production very crude and complained that had the theme been earnestly pursued the play might well have made 'a disarmingly poignant drama'. He and the other New York critics strongly condemned the over-obvious farce that had been introduced to the detriment of the play underneath. The lesson was not learned. Another farcical production of the play was tried at the Garrick Theatre, London, in December 1934, and again it failed.

4   We were unable to turn up a copy of this play when we did our research in 1977 and 1978, but when Holly Hill was searching the Rattigan archives in 1975 she came across a copy and we are indebted to her for her description of it.

5   This is how Rattigan remembered the conversation when talking to the authors in 1977.

6   Although there were a number of proposals to produce Gielgud and Rattigan's *A Tale of Two Cities* in the years immediately before the Second World War, including a production with music and lyrics, the play was not staged until 1950, when it was given an amateur production by the St Brendan's College Dramatic Society in Bristol. This was followed later in the same year by a radio production starring Eric Portman as Sidney Carton.

7   For our description of many of the events surrounding the production of *French Without Tears*, we have drawn extensively on Harold French's second volume of autobiography *I Thought I Never Could* (Secker & Warburg, 1973) and on Rattigan's introduction to Harold French's first volume of autobiography *I Swore I Never Would* (Secker & Warburg, 1970).

4
After the Dance

'I no more understand this sort of play and acting than my cat understands Euclid,' wrote James Agate in his *Sunday Times* review of *French Without Tears*. The posh Sundays brought a douche of cold water after the elation of the daily paper reviews. In the *Observer*, Ivor Brown also did not rate Rattigan as a writer, '... his play, brief and brittle, with little construction and no freshness or fun'—had, Brown claimed, only been saved by the director and cast.

Agate's outspoken criticism caused an uproar. He was accused of having arrived at the theatre fifteen minutes late, of staying only thirty minutes, and of spending most of this time looking at the audience rather than the stage. But Agate was unrepentant and continued to attack the play in his column. The row rumbled on, bursting into a final conflagration in March 1938, when Agate disparagingly named *French Without Tears* last in a list of plays running in the West End. John Gielgud, at some risk to himself, sprang to Rattigan's defence. He protested, in an open letter to the *Sunday Times*, that he had read Rattigan's play in manuscript and thought it 'particularly delightful and original both in conception and execution'. He reprimanded Agate for ignominiously baiting a promising young playwright, and reminded him that the theatre was in great need of young writers.

Agate used his speech at the annual Gallery First Nighters'

dinner, on the same day that Gielgud's letter appeared, to attack both Gielgud and the notion that popular success could be equated with quality—which was hardly Gielgud's point. Percy Walsh, a member of the original cast who was a guest at the dinner, was so incensed that he jumped to his feet in protest. There was uproar. Shouts of 'Sit down'. Cheers and counter-cheers. Percy Walsh was escorted from the room by a steward, while James Agate said that he would maintain to the grave a critic's duty to condemn work he dislikes no matter how popular it may be. A week later, Agate returned to the attack in a long reply to Gielgud in the *Sunday Times*. His central point was that plays such as *French Without Tears* are not harmless. The critic who endorsed such poor-quality work, he argued, discouraged and delayed the day when a finer theatre based on true critical standards would come into its own. Popular Piccadilly knick-knacks only encouraged the mindless, perfunctory, popular audience in its laziness.

Adverse criticism is often more deeply felt by those who receive it than praise. Rattigan was no exception. He had ambition as a writer, and broadsides like this, especially from such respected quarters, reinforced his determination to be taken seriously. But the three-year struggle for financial success, the daily confrontation with the blank sheets of paper in an upstairs back room, the stream of finished plays and answering rejection slips, had combined to deplete his stock of creative fuel. The sudden and wholly unanticipated popular success of *French Without Tears*, and the resulting transformation of his financial situation, produced an inevitable reaction—something very like a breakdown.

He abandoned himself to a life of pleasure and gave up any attempt at serious writing. With his income rising overnight to more than £100 per week, he moved out of his father's home into a high-ceilinged flat in Hertford Street, Mayfair, where he started repaying some of his friends' hospitality. His drink and gambling bills rose in proportion to his income. Always a fastidious dresser, he now indulged his taste for Savile Row tailoring and took to having his hair cut by the King's barber. He bought a motor car and formed himself into a limited liability company for tax purposes. But his accountant was soon chiding him for his extravagance, and when a year or so after the play had opened he went out and bought a Rolls-Royce, his accountant remonstrated:

'But you don't have that sort of money.' Rattigan replied that since everyone thought he had, 'It's your responsibility to see I do have!'

The first-night success of *French Without Tears* was immediately confirmed. Delighted audiences packed the theatre every night and the play settled down to a record-breaking run. Reports of the extraordinary sums it was taking at the box office and exaggerated stories of how much Rattigan was earning from it appeared regularly in the newspapers. *French Without Tears* became the most talked-about hit of the day.

Within a year of its London opening there were productions of *French Without Tears* in the provinces, in New York and Paris. In February 1937, Queen Mary made her first theatre outing since the death of the King to the London production of *French Without Tears*. Marlene Dietrich took Douglas Fairbanks to see it and soon the papers were reporting that both she and Carole Lombard wanted to play Diana in the film. Paramount were reported to have bought the film rights at Miss Dietrich's instigation for £10,000. (In fact, the film was not made until 1939 and it starred neither of these ladies.) Von Ribbentrop, the German Ambassador, was a fan of *French Without Tears*, seeing it five or six times with a series of Nazi dignitaries. It was thought that he used the play as a demonstration of how decadent the British had become—young men mocking the nation's most sacred institutions, the Diplomatic Service and the Navy.

Another regular attender, sitting proprietorially in a stage box, was Frank Rattigan. He unashamedly used his position as father of the author of the most fashionable play in London to impress young ladies he took a fancy to, and was escorted to the theatre by a succession of fluffy blondes. He quite unscrupulously promised pretty young actresses parts in his son's future plays. Although he was well into his fifties his vigour was in no way impaired. He became well known to the cast from his frequent appearances both front and backstage. He took to challenging the more athletic members of the cast to games of squash, which he still played extremely well. As the run of *French Without Tears* progressed, a number of different actresses took over the part of Diana. On the night when one of these young ladies played the part for the first time, the men in the cast had laid bets as to which of them would be the first to take her out to dinner. After the performance the young men came out of their dressing-rooms to see her walking down the corridor on the arm of Frank Rattigan.

Rattigan was now able to repay the years of subsidy from his father. He could hardly pay him an allowance, so he bought pictures and antiques and sold them to his father, who still ran an antique business, at prices far below the market value. Relations between Rattigan and his father received a rude jolt, however, when shortly after a visit to France Frank Rattigan by mistake opened a letter to his son from a Paris hotel manager. The letter complained of Rattigan's improper behaviour with a man in the hotel and asked him in future to take his custom elsewhere. Frank wrote his son a two-page letter to tell him how shocked he was. But the solemnity of this missive was undermined somewhat by a postscript in which he added that he hoped he wouldn't mind but he had taken the liberty of giving his son's gramophone to a lady friend, and would he please on no account mention this to his mother.

One inevitable consequence of Rattigan's new-found fame was the string of compliments he received. These he could normally accept with modesty and charm, but he had to develop a style of dealing with the more gushing adulation. Thus a débutante who approached him at a garden party and said, 'I think yours is the best play that's ever been written!' was parried with a smile and a question: 'Have you ever seen *King Lear*?'

In September 1937 Rattigan went to America for the New York opening of *French Without Tears*. The production was again by Harold French but with a new English cast. The reviews were varied. The New York *Herald Tribune* greeted the play as 'the first pleasure of the harassed new dramatic season ... it possesses gaiety, high spirits and an air of good-humoured freshness'. Brooks Atkinson in the *New York Times*, complimenting Rattigan on his attractive style and capricious gaiety, said the play was so light that it 'almost floats out of the theater'. *Variety* predicted that it was too light 'to stay anchored for long on Broadway'.

Rattigan had only intended a short visit to New York, but he so much enjoyed the hospitality and attention paid to him by Americans that he stayed on as *French Without Tears* settled down to a respectable New York run. Surprisingly, amid the New York parties he rediscovered the urge to write. It was well over a year since he had written anything more sustained than snippets of film dialogue. Nagging at the back of his mind had been the problem of how to follow his first success. He was afraid of anticlimax, and this had contributed to his creative paralysis. His mother had warned him: 'The poorhouses are full of people who have written one successful play.'

He was all too aware of the number of playwrights who had written one spectacular success and spent the rest of their careers writing sequel after sequel. He had to make a leap right away from comedy, to produce a play which would be taken seriously by the critics who, he suspected, would be gunning for him after such a commercial success. In the unlikely surroundings of the Waldorf Astoria Hotel in New York, where he was staying, he took the plunge and started to write *After the Dance.*

He was immediately interrupted. Irving Asher, his studio boss from Warner Brothers in England, arrived and put up in an adjoining hotel. Since the success of *French Without Tears*, Rattigan had become a valuable property and Warner Brothers were able to hire him out to other producers for huge sums, although Rattigan still only received his £15 per week. Rattigan was only in New York under leave of contract and Asher announced he was going to take him to Hollywood, for which he would receive an extra fifteen per cent on his salary. Rattigan had no intention of going. The final confrontation took place in Asher's hotel suite, which Rattigan noted gleefully was rather smaller than his own. Rattigan had had a lot to drink and, in his own words, proceeded to 'behave like an absolute shit'. Although he privately conceded that at £15 per week they had been over-paying him, he made it plain that he would not work for them for £15 a week any longer. Asher reminded him of the terms of his contract and said that he was taking him with him to Hollywood that very evening; he had already booked sleepers for them on the train. But Rattigan retorted hotly that he wasn't going anywhere and that if Asher didn't like it he could sue him. When Asher left on the train Rattigan remained behind and continued to write his play. Luckily, Asher was a benign boss. Rattigan was allowed to return to England and, although he was put on a number of assignments, the studio did not treat him harshly. Eventually, Warner Brothers British went out of business and their writers' contracts were nullified.

The play which Rattigan brought back with him from New York at the end of 1937 was about a high-living, hard-drinking, successful author and his involvement with two women—his wife and an earnest-minded younger woman. Rattigan told journalists that it was intended as a firm statement that another war was coming and that the people responsible for it were the people who had been young just after the Great War: 'It was an indictment of that generation by the younger generation.' But while he wrote, he had found that his sympathies drifted towards the older generation: 'With all their faults, they were less stupid, less boring and less priggish.'

After the Dance is set in the top-floor Mayfair flat of David Scott-Fowler, a successful thirty-eight-year-old writer of history books. The other principal male characters are John, a fat contemporary and friend of David who lives as a parasite on his wealth, and Peter, David's idealist young cousin and secretary, just down from Oxford, fresh and eager to make his way in the world, but unable to find a job 'because they are all filled, mostly by people who started at the top of something and worked their way to the bottom'.

The plot hinges on Peter's young fiancée Helen, who falls for David and makes it her mission to save him from drink, laziness and his wife Joan. Helen tells him that he and his generation have been spoiled by the war, even though they were too young to be part of it. She declares her love for him by vowing to help him back to the disciplines of writing and scholarship, so that he can realize his potential talent to the full.

Again Rattigan was clearly using a play to work through his own immediate preoccupations. At the same time he reworked recurrent themes: inequality of love, feelings hidden until too late. It is only after Helen has come between them that Joan admits to the true strength of her feelings about her husband—and then only to a mutual friend, John. John calls her a fool for not telling David how much she really loves him—'That's all he really wants—someone to be in love with him.'

JOAN: Not me. He doesn't want me to be in love with him. I'd have bored him to death if I'd ever let him see it. I know that.

JOHN: It's awful how two people can misunderstand each other as much as you and David have over twelve years.

Later Joan weakens and shows David her real need for him; she confesses that she has all along only pretended to enjoy the high life to please him, not realizing that he secretly craved someone more serious like Helen. In return David confesses that he was ashamed to show the more serious side of himself. But it is too late, their marriage is over. During a party, brilliantly handled by Rattigan, Joan commits suicide by throwing herself from the balcony of their flat.

The play ends in disillusion. Peter, once the high-principled young idealist, becomes a shameless parasite. David and Helen are clearly incompatible, their relationship cannot work no matter how much they may want it to—instinct is stronger than reason or will-power. David has stopped drinking temporarily, but he still does no real work. He and Helen have started to row.

Finally it is John, who has decided to give up his parasitic existence and settle down to a dull job, who tries to make David face the truth of his situation.

DAVID: Are you trying to tell me that Helen isn't in love with me?

JOHN: No, I'm not. She's in love with you all right, and you're in love with her. The only difference between you is that in a year's time she'll be even more in love with you than she is now, and you'll undoubtedly hate her like hell.

DAVID: What makes you think that?

JOHN: The fact that you half hate her already.

So David comes to terms with himself and resolves to give up Helen. For a moment he seems to consider following Joan and killing himself by jumping off the balcony, but instead he decides to return to his former life and the round of parties and drinking—as effective a way of killing himself as throwing himself off the balcony.

After the Dance is in some ways reminiscent of Scott Fitzgerald. Rattigan, who had himself only narrowly escaped Hollywood, undoubtedly knew that Fitzgerald, now a hopeless alcoholic, was at that time trapped in Hollywood and condemned to writing material unworthy of the talent which only a decade

94

before had dazzled the world. The moral could not have escaped anyone with Rattigan's underlying determination and self-knowledge about his own weaknesses for high living, drink and idleness. The parallels between Rattigan's fictional author and the real Scott Fitzgerald are underlined by his choice of the name Scott-Fowler.

The other writer called to mind by *After the Dance* is Noël Coward. Rattigan's student contempt for Coward had been replaced by respect for his craftsmanship, though not yet with approval of his use of it. The play seems to be as much an attack on the attitudes of Coward's 1920s bright young things as on Fitzgerald. In later years, Coward and Rattigan were bracketed together, but Rattigan always firmly, though politely, dissociated himself from the connection, pointing out that they wrote different plays and that Coward belonged to an earlier generation. *After the Dance* can be read as a reproof to Coward, the brightest talent of the previous generation, from the rising hope of the new one, implying that Coward had broken faith with his talent by not producing work worthy either of himself or of the momentous times in which he lived.

It is characteristic of Rattigan that having recently experienced such a dramatic alteration in his own style of life he should write about people living that same life. He looks not only at the wealthy people in the centre of the circle, but at the parasites who hang round the periphery; not so long ago he had himself been a hanger-on, but he was now increasingly finding himself the target of parasites and flatterers. In the play Rattigan can be seen casting an eye on both his former situation and his new one. Among the characteristic in-jokes is a delicious side-swipe at a little-liked erstwhile collaborator. David, having re-read some of the material which he has dictated, tells Peter that it stinks:

PETER: I thought it read rather well.
DAVID: That's just the trouble with it. It reads too
    well—imitation Hector Bolitho.
PETER: Well, you're writing it to be read, aren't you?
DAVID: Not by the sort of people who read Hector Bolitho.

After the Dance was not immediately snapped up and put into production by a management eager for a new play from the pen of London's most successful new playwright. It was put to one side, and by early March 1938 Rattigan had become deeply involved, with Tony Goldschmidt, in writing an openly propagandist political farce.

Rattigan, Goldschmidt and the rebellious circle from their Harrow and Oxford days had remained friends. As the 1930s progressed they had shifted further to the left. A *Daily Telegraph* reporter who interviewed Rattigan at this period formed the impression that he was 'an almost complete pacifist'. The hardening of their positions was, of course, a direct consequence of outside events. As Western governments failed to stand up to the dictators or give substance to the ideal of collective security through the League of Nations, and settled for appeasement, the Communist Party seemed increasingly attractive as the only opponent of Fascism. Although, unlike some of his friends, Rattigan did not join the Party, he certainly flirted with it. Goldschmidt joined the Labour Party and became very active in the Holborn constituency.

The catalyst for their feelings was the Spanish Civil War. Although they still denounced arms for Britain as immoral, they turned out to demonstrate for 'Arms and Food for Spain'. To them there was no inconsistency in this. Britain was a Big Power which had to set a moral example and work through the League of Nations; Spain was a small country in which democracy was being crushed by force of arms supplied to Franco by Hitler and Mussolini. So Rattigan, while enjoying the first flush of success and extravagant living, found himself increasingly in the company of such unlikely comrades as Michael Foot, being held back by the police outside Number Ten Downing Street. On one occasion, he found himself in a crowd being charged by mounted police, and the terror he felt then etched itself forever in his mind.

When Rattigan returned from America at the end of 1937, Hitler was once again making aggressive noises about the need to incorporate all people of German blood into one unified Nazi state. Rattigan, who had been contemplating for some time the idea for a satire on Hitler, was now galvanized into action. The problem was that he could no longer be sure what was funny in his idea and what was not. He needed someone like-minded to work with. Philip Heimann was no longer around, so he called in Tony Goldschmidt, whose wit, he knew, would draw the best out of him.

They secluded themselves in Shiplake so that they could concentrate undisturbed. As they wrote, Hitler stepped up his propaganda campaign for the incorporation of Austria within Germany. By mid-March the newspapers were full of the *Anschluss* and Hitler's triumphant reception in Vienna.

They set their play in a country called Moronia. It followed the rise to power of a plumber called Hans Zedesi. The national slogan of Moronia becomes 'Up Zedesi'—pronounced 'Up-si-daisy'—accompanied by a Hitler salute. Under the new dictator's programme, neighbouring countries are to be absorbed into Moronia. Next is to be Neurasthenia. To this end, it is planned to blow up the Neurasthenian Embassy when the King of that country is inside it. By mischance the British Embassy is blown up instead. The Ambassador of the appeasing British government arrives, still tattered from the explosion, to deliver his govern-ment's apologetic protests to the dictator. He tries, in his torn clothes, to maintain his dignity while both protesting and apologizing at the same time. Between the first and second acts, Goldschmidt and Rattigan planned to include newsreels showing the dictator's sensational rise to power.

By the time they had finished *Follow My Leader*, Hitler already had another campaign in full swing. His target this time was Czechoslovakia and the Sudetenland. As the Munich crisis loomed and the British government shilly-shallied about standing up to Hitler, Rattigan and Goldschmidt wanted to rush their play into immediate production. However, their script got no further than the Lord Chamberlain's office. He banned it outright as likely to give offence to a friendly country.

1939 opened with matters no further advanced. Meanwhile, at the Criterion Theatre a 'Last Weeks' notice was posted up for *French Without Tears*. Rattigan tried to get round the ban on *Follow My Leader* by arranging a club performance, but to no avail. His frustration was temporarily forgotten when he started to work with Anthony Asquith and Anatole de Grunwald on the film adaptation of *French Without Tears*. This was a new world for Rattigan. Although he had been a screenwriter, he had never been allowed to become involved as a collaborator among equals and, moreover, he was now working on his own material. It was suggested, apparently seriously, that Rattigan himself should play the Rex Harrison role, Alan. He wisely declined. Eventually the

British actor, Ray Milland, returned from Hollywood to play it. Roland Culver and Guy Middleton remained from the original stage cast, and a promising twenty-one-year-old actor, Kenneth Morgan, came in as Babe Lake, the youngest of the students. He eventually won the Best British Screen Newcomer Award for his work in the film. Later this talented and very attractive young man was to play a crucial role in Rattigan's life.

By the summer of 1939 Rattigan was almost broke again. He had made more than £20,000 from *French Without Tears*, including the sale of the film rights. He had spent heavily throughout the run, and lost still more by investing in his father's tips on the Stock Exchange. When *French Without Tears* finally closed at the beginning of May, after 1,030 performances, he went to France and in three weeks lost the remainder of his accumulated savings, by playing the casinos.[1]

That summer *After the Dance* was at last about to open at the St James's Theatre, but Rattigan knew it was unrealistic to expect the same sort of financial reward as from *French Without Tears*; even so he hoped he might get a six-month run out of it. That it was to be produced so soon after the closure of *French Without Tears* seems to have been due once again to the tireless efforts and faith of his agent, A. D. Peters. As with *French Without Tears*, Peters put some of his own money into the production. In addition he enlisted the support of another client of his, J. B. Priestley, who was at that time running the Westminster Theatre. Priestley approached Michael Macowan to direct, and a strong cast was assembled, headed by Robert Harris and Catherine Lacey as the Scott-Fowlers.

On Monday 12 June the play opened at the New Theatre, Oxford. The try-out went well and rumour of an exciting and unexpected new play from the author of *French Without Tears* had got round theatrical circles by the time the play opened in London nine days later. When Rattigan arrived at the St James's with his mother and father on that Wednesday evening, it was packed with celebrities; the expectant mood was in sharp contrast to that previous first night on a rain-sodden evening at the Criterion almost three years earlier. In her handbag Vera Rattigan carried the champagne cork from the tense dinner before that earlier first night as a good luck token, along with another from the dinner they had just had together. Rattigan had again had his hair cut. These were to become the elements of a ritual they went through before the London first night of each new play.

The newspapers all agreed that this first night would be the theatrical event of the week. They asked, 'Can he do it again?' Those who attended the first night hoping to see a bright young author fall flat on his face—and there must have been quite a few—were quickly disappointed. The evening went well from the start and at the end the audience broke into cheers and called for the author. This time clear arrangements had been made about curtain speeches. Rattigan had categorically refused to speak and had given instructions that Robert Harris and Catherine Lacey should thank the audience on his behalf.

In the small hours of the next morning Rattigan anxiously rushed through the reviews. They were uniformly good. CAN HE DO IT AGAIN? was transformed to RATTIGAN DOES IT AGAIN. *The Times* said that Rattigan's 'method of allowing his people gradually to reveal themselves gives to his play a genuine distinction'. In the *News Chronicle* the final paragraph of Anthony Squires' glowing review read: 'It only remains to wish this play the long and prosperous run that it deserves, to congratulate its author on having justified so conclusively his departure from the realms of comedy and to look forward to a long series of his triumphs during the next forty or fifty years.'

On Sunday came perhaps the sweetest praise of all. In the *Sunday Times*, James Agate praised Rattigan for having the courage not to take the easy way out by continuing with a line of commercial but vacant comedies. While he did not totally surrender to the play, he found many things in it to praise. He concluded his long article by saying: 'Nevertheless ... I suggest that this play is worthy of respect.'

Three weeks later Rattigan celebrated at Lord's with Tony Goldschmidt and other school friends during the annual Eton v. Harrow cricket match. It was a moment of supreme happiness. In bright sunshine Rattigan moved among the fashionable throng, at twenty-eight the best-known young dramatist in London, the acknowledged hope of the rising theatrical generation. At last he was acclaimed and respected. He was among friends, and to crown it all Harrow won. The captain was carried shoulder high; it was the school's first victory since 1908.

The enjoyment of the moment was the sharper for the sense of approaching catastrophe. An observer[2] looking back on those two days in July 1939 recalled Rattigan and his young, seemingly carefree friends, standing out like figures bathed in the last brilliant rays of the sun against the background of an approaching thunderstorm. Appeasement had failed and another war was imminent. The collapse into war and the collapse of Rattigan's hopes went hand in hand. Despite the good notices and the fashionable crowds at early performances, attendances at *After the Dance* soon fell off and on 12 August, after sixty performances, it closed. Simultaneously negotiations between Russia and the Allies which might have staved off war collapsed. Ten days later, Russia and Germany concluded the Nazi-Soviet Pact, and on 1 September Hitler attacked Poland. Two days later, a few minutes after 11 a.m. on Sunday, 3 September, Rattigan listened to Chamberlain's wireless announcement that Britain was at war with Germany.

Unlike their left-wing friends who had actually joined the Communist Party, Rattigan and Tony Goldschmidt did not find their reaction to the outbreak of war complicated by the Nazi-Soviet Pact. Hitler was plainly an aggressor who had violated all the ideals that lay behind their admiration of the League of Nations. For all their pacifism, their immediate impulse was to enlist. But like thousands of others they were rebuffed. The machine did not yet exist for taking huge numbers into the Forces and the government as yet seemed half-hearted about the war. As autumn progressed, Rattigan began to accept the growing popular feeling that it was just a phoney war, and returned to a country cottage he had taken at Frensham Ponds in Surrey.

Notes

1   Rattigan to Kenneth Tynan, *Evening Standard*, 1 July 1953.
2   Tony Goldschmidt's sister.

5
Per Ardua

'There was a young man called Terry Rattigan;
Had one hit and then fell flat again;
Sat right down and then begat again;
Tireless Terry Rattigan.'

Whoever put that verse about in the theatre in 1939 did not know
the truth about the struggle Rattigan went through ever to write a
play again. *After the Dance* had been composed late in 1937 and
two years had elapsed. The writing had been on the wall when
Rattigan called in Tony Goldschmidt to help him with *Follow
My Leader*. In March 1938, he told a journalist who asked him
why he was working with a collaborator: 'If I hadn't I should
have gone stark, staring mad ... I brooded over the plot for so
long that I completely forgot how to hatch ...'[1] Since then he had
written nothing original at all. There had been work adapting two
foreign plays for an American impresario and collaboration on the
screenplay of *French Without Tears*. During the summer of 1939
he gave the impression to Michael Macowan, who was meeting
him for the first time during the production of *After the Dance*,
that he rather regretted becoming a playwright at all and felt that
perhaps he should have concentrated harder on becoming a
historian when he had the chance at Oxford. He was obsessively
concerned that he had nothing on the stocks and repeatedly turned

over possible historical themes. He rejected them all. By the autumn of 1939 he had still not managed to settle on a new play.

Rattigan became so desperate about his 'block' that he sought advice from a psychiatrist, Dr Keith Newman of Oxford City and County Hospital. Newman was a strange figure, well known around Oxford during Rattigan's time there. From an Austrian background, with blue eyes and fair to gingerish hair, he had always seemed to enjoy exercising his influence over the young men he met. An actor who suffered particularly badly as a result of falling under his mesmeric attention suggested to us that having discovered that Rattigan was frightened that he had writer's block, Newman encouraged his belief in the block so as to increase his own influence over him, as the man who could cure him. Be that as it may, Newman advised Rattigan that the best way to cure his block was to get into the RAF and see some active service.

As Rattigan became involved with Newman, so did Anthony Asquith. Asquith and Rattigan had met during the filming of *French Without Tears* and had become very close friends. Asquith was the youngest son of Herbert Asquith, the Prime Minister at the time of Rattigan's birth. By 1940 he was one of the highest paid film directors in Britain. Initially, Rattigan had been very much in awe of him. They met for the first time at a dinner party, but by the end of the evening Asquith's boundless enthusiasm for *French Without Tears*, and his evident enthusiasm about Rattigan, had broken the ice. Rattigan recalled: 'Frankly at that moment I more or less fell for him—fell for his personality, fell for his charm, fell for his enthusiasm and for his eagerness, for his way of life.' Asquith was nine years older than Rattigan, but they found they had many things in common. Asquith had broken with family tradition to enter the film industry. Since his youth he had loved films with the same single-minded enthusiasm Rattigan had for the theatre. His financial affairs were chaotic, out of carelessness rather than deliberate extravagance, and like Rattigan he had to have an accountant to keep them in order. In total contrast to Rattigan, he cared little about his appearance or his creature comforts.

When Rattigan began work with Asquith on *French Without Tears* he found his first impressions confirmed. 'Working with Puffin [Asquith's nickname] was an absolute joy because instantly we discovered we had a lot of private jokes ... those weeks of my introduction into films were weeks of giggling and laughing, and at the same time weeks of rewriting a not very good film script, which however turned out to be a good one; mostly through Puffin's inspiration.'[2] The film was not completed until after the war had begun and the government had decided to close all the cinemas for fear of bombing. When Asquith heard this he persuaded his mother, the widow of the former Liberal Prime Minister, to get the members of the Cabinet concerned to meet her son and representatives of the film unions at their family house, and the government decision was reversed. *French Without Tears* was released during the first months of the war and played to large audiences.

After the completion of the film Rattigan and Asquith continued to spend a lot of time together. Between September 1939 and the summer of 1940 it was his film work with Asquith that kept Rattigan financially and creatively alive. However, it was Asquith who was having all the ideas. Rattigan seemed to lack creative inspiration—a symptom of his 'block'. Towards the end of 1939 Asquith had suggested writing an original film script about a ballet company stranded by the outbreak of war—based on what had happened to the Sadler's Wells Company while playing in Rotterdam. Rattigan had poured cold water on the idea. Then in 1940 Asquith persuaded Rattigan to work with Anatole de Grunwald on the script of a film he was making of Esther McCracken's stage success, *Quiet Wedding*. The film was a chore to all three of them but they got through the work on giggles and private jokes. They worked together in a room with a shorthand typist who took down everything they said and typed it up for the producer—a man called Soskin. If they were not careful, pages such as this reached him: 'Dallas enters left. Sits down. Camera comes into closer shot ... then into close-up. Oh god why have we to do this bloody script for this man Soskin.'[3]

With the coming of the war, the Lord Chamberlain's objections to *Follow My Leader* were no longer valid. The play was tried out in Cardiff in the week before Christmas, with Reginald Beckwith as the plumber-dictator, Walter Hudd and Francis L. Sullivan as the political rivals who put him in power, and Marcus Brown as the British Ambassador. Also in the cast was Kenneth Morgan—the young actor Rattigan had met when he played Babe Lake in the film of *French Without Tears*. Rattigan's co-author,

Anthony Goldschmidt, adopted the very English sounding nom de plume of Anthony Maurice for the posters and theatre programme.

The production transferred to London immediately, opening on 16 January 1940 at the Apollo. It was a bitterly cold, snowy night. Although the audience laughed enthusiastically, there was no real spirit to the evening. The bite had gone out of the comedy. What would have been pointed at the time of Munich in 1938 now seemed obvious and too easy. It must have been galling for Rattigan to read the notice in *The Times* next morning which began 'The very ease with which dictators may be ridiculed on a democratic stage constitutes a difficulty for the dramatist. How can he hope to fantasticate the fantastic?' The reviewer chose not to reflect on the fact that this 'comic strip' had not been allowed on London's democratic stage in 1938, when it might have had more point and even done some good. Even so, *The Times* critic did concede that the scene where the British Ambassador, who has been blown up in his Embassy, comes in in clothes that are torn and dusty but still correct, to draw the Foreign Minister's attention to 'the irregularity', was brilliant farce. The *Manchester Guardian*, which had not thought much of Rattigan's previous plays, called *Follow My Leader* 'thrice as witty as the same author's *French Without Tears*'. But events had overtaken the play. How it would have fared or what the effect of it might have been for Rattigan's reputation if it had been put on when it was written we shall never know. By 1940 the public were not in the mood for jokes about Hitler and the British policy of appeasement. *Follow My Leader* ran for only eleven days.

On 4 April, Hitler attacked Denmark and Norway. Rattigan, like everyone else, was stunned. He acted on Dr Newman's advice and applied to join the RAF at once. He had heard that the RAF needed officer air-gunners, but Hitler's attack in the West had produced a new rush of volunteers and again Rattigan nearly didn't get in. The interview was going badly until he mentioned that he had written *French Without Tears*. One of the interviewing officers had heard of it and the selection board decided to take a chance. They assured him that he could always write for camp concerts in his spare time.

Rattigan packed up his flat and sent his valuable papers to his mother for safe keeping. During the interval between his acceptance for the RAF and his call-up, *Grey Farm*, the play he had adapted with Hector Bolitho, opened in New York with an Austrian refugee actor, Oscar Homolka, in the lead. The critics hated it, and it closed within days. Rattigan had one final gloomy meeting with Hector Bolitho over lunch in a London restaurant, and paid the bill with their meagre royalties. It was now May 1940.

As France fell and the Battle of Britain raged, Rattigan went through his basic training. It was a new world and there was a great deal to learn: basic theory and practice of radio, Morse, airmanship, gunnery. Rattigan was totally absorbed. Towards the end of his training he wrote to Dr Newman: 'Since I last wrote to you I have sprouted a few tiny feathers on my uniformed wings ... I have passed my tests 100 per cent which is not unprecedented, or anything like it ... Such exercises aren't at all difficult. What is difficult is to do correctly all the hundred little things connected with the whole business—to forget none of them or, if one does (and one nearly always does) forget one, to be able to find the fault and not to panic. Which sounds like Kipling's "If", I'm afraid, but to a person like myself, always prone to intense panic and by no means the cool-headed unimaginative type, it was a triumph to find I had managed to stumble through all the tests while other worthier people were coming down from the skies in tears of desperation ... The concentration is so enormous that from the moment one fell into the plane till the moment one jumped out and leant nonchalantly against the plane in the hope that someone on the road would think one was a fighter pilot, one was utterly and completely oblivious of one's surroundings and conscious only of that infuriating medley of knobs and dials before one's face. However I become a bore on the subject and indeed think and talk of little else. Forgive me ...'[4]

Once Rattigan had completed his training, he was posted as a Pilot Officer air-gunner wireless operator to Coastal Command. His duties entailed long sorties of twelve to eighteen hours in Sunderland flying-boats out over the Atlantic searching for German submarines. It was not immediately dangerous in the way people imagine war in the air to be, but called for enormous stamina and concentration. For the duration of the flight the whole crew was called upon to maintain the highest level of observation. The smallest lapse of concentration meant not only the possibility of missing an enemy submarine or surface ship—indistinct grey blobs on a grey sea—it could bring about their own destruction. Marauding long-distance enemy planes patrolled much of the ocean, waiting to pounce on any unwary Sunderland. The danger was at its greatest when the crew were returning to base after a long mission and were tired and inattentive. Responsibility for the plane's communications and the level of the crew's awareness fell particularly on Rattigan's shoulders as an officer air-gunner.

His new companions were a tough and varied bunch, mostly very different from people he was used to. Most had never encountered a writer before and did not know quite what to make of him at first. They found Rattigan a friendly man who was every bit as tough as they were, and he soon became extremely popular. One officer he served with, unlike many of the others, had an interest in the theatre and was well aware of Rattigan's considerable reputation; he described the quality of Rattigan's relationships in the RAF: 'He and I both liked the theatre, we both liked music. This seemed to bring us together and I felt that I had a very special relationship with him. He made one feel bigger and better, because of his friendship, and he had the same effect on the other people because of his friendship with them. When I first noticed that he was getting on well with other people I was a bit annoyed, I thought I was the only special one. But I was quite wrong. There were thirty-two of us all in the same boat, all loving Terry very much.'

Later, when Rattigan was promoted to the rank of Flight Lieutenant, he became the Gunnery Officer with 422 Squadron. This meant that on top of flying normal missions, he was responsible for maintaining the efficiency of both the guns and the gunners. He had to devise training programmes and see that each gunner fired the necessary number of training rounds each month. He would take his place in each crew in turn and go out with them on a long patrol of perhaps twenty hours, putting them through exercises in gunnery and observation. This was a particularly tough squadron, made up of Canadians, South Africans and Rhodesians. The officer quoted earlier said of Rattigan at that time: 'He was as tough as anybody else, but he was both a gentleman and a gentle person. He never hurt anybody, never said anything at all damaging. He would criticize and people would improve their performances because of what he had said, but he never criticized anybody for the sake of criticism and never aimed to hurt.'

By 1941, Dr Newman's prescription had worked. Both the impulse to write and the uninhibited flow of dialogue returned unimpaired. His total absorption in his new occupation had slackened. There were long intervals of boredom between missions; days or even weeks of sitting about in Nissen huts waiting for the weather, for engines to be fixed, for replacement aircraft to arrive. War for Rattigan, as for so many others, was indeed long periods of boredom and inactivity interspersed by brief intervals of fear. Rattigan found he wanted to write a play about the RAF and his companions, about the war and how it was affecting them and their loved ones.

He began to write at Calshot on the Solent, where he was grounded for a fortnight by bad weather, while waiting to fly out to join a new squadron in Freetown, West Africa. For those two weeks he wrote in a hard-covered exercise book, and by the time the weather had improved enough for them to take off he had completed the first act of *Flare Path*.[5] When they eventually took off, Rattigan took the exercise book with him. On the first lap of the flight to Gibraltar they were pounced on by a Heinkel over the Bay of Biscay. Luckily they spotted it and were able to make their getaway with nothing worse than some shots in the tail. The damage was serious enough, however, to mean a further two-week delay in Gibraltar while repairs were carried out. During that time Rattigan completed Act Two of his new play.

Then they set out again on the longest leg of the journey, 1,200 miles to Freetown, the absolute limit of the aircraft's range. When they had reached just over halfway, one of the engines spluttered and died. There was no turning back, and unless they could reach Bathurst in Gambia it looked as if they would have to ditch in the sea off Spanish Morocco, which would mean being interned for the rest of the war. After calculating the amount of fuel the aircraft had left, the captain decided to fly on and try to ditch near enough to the Gambian coast to get picked up by Allied Forces there. The plane had to be lightened as much as possible. It was Rattigan's job to supervise this. He ordered that everyone's luggage and personal possessions were to be thrown overboard. Even the frames of photographs of the men's girl friends had to go. All the loose equipment was wrenched off the aircraft and an axe was taken to the stubborn parts. Just as Rattigan's kit bag was poised to go over the side, he remembered the hard-backed exercise book with the first two acts of his play in it. He called for the kit bag to come back. Watched with great suspicion by the rest of the crew, he opened it and took out the exercise book. He ripped the covers off and put them back into the kit bag; then, showing the others what they were, he stuffed the loose pages into his pocket. The plane flew on uneasily. Aided by a strong tail wind, they made Bathurst with two minutes' fuel to spare.

The third act of *Flare Path* was written while they waited in Bathurst for a replacement plane. When he finally reached Freetown, Rattigan set about copying out his fractured manuscript. He planned to send it back to his agent with someone who was flying home on leave. But he did not want to risk parting with his only copy, and since he could not get the use of a typewriter, he copied it all in longhand into another exercise book. In the humidity of Freetown this was no easy task. There was nowhere to work in private. Since the officers were crowded four to a bedroom, he sat out on the verandah of the officers' mess and wrote there. This was open to everybody and he felt he was making rather an exhibition of himself, but there seemed no alternative. 'It was a verandah of a former school with monkeys clambering about and everybody drinking gins and tonics going spectacularly to pieces in the White Man's grave—all of them looking over my shoulder while I wrote the thing,' he recalled. ' "I say, Rattigan, that's not a very good line, is it?"—"Well, I think it's all right, sir."—"Well, if you think it's all right, Rattigan, keep it, by all means."—"No sir, I'll take it out if you think ..." '6

He dedicated the play to Keith Newman. Back in London, two managements and a film company turned it down, saying the public did not want to see war plays, before H. M. Tennent Ltd agreed to produce it. The Air Ministry made it fairly easy for Rattigan to be in London between flying duties during the rehearsals; they hoped the play would be a good piece of public relations for them. Anthony Asquith, who had not previously directed in the theatre, was to direct and casting began in May 1942. A young actor was needed to play the hero, an RAF bomber pilot. Eric Portman suggested a nineteen-year-old actor who had not yet been called up, Jack Watling. He was a working-class lad, still green and quite unused to people from privileged backgrounds like Asquith and Rattigan. He was summoned to meet them one evening in the cocktail bar at the Savoy. They did not tell him that there would be a third member of the party scrutinizing him—the psychiatrist Dr Newman.

When the overawed Watling arrived at the Savoy the bar was already fairly full. Rattigan and Asquith gave him a script and asked him to study it for a few moments. Then they asked him to read for them: 'Read quietly, old boy, there are other people about.' After he had read a page or two they said, 'OK, you've got the part. Dr Newman will be directing you.' It was not until rehearsals got under way that Watling discovered the meaning of this last remark. Asquith, of course, was directing the play, but Newman gave Watling special advice and took a close interest in him. Slowly the impressionable young actor fell under the domination of Newman until, after a year or two, he seemed to have almost no will of his own. Watling's was an extreme case, but Newman exerted a similar Svengali-like influence in varying degrees over Asquith, Rattigan and Tony Goldschmidt.

Flare Path went on a four-week tour, and then opened at the Apollo Theatre in London on 13 August 1942. Rattigan attended in uniform and hovered nervously at the back of the stalls with Anthony Asquith. It was a 'top brass' night as far as the RAF were concerned. Looking back on that evening, Rattigan remembered spending most of it 'standing rigidly to attention, while Air Marshal after Air Marshal approached the humble Flying Officer to tell him how his play should really have been written!' It was an emotional evening rather than a glamorous one. A number of people in the audience, especially the wives of airmen, were moved to tears which they did not try to conceal. Just two pages before the final curtain, Rattigan turned to Asquith and whispered, 'I think we've brought it off.' It was tempting fate. At that moment the curtain descended to halfway and stuck there. After a moment which seemed like an age, it slowly rose again and the audience broke into applause. The cast completed the play and the final curtain came down. It was the warmest reception Rattigan had received from a first-night audience since *French Without Tears*. Air Chief Marshal Sir Charles Portal, the Chief of the Air

Staff, sent a message asking Flying Officer Rattigan to his box. He wished to be the first to congratulate him.

More important to Rattigan than the praise or blame of Air Marshals was the reaction of the critics. 'At long last I found myself commended, if not exactly as a professional playwright, at least as a promising apprentice who had definitely begun to learn the rudiments of his job.'[7]

In the *Observer*, Ivor Brown claimed that Rattigan had made an able compromise between the routine war comedy and the grimmer reality of battlefield tragedies like *Journey's End*. He concluded: 'Altogether Mr Rattigan has scored his double: his play is guaranteed alternately to tickle all ribs and to raise a few lumps in the larynx.' James Agate, in a long article in which he quoted Byron and Milton and invoked Shakespeare, Schiller, Sherriff and Euripides, questioned whether it was morally permissible for a playwright to make capital out of the present storm and stress when there might be wives and sweethearts in the audience whose RAF menfolk were actually undergoing the tragedies depicted on stage. He wondered if the defence that the play reminded 'anybody who needs reminding that war is not all beer and skittles, leave and laughter', and that such pieces 'jolt us out of the escapist rut', was enough. He concluded by saying that the play was better than simply good entertainment, but too sentimental to bear comparison with what Ibsen might have done with the same material. In an extremely perceptive review in the *New Statesman*, Roger Manvell said that 'the play was immensely effective alike in comedy and pathos', but accused Rattigan of not having the courage to give it the tragic ending that his story so clearly called for: 'This seems to me a wanton sacrifice to the wishes of the audience.' It was an accusation to be levelled at Rattigan with cumulatively deadly effect as one popular success succeeded another.

Flare Path differs from Rattigan's previous plays in that the plot is not built up organically out of an accumulation of small incidents and scenes between an ensemble of characters, but depends on a central outside event—a night bomber raid on Germany. The action is confined to the residents' lounge of a hotel close to an RAF bomber base in Lincolnshire.

The action of the play covers one night and the following morning as the womenfolk wait anxiously to see if their aircrew husbands will return safely from the bombing raid. One husband, a Polish Count married to an English barmaid, Doris, seems to have been killed and is only restored to his stoical wife moments before the fall of the final curtain. News of his safe 'ditching' and rescue does not arrive until after Doris has had the contents of a letter left by him, to be opened 'only in the event of something happening' to him, read to her. It is only through this letter that she discovers the true extent of his feelings for her—love he has been unable to express because of the language barrier between them.

Once again, even in the guise of a war play, Rattigan is pursuing his familiar motifs. The main suspense of the play hinges as much on a central triangle situation between a young bomber pilot, his actress wife and an ageing Hollywood star, as on the outcome of the off-stage bomber raid. The Hollywood star, Peter, has come to the hotel to try to reclaim the pilot's wife, Patricia, with whom he had an affair before she married. Peter now needs Patricia. His studio has decided to drop him. He is becoming too old to play young heroes and is not a good enough actor for the older starring roles. Since the war he has felt cut off. He can talk glibly about the fight for democracy, freedom and the rights of man, but they don't really mean anything to him. The rest of the world has turned its back on him and his pre-war world.

Patricia has secretly continued to love Peter. Her boyish, extrovert, RAF-slang-talking husband Teddy treats her as a possession to show off, but is unable to satisfy her real emotional needs. At first it seems that she will return to Peter. However, during the course of the play Patricia discovers the extent of Teddy's vulnerability and need for her. After returning from the raid which, as one character says, has been 'a proper muck up from beginning to end', Teddy breaks down, revealing to his wife, the only person in the world he can tell, all his accumulated strain, fatigue and fear:

You don't know what it's like to feel frightened. You get a beastly bitter taste in the mouth, and your tongue goes dry and you feel sick, and all the time you're saying—this isn't happening—it can't be happening—I'll wake up. But you know you won't wake up. You know it's happening and the sea's below you and you're responsible for the lives of six people. And you pretend you're not afraid, that's what's so awful ...

Patricia cannot leave Teddy after what she has discovered. She confronts Peter:

... I used to think that our private happiness was something far too important to be affected by outside things like war or marriage vows ... Peter, beside what's happening out there, it's just tiny and rather cheap—I'm afraid. I don't want to believe that, I'm an awful coward. It may be just my bad luck, but I've suddenly found that, I'm in that battle, and I can't—
PETER: Desert?
PATRICIA: Yes, desert.

Flare Path was the first play of Rattigan's of which almost all the critics remarked specifically on the excellence of his theatrical technique. His reputation as the country's leading theatrical craftsman was established. Although it is ostensibly a war play, *Flare Path* has Rattigan's trademarks stamped all over it. Doris and Patricia both have husbands who have been unable to find words to express their feelings. They only discover how much they are loved when it is almost too late, and in a sense by accident. At the time of its original production, the critics' major quarrel with the play was with the false happy ending which restored the Count to his wife just in time for the final curtain. Rattigan can be accused of sacrificing a dramatically honest ending to the war effort, yet this ending is consistent with his other work. Patricia has chosen reason over instinct by sticking with Teddy, but she has by no means solved all her problems. James Agate told Rattigan that he had taken the easy way out by having Patricia opt for Teddy and duty, but had thereby avoided the need to examine the consequences of her decision. He suggested that Ibsen would have started his play two years after the fall of Rattigan's curtain and would have shown Patricia's struggle between the torture of physical hunger and spiritual thirst when the moral self-righteousness of her decision to do her duty had faded. Agate was not the only critic at the time to complain that the central love story did not carry conviction or live up to the theme of the interaction between the war and personal relationships. The play's major weakness lies in Rattigan's failure to explore Peter's character or Patricia's feelings about him. He gives enough to leave the audience in suspense but no more, thus ultimately undermining the play's credibility.

Another fault, to modern eyes, is the one-dimensional staginess of the working-class characters, particularly the Sergeant Air-Gunner, Dusty Miller, and his wife Maudie. It was a weakness which Rattigan never overcame, and on the whole he avoided working-class characters, except for butlers and servants whom he had observed often enough to do well in a conventional way. The fact that this failure of characterization went unremarked at the time was partly due to the excellent performances of Kathleen Harrison and Leslie Dwyer, but more particularly to the fact that in such stagey characters Rattigan was only following the convention of the period which still depicted the working class on the stage as 'comic-cuts'.

The real achievement of *Flare Path*, however, was that it caught precisely the public mood of the moment. It is the major reason for Rattigan's amazing popular success, and arguably his chief claim to enduring reputation, that he managed to mirror and focus the public and private concerns of a vast British audience over a period of almost twenty years. This audience extended beyond middle-class theatre-goers to millions of cinema-goers in every part of the English-speaking world and from every stratum of society. Rattigan gives Maudie a speech in Act Two about her husband in which he plucked a string which harmonized perfectly with public sentiment:

'Mind you, I'm not saying I like him being a gunner; it's not good for him in those turret things. They're wickedly cold. He told me so himself—and he gets horrible backaches. He used to get them when he was working on the buses. Besides it's no good saying they always get back from these raids, because they don't—not all of them. Then I'm not saying I liked being bombed out and going to live in St Albans with Dave's Aunt Ella, who I've never got on with and never will—and working at the Snowflake—but what I say is, there's a war on and things have got to be a bit different, and we've just got to get used to it, that's all.'

Reading that today, one cannot miss the patronizing flavour, but the speech worked perfectly in a London theatre where the

113

air-raid siren was likely to go at any minute and the audience was made up of people who were either in the Forces themselves or had menfolk who were.

Rattigan and Asquith reworked much of *Flare Path* about two years later in their film *The Way to the Stars*. They achieved an even greater degree of universal appeal and succeeded at the same time in making a memorable film. It was as though they had heeded the criticism levelled at *Flare Path*. The film was also set on the ground in and around an airfield and dealt with airmen and those who wait for their return. But this time, although there were love episodes, inequality of passion and emotion that went unspoken or was suppressed because of the exigencies of war, the unconvincing and inappropriate triangle story was avoided. The problem of matching a need for a characteristically British style of understatement with the need for dialogue which rose above the confines of naturalism was brilliantly solved by the introduction of John Pudney's poem, 'For Johnny'. When an officer breaks the news of a brother officer's death in action to his wife, he brings not a letter but a poem he has found among his dead comrade's personal effects.

It was a weakness in Rattigan as a dramatist that he was unable to write anything other than naturalistic dialogue, no matter how skilful. It was a failure that came to count against him more and more as the demand grew for something beyond vernacular speech to be heard in the theatre.

Flare Path was in every sense a turning point for Rattigan. It marked not only the end of his block as a writer, it also saw the end of him as in any sense a writer of protest, as one who was out of step with the accepted views of the establishment. His commitment to the socialist and pacifist views of his Oxford contemporaries was always more liberal than radical, but from now on, his was the acceptable voice of protest that would not embarrass or annoy those who dictated what was politically or artistically acceptable.

None of this, however, should detract from the power and effectiveness of *Flare Path* in its day. A statement by an officer in the same squadron as Rattigan is eloquent testimony to its impact:

I felt that it was too true. Something in me, something in all of us who had flown, was exposed. He knew us better than we knew ourselves and he perhaps expressed thoughts and words for us which we had just fumbled around. I felt he's exposing us. He's come into our lives, he's taken our secrets and is now putting them out in public. He shouldn't do this. Then I realized that he was not exploiting us, he was talking about us, he was demonstrating us, our lives and the way we worked in war. He was quite right to do this. But at the time it was something of a shock to realize that he had seen so deeply into us.

Notes

1   *Sunday Referee*, 8 March 1938.

2   *Puffin Asquith: A Biography* by R. J. Minney, Leslie Frewin, London, 1973.

3   Ibid.

4   Quoted by K. O. Newman in *Mind, Sex and War—Blackouts, Fear of Air Raids and Propaganda*, Oxford, Pelago, 1941.

5   Flare Path was the name given to the lines of flares which lit the runway at night for returning aircraft.

6   Rattigan interviewed by Sheridan Morley for *Kaleidoscope*, BBC Radio 4, July 1977.

7   Preface to *Collected Plays*, Volume I.

6
Ad Astra

Flare Path ran for 670 performances. For the first five months of the run Dr Keith Newman attended every single one. At the end of this marathon he published a book entitled *Two Hundred and Fifty Times I Saw a Play—or Authors Actors and Audiences.*[1] It is a very strange book, which does not actually reveal which play it was that Newman had been watching. Newman's interest was in the creative process and the interaction between the play and the personalities of the author, actors and director, as well as the effect of different audiences on the play and its cast. Newman knew Rattigan very well by this time, and what he says about the way his mind worked during the creation of a play is instructive, even if it sometimes seems deliberately obscure. He says that through his own knowledge of Rattigan's personality he quickly became aware of a 'commissariat which provisions the characters and, different as they may be, makes them appear as belonging to one and the same family'. Of Rattigan's play-making process he says:

> Factual events and characters are, unconsciously, reduced to their elements and these particles, suspended in the air, create the very atmosphere the author must be susceptible to. Words and facts have disappeared and for a varying time his mind is filled with indefinite, yet strong, impressions and feelings. He

has dissolved words and facts and has created a general atmosphere. The next step is the re-embodiment of both, still shapeless yet solid. They have become the author's personal property. Finally facts and characters are re-shaped into their original form and they emerge, though apparently unchanged, with a different quality. These three distinct processes I call dissolution, condensation and organization.

Newman says that the author is then ready to produce a plot and that from that point on, the conscious mind takes over the actual writing and application of stage craft to the technical problems of making a theatrically effective play. He says also that the author seemed to have a skeleton audience within himself at the time of writing

as a silent collaborator. The silent audience is not just the critical sense of the author, telling him what is technically right or wrong, or what is effective and what is not. The members of the silent audience represent the practical experience of the dramatist in life. They curb the idiosyncrasies which brought him into trouble before and they encourage those sides of his character from which he benefited in his social contacts.

He tells us that the author has to survive a conflict of high intelligence and a lowest common denominator of taste or reaction—a mass mind. The combination and conflict between these two produces drama and vitality. His common mind will produce rubbish, his intellect something lacking in life and excitement. Newman comments that Rattigan 'on the whole seems to enjoy himself most in occupations he does not excel in, while those of which he is a master find him rather bored'. The book is peppered with allusions to the dangers of success and the enjoyment of applause, which can turn the author from artist to hack businessman. He comments that too much looking at the box office during conception can cause the baby to be born with a squint. The book also gives some useful insights into the increasingly corrosive relationship between Rattigan and Newman.

Newman's sessions with Rattigan and Asquith continued through 1943. While Newman was closeted with one or the other, no one was allowed to disturb them, no matter who they were or how pressing their business. No one really knew what they were up to, and a great air of mystery surrounded their sessions. On Newman's death, the man who inherited his papers approached Rattigan and told him that he had found a number of pieces of paper in his handwriting. 'Oh, My God,' said Rattigan, 'destroy them. Whatever you do, don't let anyone see them!' By then Rattigan wished to forget the extent to which he had revealed his mind and working method to Newman. Rattigan was no different from other artists in not wanting to enquire too deeply into how his own creative process worked, or what triggered it off, for fear that self-consciousness might destroy it. Newman's interest in Rattigan and Asquith extended beyond the doctor-patient relationship and scientific enquiry into the creative process. He even persuaded them to form a canal company. (It never seems to have traded.)

In the autumn of 1942, after the opening of *Flare Path* in London, Rattigan accompanied his squadron to New York. They were going to pick up new aircraft—Catalina flying-boats—from the Americans. At the start of the crossing, the entertainments officer on the troopship cornered Rattigan and said, 'I hear you write plays. Well, write me a short one for next Thursday would you? About twenty minutes?' Rattigan said no, he couldn't do that, and went to his Squadron Leader to complain. The Squadron Leader sympathized; nevertheless, Rattigan went away and wrote a frothy comedy thriller of exactly twenty minutes' duration, involving a house party and a butler who stole the silver, which was performed during the crossing by volunteers and was a tremendous success with the passengers. During the crossing there was a storm and everyone was very sick—everyone except Rattigan. No matter what he may have felt like, he stalked about the ship, a picture of composed self-control. Finally, his Squadron Leader asked him, 'Terry, how do you manage to avoid this sea-sickness? Everybody else has got it.' Rattigan replied, 'Ah, I have a special arrangement with the management. They keep the ship still for me and someone else moves the scenery up and down.'

On arrival in New York, the squadron was billeted in a rather dowdy brown hotel until they moved on to pick up their new aircraft. But not Rattigan: *Flare Path* was about to be staged in New York, and as a Broadway author he was not going to stay in a cheap hotel. He moved himself into the Waldorf Astoria. From there he entertained his less fortunate RAF colleagues—at that time an RAF officer's pay compared with that of only an American rating. As well as standing them dinner in the evenings, he issued an invitation to them to watch him taking breakfast. For this he would put on a great act. Sitting in a silk dressing-gown, he would order an enormous tray of food to be wheeled in by uniformed waiters while he played the great man. When they had gone, everyone fell to and tucked in.

Flare Path opened in New York on 24 December 1942, with Alec Guinness making his first Broadway appearance as Teddy Graham. It was a flop. The *New York Times*, while praising the impeccable production, said the play seemed 'sentimental, slow and confused'. But Rattigan was not in New York for the first night. He had left the day before to fly in one of the new Catalinas back to Britain, via Bermuda to Prestwick. The leg from Bermuda to Prestwick, on Christmas Day 1942, turned out to be one of his worst experiences during the war. They passed through seven fronts and got hopelessly lost. Rattigan had lost his flying-boots in New York and was freezing cold and very frightened. After flying for more than twenty hours, they spotted the coast of Northern Scotland in the first light of Boxing Day. They turned right and made their way down to Prestwick.

One of the first things Rattigan did when he finally got back to London was to check up on how *Flare Path* was doing at the Apollo. He sneaked up into the gallery to watch a performance. Unknown to him, Mrs Churchill had persuaded Winston to make one of his rare visits to the theatre that evening. Eleanor Roosevelt had seen the play on a visit to London a month or two earlier and had told Mrs Churchill that she must get her husband to see it. From his position at the back of the gallery, Rattigan could not see down into the stalls well enough to see who was in the audience and he was unaware of Churchill's presence. After the performance, Rattigan did not bother to go round and see the cast, and so when Churchill asked to be taken backstage to meet the actors, Rattigan was not among the people presented to him. Churchill told one of the actresses how moved he had been by the play. He said, 'It's a masterpiece of understatement,' adding with a smile, 'but we're rather good at that, aren't we?' The first

Rattigan heard of Churchill's visit was when a newspaper rang him for a reaction. He said, 'No one tells the author anything!'

More and more now, Rattigan was becoming a celebrity in battledress. During 1942 he had been seconded by the RAF to script *The Day Will Dawn*, to be directed by Harold French, a drama about resistance work in Norway; the main achievement of the film was the successful way in which it blended documentary footage of a real Commando raid with its fictional story. Later in the same year Rattigan worked with Rodney Ackland on the script of an Anthony Asquith film called *Uncensored*. This was a critical failure, its redeeming feature being the performance of Peter Glenville, Rattigan's digs-mate at Oxford, as a jealous lover who turns informer and betrays a Belgian underground newspaper to the Nazis.

In March 1943, Rattigan was seconded by the RAF to work with a well-known American novelist and screenwriter, Richard Sherman, on a film dealing with an airfield during its transition from RAF to American Air Force use. The project had arisen out of Twentieth Century-Fox's interest in *Flare Path* as a film. Fox had announced that Merle Oberon would play the leading female role. The Allied propaganda services (more correctly known as the Ministry of Information) also favoured the film. It was to be directed by William Wyler, who had made the tear-jerker, *Mrs Miniver*, which had done a lot to promote support for Britain among American audiences in the days before the United States had come into the war. As America started to step up its contribution to the war effort in Europe, and particularly to the bomber offensive against Germany, this new film was intended to promote harmonious relations between the British and the Americans. At the time there was considerable mutual resentment—Americans feeling that their boys had no business risking their lives in Britain in someone else's war, the British resenting the increasing number of American servicemen in Britain with money in their pockets to spend on local girls.

London was filling up not only with Americans, but with men in the uniforms of all the Allied countries—Australians, Canadians, South Africans, New Zealanders, Czechs, Poles and Frenchmen. While Rattigan was working on the grandiose Anglo-American film project, he had the idea for a stage comedy based on the petty national rivalries and broken hearts fostered by

120

casual pick-ups made in London. The black-out, and the feeling of transience engendered in men on leave for a few days before returning to active service, led to an era of sexual licence among heterosexuals and homosexuals alike. During a three-week leave, which he spent in borrowed rooms in the Albany, Rattigan wrote *While the Sun Shines*, a comedy about life in wartime London. He set the play in the Albany chambers, and dashed off the first draft in a hectic ten days. It was completed a week later. The theatrical managers H. M. Tennent and Linnit and Dunfee, who already had *Flare Path* running, accepted the new play for immediate production.

The cast, directed by Asquith, was headed by Michael Wilding, Ronald Squire, a brilliant veteran comedy actor, and Jane Baxter, making her first comedy appearance since her success in *George and Margaret*, the play which had vied with *French Without Tears* as the comedy hit of the late 1930s. An eighteen-year-old actress called Brenda Bruce was cast as a typist/tart-with-a-heart-of-gold, Mabel Crum. She had just come to London from the Birmingham Repertory Theatre, where she had played serious heroines. She was inexperienced at light comedy, and when the play opened on tour Asquith and Hugh (Binkie) Beaumont of H. M. Tennent were still very worried about her performance. Noël Coward, who had money in the production, attended a performance in Oxford and his opinion was sought about possible changes. The cast were lined up on the stage and Coward went down the line making ribald comments on each person's performance, imitating their mannerisms. Everyone else was laughing, but the young actress knew that the management were not very pleased with her, and dreaded what Coward might say about her. When he reached her, he said, 'And as for you, you're a very dim little actress.' Brenda Bruce burst into tears and through her sobs said, 'I know, I want to go back to Birmingham.' Binkie Beaumont said, 'Yes, well, I really think that if it hasn't improved at the end of the month that'll be it. It just doesn't work. It isn't right. You're much too sad.' Ronald Squire and Rattigan took pity on her, Squire coaching her every morning for the rest of the tour in his hotel room and Rattigan rewriting her scenes until they came right. When things went wrong Rattigan would say to her, 'It could be my fault, there must be a reason why you can't get it right.' Then he would go off and change a scene or the placing of a laugh line. Although he was an established author and she only a young actress in a subsidiary role, he never made her feel that she was putting him to any trouble. He devoted a lot of time to her, inventing word games to amuse her and break the tension when the company were on long train journeys, giggling, making jokes and generally helping to put her and everyone else at ease. When the month was up, Brenda Bruce was allowed to stay in the cast and when the play opened in London, she was one of the successes of the production. Understandably, Brenda Bruce fell for Rattigan, the kind, immensely successful and glamorous young man who always appeared in the theatre in immaculate Flight Lieutenant's uniform. She remembers him at that time as 'quite fantastically good-looking. Really incredible'. He took her out to dinner a number of times after the show and she hoped that a romance would develop. She was young and naïve; there was a feeling of constraint when they were alone together that she put down to her own inexperience. Both seemed shy, and slowly the meetings petered out. She never suspected that he was homosexual, and no one told her. Very few people, even in the theatre, knew.

While the Sun Shines opened in London on Christmas Eve 1943 at the Globe, next to the Apollo, where *Flare Path* was still playing to capacity houses. Since it was Christmas Eve, many theatres were closed and the first-night audiences included many artists from other London shows. The evening was a tremendous success—Rattigan's most trouble-free first night to date. The reviews could hardly have been better. Although most said the play was an inconsequential piece of nonsense and some that the last scene was weak, all agreed that it was brilliantly funny. The *Manchester Guardian* began: 'There are at least nine reasons for justifying a visit to *While the Sun Shines*: the seven members of the cast who act with subtlety and polish; Mr Rattigan's light-hearted text, which has the inspired lucidity and economy of P. G. Wodehouse at his best; and Mr Anthony Asquith's production which has timing and authority.' Most astonishing was James Agate in the *Sunday Times*, who began: 'About *An Ideal Husband* on its first production Mr Shaw wrote, "It is useless to describe a play which has no thesis: which is, in the purest integrity, a play and nothing less." And about its author: "In a certain sense, Mr Wilde is our only playwright. He plays with everything: with wit, with philosophy, with drama, with actors and audience, with the whole theatre." The same might be said today of Mr Rattigan, a playwright with the brains not to take himself seriously.' He continued: '... This piece is delightful, a little masterpiece of tingling impertinence.'

The play ran for three years—1,154 performances—making Rattigan the only author up to that time to have written two plays which ran for over 1,000 consecutive performances in the West End. He received more than £21,000 from the London run and a further £30,000 for the film rights, plus generous royalties from provincial and foreign productions.

The setting of *While the Sun Shines* is young Lord Harpenden's chambers in the Albany. It is the morning of the day before his wedding to Elizabeth, daughter of the Duke of Ayr and Stirling. Despite their aristocratic backgrounds, neither Bobby nor Elizabeth has been able to impress officer selection boards sufficiently to get a commission, so both are doing their war service in the ranks. The play's plot revolves around two allied officers—a Frenchman and an American—on leave in London, who try to make love to Elizabeth and to dissuade her from going through with her marriage to Bobby. Matters are complicated still further by the appearance of an extremely amenable ex-girl friend of Bobby's called Mabel Crum—a lovely girl 'but not the kind you marry'—and the self-interested interference of Elizabeth's crusty old father, who is notorious for his delight in pretty girls and unrelenting efforts to relieve his own shortage of cash by involving others in doomed business ventures and unsound investments.

The play consists of a steadily escalating series of hilarious misunderstandings and complications, but finally ends happily when Elizabeth decides to settle for 'ordinary quiet restful love' and marriage to Bobby in preference to the glamour of the American or 'the white hot burning passion of the heart' proffered by the Frenchman.

Together with *French Without Tears* this is Rattigan's best comedy. Its long-term durability could be threatened by its many allusions to the war and the extent to which so many of the jokes depend on understanding the prejudices and conditions of life in wartime London. Nevertheless, the *Manchester Guardian*'s original comparison with the 'inspired lucidity and economy of

P. G. Wodehouse at his best' is certainly justified. Even Agate's comparison with Oscar Wilde is not too far-fetched—it is certainly 'in the purest integrity, a play and nothing less'. The one area in which it fails to match Wilde is in memorable language. Although Rattigan's dialogue is extremely skilful throughout, there is nothing that raises the words above the simply naturalistic. Sharp though the exchanges are, the lines do not of themselves have the brilliance or sheer tingling pleasure characteristic of the very finest Wilde and Shaw. But if by the very highest standards Rattigan just fails in this one department—his Achilles' Heel—he nevertheless succeeds triumphantly in every other.

The comic invention, and the way the hilarious lines and situations not only grow out of but top what has gone before, is masterly. The unity and economy of the play point to Rattigan's observation of the classic dramatic unities. The integration of the characters into the mainstream of one central plot is superior to *French Without Tears*. So is the unity of tone. Here, as Agate says, Rattigan has the wit never to take himself too seriously, and one is never aware of undigested bits of a different and heavier play protruding through its glossy texture. This does not mean that the play is, in Rattigan's phrase, unaware of the time in which it was written—far from it—but everything in it is handled with a uniform and graceful lightness. This play is the reverse of *Flare Path*. Here we see, not the tragedy of war nor the ennobling determination to grin and bear it, but the petty stupidities and ludicrous muddle on the one hand and the opportunity for release in drink, parties and casual encounters on the other. Here we see not so much the triumph of Allied co-operation as the confusion, rivalry and chaos. Talking about the play thirty years after it was written, Rattigan said that he saw the three central young men as pathetic figures because he assumed that all would perish in the war. This does not really come across in the play, except in the shared sense that the war pervaded everyone, both on stage and in the audience. Such awareness of impending doom as there is in the play relates almost exclusively to the sense of coming social change, and this is put to fine comic use. Colbert, the Frenchman, describes himself as 'socialiste' and often refers to Bobby and his class as 'doomed'. Bobby himself jokes about 'swinging from a lamp-post' outside the Albany and nasty Willie Gallacher (the

British Communist leader) taking all his millions. The fact that he is not an officer he puts down to modern class prejudice—he went to a public school. In contrast, his butler's son is a Lieutenant Commander.

The autobiographical elements in the play are both obvious and comparatively unimportant, although it is worth noting that Rattigan told friends after the war that the general impression of a selection of young servicemen casually picked up and taken to bed in blacked-out London was correct. Rattigan said that he took stock 1930s figures and put them into a contemporary but escapist situation. The only partial exception to this might be the Duke—Rattigan's first major elderly figure. Many of the Duke's characteristics are from time-honoured comic stock, yet there are elements which tempt one to suspect that we have here the first of a long line of characters drawn from Rattigan's own father. The enthusiasm, the gambling, the impecuniousness, the taste for suspect business ventures and unsound shares, the partiality to girls, are all echoes of Frank Rattigan. By 1943 he had lost none of his vigour or old-world zest. He was still much in evidence backstage, nudging the girls in the cast and inviting them to dinner.

London audiences' sense of shared experience with the characters in *While the Sun Shines* was heightened, and their enjoyment was, if anything, increased, with the start of the doodlebug raids on London in June 1944. London had been free of serious air-raids for some time; the Allies had landed successfully in France and everyone had decided that the war was as good as over when these pilotless jet-planes, crammed with high explosives, began to rain on London. They were extremely unnerving, but *While the Sun Shines* continued playing to packed houses. When the air-raid sirens sounded, hardly anyone left the theatre to take shelter. The cast continued with the play, but with an ear cocked for explosions. Once, towards the end of the third act, there was a deafening roar and the Globe shook to its foundations. The theatre next door, the Queens, had received a direct hit and was flattened; luckily, it was empty at the time. The audience for *While the Sun Shines* remained in their seats and the cast finished the third act and took their curtain calls in the normal way.

On the night of 12 July, a doodlebug hit the Aldwych where

the Lunts were playing Robert Sherwood's propagandist drama *There Shall Be No Night*. Although the performance was over and there was no one in the theatre, the damage to the building closed the production. The Lunts decided to look for a new vehicle. They wanted a representative British play to suit their combined talents, which they could open in London and then take back to Broadway. Alfred Lunt, who normally directed the productions in which they appeared, was an American, and at that time just over fifty. Lynn Fontanne, his British-born wife, was six years his senior. What they sought was a sophisticated vehicle in which they could play opposite each other—he preferably in the character of an American and she as an elegant Englishwoman.

Rattigan already had a comedy well on the way to completion, which he had hoped to get Gertrude Lawrence to play. Gertrude Lawrence was synonymous with theatrical glamour, and Rattigan intended his play, which was built round a beautiful woman, to be a defence of glamour in an age of austerity, of charm in an age of utility, of the freedom of the individual in an age of conformity. She had encouraged him in his idea for the play during a brief chance meeting while she was touring in a wartime show in England. However, when Rattigan reminded her of their meeting just before she returned to the United States, she did not recollect giving him any encouragement and left expressing no interest in the play which by then he had drafted. He was desolate. He had built his whole play round the idea of her playing it.

The Lunts' sudden need for a new play came as a potential god-send but, as Rattigan diffidently explained to Alfred Lunt when Ivor Novello arranged a meeting, the part of the woman's lover had been created as a supporting rather than a starring role. Lunt reassured Rattigan that the relative sizes of his and his wife's roles did not matter: 'Sometimes Lynn has the play and sometimes it's my play. Mr Rattigan, if your play is good, I'll be satisfied to hold a tray and let it be Lynn's play. The play is what matters.' Two days later the Lunts told Rattigan that the play needed a few adjustments here and there, but fundamentally it was splendid and they would both be happy to appear in it, with Lunt himself directing. They wanted to start rehearsals right away.

By the time he got the Lunts' commission, Rattigan had

already that year been involved in scripting three films. The first of these saw the light of day that autumn. It was a comedy of manners about a titled lady who falls in love with her butler, Gilbey (a name plucked from one of his more outrageous schoolboy associations). The butler enlists and becomes an officer. There are endless misunderstandings of the ways of foreigners who have come to Britain to fight in the Allied cause before co-operation and mutual trust are achieved. Any similarity to discarded bits of *While the Sun Shines* must be regarded as far from accidental. Rattigan became progressively more inclined to put his theatre cast-offs to profitable use in the cinema, which he always regarded, despite his serious excursions into it, as an undemanding way of making money. This piece, called *English Without Tears*, was generally liked and was, appropriately, directed by Harold French.

Work on the film to promote Anglo-American co-operation, developed from *Flare Path*, had continued throughout 1943 and 1944, but in the end Rattigan's idea of building the story round the changing role of a British airfield handed over to the Americans was not used. Major William Wyler returned to America and Rattigan was left with his material. Anatole de Grunwald believed in Rattigan's basic concept enough to take it to another producer, Filippo del Giudice (who had already produced the film version of *French Without Tears*), and get him to set it up for Puffin Asquith to direct. So, through the doodlebug raids of 1944, de Grunwald, Asquith and Rattigan worked in chambers which Rattigan had now rented for himself in the Albany. In contrast to Rattigan, who was always immaculate in uniform, Puffin Asquith wore his so that he looked like a tramp. He had joined the Home Guard, although neither Rattigan nor de Grunwald could discover what, if anything, he ever did in it. He always wore his khaki battledress and heavy boots—in which he clattered up and down the Albany's echoing stone steps. One evening Rattigan was waiting for him to arrive for a script conference when the liveried porter telephoned: 'Excuse me, sir, there's a person down here who says he's Anthony Asquith, but I can see that he's not, so I've sent him about his business.' Rattigan was horrified, but he couldn't help being amused. A few minutes later, the phone rang again and this time it was Asquith from a call box: 'I don't understand what they're doing—they've turned me out,' he said furiously. Trying not to giggle, Rattigan told him, 'Puffin, you see, the point is there are a lot of deserters about—in fact there are quite a number trying to hide in odd corners round Albany.' Far from laughing, Asquith protested: 'I don't look like a deserter.' 'To him,' Rattigan replied, now forced to keep his joke going, 'you must have looked like one. I'm awfully sorry, Puff. Do come along. I'll talk to the porter and see that it is put right.'

Their script conferences went on at all hours of the day and night regardless of the doodlebugs. Rattigan and de Grunwald listened for them with half an ear while talking. They had decided that when they heard the engine cut out they would dash out into the passage, which was the only place in the old building that might afford some shelter, and throw themselves on the floor. 'Puffin kept walking up and down the room, talking rapidly as always and incessantly. We heard the buzz-bomb but he obviously was quite unconscious that there was any sound other than his own voice. The bomb came closer and closer and then suddenly we heard the cut-off. Tolly de Grunwald and I dashed into the passage, knowing that within seconds the bomb would drop and explode. I quickly threw myself on the floor and Tolly fell on top of me—or perhaps it was the other way round. After the explosion—the bomb fortunately missed our building—we came back. Puffin was still walking up and down the room. On seeing us come through the door he realized that we hadn't been listening to what he had been saying. "This is no time for games," he said, "we're supposed to be getting on with the script ..."'[2]

The film, now called *Rendezvous*, from Roosevelt's exhortation 'Our generation has a rendez-vous with destiny', began shooting in September 1944, but by the time the shooting was complete it was clear that the war would be over before the film could be edited and released. Accordingly, a new beginning and ending were devised which showed a disused and overgrown airfield, from which the film flashed back to tell the story of the successive groups of airmen, British and American, and their wives and girl friends, who had flown from it during the war. When it was released the film was hailed as a patriotic masterpiece—a reputation which has endured. It was popular with the public on both sides of the Atlantic, and won the *Daily Mail* National Film Award.

Rattigan, de Grunwald and Asquith had confined the story of

Rattigan's father

Rattigan's mother

Rattigan, aged three, with his elder brother Brian

Rattigan (left) with Dorian Williams as Calpurnia in Harrow School's
production of *Julius Caesar*

(*Keystone Press*)

Harrow School First XI Cricket, 1929. Rattigan back row left   (*Hill and Saunders*)

Rattigan's father and mother at a first night

Flying Officer Terence Rattigan 1942 (*Paul Tanqueray*)

Rattigan photographed by Gordon Anthony in 1946
(*Radio Times Hulton Picture Library*)

Rattigan aged thirty-seven in his Albany chambers

their film, which was finally called *The Way to the Stars*, to the airfield and a hotel in a near-by town. Although it was a war film, there were only a few flying sequences and no scenes of combat.

In the autumn of 1944 Rattigan also had in production another, rather different film script about life in the Air Force. For this he had been seconded to the RAF Film Unit. The director was a young Flight Lieutenant, John Boulting. Until this time all the RAF's propaganda efforts had been directed to showing how brave and effective were the operational Commands, such as Bomber, Fighter and Coastal. Now Flying Training Command wanted a look in as well. After months of research, including a tour of America where a lot of the aircrew training was done, Boulting and another writer had returned with material for a three-hour script. They needed someone to reduce this unmanageable material into a taut dramatic narrative, so Boulting went to the head of the RAF Unit and said that he needed a first-class writer to dramatize his material and turn it into a story centred round a limited number of characters. Flight Lieutenant Rattigan was seconded to Pinewood Studios to do the job. Boulting could not believe his luck. It improved still further when Sergeant Richard Attenborough and Aircraftman Jack Watling, both on RAF pay of a few shillings a day, were seconded as his leading players.

Boulting was in considerable awe of Rattigan when he met him for the first time. However, he found him charming and gentle, with a boyish giggle in spite of his obvious sophistication. 'Of course,' Rattigan said, referring to Boulting's bulky projected script, 'it's perfectly splendid.' Then he tactfully set about suggesting possible changes. Rattigan worked to create a 'humanized documentary', as both men liked to call it. The story that Rattigan eventually came up with, called *Journey Together*, served the purposes of Flying Training Command admirably, while at the same time providing him with the opportunity to explore further the way in which the war made people from different backgrounds mix and grow dependent on one another.

This is the persistent theme of all Rattigan's wartime writing, and *Journey Together* was its most realistic expression. The film remains one of the most satisfying blends of documentary and fiction achieved in the cinema.

During the months of their work together Boulting found that Rattigan's mood never changed. He was continually calm and charming, even when his young director questioned his most carefully thought-out lines; he would patiently explain what he meant, how they should be played and, if Boulting was still unconvinced, would offer to change them. On only one occasion did Boulting see a change come over Rattigan and this was the result of deliberate provocation. He had begun to suspect that Rattigan was 'too good to be true', so he set out to needle him. One day, walking round the grounds at Pinewood, Boulting brought up the subject of Shakespeare: 'I think *Hamlet*'s greatness is highly questionable.' Boulting watched Rattigan shudder. Then with a visible effort at self-control he asked in his usual even tone, 'What do you mean, John?' Boulting expanded on his obviously blasphemous theme: 'Well, would you solve the climax of that play by a stage strewn with bodies and "Goodnight sweet Prince"?' As their gentle stroll continued, Rattigan launched into a thirty-minute model lecture on the play, its characters and its resolution.

The conversation about *Hamlet* seems to have had a bearing on the play which Rattigan rewrote for the Lunts. *Love in Idleness* has a *Hamlet* theme, the plot being consciously modelled on Shakespeare's play. Interestingly, Rattigan does not resolve it with a stage strewn with bodies and 'Goodnight sweet Prince'. The play concerns an eighteen-year-old boy, Michael Brown, who returns from five years' evacuation in Canada to find his mother living with a wealthy industrialist, Sir John Fletcher, who is a Tory member of the War Cabinet, Michael's father having died three years previously. Michael, who has grown up into an enthusiastic young socialist in Canada, is horrified to discover not only that his mother, Olivia, is living in sin with such a reactionary, but that she seems to have adopted his expensive tastes and become a 'useless parasite'. He broods—his 'antic disposition'; takes to wearing a black tie—his 'inky cloak'; studies a book on poisoning; invites Sir John and his mother to a play called 'Murder in the Family'; and confronts his mother—in Rattigan's equivalent of the 'closet scene'—with her treachery to his father's memory, finally breaking down with his head in her lap and pleading with her to leave Sir John: 'Don't go on with it, Mum! Please don't! Please! I can't bear it!'

130

He forces his mother to choose between her lover and her son. Olivia chooses Michael, and they move out of Sir John's expensive Westminster home into a small flat in Baron's Court, near Puffin's Corner (Rattigan's obligatory in-joke). Rattigan is writing a comedy and therefore fashions a happy rather than a tragic ending. His Hamlet, Michael, sees that he is being a prig and that it is to his advantage to get along with Claudius (Sir John). So Gertrude (Olivia) is reunited with Claudius and they live happily ever after with Sweet Prince Hamlet. The rather irritating parallels with *Hamlet* serve to underline the extreme cynicism of Rattigan's play. His Hamlet comes to see inconsistency and error in all his noble ideals, and finally abandons them because Sir John's wealth and position will help him impress a reluctant girl friend. By implication the idealist and socialist accepts Sir John's mellow affluence as good taste and his use of privilege as realism—living in the world as it really is. In *Love in Idleness*, at least as it was staged by the Lunts, Michael—and Rattigan—finally repudiate all that they have believed in.

The qualification about what the Lunts made of Rattigan's original conception arises from the fact that almost twenty years later Rattigan was to claim that their production had turned his intention on its head. Rattigan claimed that in his original draft Michael had been the sympathetic character and Sir John the unscrupulous and unsympathetic one; that Michael was not a villain or the figure of fun which he became in the production, but a confused and vulnerable adolescent. He intended to show Michael's distress as he struggles with his ideals and the attraction of money and gracious living. He did not intend him as the posturing caricature of Hamlet that ultimately appeared on stage.

Rattigan complained that by building up Alfred Lunt's part, the Lunts changed the play to make the love affair between Sir John and Olivia the centre of interest; Michael's function was consequently reduced to that of the villain who comes between true lovers. Recalling those re-writes and rehearsals, Rattigan said, 'He [Lunt] was so subtle about it that I didn't realize he was making me write a new play ... As I'd written it, Olivia's son was constantly scoring off Sir John. Gradually, so gradually I didn't know it myself, the minister began scoring off Michael, the son. In fact, Michael became a snooty character, while Sir John changed into a fine fellow, good hearted, a worldly chap doing his best for God, for England, and for Lynn Fontanne, and having to put up with this beastly little bugger of a left-wing socialist.'[3] In the end the point was reached where Sir John is credibly presented as the real upholder of the individual's rights and the bastion against a new order which will do away with charm and beauty in the name of drab uniformity.

No copy of the draft which Rattigan originally submitted to the Lunts seems to exist. Nevertheless, although there is no reason to doubt that Rattigan found working with the Lunts a trying experience, and that they did make a number of changes to the play so that it became a suitable commercial vehicle for their combined talents, there are also good reasons to doubt Rattigan's belated claim that they perverted the fundamental attitudes of his original play. By 1944 Rattigan was a powerful writer. If he did not like what was going on—and he must have realized what was happening, at least in the provincial tour which preceded the London opening, if not during the rehearsals—he was in a position to cry halt. He was the most commercially successful playwright in Britain, with a new-found critical reputation which he wanted to enhance; and as the play's author he had the ultimate sanction. Nor was he short of money. If he disapproved so much of what the Lunts were doing, why did he not stop them? Either they did not alter the play in ways of which he fundamentally disapproved, or he was short of moral courage.

The answer is almost certainly that it was a little of both. Rattigan had a pathological dislike of unpleasantness—later in his life we shall see him going to inordinate lengths to avoid scenes, allowing himself to be robbed by his servants to avoid having to confront them. By the early 1960s, when Rattigan accused the Lunts of having turned the values of his play upside down, he was preoccupied with trying to defend himself against charges from a new generation of writers and critics that he was a dyed-in-the-wool reactionary. *Love and Idleness* is his most cynically reactionary play, and it was useful to be able to shift the blame elsewhere. Yet even in the course of the interview in which he made this accusation against the Lunts, he said, 'In the end he was right. I wrote a far better play because of his suggestions.'[4] Lynn Fontanne said in a recent interview that she, far from being worried that Sir John was too unsympathetic a character, was concerned from the start because Michael was too unpleasant: 'He spoiled the play every time he came on. Everybody hated him and he was a lot of the play.'[5]

Rattigan's own life at this time supports the contention that from the outset *Love in Idleness* was a repudiation of his previous values. The fact is that the play witnessed, and to some extent attempted to justify, a change in his own life and ideals.

The shift in Rattigan's position by the time of *Love in Idleness* represents a development of the position he seems to have reached in *After the Dance*. In the earlier play he proclaims the need and right of everyone to be true to themselves. He restates this theme in *Love in Idleness*, but by now the only defender of this right is the reactionary Sir John. Individuality is a house in Westminster, dinner at the Savoy, and entertaining the fashionable social élite to smart little dinner parties. In *After the Dance*, the young idealists are well-intentioned, even though in practice their ideals lead to disaster. In *Love in Idleness*, Michael merely recites other people's ideas and is himself revealed to be a self-interested hypocrite.

Love in Idleness reflects the upsurge of socialist ideas during the war, which would put Labour into power in 1945. Rattigan seems to be about to confront the political and emotional implications of this in the contest between Michael and Sir John, but instead he merely scoffs at the idealists—among whose ranks he had so recently counted himself. Despite the Beveridge Report (which he refers to in the play), the 1944 Education Act and a new forward-looking spirit, Rattigan, like most of the new circle of Conservative friends to whom he was becoming steadily more attached, did not really believe that this new mood was as widespread as the results of the 1945 Election were to indicate. In the short term, *Love in Idleness* pandered to the prejudices of comfortably-off theatregoers. In the longer term, such a misreading of the public mood boded ill for Rattigan's lasting popularity.

Technically also, *Love in Idleness* was a backward step. Instead of the play building up through the interaction of a number of fully realized characters of more or less equal weight, we have only two complete characters—Sir John and Olivia, plus one two-dimensional character, Michael, who seems little better than a caricature. Also, there is no reason why a comedy should not carry weighty ideas; but simply on the level of provoking laughter *Love in Idleness* fails. There are far too few good comic situations, funny lines or shafts of wit.

The play opened on tour in Liverpool on 27 November 1944. Although the reviewers praised the artistry of the Lunts, the notices were not good. There were three anxious weeks in provincial theatres devoted to frantic work by the Lunts, with Rattigan in worried attendance. When Noël Coward, who again had money in the production, came to a performance, he advised them to abandon the production immediately without incurring the additional costs of a London opening. Rattigan and Alfred Lunt sat in a dressing-room gloomily polishing off a bottle of whisky, while in the next room Coward made devastating comments about the play to Lynn Fontanne. Back in the Lunts' hotel room, as Coward continued to analyse the play and Rattigan tried in vain to get drunk, Lynn Fontanne motioned Rattigan to follow her into the bedroom. 'Look,' she whispered, 'nothing that Noël has said, or will say, can affect me. This is an enchanting play and we're going to do it in London. I know Alfred will want to close it. But don't worry. I shall talk Alfred round. I have faith in the play.' An hour later, Lunt beckoned Rattigan into the bedroom. 'My boy,' he murmured, 'as you can see, Lynn is disheartened by Noël's reaction. She's going to want to close the play. But no matter what Lynn says, we shall do it. It's a good play. Now don't say anything. Leave it to me to talk Lynn round to my way of thinking. I have such confidence in your play that I'm going to buy Noël's share in it.'

The London opening night was Wednesday 20 December 1944 at the Lyric Theatre, next door to the Apollo where *Flare Path* was still running, and next door but one to the Globe, home of *While the Sun Shines*.

In the event, although nobody had thought much of the play, the evening was a triumph and 'The Audience Went Wild With Delight', as one headline writer put it.

The play was billed as being limited to a three-month run because the Lunts were committed to taking it back to America. The Lyric rapidly became 'the theatre you can't get in to', and when the play was taken off, after the run had been extended to six months, it was still playing to capacity houses. In America, it became the Lunts' greatest success. They enjoyed 451 performances on Broadway, and played it altogether, in Europe, in New York and on tour, for almost four years.

Rattigan had started the war with a reputation based on one commercial success, which most people suspected was a fluke anyway, and two flops, which together had gained him only a small amount of grudging critical respect; he had been broke and suffering from a writer's block so severe as to need psychiatric help. Six years later, by the end of the war, a total transformation had been effected. He was, at thirty-four, the highest-earning playwright in Britain, reputed to be receiving over £600 a week in royalties—although he told journalists that the Inland Revenue only allowed him to keep £12 of that. All three plays he had written during the war had been smash hits; he was the only playwright to have had two plays with runs of over 1,000 consecutive West End performances; he had written four films, all of which had been well received and one of which, *The Way to the Stars*, was hailed as an undoubted masterpiece. Despite the critical dismissal of *Love in Idleness*, a new Rattigan play was now an event with critics, just as it was with theatre managers; and new plays seemed to be flowing from him in effortless succession. Yet Rattigan nursed still greater ambition. He wanted to be a great playwright. This most publicly modest of men admitted to his most intimate friends that he wanted to be numbered with Shakespeare and Shaw. With the war over, he could devote his life to the realization of that ambition. On the surface, Rattigan's life was a success story, yet there were dark clouds. One of the reasons that Michael, the son in *Love in Idleness*, was such a harsh portrait, was that it was, in part, a self-portrait. In *After the Dance*, Rattigan had revealed a pessimistic side of himself in his picture of David Scott-Fowler, the writer who wastes his talent and destroys himself. In *Flare Path*, Teddy, the brave pilot who fools around to show how little he cares when he is in truth scared almost to death, and Peter, the smoothly self-confident film star who is underneath a vulnerable child begging for mother love from his mistress, are both portraits in which Rattigan identified elements of himself. So too, in *Love in Idleness*, Michael is a cruel portrait of Rattigan past and present: the earnest young student and poseur who takes himself too seriously; the dogmatist whose youthful ideals achieve nothing. Pacifism had not prevented war, and at least one of Rattigan's close friends, Tony Goldschmidt, had been killed in action. Now that he had money he found that, like Michael, he enjoyed it, not because it gave him the freedom to write what he liked, but because he could splash it about and impress others. At the end of *Love in Idleness*, Michael abandons all his principles and objections to Sir John Fletcher and what he represents. By 1945, Rattigan had found that he too enjoyed the flattering attention of those very Tories he had howled abuse at outside Downing Street and at Oxford; he could not resist dropping into conversations just how much he was earning, or offering a cigarette from his newest gold cigarette case to impress his friends; he enjoyed being seen in the most expensive restaurants, having chambers at one of London's most exclusive addresses, driving the newest Rolls-Royce. Rattigan drew characters with irreconcilable sides to their natures. Could he reconcile the conflicts in his own?

Notes

1   Newman's book was dedicated to the memory of Anthony Goldschmidt, killed in battle on Easter Day, 25 April 1943.
2   *Puffin Asquith: A Biography*, by R. J. Minney, Leslie Frewin, London, 1973.
3   For an account of the changes made to *Love in Idleness* and problems surrounding the original production we have drawn extensively on *Stagestruck—Alfred Lunt and Lynn Fontanne* by Maurice Zolotow, Heinemann, London, 1965.
4   Ibid.
5   Lynn Fontanne, in Anthony Curtis' BBC Radio 3 programme, *Rattigan's Theatre*, March 1976.

7
The Winslow Boy

'Terry came to lunch about 12.55. He said (he is a wireless addict), "Turn on the news," and we did, as we sipped our pre-prandial cocktails. The wireless announced that Japan had asked for peace, but insists on the rights of the Emperor. They want to save the Mikado. At long last the war is over, or ending. The streets were crowded with celebrating people singing and littered with torn paper ...'—Henry 'Chips' Channon's diary entry for 10 August 1945. In his book *Ruling Passions*, Tom Driberg, who knew him well, said of Channon at this time: ' "Chips", of American origin, was a social figure at least as glittering as Lady Cunard. He had a large house and a lot of money—the latter, I suppose, largely through his marriage ...' Chips Channon was the forty-eight-year-old Conservative MP for Southend. He entertained the high and the mighty—cabinet ministers and royalty—at his house in Eaton Square. He counted among his intimates the Duchess of Kent, the Duff Coopers, the Wavells (then Viceroy and Vicereine of India) and members of Churchill's cabinet. He knew about the courtship of Philip Mountbatten and Princess Elizabeth long before it was public knowledge, and was approached by Buckingham Palace to loan them his house as a first home after their marriage. He was married to, but about to be divorced from, Lady Honor Guinness, the eldest daughter of the second Earl of Iveagh. Tom Driberg continues: 'For Chips was one of the better known homosexuals in London, and he was rich enough to rent almost any young man he fancied—a handsome German princeling, a celebrated English playwright. His seduction of the playwright was almost like the wooing of Danae by Zeus: every day, the playwright found, delivered to his door, a splendid present—a case of champagne, a huge pot of caviar, a Cartier cigarette box in two kinds of gold ... In the end, of course, he gave in, saying apologetically to his friends, "How can one *not*?" '

Rattigan, who was of course the 'celebrated English playwright', had met Chips Channon on 29 September 1944 when he was deeply engaged in writing *Love in Idleness*. The social world, the glamour which Rattigan described and sought to defend in that play, was the social world of Chips and his friends. This is how Chips recorded their first meeting: 'I dined with Juliet Duff in her little flat stuffed with French furniture and bibelots—also there, Sibyl Colefax and Master Terence Rattigan, and we sparkled over the burgundy. I like Rattigan enormously, and feel a new friendship has begun. He has a flat in Albany.' However, the seduction did not go easily. Rattigan resisted for some time. Here is how one close friend remembers it: 'It was pathetic really. Channon used to buy him these presents, which Terry could have bought six times over, but he was flattered by the social side, Princess Marina [The Duchess of Kent] and all that stuff. The trouble was he didn't want to pay the price. He would bring him here and he would say, "Oh, for God's sake get him drunk so that I don't have to go to bed with him".' When *Love in Idleness* was published it was dedicated 'to Henry Channon', a fitting acknowledgement of his capitulation; Rattigan had surrendered more than his body.

Something of the quality of the time Chips and Rattigan spent together can be gleaned from this entry in the expurgated published version of Channon's diaries:

20th May 1945. From Sturford Mead—where we are staying—I took Terence Rattigan over to Longleat ... Henry Weymouth [the Marquess of Bath] took us all over the house and showed us the famous Shakespeare folios of which they have the first, second, third and fourth. Terry was fascinated and impressed and I saw his face light up as he took one down from the shelf and fingered it ... In the evening we drove to Ashcombe to dine with Cecil Beaton, a long melancholy beautiful drive through isolated country. The house is romantic and amusingly arranged, and Cecil received us in Austrian clothes. Also there, an uninteresting couple, the Graham Sutherlands. He is a painter.

By the late summer of 1945, Chips Channon, although he himself had retained his seat, was in a state of shock from the rout of Churchill and the Conservatives in the General Election. To Channon, and most other Tories who had assumed that having won the war Churchill would win the election, defeat had come as a rude surprise. He and his friends feared what a Labour government, bent on socialism and with a powerful majority, might do to them and their privileged way of life. Rattigan, too, shared their surprise. Only a few years previously he would have been overjoyed at Attlee's victory; his feelings now were much more equivocal.

His political opinions, like much else, were in turmoil. With the exception of Puffin Asquith, who was by family tradition a Liberal, he had lost touch with the radical friends of his youth. Tony Goldschmidt had been killed. Many of his surviving radical friends had moved firmly into the Labour movement during the last years of the war, while Rattigan had drifted in the opposite direction. Despite sharing comradeship and danger with men from quite different backgrounds during his active service in the first years of the war, and getting so much out of it, Rattigan had found himself irresistibly attracted by the powerful and glamorous people with whom he came into contact as a 'war personality'. Inevitably, most of these people were philosophically and politically conservative. The 1945 Election had been the watershed. Rattigan almost certainly voted Liberal; but when the floodwaters of excitement subsided the Liberal Party, along with most of the middle ground in politics, seemed to have been washed away. Rattigan found himself uneasily alongside the Tories. It was perhaps inevitable, considering his family background, his education and his new wealth which he wished to protect from Labour, the traditional party of high taxation.

On 19 August 1945, Chips Channon recorded in his diary: 'Terry read me out the first act of his new play about the Archer

Shee case. I suggested the title of *Ronnie versus Rex*, and he has temporarily adopted it. So far, it is brilliant, dramatic and full of a sense of period.' The Archer Shee case was the one that had so excited his parents' generation around the time of Rattigan's birth, in which a father had defied a reforming government by fighting for the rights of his son. When those who had taken up Archer Shee's case succeeded in getting Parliament to suspend a debate on naval rearmament in order to discuss compensation for a thirteen-year-old naval cadet wrongfully dismissed for the theft of a postal order, they had hailed it as a vindication of democracy in the face of galloping dictatorship by state bureaucracy. An immediately suitable subject, then, as far as someone like Chips Channon was concerned, for 1945; or, as the virulently Conservative *Daily Mail* put it when the play eventually appeared: 'Mr Rattigan's tract for these particular times'. However, in Rattigan's hands it turned out to be something rather more complicated.

One of Rattigan's hobbies was famous trials and he maintained a whole shelf of books on famous cases, to which he added continually. He had read various accounts of the Archer Shee case, the most recent published in 1943. Rattigan and Puffin Asquith used to play a party game with friends which consisted of thinking up the most ludicrous crimes and holding a mock trial in which each guest took on a role—as judge, defending counsel, prosecuting counsel, jury and so on. Rattigan's favourite role was prosecuting counsel. It was probably as a result of participating in one of these mock trials that Anatole de Grunwald suggested to Rattigan and Asquith that they should collaborate on a film about British justice—it was just before the end of the war and there was still pressure from the authorities for films which would advertise traditional British democratic institutions. Rattigan suggested the Archer Shee case and gave him the book. De Grunwald rejected it as too dull. However, the idea had been growing on Rattigan: 'I got very angry and said that if he didn't want to do the bloody thing as a film I would do it as a play.' With the end of the war and Labour's victory in the General Election, the appeal of the subject and its implications grew stronger for Rattigan. But Asquith warned that it would never work on the stage. It would have to be far too elaborate and expensive—as well as domestic scenes there would have to be an enormous court scene. But Rattigan had got the bit between his

140

teeth; he would do it without any court scene, he said. He would have one character, the defence barrister, who would represent all the legal side of the story. The two men argued enthusiastically and eventually laid a bet on whether Rattigan could bring it off. In his excitement Rattigan undertook to write it in the manner of a Granville Barker period piece.

When he sat down to do it he encountered an unexpected difficulty. 'For the first time I was faced with a ready-made plot, before I had worked out the setting in which to put it and the characters through whom to tell it. I had therefore to fashion characters who could, because they actually did, only behave in a certain way. I found it a dreadful task and, after hurling the play many times into my mental waste-paper basket, I decided that the only way that the impossible equation would work out was by dint of some judiciously concealed cheating ... Once again, in fact, I found I could only write my play by allowing my characters to make their own story.'[1] Once Rattigan had made this discovery he found that 'the task, though not easy, proved on the whole a good deal less arduous than that of writing a light comedy.'[2] On 17 September 1945 Chips Channon could record: 'Terry returned to London, and we discussed his play, which he has now all but finished. It is being typed, and there are only a few touches still to do. I advised against the title *The Hamilton Boy* [Rattigan had also tried *The Thompson Case*] and we decided on *The Winslow Boy*, which I suggested. Terry thinks only of his play, dreams and lives it, and it really is magnificent. What a genius he is. He has completed it in six weeks.' Two days later Rattigan read Chips the completed typescript of the finished play. He dedicated it to Chips' son: 'For Master Paul Channon. In the hope that he will live to see a world in which this play will point no moral.'

The major problem that Rattigan had set himself by his determination to keep the court scene and other public events on which his plot ultimately hinged off stage, was to find some way of describing those events in dramatic terms without resorting to having one character come on to the stage to give another information he or she would in real life have already known. Rattigan avoided this trap by establishing the growing interest of the press in the story as a small man's fight for his 'ancient freedom' against 'the new despotism of Whitehall'. The latest

141

editions of the newspapers are brought in, and choice chunks are read by one excited member of the Winslow household (as he had renamed the Archer Shees) to another; an empty-headed woman reporter, who is more interested in the elegance of the curtains than in Arthur Winslow's explanation of the intricacies of the case, arrives with a photographer to do a 'human interest' story on Ronnie and his father's campaign. Through such devices we discover that after weeks of blank refusal Winslow's solicitor has at last got permission to view the evidence on which young Ronnie has been expelled from Osborn Naval College. Similarly we hear how public pressure, brought to bear through letters in the press and questions in the House of Commons, gets the case reopened. Throughout, Rattigan remains close to the essential facts of the Archer Shee case. The only question he ignores that might interest a present-day author dealing with the same material is how the campaign of public pressure was orchestrated. By changing the characters so as to exclude Archer Shee's half-brother who was a Tory MP and therefore well placed to initiate such a campaign, Rattigan allows his audience to assume that the British press and MPs will respond vigorously enough to cause a national outcry whenever their suspicions of a case of injustice are aroused by an ordinary citizen who has sufficient belief in his cause to persist in it. Today that would seem a rather complacent assumption, and even in 1945 it reinforced the view of conservative-minded people that traditional British institutions were best left unquestioned.

As the play develops, Rattigan makes it increasingly clear that the real issue at stake is not Ronnie's guilt or innocence but his right as a citizen, although only a child, and accused of something as trivial as the theft of five shillings, to a full and fair trial with legal representation before a properly constituted and independent court. Against this human right Rattigan sets the opinion of those who believe that it is out of all proportion to create such a public storm over a five-shilling postal order, when the nation is faced by mounting crisis in Europe and the potential threat of the fast-growing German navy. He poses too the question of the human priorities within the Winslow family. Arthur Winslow's health deteriorates under the strain. His elder son's career at Oxford is terminated because the cost of the case makes it impossible for his father to keep him there.

Perhaps the most famous scene in the play is the one that

brings down the second act curtain. On the advice of their solicitors the family hopes to brief the country's most highly esteemed advocate, Sir Robert Morton. He is to interview Ronnie, and on the outcome of that examination hangs his decision whether or not to take the case. He is a Conservative—'for a large monopoly attacking a Trade Union or a Tory paper libelling a Labour leader, he is the best', the Winslows' campaigning suffragette daughter Catherine says, but not for a small case of this sort. He could not possibly have his heart in it. Sir Robert finally appears and Ronnie is brought in to face him. He subjects the boy to a fierce cross-examination, outlining the powerful evidence against him, making the boy contradict himself and finally reducing him to tears by venomously denouncing him as 'a forger, a liar and a thief!' While the family are still reeling under the shock, Sir Robert blithely sweeps out, announcing almost casually at the door: 'The boy is plainly innocent. I accept the brief.' The curtain rings down on a great Edwardian *coup de théâtre*, the audience left stunned and mystified for the interval by this sudden and totally unexplained reversal of what they had expected. Rattigan himself confessed that he had misgivings about that Act Two curtain—'which when I wrote it made even me ashamed. I thought you can't have so theatrical a curtain as that these days, but then I thought, well, of course, in 1912 you could. So I left it in. Thank God I did!' On the first night, that Act Two curtain was greeted with great cheers.

Rattigan depicts Sir Robert as cold and supercilious, maintaining an almost unwavering professional detachment throughout, whereas Sir Edward Carson, who was the Archer Shees' counsel in the original case, was emotional and hot-tempered about the issue from the outset. The reasons for Rattigan's characterization only become fully apparent at the end of the play. The case is not finally brought to proper trial in open court until Sir Robert has successfully brought a Petition of Right on the Winslows' behalf before Parliament. This was an ancient and complex procedure which taxed even Rattigan's mastery of stagecraft to explain convincingly in the theatre. Put simply, a Petition of Right proceeded from the medieval assumption that the King could do no wrong and that a subject could therefore only sue him, or his government, if he received royal assent for such an action. In practice this meant presenting a petition to Parliament, which the

Attorney General might sign on the King's behalf—the form of words then used being 'Let right be done'. Only after such endorsement could a case be brought to court. However, as endorsement of all such Petitions was at the discretion of the government the only way in which an unyielding government could be forced to endorse a Petition was through a defeat in the House of Commons.

The Petition of Right system was not done away with until after the publicity surrounding the success of Rattigan's play—when, ironically perhaps, it was a Labour government which abolished it as an anachronistic curb on the liberty of the subject and a survival from a less democratic past.

While the parliamentary debate over the Petition rages off-stage, Catherine sums up the democratic principle which is one of Rattigan's principal themes. She tells her doubting fiancé: 'If ever the time comes that the House of Commons has so much on its mind that it can't find time to discuss a Ronnie Winslow and his bally postal order, this country will be a far poorer place.'

News of the result of the court case comes early in the fourth and final act of the play. It is brought by the family's faithful maid, who has been established as a 'character'. She has been in court and tells of the emotional scenes that have greeted the Admiralty's admission of Ronnie's innocence. The Winslows have won; but each member of the family has sustained lasting damage as a result of their fight: the compensation paid is unlikely to cover the full financial outlay on the case; Arthur's health has been impaired; the elder son has no degree; Catherine has not made the marriage she wanted because, in an attempt to halt the Winslows' fight against the establishment, her fiancé's conventional family have withdrawn their consent. However, it is clear that the result of the case is not the play's main subject. Rattigan clears the stage for a final confrontation between Catherine, the progressive, and Sir Robert, the conservative, the two characters upon whom the play has increasingly focused. Each has betrayed an increasing interest in and respect for the other. Not only has Catherine's admiration for Sir Robert's skill grown, but so has her respect for his motives—she has been told that he passed over the chance to become Lord Chief Justice in order to continue with the case, which he has fought out of principle. She is surprised to find that he has emotions—he wept

144

when the verdict was announced. For his part, Sir Robert has expressed admiration both for her pretty hats and for her intellect. Rattigan leaves his audience waiting to see if there will be a conventional happy ending.

Catherine starts the scene by apologizing for having misjudged Sir Robert. Then she asks why he is at such pains to prevent people knowing the truth about him; he replies that it is perhaps because he does not know the truth about himself. But why is he ashamed of his emotions, asks Catherine. 'Because as a lawyer I must necessarily distrust them.' We are right back in the heart of Rattigan country. Sir Robert goes on: 'Emotions muddy the issue. Cold, clear logic—and buckets of it—should be the lawyer's only equipment.' He wept at the verdict only because 'Right had been done'. Rattigan does not dwell on the conflict between intellect and emotion but moves swiftly on to the final statement of the play's theme. 'Right had been done,' says Sir Robert. 'Not justice?' counters Catherine. 'No, not justice. Right. It is easy to do justice—very hard to do right.' Finally, Catherine asks him how he can reconcile his support for Winslow against the Crown with his political beliefs. 'Very easily,' Sir Robert replies, 'no one party has a monopoly of concern for individual liberty. On that issue all parties are united.' Catherine qualifies the sentiment: 'No, not all parties. Only some people from all parties.' Sir Robert accepts this—'We can only hope, then, that those same people will always prove enough people.' And so they part, leaving Catherine, who only a little earlier had been despairing of the cause of women's suffrage, determined to continue the fight for women's rights. Not a conventional happy ending nor a rounding-off, but an ending characteristic of Rattigan; one where the audience can sense that the characters will continue their lives after the fall of the curtain, but with the courses on which they are set radically shifted by the events witnessed. Catherine accepts the loss of emotional happiness, embracing instead the opportunity for fulfilment in duty, a cause, an ideal for which to struggle.[3]

The Winslow Boy is a finely detailed statement of Rattigan's beliefs as a dramatist. While it may have started out as a reactionary tract, and in production may have given succour to reactionaries who did not wish to recognize its full implications, it emerges as a reworking of Rattigan's philosophical and emotional position in the light of the changed circumstances of the world at the end of the war.

Most of the play's faults stem from the circumstances of its conception and the limitations Rattigan imposed on himself while writing it in arguments with Anatole de Grunwald and Anthony Asquith. Rattigan brilliantly won his bet with Asquith by telling the story in the manner of an Edwardian play, without including a court scene. Indeed, he went one better, never moving his scene from the Winslow drawing room. But while one cannot fail to admire the brilliance of Rattigan's technique, one is conscious of contrivance. Holly Hill has pointed out[4] that keeping the action away from the court focuses attention on the principle of fundamental rights and on the sacrifices which people of principle—Sir Robert, Arthur and Catherine—have to make to uphold such vital principles, rather than on the lesser issue of justice and whether Ronnie is innocent or not. Nevertheless, the play is too domestic to encompass the full implications of its theme. None of the characters, with the exception of Catherine, is quite rounded enough; and although all are given motives for their behaviour, their actions do not spring from revealed character. In other words, one senses the manipulative hand of the author. *The Winslow Boy* is a fine engrossing play but never a great one.

In the autumn of 1945, Dr Keith Newman went finally insane and had to be permanently confined in a mental institution, a fate which relieved Rattigan of the hold Newman had over him. At the same time it released the young actor Jack Watling from a hold so total that he was himself in imminent danger of mental collapse. Rattigan offered Watling shelter and a chance to relax in a house that he had acquired in Sonning-on-Thames. While Watling was staying in Sonning, Rattigan read him *The Winslow Boy*. 'It was the best performance of the play I ever heard,' recalled Watling, who later played the elder son in the London production.

The Winslow Boy was accepted for production as soon as a theatre and a suitable cast could be got together by Binkie Beaumont of H. M. Tennent, now well on the way to being London's biggest and most influential management. Rattigan wanted Gielgud to play Sir Robert Morton, but he turned it down. Eric Portman was also approached but he also turned it down—perhaps because he did not think the part was big enough. Finally Emlyn Williams accepted it.

146

The play opened on tour in April 1946, and was a success even before it opened in London. Rattigan's royalties from it in the provinces alone were reputed to have reached £200 a week which, even allowing for exaggeration, was a phenomenal sum for those days. The management received a letter from the surviving Archer Shee daughter, on whom the character of Catherine was based, announcing that she was coming to see a performance when the production reached Bristol. It seems that she was a high-minded Tory and was annoyed to hear that Rattigan had made Catherine a liberal and a suffragette. Nervously, Rattigan travelled down to Bristol to meet her. He took her out for a champagne supper and charmed her into dropping her objections to the play.

The Winslow Boy opened in London on 23 May 1946 at the Lyric Theatre, previously the home of *Love in Idleness*. It was another huge success, Rattigan's fourth in a row, and did almost as well in America as in Britain. The play ran for 476 performances in London and 218 performances at the Empire Theatre, New York. It won for Rattigan the Ellen Terry Award—the first time the award was made—for the best play produced in London in 1946, and the New York Critics' Award for the Best Foreign Play of 1947. The reviews were the best he had ever had. As Rattigan himself wryly recalled a few years later,[5] the play caused 'something of a critical sensation. It was generally felt to be very strange that a notoriously insincere farceur could so readily turn his hand to matters of fairly serious theatrical moment, and I found myself on the one hand warmly commended for my courage, and on the other sternly reprimanded for having hidden for so long my light under a bushel. I was myself conscious neither of the virtue nor of the vice, but for all that basked happily, if with a few pangs of conscience, in the sun of the critics' praise.'

Notes

1   *Strand Magazine*, February 1947.

2   Preface to *Collected Plays*, Volume I.

3   When the play was produced in America, the Broadway producer tried to persuade Rattigan to give it a conventional happy ending by suggesting romance between Sir Robert and Catherine. Rattigan demurred.

4   In 'A Critical Analysis of the Plays of Terence Rattigan', 1977.

5   Preface to *Collected Plays*, Volume I.

8
Playbill

'Play-as-you-earn Rattigan', said a *Daily Express* headline in
April 1946, over an article on his phenomenal earnings and tax
liability. 'Mr Terence Rattigan, the playwright, has chambers in
18th-century Albany which are an example of the combination of
selection, contrast and restraint in decoration and furnishing
necessary to provide modern comfort without undue formality,'
began a photographic feature in *Ideal Home* for April 1947. 'My
ambition is static,' Rattigan responded to an *Auckland Weekly
News* reporter in November 1946, when asked if his ambitions
had been affected by success. 'It always remains the same—not to
be content with writing a play to please an audience today, but to
write a play that will be remembered in fifty years' time.'

These three press stories give a fair impression of the public
Rattigan in the period immediately following the production of
The Winslow Boy. The article in *Ideal Home* illustrates the
extent to which Rattigan was now regarded as one of the most
fashionably elegant young men in London. Almost any article on
the haunts or style of celebrities was likely to include a picture or
comment from Terence *(French Without Tears)* Rattigan—in
spite of his subsequent successes the label still stuck. For example,
when the *Tatler* did an article on London's most famous
show-business restaurant, the Ivy, there was a picture of Rattigan
with a film producer, in perfectly cut double-breasted chalk-

striped suit, beaming boyishly. He featured in the *Tailor and Cutter*'s selection of best-dressed men in London; his attendance at fashionable parties, discreet dinners with Greta Garbo, and trips to New York aboard the *Queen Elizabeth* were all fodder for the gossip columnists. When the *Daily Sketch* did a feature on the famous, not to say superior, persons who inhabited the Albany, it was inevitable that the first photograph in the spread was of Rattigan elegantly cross-legged on a sofa, his left hand resting lightly on his white French poodle Tiffin. The fact of his residence in the Albany was regularly slipped into news items covering his many activities. It was something of which he was proud—proof positive that he had 'arrived'.

At the time *The Winslow Boy* opened, a new vogue for what John Russell Taylor has called 'theatricalism' was already discernible in London. Verse plays by Christopher Fry and Ronald Duncan were receiving critical acclaim, if not commercial success. Poetic, colourful but ultimately vaporous, the work of Fry and Anouilh looked like a reaction to the war, Stafford Cripps' austerity budgets and continuing rationing. The new playwrights were the very opposite of Rattigan—their work was over-statement, where his was understatement. As far back as 1944, after *Love in Idleness*, Beverly Nichols had suggested to Rattigan in his column that he should write 'a play that will cause the sort of social uproar which it is one of the theatre's functions to create'. It would not have been surprising if Rattigan now attempted a problem play in a contemporary setting or an epic, but his mind was working in a totally different direction. Among friends he had started to argue that the intervals between acts in the normal play disturbed the dramatic illusion—he had no time for alienation techniques. Although he later used long sequences of short impressionistic scenes, this was always to create illusion. Rattigan forecast the development of generally shorter plays in the theatre with running times of sixty to eighty minutes. He is generally accused of being behind his time but here he was demonstrably ahead of it.

Voices had recently been raised criticizing the dearth of new plays by British dramatists. Rattigan himself had been one. As guest critic of the *Sunday Chronicle* he had lambasted an adaptation of a foreign play and called for original work in the British theatre. Among the older playwrights, Bridie had also been vociferous, laying much of the blame on commercial management of London theatres and the unhealthy policy which sought to increase the length of runs in order to maximize profits—thus reinforcing proven success and hampering experiment. Bridie was now writing largely for the Citizens' Theatre in Glasgow—a repertory theatre. Repertory and the notion of state subsidy seemed the best hope of salvation for the serious theatre. The wartime creation of CEMA, the Council for the Encouragement of Music and the Arts, later the Arts Council, had grown out of the belief that the arts should not be the prerogative of a cultured few, living in London and the big cities. Although this had resulted in worthy productions of Shakespeare and support for touring companies, it had, as yet, done little to encourage new writing. This was almost wholly left to daring amateur companies or professionals working for very little in a few small theatres and societies. But Rattigan's run of successes made him one of a select band of writers who could hope to get almost anything he wrote accepted for professional production.

Keith Newman had observed that Rattigan became bored repeating things he had mastered. Having succeeded with three-act plays and a throw-back to the Edwardian four-acter, he decided to try his hand at one-act plays. He announced that he was writing four one-act plays which would be produced by John Gielgud the following year. Gielgud seems to have given him some encouragement, telling him he was interested in the idea of playing four separate characters in the course of two evenings, if only because it broke up the monotony of a long run. Rattigan was notoriously inclined to take a polite expression of interest as encouragement to go ahead with a project, and he put it about that each play would be an hour and a quarter long and they would be put on two each night, turn and turn about. It was a dangerous scheme. The one-act play had fallen into almost total disfavour and it would be a brave management which put on a double bill, even with Rattigan's name behind it. For his first two one-acters, he chose subjects which touched on his deepest personal concerns. In both he drew on his past, making extensive raids on his 'writer's cupboard'. One was a deeply serious play, *The Browning Version*, which owed its origins to his time at Harrow. The other, *Harlequinade*, was little more than a skit on a theatrical family staging *Romeo and Juliet*, which owed a good deal to working with the Lunts and his experiences with Gielgud's Oxford production. Beneath the jokey surface, however, Rattigan's total addiction to his first love, the theatre, is clearly visible.

The Browning Version is about intellectual failure and the anguish resulting from emotional atrophy. Rattigan was enjoying greater critical and financial success than he had ever known, and at first sight it is surprising that he should choose this moment to write such a play. However, one has only to examine Rattigan himself and the events of his private life to see how such a theme seemed almost inevitable at this point in his career. Rattigan had enjoyed the critical praise of *The Winslow Boy*, but deep down he distrusted it. Although he freely admitted to reading critics avidly, to being lifted by their praise and cast down by their condemnation, he knew enough about their fickleness to rely on the inner conviction that the ultimate judge of success or failure was himself. When Agate had compared *While the Sun Shines* with Oscar Wilde, Rattigan reminded his public that the same critic had only a few years previously dismissed *French Without Tears*, on which the later play had been consciously modelled, as 'nothing'. 'No writer,' he remarked, 'can grow from nothing into Oscar Wilde between one light comedy and another.'[1] Rattigan's own assessment of his achievement so far was less favourable than that of some recent critics, but then he was measuring himself against the highest standards and not merely technical facility.

The intellectual disillusionment at the time of the production of *After the Dance*, which had made him ask whether he should have concentrated on history rather than becoming a playwright, had not been totally dispelled by his success. He still doubted whether he was fulfilling his intellectual potential. He had friends who criticized his work because it demonstrated no spiritual or philosophical quest. There was a growing suspicion that he was spending too much time surrounded by people who were not his intellectual equals. But the most important factor, the one that did most to precipitate the writing of *The Browning Version*, was undoubtedly emotional in origin.

Chips Channon was a glittering social figure—'the iron butterfly', as Rattigan and his friends called him behind his back. For all his gaiety and social poise, Channon was at heart a failure. He had accepted gracefully the frustration of his political and creative ambitions and long ago decided on an observer's role. His distinction was to fill his butterfly role with such luxurious wit and elegance that he seemed to belong to Regency England rather than to the 1940s. His considerable creativity was poured into elaborate entertaining and his diaries, which he packed with outrageously frank observations on the foibles and follies of the important figures of his time—all of whom he went out of his way to meet. He intended his diaries to be a unique record that would, after their deaths, be published. But his marriage, which had done so much at the outset to buy him his social position, had just ended in amicable divorce. Now fifty, Channon had begun to feel himself a prematurely old man. His feelings for Rattigan were undoubtedly much stronger than for most of the young men he 'rented'; but they were not feelings Rattigan could reciprocate. He found Channon's demands increasingly difficult to meet. The consolation Channon might have found in Rattigan was not forthcoming.

After the completion of *The Winslow Boy*, but before finishing *The Browning Version*, Rattigan made up his mind to break off the relationship with Channon. He must have brooded on his decision for some time before telling Channon. The irony was that the feeling which he could not reciprocate for Channon he had begun to feel for someone else. He would himself soon be racked by the very possessiveness he resented from Channon.

Kenneth Morgan, the young actor who in 1939 had played Babe Lake in the film of *French Without Tears*, seems to have largely dropped out of Rattigan's life while he was in the Forces. Ken Morgan's post-war career in the theatre did not quite realize his early promise. He was seven years younger than Rattigan, and those who remember him recall him as charming but quiet—'a very nice young lad', but not a colourful personality. Whether Rattigan had been seriously attracted to Morgan when they met before the war is not clear. If so, he seems to have done little about it, since he already had a fairly regular relationship with another actor. But whatever had or had not happened before, Rattigan found himself very strongly drawn to him now. His role in the relationship with Chips Channon was now reversed: Rattigan became the pursuer, Morgan the pursued. And of course, relative to Ken Morgan, Rattigan was in the financial position of Chips Channon; he could now play Zeus to Morgan's

Danae. Morgan moved in with Rattigan, who smothered him with gifts and affection. He had never felt so strongly about another person. But, like Rattigan with Channon, Morgan seems to have been unable fully to return his feelings. What Rattigan had observed in others he now began to experience in himself—the more desperately you try to make someone love you the less they do.

All this had, of course, to be concealed from the public. One of Rattigan's reasons for breaking with Channon had been the fear that their relationship was becoming too public. To be seen so much in his company might cause speculation. The cruel repression engendered by the law, which still made those found guilty of homosexual acts, even between consenting adults in private, liable to severe prison sentences, is too easily overlooked today. Blackmail was not uncommon and criminal prosecution by no means unknown. It was understandable then that Rattigan, who was in any case naturally shy, was cripplingly reticent about his sexual relationships. It went deeper than his fear of offending convention or earning the disapproval of his parents. There were occasional lapses, but only among his friends or when he had been drinking—on one famous occasion he tried to pick up an actor at a party in front of the man's wife, and when the actor seemed reluctant told him he was missing out on the best chance of his life. But normally he was extraordinarily discreet.

The degree of falsity and artificiality imposed on Rattigan by this necessary concealment can to some extent be gauged by the replies he gave to a reporter from *Woman* magazine in 1947. 'He talked about the difficulty of writers who are essentially creatures of mood—marrying' the reporter wrote. 'He believes friction is bound to arise if writer marries writer. Wouldn't want a wife to have anything to do with either the theatre or films, at least she should have to give up her work on marrying. Puts tact high on the list ... He wants a good companion, someone with whom he could be silent for two hours and yet feel wonderfully entertained. He prefers someone of whom men will say "I don't understand what he sees in her." He would want her to enjoy the things he likes, travel, tennis, golf, watching cricket. He thinks jealousy, justified or not, the most infuriating of emotions, hates dominating women, those who smother a man with devotion and drown him in glasses of milk.'

154

The Browning Version, although based on an incident from his boyhood, is a reflection of Rattigan's enforced endurance of such concealment. Beautifully but unobtrusively shaped, it deals with emotional repression, falsity, failure and love, in a densely packed yet completely satisfying hour and a quarter. The plot through which Rattigan opens up such large themes, while maintaining a completely convincing naturalism and a poignant, essentially English quality of understatement, is deceptively simple. The setting is that most British of institutions, a boys' public school. After eighteen years of increasing failure as a teacher, Andrew Crocker Harris is being driven into premature retirement by heart trouble. During his time at the school he has progressed downwards; a brilliant and idealistic scholar when he started teaching, dedicated to communicating his own great love of classical Greek literature to the boys, he is now a desiccated pedant, held in contempt by his fellow teachers and feared by his pupils: 'the Himmler of the Lower Fifth.' He has been unable to satisfy the sexual needs of his wife, Millie, who with calculated destructiveness has turned to other men. She is carrying on an affair with a popular young master, Frank Hunter, which she has deliberately advertised to her husband. However, Frank is tiring of her, unable to reciprocate the feelings she has for him.

It is the penultimate day of term. The headmaster conveys to Crocker Harris the school governors' decision not to grant him a badly-needed pension, and asks him to forgo his right to speak last at the next day's prize-giving ceremony, in order that the speech of the master who coached the school cricket team to victory at Lord's may bring the proceedings to the popular climax. To all this, as to his wife's cruelty, Crocker Harris placidly assents, registering no protest or show of feeling. He treats his situation as if it had no emotional meaning to him. 'You can't hurt Andrew,' his wife tells her lover. 'He's dead.'

Years of pent-up emotion are released by one small gesture: an act of kindness in which a boy, Taplow, who likes Crocker Harris in spite of his forbidding exterior, gives him a leaving present—a second-hand copy of Browning's translation of his favourite play, the *Agamemnon* of Aeschylus. Crocker Harris breaks down. This, for him, is the single success which 'can atone and more than atone for all the failures in the world'. With courage born of this one small show of gratitude, Crocker Harris himself makes a small gesture of defiance and reclaims a shred of self-respect; he will, after all, exercise his right to speak last at the school prize-giving.

Rattigan said more than once that to a great extent the boy Taplow was himself while at Harrow, telling us quite specifically that the central incident in the story—Taplow's gift to the retiring master—was based on his own school experience; and that the character of Crocker Harris grew out of his speculation about how a human being reached the point, as his own Greek master Coke Norris had done, where he responded to an act of ordinary human kindness with unkindness. The *Agamemnon* had been Rattigan's favourite play at school, and he ascribed a large part of his determination to become a dramatist to having read it in translation in the Harrow school library after his discovery, despite Coke Norris's dry-as-dust teaching methods, that it was a living play and not a dead text.

But Rattigan's identification with the play and its characters goes much further than a few autobiographical details. One day while he was at work on it, his manservant came in to find tears streaming down his face. The character in whom people have seen most self-identification is obviously Crocker Harris; but, as always with Rattigan, it extends in varying degrees to all the characters. It is most in evidence in the central trio—Crocker Harris, Millie and Frank—both individually and in their relationship to each other.

Early in the play Frank Hunter, who Rattigan describes in his stage directions as 'wrapped in all the self-confidence of the popular master', admits to Millie Crocker Harris that after only three years as a schoolmaster he has slipped into an act with his pupils which he just can't get out of. 'My God, how easy it is to be popular,' he says, but goes on to explain that this is achieved at the expense of being oneself. The theme of deceit and falsity in relations between people pervades the play. Characters who hide their feelings, relationships which are not as they appear, bonhomie which hides pain, all have been much in evidence throughout Rattigan's writing. Yet in *The Browning Version* the full destructive force of these elements is revealed for the first time. He shows how deceit in personal relationships, the pursuit of popularity and emotional repression all lead to tragedy; not just to personal unhappiness but to a betrayal of integrity, the

156

undermining of ideals and the destruction of the emotional security on which ultimately everyone depends.

The principal characters inhabit an emotional wasteland of unsatisfied longings, in which life has been almost extinguished by years of starvation from true human feeling or responsiveness, and this is heightened by the way in which the social relationships between even the minor characters are based on a polite dishonesty. The headmaster, whom Rattigan describes as being 'like a successful diplomat', is the most obviously socially correct, and therefore socially dishonest, of the minor characters. Like a diplomat he uses his charm to blunt the edge of his encounter with Crocker Harris. When he pays a compliment by saying that it is hard to remember that Crocker Harris was the most brilliant classical scholar the school has ever had, it also deftly underlines the man's failure and the dismal circumstances surrounding his forthcoming departure; he evinces concern about the Crocker Harrises' future while bringing them the news that the school governors have decided not to grant them that much-needed pension. Social etiquette requires Millie to visit and say farewell to the other masters' wives, whom she despises. She has in turn to endure their transparently insincere expressions of sorrow about the bad luck that has forced her husband to retire before he has become a housemaster. Throughout, Millie gives herself airs, making out that her father runs a large business, when in fact he has a clothing shop in the Bradford Arcade. The very first action of the play is a piece of deceit—before anyone else has appeared the boy Taplow surreptitiously takes two chocolates from a box on the table in the Crocker Harrises' room but, judging that he might not get away with the theft of two chocolates, he replaces one.

Central to Crocker Harris's failure as a master has been his attempt to win popularity by encouraging the boys to laugh at him. By playing up to their delight in his mannerisms and tricks of speech, he has tried to compensate for his lack of natural ability to make himself liked. He rationalizes his behaviour by saying that more things can be taught by laughter than by earnestness, yet he knows in his heart, even though he is afraid to acknowledge it, that this has undermined his ability to communicate his true feelings for the great literature of the past. By being afraid to be himself he has betrayed both himself and the literature he loves.

157

He knows that the origins of his failure go deeper than his illness: 'Not sickness of the body, but a sickness of the soul', he says.

The same cankerous deceit and repression of true feelings have entered the emotional relationships of the principal characters. All three central characters pretend to a concern for each other that they do not really feel; all become, with the possible exception of Millie, better off at the end of the play, after they have shed their pretences, by being themselves. Even the lovers are dishonest with each other. Frank has tired of Millie but has not told her, and has in any case never felt as strongly about her as he has allowed her to believe. Millie admits eventually to using Frank for emotional and sexual gratification. The ultimate irony is that Crocker Harris knows about Millie's affair with Frank because she has told him, as she has told him about all her previous affairs. She tells Crocker Harris the truth, but to her the truth is a weapon to be used specifically to hurt him. The use of the truth is Millie's greatest cruelty. Frank goes so far as to warn Crocker Harris that she intends to kill him with it. It is Rattigan's central paradox: honesty is a prerequisite of emotional fulfilment, but at the same time it is the vehicle of deadly pain. Without honesty there may be no hope; with it there may be no comfort. It was a paradox which permeated Rattigan's own life.

In the film of *The Browning Version*, Rattigan added a scene in which a group of masters' wives discuss the Crocker Harrises: 'Yes, a marriage of mind and body. It never has worked since the world began.' Here, as in so many film scripts based on his own plays, Rattigan makes a blunt statement of one of the work's major themes: inequality of emotion and mismatching of relationships. In both play and film, Crocker Harris explains that he and his wife are equally to be pitied: 'Both of us needing from the other something that would make life supportable for us, and neither of us able to give it. Two kinds of love. Hers and mine. Worlds apart ...'

Millie, unable to find what she requires in her husband, has turned elsewhere. She has become an embittered neurotic, not simply through lack of physical satisfaction, but through years of deprivation of emotional fulfilment and release which ought to come from the sexual expression of love—Rattigan is never interested, through his characters, in the damage caused by purely physical sexual deprivation.

The pain inflicted on those who love by the petty cruelties of their loved ones is beautifully observed. While Millie deliberately inflicts repeated petty humiliations on her husband, she in turn suffers from Frank's petty oversights. She has bought him a seat for a school cricket match at Lord's; he fails to turn up, and she asks if he has ever been in love with anyone: 'Do you realize what torture you inflict on someone who loves you when you do a thing like that?' When he confesses that he clean forgot, she begs for pity: 'Do you think it's any pleasanter for me to believe that you cut me because you forgot? Do you think that doesn't hurt either?' At another point, she notes triumphantly that Frank is still using a gold cigarette case she gave him—that he hasn't given it to another girl friend. This sails very close to Rattigan's own experience: not only had Chips Channon been in the habit of showering him with similar presents, but Rattigan was also in the habit of giving his boy friends gold cigarette cases, which may well have turned up in other hands.

But the love, and the failure of love, in *The Browning Version* is not cast in the mould of heroic tragedy or theatrical grand passion. It is more in keeping with its subject—the failure of a rather colourless schoolmaster. Devoid of human affection, such people become devoid of human dignity. One small gesture of human sympathy transforms the situation, and in the end Crocker Harris's little act of defiance takes on great force as a symbol of the reassertion of human dignity. Crocker Harris himself belittles his own situation, saying that it is not very unusual 'or nearly as tragic as you seem to imagine. Merely the problem of an unsatisfied wife and a hen-pecked husband ... It is usually, I believe, a subject for farce!'

The dénouement of the play caused Rattigan much trouble. He recognized that a neat tragic ending—probably Crocker Harris's death from his heart trouble—might win him praise from critics and audience alike. He was very tempted to send his audience home crying happily, and confessed that in his youth he would have contrived just such an ending. However, he felt that this was too easy—it was not only too pat, it evaded the issues he had raised. Later he was accused of having given *The Browning Version* a quasi-happy ending. This he disputed, but he did recognize that by giving the play an inconclusive ending he had upset the more conventional members of his audience. This was, of course, not the first time he had given one of his plays an ending which left the characters with problems to solve and lives to continue. Most of his endings are to a certain extent inconclusive. However, *The Browning Version* is perhaps the first occasion on which he took a calculated risk, deliberately leaving the play unresolved, in the hope of making the audience continue to ponder the implications of what had been placed before them. Crocker Harris's final act of defiance to the headmaster restores his dignity but does not solve any of his problems or wipe out his years of failure. He still has to live with the reality of his situation.

This is the message of many of Rattigan's mature plays: human beings cannot live unless they come to terms with themselves and their circumstances, no matter how painful that truth may be. Without self-knowledge there is no hope. However comforting self-delusion may be, it leads finally, like an addictive drug, to death. Rattigan sees men as ultimately the masters of their own fate, and says uncompromisingly that they may not opt out but must confront their lives for themselves. Love and friendship may help, but in the end each person is on his or her own. This is not a comforting view—despite the sneers of Rattigan's detractors—nor is it a bleak one. Rattigan's position is profoundly humanistic.

The mastery of the play is brought out by comparing it with the film, which is itself widely accepted as a classic of the British cinema and perhaps the finest of Anthony Asquith's films. In the theatre Rattigan manages to pack the wealth of feeling and implication we have described into one set, in one scene lasting little over an hour, without strain or apparent contrivance. The film, although it conveys much of the same feeling, is both longer and more explicit, and therefore weaker. By opening out to include the life of the whole school and the Crocker Harrises' relations with the other members of the staff, the film detracts from the universal implications of Crocker Harris's tragedy and focuses attention on his role as a master in a public school. Universality, in spite of the remarkable performance of Michael Redgrave in the central role, is reduced. At the end of the film the Crock is seen making his prize-day speech to the school. He movingly confesses his failure, apologizing to the boys for having let them down. After a stunned silence the boys break into cheers.

Rattigan at the time of the production of *The Browning Version* —
one of a series of press photos entitled 'Playboy Comes of Age'

(*Central Press*)

Terence Rattigan and Anatole de Grunwald at the formation of
their company International Screenplays

(*Keystone Press*)

Rattigan aged fifty and his mother on the *Queen Mary*

(*Cunard Lines*)

Rattigan in his mid-fifties (*Angus McBean*)

opposite: Rattigan aged forty-five with Vivien Leigh at the first night of
   Summer of the Seventeenth Doll (*Keystone Press*)

Rattigan at sixty (*Anthony Crickmay*)

Rattigan on stage with the cast of *Separate Tables* at the performance
to celebrate his sixtieth birthday

(*Evening Standard*)

Rattigan with Sir Noël Coward   (*Evening Standard*)

The audience is allowed to leave the cinema suffused in a glow of sentimentality, excused from thinking any further about the fundamental issues raised by the script. Its tragedy and challenge are undermined.

The second play in the projected quartet of one-acters was *Harlequinade*. This companion piece to *The Browning Version* was a sharp and deliberate contrast. Where the first play had been a tragedy centred on emotional repression and an introverted character, *Harlequinade* was a farce about a theatrical family—the Gosports—who exhibit their changing feelings with the same extrovert panache as their theatrical costumes. Rattigan made no secret of the fact that his characterization of the Gosports—Edna Selby and Arthur Gosport—owed a lot to the Lunts. In *Harlequinade*, a reporter on a local newspaper enquires about the fact that the Gosports always act together and asks if they always play as husband and wife; he is told: 'No, usually as lover and mistress. The audience prefers that. It gives them such a cosy feeling to know they're really married after all.'

Harlequinade is set in a theatre in a Midlands town where the Gosports are dress-rehearsing their production of *Romeo and Juliet*, prior to opening on an Arts Council tour. Edna is playing Juliet and her husband is directing as well as playing Romeo. The way in which they needle each other in rehearsal, and wheedle to get their own way, while keeping up a front of mutual admiration and adoration, is very reminiscent of descriptions by eye-witnesses of the Lunts' rehearsals. The fact that they are rehearsing *Romeo and Juliet* leads one to expect references to Rattigan's own experiences in Gielgud's Oxford production, and one is not disappointed. The actor playing the one line, 'Faith, we may put up our pipes and be gone' (Rattigan's line at Oxford), leaves the production and a breathless, incompetent youngster is selected to replace him. He proudly tells his mother, whom he has sneaked into the back of the gallery, of his new-found pre-eminence. He then sets about trying his one line with a series of different inflexions, with the emphasis on a different word each time, to the increasing annoyance of the company.

Arthur Gosport's rehearsal methods and mannerisms owe something to Gielgud as well as to Alfred Lunt—particularly his absent-mindedness, caused by his total absorption in the production. His way of remembering the date of outside events by recalling which play he was appearing in at the time is reminiscent of Gielgud, while the fact that he can only remember the date of the General Strike by recalling that 'it was the year Gladys Cooper opened in *The Sign of the Door*', caricatures many elderly actors. The habit of seeing important public events only in terms of their consequences for the theatre or the current production is a characteristic of almost the entire acting profession. Accordingly Rattigan has Gosport's aunt, Dame Maud—a formidable old actress who is playing the Nurse—recall playing Juliet in 1914: 'I remember the date well, because the declaration of war damaged our business so terribly.'

The plot of *Harlequinade* is extravagant, in the best traditions of farce. Amid the routine but hilarious chaos of their dress-rehearsal, the Gosports discover that they are bigamously married—Arthur having previously contracted marriage to a lady which he has absent-mindedly overlooked. In resolving this difficulty, Rattigan, unlike conventional farceurs, allowed his play to develop out of his characters. While he was working on the play, he wrote an article in *Strand Magazine* called 'How I Write My Plays'. In it he said that he had a formula for farce: 'a formula which, though extremely simple, has not, up to now, been generally followed. I believe in the farce of character—a contradiction in terms, most purist minded critics would say, but wrongly, as I think.' He argues that by creating believable characters and rooting the plot, however farcical, firmly in their behaviour he encourages continuous audience laughter because he does not excite disbelief. The plot then becomes the vehicle through which he can exhibit the follies and foibles of recognizable theatre characters. Most of the best laughs have the double-edged quality, typical of Rattigan's best comedy, of tickling the ribs while telling a truth.

Rattigan himself later declined to defend the play as anything more than a soufflé designed to round off a meal of which *The Browning Version* was the main course. But, like all good chefs, he concocted a soufflé worthy of the rest of his meal which was distinctively his own. Nothing concerned him more than the theatre, and in *Harlequinade* he expressed his attitude towards it more clearly than anywhere else in his writing. The Gosports, we are told, '*are* the theatre'. They are the theatre at its best and worst—'They're true theatre, because they're entirely self-centred, entirely exhibitionist and entirely dotty, and because they make no compromise whatever with the outside world ... All through the ages, from Burbage downwards, the theatre—the true theatre—has consisted of blind, anti-social, self-sufficient, certifiable Gosports.'

Edna Gosport tries to explain the immense change that has come over the theatre in recent years—'The theatre of today has at last acquired a social conscience, and a social purpose. Why else do you think we're opening at this rathole of a theatre instead of the Opera House, Manchester?' Dame Maud says she didn't know it was social purpose that had brought them there, she thought it was CEMA. Edna replies scathingly, 'CEMA is social purpose.' Later, the Stage Manager explains that theatre with a social purpose is a contradiction in terms: 'Good citizenship and good theatre don't go together. They never have and they never will.' As far as the Stage Manager is concerned, social purpose in the theatre seems to mean 'playing Shakespeare to audiences who'd rather go to the films; while audiences who'd rather go to Shakespeare are driven to the films because they haven't got Shakespeare to go to. It's all got something to do with the new Britain and apparently it's an absolutely splendid idea.' If that is a true reflection of Rattigan's theatrical beliefs—and there is every reason to believe it is—then it is hardly surprising that, apart from *Follow My Leader*, he never wrote a didactic play. Ironically *Harlequinade*, along with the earlier farce, comes as near to being didactic as anything he wrote.

Although he completed a third play, Rattigan dropped the idea of a second pair of one-act plays to be alternated in repertory with *The Browning Version* and *Harlequinade*. Binkie Beaumont, the head of H. M. Tennent, which was now the management which normally presented Rattigan's work in London, was less than enthusiastic about pairs of one-act plays; the last new one-act play to succeed in London had been Coward's *Tonight at 8.30* in 1937. Since then only Olivier, doubling in *The Critic* and *Oedipus* in 1945, had got away with such a thing. Disturbing London theatre-goers spelt danger at the box office. By the autumn of 1947 Gielgud, who was playing on Broadway, had had plenty of time to read both plays and make up his mind about them. The prospects for their London production now seemed to hang on his decision. In October of that year, Rattigan sailed to New York for

163

the Broadway opening of *The Winslow Boy.* The two men met and strolled in Central Park, Rattigan waiting anxiously for Gielgud's decision. There was a long silence, suddenly broken by Gielgud. 'They've seen me in so much *first-rate* stuff,' he said, thinking aloud with more candour than tact. 'Do you think they will like me in second-class stuff?'[2] Gielgud had not intended to hurt Rattigan and Rattigan was far too well-bred to show his feelings. He replied mildly, 'Oh, I think they will, John.' Although Rattigan knew that Gielgud did not realize what he had asked him, it was nevertheless a shattering blow. Gielgud had now turned down two successive roles which Rattigan had written for him—Sir Robert Morton in *The Winslow Boy* and Crocker Harris in *The Browning Version.* Five years later, Kenneth Tynan found that Rattigan still could not speak of that moment in Central Park when Gielgud made it clear he would not do *The Browning Version.*[3] That apparently casual conversation was one of the sharpest setbacks of his life so far.

Rattigan had plenty of other work on hand to take his mind off his disappointment over Gielgud's rejection. So while his agent sent his one-act plays round other managements, he concentrated on film work. Early in 1947 he and Anatole de Grunwald had set up a film company called International Screenplays. They had announced that their first film, directed by Anthony Asquith, would be *While the Sun Shines.*

Since the last years of the war, Asquith had been drinking heavily, and de Grunwald and Rattigan, though no mean drinker himself, had become increasingly anxious. Frequently they wondered whether he would be fit to direct at all when he went on to the studio floor. One day de Grunwald and Rattigan were asked to lunch at the Berkeley by Alexander Korda, the film producer. That morning, de Grunwald phoned Rattigan and suggested they meet beforehand to decide what to do about Asquith's drinking, recalling that the last time they had lunched with Korda, Asquith had slumped into the soup. Luckily Korda, who was perhaps the single most powerful person in films in Britain at the time, had merely commented, 'Even that he does with so much grace.'

De Grunwald and Rattigan met at the Ritz, just across Piccadilly from the Berkeley. They ordered two dry Martinis, and de Grunwald suggested that as Rattigan was Asquith's best friend *he* must talk firmly to him. Rattigan thought de Grunwald should do it. As they talked, a waiter kept refilling their glasses. They had got no further than agreeing that one of them must say to Asquith that he *must* stop drinking, because it was ruining his career, when they noticed that by now they should have been at the Berkeley for lunch. Now more than a little befuddled themselves, they dodged through the traffic and staggered unsteadily into the Berkeley, to be confronted by a stone-cold sober Asquith, who demanded to know where they had been: 'Why are you late? Are you both drunk?'[4]

By sheer will-power Asquith managed to keep himself sober enough to complete at least a film a year during the six years between 1944 and 1950, at the end of which period he underwent a most rigorous cure and never drank again until his death in 1969. During the six years when he was fighting alcoholism, Rattigan tried to support him in his battle. While filming *The Way to the Stars*, Asquith had discovered a café used by long-distance lorry drivers on the Great North Road. It was run by an ex-regimental-sergeant-major and his wife. No alcoholic drinks were served and Asquith and Rattigan had formed a lasting friendship with the proprietor during the filming. Asquith found that by going up there when he was not working and living as the family did, rising at five in the morning and serving behind the counter, he could stop drinking altogether. It became a refuge for him. Rattigan seems to have accompanied him a number of times when he stayed there.

By the summer of 1948, a smaller but more adventurous management than H. M. Tennent had been found to present *The Browning Version* and *Harlequinade* as a double bill, under the title *Playbill*. This was Stephen Mitchell, who had presented Emlyn Williams' *The Corn is Green*. But Glen Byam Shaw, who had directed *The Winslow Boy*, refused to direct *Playbill*, so Peter Glenville was called in. Glenville had in the last few years branched out from an acting career to direct with the Old Vic Company in Liverpool and subsequently, with increasing success, in London. This reunion was the beginning of a long professional association. When *The Browning Version* was published, it was dedicated 'to Peter Glenville in Gratitude'.

Eric Portman, one of those who had turned down the part of Sir Robert Morton in *The Winslow Boy*, did not repeat his mistake, and accepted the roles of Crocker Harris and Arthur Gosport. Mary Ellis played his wife in both plays, and Campbell Cotts, a redoubtable baronet and raconteur in private life before he had been induced to take to the stage, played the headmaster and the theatre manager.

Playbill opened on 8 September 1948 at London's Phoenix Theatre. It was an immediate success with audiences and critics alike. For the second year running Rattigan received the Ellen Terry Award for the best new play, and Eric Portman won the award for Best Actor. The critics thought both plays perfectly judged. The *Daily Mail*'s reviewer said that in both plays Rattigan's acute perceptive talent pierced to the very essence of his characters: 'one is looking at the workings of real human souls.' J. C. Trewin placed *Harlequinade* among the classic plays about the theatre, comparing it favourably with *The Rehearsal, The Critic* and *Trelawny of the Wells.*

As so often before, Rattigan found that work which the critics and public had hailed in England was damned in America. *Playbill* ran for 245 performances in London but for only 62 when it opened a year later in New York. Although one American critic called *The Browning Version* a masterpiece, the majority were at best dismissive, at worst downright rude ('As playwriting, it is not too far from double bilge,' said *Time Magazine*).

In the *New York Times*, where Brooks Atkinson had dismissed *The Browning Version* as 'superior hackwork', Rattigan wrote a thoughtful article entitled 'Sea Change Problem', on the differing receptions his plays had in Britain and America. He wondered whether plays of character, such as his, faced greater hazards when exported from their native countries than plays of ideas: 'plays of character, be they Russian, American, English or French, really demand a contribution from an audience which, when that audience is foreign and unversed in the customs, idiom and idiosyncrasies of the dramatist's native country, cannot readily be given. The portrait, however meticulously drawn, becomes blurred and coarsened and emerges often merely as a type, confused in the audience's mind with a hundred other such Russians or Americans, or Englishmen or Frenchmen, all very like each other and totally unlike anyone else.' However, the 'sea change problem' did not beset *The Browning Version* everywhere it went. While Brooks Atkinson was condemning it as 'sentimental' in New York, a Danish critic, reviewing a production in Copenhagen, called it 'a modern version of *The Dance of Death*'.[4]

Rattigan himself said later that if he had one day to justify his choice of career before a heavenly jury, then *The Browning Version* would be the play he would want to represent him. Writing about the play at the time of its original production, Harold Hobson, who had now replaced James Agate as drama critic of the *Sunday Times*, said in the course of an extremely perceptive appreciation of Rattigan's distinctive qualities: 'As one listens wearily night after night to the banal, clipped, naturalistic dialogue of the modern drama, one's heart cries out for writing of courage and colour, for the evocative word and the mannered phrase. But Mr Rattigan makes one doubt the necessity of that cry. In *The Browning Version* there is not a single sentence that in itself would raise the emotional level of a railway timetable. There is hardly a word that would be out of place in giving an order for a pound of vegetables.' Yet, Hobson points out, the audience is moved to tears. And when Crocker Harris makes his act of defiance at the end of the play, the heart responds 'as to the sound of a trumpet. It is not, Mr Rattigan reminds us, the intrinsic quality of the words that matter, but the amount and nature of the emotion they can be made to convey.'

Notes

1 Preface to *Collected Plays*, Volume I.

2 This is Rattigan's version of what was said. Gielgud's biographer, Ronald Hayman, reports Gielgud's words as 'I have to be very careful what I play now.' Either way, Gielgud's motives for turning down *Playbill* are clear.

3 Gielgud eventually played Crocker Harris in both a BBC radio production in 1957, which Rattigan himself introduced on the air with a eulogy to Gielgud's talent and a paean of gratitude for his kindness to him as a young man, and on television in America in 1959. This latter version was directed by John Frankenheimer and marked Gielgud's American TV debut. It was a triumph and Gielgud received glowing notices.

4 *Puffin Asquith: A Biography*, by R. J. Minney, Leslie Frewin, London, 1973.

5 G. O. Harris, *Berlingske Tidende*, 12 October 1949.

9
Adventure Story

By the time *The Browning Version* and *Harlequinade* opened in London, Rattigan already had another play nearing completion. This play, *Adventure Story*, was to open up not only the question of Rattigan's distinctive use of language, but the very nature of his claim to be considered a great playwright. People had long speculated about whether Rattigan, with enough money to last him for life and an established reputation as a master craftsman, would now change his style and write to please himself. They could not accept that he might have been pleasing himself all along. To them, the fact that his plays had been commercially successful suggested that he must have been writing down to his audience. They made the illogical assumption that the best, most personal and most deeply-felt work was incompatible with commercial success. They ignored the examples of Shakespeare, Marlowe, Congreve, Wilde and even Shaw, who were popular successes in their own day, as was Dickens, with whom Rattigan shared an uncanny ability to appeal to popular audiences.

Although Rattigan professed that he chose to tell the epic story of Alexander the Great in *Adventure Story* with no loftier intention than the one that had motivated him in writing all his plays, namely that be believed 'the chosen subject would make a good play', he admitted later that there was also the element of deliberately measuring himself against the demands of the commonly-held view of the great play: an epic story, a central figure of heroic stature and a great, universal theme; in this case, the story of Alexander's twelve years of conquest in Asia which turned him from plain Alexander of Macedon into Alexander the Great, the subject of legend. Rattigan's aim was to explore the character of his hero in relation to the paradox of his unsurpassed material success and ultimate spiritual defeat.

The story of Alexander (which his grandfather had touched on in his history of India) had appealed to him since he was a boy. Having made up his mind to write the play, he read all the available books but found that, while they more or less agreed about Alexander's achievements, they failed to agree about his character. Rattigan preferred the story as told by Plutarch and decided to rely on it for his outline. As he believed that 'action should arise out of character, not character out of action', and very little was commonly accepted by historians about Alexander the man, he was free to interpret the character of his hero in the way he felt was most likely to have given rise to his deeds. 'I tried to discover what was in Alexander's heart that drove him on in his tempestuous, ruthless, invincible march ... "Absolute power corrupts absolutely," said Lord Acton, and the story of Alexander does not belie this universally-held belief. Yet the corruption of power is not the theme of *Adventure Story*. For even absolute power can only corrupt the corruptible and Alexander's tragedy was that he set out to conquer the world before he had succeeded in conquering himself. "For what shall it profit a man if he gain the whole world and lose his own soul?" ' Rattigan pointed out that, measured by what he did, Alexander might well have been the greatest man who ever lived. 'But is it right to measure man's greatness simply by his deeds, isn't what you are more important that what you do?'[1]

At the beginning of the play, in a prologue in which he is seen on his death bed, Alexander asks despairingly, 'Where did it first go wrong?' Eleven scenes follow, spanning Alexander's life from the age of twenty when he embarked on his conquests, returning finally to his death at the age of thirty-two. Each scene attempts to supply part of the answer to that initial question. Rattigan answers the opening question in terms of his own life and inner experience; large elements of his portrait of Alexander are yet another projection of aspects of himself.

The most striking merit of the play is the economy with which Rattigan manages to encompass his epic story. Yet the play's recurring theme is stated at the outset when the Pythia at Delphi warns Alexander that there is one conquest he must make before any others—himself. 'Know yourself, Alexander,' she admonishes him. So the play's recurring theme, the importance of self-knowledge (the lack of which is the cause of Alexander's eventual spiritual downfall), is stated at the outset. Up to now, Rattigan's plays had hinted at the dangers inherent in the failure to express feelings, but *Adventure Story* was the first of a series of plays in which he explored both the importance and the devastating effects of self-knowledge.

Rattigan's Alexander, like Rattigan himself, must conquer to impress his father. After his first great victory over Darius and the Persian Empire, he asks the gods to ensure that his father knows what he has achieved: 'Let him see me now—in Darius's tent, wearing Darius's mantle—and let his eyes burn with the sight.' Later, on the eve of his decisive battle against Darius, after which he will either be 'Master of the World' or dead, Alexander prays: 'Father! Father! Philip! I invoke you, then. Look down at me now and sneer. Say—"See what a weak, effeminate coward I have for a son!" Say that, Father! You used to say it often enough in your lifetime. Say it now, and help me, for only anger can conquer fear!' (Rattigan, the leader of the Harrow OTC revolt and the pacifist who had voted against fighting for 'King and Country' at Oxford, had to some degree always been concerned to justify himself.) In contrast to his relationship with his dead father, Alexander takes his greatest risks, even leaving himself open to being poisoned, to demonstrate his trust in and love for Darius's mother who becomes a surrogate for his own absent mother. Alexander's need, thwarted in childhood, to give and receive affection and approval, conditions all his adult relationships.

With success Alexander turns slowly into a despot and begins to adopt the finery and manners of a god. He has established his hold over the Persian Empire but continues to pursue conquest not for strategic advantage but for its own sake. Alexander's single-minded dedication to achieving his ambition of world conquest causes him to question his own sanity. Increasingly troubled by uprisings, he becomes steadily more ruthless, less tolerant of criticism and distrustful of his lieutenants and friends.

170

He justifies his own retention of power: 'Despot I am, because I must be.' He tells Hephaestion, his closest friend, that his ideal—'The world state ruled over by the man-god, whose word is law, and who has dedicated his whole life and being to the welfare of all his many million subjects. No more war ...'—justifies everything. These, of course, are the words and excuses of every despot. The obvious parallel is Napoleon; but Hitler, Mussolini and Stalin were more immediate parallels for Rattigan's intended audience. Also, though many of them would not have chosen to recognize it, they were the sentiments of those who were at that time opposing the dismemberment of the British Empire.

After the death of her son, Darius's mother vows never to speak to Alexander again, but at the end of the play she goes back on her word. Alexander calls their reconciliation his greatest victory. Yet he is driven by his devil to continue with conquest until the bitter end—bitter because as the Queen Mother warns him, his devil must therefore conquer him. Alexander asks whether it matters if he loses his soul, after conquering the world: 'I shall be remembered not for what I am but for what I do.'

Noble though Rattigan's intentions were in trying to grapple with great issues and to make understandable, and human, a legendary figure, and skilfully as he condensed his mass of material into a free-flowing narrative, *Adventure Story* was a failure, even on Rattigan's own terms. Towards the end of his life, in an interview with Holly Hill, Rattigan admitted that he had funked issues raised in the play. As we have seen, Alexander defended his actions in the play by the time-honoured formula of the end justifying the means, but the inherent evil of Alexander's vision is not spelled out in the play. Holly Hill asked whether Rattigan himself had recognized that evil:

'Of course, I didn't think it was a noble ideal,' Rattigan replied. 'But I think I was worried that it was very close to '45, wasn't it? It was '49 and with the memories of the Bunker in everybody's minds I didn't want to go on very much about it ... I was afraid of the obvious cliché, you know—all conquerors are necessarily dictators, which I don't think is necessarily true, but it seems to have proved true up to now, hasn't it? I suppose I was trying to say that it depends on who has the ideal. I think what I meant is that if Alexander failed, then everyone would. It would seem to me to make the most sense, because Alexander was a very special person. A world ruled by force of arms, and by one man—that is where the ideal must crash. Although he was taught by Aristotle and worshipped Athenian democracy, the fact remains that he still had to be the Persian tyrant, didn't he?'

So the play fails on this important philosophical level, but it fails also as a study of character. Alexander does not carry conviction. What we are shown is a charming, idealistic, adventurous young man with a single-minded and eventually soulless ambition, whose character changes for the worse. In trying to humanize a larger-than-life figure, Rattigan only succeeds in trivializing him. As Ivor Brown said in the *Observer*, he could not altogether believe in Rattigan's Alexander: 'shadowed o'er with the pale cast of Freud and always aching to lay his head on mother's knee'.

The play's major interest today is for what it tells us about Rattigan—a man who made no secret to his friends of his ambition to conquer his own chosen world, here writing about a legendary figure who succeeded in conquering his. In this play he put a mother-figure on the stage and showed his love of her; in his next, which he was already forming in his mind, he intended to put his father on the stage and to damn him.

On the day of the first read-through of *Adventure Story* early in December 1948, Rattigan had lunch with Harold Hobson. He told him: 'Hitherto I have written plays with six characters and one drawing-room set. I have never written anything with such satisfaction as the stage direction to the second scene, "The Hanging Gardens of Babylon", and left it to the scene designer to do the rest.' Rattigan had written most of *Adventure Story* at a pub in Binfield in Berkshire—The Stag and Hounds. This was a small unpretentious place with a green in front of it where the local hunt met. It was conveniently near his favourite golf club, Sunningdale, where he played to a handicap of fourteen. 'I read every book that is published on golf and study the game terribly seriously,' he said at this time, 'and the more I study the worse I play.' Mr and Mrs Newport, who ran the pub, kept a small upstairs room for him—this later became a small bedroom, a sitting room and a bathroom which he retained for a number of years for about five pounds a week. He later dedicated *The Deep Blue Sea* to Mr and Mrs Newport in 'affection and gratitude'. The gestation of that play, which did not finally appear until 1952, spanned most of the time that he made use of The Stag and Hounds.

By late 1948, Rattigan's relationship with the young actor Ken Morgan was in turmoil. Morgan, having allowed himself to be successfully wooed by Rattigan, was still unable to return his strength of feeling. By late 1948, Morgan was becoming restless; he was interested in things outside his exotic champagne life as satellite and lover of Rattigan. It cannot have been easy for a young man, a talented actor himself, to live in the shadow of Rattigan's popularity. Each night Rattigan, immaculately dressed for dinner, could be seen in the fashionable restaurants, moving from table to table, from friend to friend, basking, albeit modestly, in the easy social life of his own celebrity and the ready adulation that is part of theatrical success. At some time during the course of that year, Ken Morgan became seriously attracted to another man.

Adventure Story began its rehearsals and run up to its West End opening. As was to be expected with such an ambitious project, there were a number of complications which required a good deal of Rattigan's time. Binkie Beaumont, who had turned down *The Browning Version*, was putting on this new play. He had decided on an elaborate production, with set by Georges Wakhevitch and music specially composed by Benjamin Frankel. The production was to cost £8,000, three times the normal amount for a new straight play. It called for twenty-two actors and actresses. Peter Glenville, who had made such a success of *Playbill*, was to direct and the cast was headed by a twenty-six-year-old actor playing his first starring West End role, Paul Scofield. Gwen Ffrangcon-Davies was playing the Queen Mother and at least two stalwarts from Rattigan's youth had important parts—Robert Flemyng (Kit Neilan in the original production of *French Without Tears*) as Philotas and William Devlin (who had been in the OUDS *Romeo and Juliet*) as Bessus. Listed among the Greek soldiers was a young actor called Stanley Baker. The try-out tour was to open in Brighton and then move fairly swiftly to the Lyric Theatre, Hammersmith. But the plan went wrong.

173

The tour turned out to be longer than usual and the play did not reach London until mid-March 1949.

On the tour, tragedy struck Rattigan. Ken Morgan left him and moved out to live in a flat in Camden Town. Rattigan was shattered but told himself that Morgan's new liaison would not last as he would miss the glamour and luxury of his life with him. He decided to play it cool.

Chips Channon drove down with the Duchess of Westminster and his son Paul for the first night of the tour of *Adventure Story* in Brighton. Before the show he met Rattigan in his room at the Grand Hotel. Channon recorded that he found Rattigan 'half-dressed, rather tight and maudlin, but lovable, as he always is before a First Night. I gave him, for luck, a coin minted in the reign of Alexander.'[2] The Brighton opening was attended by a galaxy of celebrities. Everyone wanted to see the show ahead of its London production because of the intense anticipation aroused by rumours of a completely new departure by the country's most successful playwright. That night Channon recorded in his diary his own impression of the first performance: 'The play is an ambitious drama, or rather a series of episodes strung together on the theme of the general decay of Alexander's character. Though it is magnificently produced, Paul Scofield as Alexander did not particularly impress any of us. As the rich drama unfolded there were some of the usual mishaps which can occur in the provinces. The Brighton audience was puzzled by the play ... We refused Terry's invitation to supper, and drove back to London.'

The final week of the tour was in Liverpool, starting on 28 February. Rattigan was by now visibly edgy. Ken Morgan had still not returned; he had not so much as been in touch with Rattigan since his departure. Peter Glenville, the director of the play, knew of Rattigan's anxiety. One afternoon the two men were sitting in Rattigan's hotel suite in Liverpool drinking tea and discussing the play when a porter appeared and delivered Rattigan a note. Rattigan read it, obviously very shaken. Then he handed it to Glenville, telling him to burn it when he had read it before the police arrived. The note told Rattigan that Ken Morgan had committed suicide. It appeared that Morgan had been increasingly left on his own by the man he had gone to live with. He had also discovered that the man was bisexual. Overwhelmed, he swallowed a large quantity of sleeping tablets, and when this did not have the desired effect he gassed himself in his room. Rattigan was broken-hearted. He felt that in some way he was personally responsible for the tragedy. Its effects lasted for the rest of his life, influencing all his subsequent relationships.

Later that evening, as Peter Glenville and he went down together in the hotel lift, Rattigan seemed to have regained his composure. Apparently lost in thought, Rattigan suddenly said to Glenville, 'The play will open with the body discovered dead in front of the gas fire.' Glenville is convinced that the seed that was eventually to grow into *The Deep Blue Sea* had already been planted. Later still, at Morgan's funeral, Morgan's mother asked Rattigan what he was engaged in writing at that moment. Again Rattigan started to outline the plot of a play that bore a distinct resemblance to the play that became *The Deep Blue Sea*. However, realizing who he was talking to, Rattigan quickly checked himself and did not go on. Rattigan's emotional fulfilment had always been dependent on the theatre and his success in it. With the death of Ken Morgan, that dependence became, if possible, yet more absolute.

In the two weeks that remained before the London opening of *Adventure Story* there was no opportunity for grief. Rattigan threw himself into the task of promoting the play, granting even more personal interviews to journalists than usual; giving his views about the theatre, allowing them to photograph him in his Albany chambers; answering the inevitable questions about his bachelor status and his ideas about an eventual marriage. He told one reporter that, like Arnold Bennett, he would have time enough to consider marriage when he was forty. 'I have three years to go,' he said, touching a gold signet ring on his little finger. 'I wouldn't say I'm a confirmed bachelor, but I will say that I don't think writers make the best husbands.'

The London opening of *Adventure Story* was on 17 March. Rattigan went through his usual first-night routine. During the day, a Thursday, he had a haircut in the morning and a champagne dinner with his mother and father before the show. Chips Channon accompanied Rattigan's parents to the theatre and sat with them in a box. The theatre was packed with celebrities: Sir Alexander Korda was prominent in the front row of the stalls; near by were Lord Kinross, Cecil Beaton and Lady Juliet Duff. Everybody seemed to think that this evening would mark either the acceptance of Rattigan as a playwright of real stature or his final relegation to the ranks of the nearly great. Rattigan hovered nervously at the back of the Dress Circle. The tension in the theatre was unusual even for a first night. It lasted for the whole performance.

When the final curtain fell, the stalls celebrities started a chorus of cries for the author, while the circle cheered for Scofield. The curtain calls were still continuing—there were eight in all—as Rattigan slipped unobtrusively from the theatre. In the small hours of the morning he read the reviews in the early editions of the papers. As he feared, he had not quite made it. Most of the critics commended him for his bravery in attempting a play about Alexander—a subject avoided by both Shakespeare and Shaw—but felt that Rattigan had over-reached himself. 'A gallant failure worth a dozen so-called successes' (Ted Willis in the *Daily Worker*) was a fair summing-up of the views of critics of all political complexions that morning. The evening papers were less kind: 'The Rattigan Tragedy' was the *Evening News* banner heading to a review which began: 'Whenever a man finds he can do something supremely well, he itches to do something else that he can do only moderately well.' Beverly Baxter went on: however much he might wish to salute Rattigan's courage 'the stern fact remains that Shakespeare did this sort of thing much better'. The Sunday papers seemed to feel much the same. Harold Hobson in the *Sunday Times* opened by pointing out that Rattigan's play never answered Alexander's opening question—'Where did it all go wrong?' In the first act Rattigan presented Alexander the open young prince, and in the second Alexander the crafty, lecherous tyrant—but the gap between the two was never bridged. It was simply marked by the interval. Hobson did say, however, that the play was the most adult political comment in the modern theatre, which breathed a message as poetically beautiful as it was politically sad—that the ideal of peace cannot be maintained except through power and that such corrupt means distort their noble ends. But this was a minority view. The *Sunday Express* asked: 'Why does the author of plays noted for sharp observation, dexterity and wit want to plod through thirteen years in the life of Alexander the Great? To show that power corrupts? It is not new, profound or dramatic.' In the *Observer*, Ivor Brown found Rattigan's Freudian interpretation of Alexander's character disappointing. Rattigan had failed in his attempt to measure up to the great dramatists.

Some of Rattigan's friends have suggested to us that the critical reception for *Adventure Story* hurt him so much that he was prevented from ever attempting to write the great play of which he was capable. This seems to us to deny the measure of Rattigan's real achievements. His own comment was that it taught him to know his limitations. Yet to the end of his life Rattigan recalled *Adventure Story* with sorrow. It remained his favourite play: 'no doubt for no more reason than that, like all parents, I nurture a special fondness for the child that dies in infancy'.[3]

Notes

1   *Radio Times*, 29 April 1949.
2   *Chips—The Diaries of Sir Henry Channon*, edited by Robert Rhodes James, Weidenfeld and Nicolson, London, 1967.
3   Preface to *Collected Plays*, Volume II.

10

The Play of Ideas Debate

As soon as he could get away from London and his involvement with launching *Adventure Story*, Rattigan returned to the privacy of The Stag and Hounds at Binfield. Despite the lukewarm critical reception, it still looked as if *Adventure Story* might run. So great had been the enthusiasm and the interest generated on the first night that, next morning, the management had clinched a record ticket-agency deal. Rattigan meanwhile seemed intent on overcoming his grief at the death of Ken Morgan and his disappointment over the critical reception of *Adventure Story* by throwing himself into his work.

He concentrated on a play he had already been working on about his father, his affaires and his treatment of Rattigan's mother. He intended it to be a serious comedy. 'I knew I was going to touch on some very sore places,' he said later. But the play refused to take shape. In his present mood it looked as if it might well turn into a full-blown tragedy. He was unable to concentrate. Normally it took him two months to complete the draft of a play, but after only three weeks he was back in London. He threw himself into a defence of *Adventure Story*, which was already showing signs of failing at the box office. In a series of articles and interviews he defended the play and his writing method by saying that 'Plays should be about people rather than ideas'; the theatre was escapism from the difficult, austere times

178

through which people were living—'I have always believed that most people go there for amusement and relaxation, which, of course, includes mental stimulus, but always in terms of characters.'[1] It was a theme he was to nag at repeatedly over the ensuing months.

As the summer progressed, he accepted a commission from the BBC to write a television play for the Festival of Britain, and he toyed with at least two abortive film scripts, including an adaptation of *Love in Idleness*. At the same time, he commented on how much he hated adapting his own work for the cinema: 'I detest writing film scripts, the material is dead to me as soon as I have written it up for the stage, but neither will I let anyone else do it, as then the whole spirit of the play is lost.' The general disenchantment of these months bore fruit in a witty contribution to an anthology compiled by John Sutro called *Diversion*.[2] His essay, entitled 'A Magnificent Pity for Camels', has perhaps even more relevance today than it had then. Rattigan guyed the exaggerated credit accorded to film directors as the only creative begetters of films. Encapsulating a bitterness for the way writers were treated by the cinema which went right back to his experiences as a screenwriter at Teddington, Rattigan said: 'I believe the camera to be the enemy of the screenwriter's art ... drama is inference and inference is drama.' He pointed out that that nonentity, the writer, provided not only the words for the actors and actresses to speak, but often the story around which the director chose his fancy camera angles as well. He ended his light-hearted essay with this exhortation: 'So let the screenwriter throw off the shackles of the director (and the camera) and remember that the screenplay is the child not only of its mother, the silent film, but also of its father, the Drama; that it has affinities not only with Griffith, De Mille and Ingram, but also with Sophocles, Shakespeare and Ibsen.'

'The Babylon of Alexander has fallen; but here again is the babel of Maingot's', began the *Daily Sketch*'s Theatre Notes on 6 July 1949. *Adventure Story* had closed after only 107 performances and a new production of *French Without Tears* was being mounted. Robert Flemyng from the cast of *Adventure Story*, and a survivor from the original production of *French Without Tears*, was to star as Alan and direct.

Rattigan continued to be restless. At the beginning of August he set out in his new Rolls-Royce accompanied by his chauffeur and his secretary, to drive to Copenhagen. He passed through war-shattered Germany, where he felt the people were hostile to him because they recognized from his Rolls-Royce that he was an Englishman. But he was overjoyed by the warmth of his reception in Denmark. Everywhere he went he was treated with the deference accorded to a great writer. He put up in Copenhagen's grandest hotel, the Angleterre, and luxuriated in comparing this visit with his first impecunious visit to the city in 1935. Then, he had sat in cheap bars eking out his pilsner and struggling with his doomed play *Black Forest*. Now, he was conducted round the plushiest tourist spots by eager hosts; had some leisurely discussions with the Danish theatre company which was shortly to present *The Browning Version*, and held court, sitting up in bed in a silk dressing-gown, to journalists who queued to see him while he ate his way through substantial English breakfasts.

A few days later, he made his leisurely way back to England. But again he did not settle to a prolonged spell of writing. By September, he was preparing to leave again—this time for New York and the Broadway production of *The Browning Version* and *Harlequinade*. He was away six weeks, but the New York production was another disappointment and the plays were not well received. While there he wrote more articles defending his dramatic methods. When he returned home in November, the subject of his ideals as a writer was still very much on his mind, and he started to collect his thoughts for a major statement of his theatrical credo. He intended to challenge what he saw as the dominating dramatic doctrine of the day—a doctrine by which he felt he had been unfairly judged and found wanting. In the statement, he brought together thoughts that had nagged him during the months since the critical rejection of *Adventure Story* and the hostile reception of *The Browning Version* on Broadway; they were ideas that had gathered throughout his struggle to get himself taken seriously, and went back to the reception of the original production of *French Without Tears* and his resentment at being tagged too popular to be really good.

In submitting his finished article—'Concerning the Play of Ideas'[3]—to the left-wing *New Statesman and Nation*, he was deliberately taking the battle to the enemy. He fully realized that he could expect a hostile reaction. His article opened: 'I believe that the best plays are about people and not about things.' He amplified this by saying that he believed that the intellectual avant-garde of the British and American theatre 'are, in their insistence on the superiority of the play of ideas over the play of character and situation, not only misguided but old fashioned.' He blamed Bernard Shaw for driving the theatre off course by his campaign, begun in the 1890s, in support of Ibsenite theatre—the theatre which Shaw described as 'theatre as a factory of thought, a prompter of conscience, and an elucidator of social conduct'. He argued that after fifty years of domination by Shavian ideas the time had come for a change of critical values:

> ... the history of artistic endeavour is surely the history of change, and our painters are not still urged to paint like Burne-Jones, nor our poets to compose like Swinburne. Why then should our dramatists still be encouraged to write like late Ibsen or early Shaw?

So complete had been the Shavian-Ibsenite victory, he claimed,

> that in 1950 any defence of the theatre they defeated is considered to be no more than a naughty heretical joke. Daily, we playwrights are exhorted to adopt themes of urgent topicality, and not a voice is raised in our defence if we refuse. That refusal is universally and blandly taken to indicate that our minds are empty of ideas, and being so, are despicable ... Where are we then, those of us who hold, as I do, that the whole cult of the play of ideas is itself a heresy and is founded on a misconception and a misreading? In the intellectual and critical soup, without a doubt, so shunned and scorned and abhorred that no one is ever likely to take us seriously enough even to enquire what we mean.

He went on to explain that the misconception that the play of ideas was founded on was that

> ideology equals intellect. It doesn't. The misreading is of Ibsen, who was considerably less interested in his own ideas than were his followers, and considerably more interested in his own characters than were his critics.

Rattigan concluded with a defence of his own theatre:

From Aeschylus to Tennessee Williams the only theatre that has ever mattered is the theatre of character and narrative ... I don't think that ideas, *per se*, social, political or moral, have a very important place in the theatre. They definitely take third place to character and narrative anyway. You see, if the ideas are of contemporary significance they tend to divide the audience, and if they are not they tend to confuse it ... The trouble with the theatre today is not that so few writers refuse to look the facts of the present world in the face but that so many refuse to look at anything else.

When the article appeared, the editor announced that James Bridie would contribute an article the following week taking up the challenge Rattigan had thrown down, and invited others to join in. No one expected the storm of controversy that broke out. The argument raged for the next two months and spread beyond the *New Statesman* to the columns of the national press. It was reported around the world. Bridie argued that Rattigan had completely misunderstood Shaw: 'It is difficult to believe that he has ever read or seen a play by Shaw. Dear Terence, *are* these plays sociological tracts? *Are* their characters emotionally sterile gramophone records, or have you only been told that they are? Do tracts make us laugh? Do automata make us weep?' Bridie then turned to Rattigan's own plays, asking 'is there no sociological content in *Adventure Story*? Is *The Browning Version* barren of ideas?' Other correspondents rapidly supplied an answer. They implied that the reason Rattigan attacked the play of ideas was that when he tackled such big themes his ideas, his intellect and his means of expressing them were all found to be deficient. Even Peter Ustinov, who on the whole sided with Rattigan, pointed out that the thoughts of a creative artist about his medium are usually a blend of pride and prejudice and therefore suspect. A number of correspondents pointed out that vital and living drama was dependent on blending both people and ideas and that the two could not be separated—a fact so obvious, Rattigan said in his reply to the correspondence, that he had not seen fit to make it. Christopher Fry said that all this labelling was dangerous; a point which Sean O'Casey took much further by saying that 'we'd have to get ideas out of life before we could remove them from drama.' He went on to point out that Ibsen and Shaw, far from killing drama, had brought a dead drama back to a serious and singing life. He reminded Rattigan that throughout history writers, poets and dramatists had commented on, and often condemned, the activities and manners of their time. It was part of their glory: 'The thinker, the playwright and poet have shared in the struggle for the rights of man—and, if they didn't wield a sword, at least they carried a banner. They have helped to immortalize man's fight against intolerance, cod custom, ignorance and fear.'

Finally, Shaw himself joined the debate, pointing out that Rattigan was vulnerable as a reasoner, 'but he is not a reasoner, nor does he profess to be one ... Mr Rattigan does not like my plays because they are not exactly like his own, and no doubt bore him; so he instantly declares that plays that have any ideas in them are bad plays, and indeed not plays at all ...' (Rattigan was later to admit that his antipathy to Shaw's views stemmed in part from the fact that he had never found himself moved by any of his plays.)

Rattigan replied to the debate by characterizing himself as a fourth-former who had been caned by the senior boys for his cheek; nevertheless he was flattered to have been found worthy of the honour of a birching from the head boy himself. But, he said, he was unrepentant. He suspected that what he had said must have made some, perhaps dangerous, sense to have aroused such thunderous indignation. He clarified what he had said in the original article; he had not meant that no good plays contained ideas, nor that all plays of character were necessarily good plays. All he meant was that 'the successful creation of living characters upon the stage ... has always been, is now and will remain a higher achievement for the dramatist than the successful assertion of an idea, or series of ideas ...' Unrepentant though he claimed he was, this was a considerably less dogmatic statement than the one he had opened with.

Rattigan's articles gave ammunition to those who suspected that he was only really interested in commercial success. Looked at from the vantage point of today, it seems a truly amazing piece of over-emphasis to claim that the trouble with the theatre of 1950 was 'not that so few writers refuse to look the facts of the present world in the face but that so many refuse to look at anything else'. In 1950 there was no English Stage Company, no network of subsidized theatres; Kenneth Tynan was still an undergraduate, and John Osborne a struggling actor. In a country still in the grip of rationing, with the centres of its cities still scarred with bomb damage, living under the threat of atomic weapons and struggling towards national recovery after being bankrupted by the war, the theatre seemed enslaved not so much by ideas as by wilful empty-headedness. True, the critics may have been guilty of overpraising the few half-good new plays that came their way, but for five years Rattigan had presided over the London theatre as its leading practising playwright. Even his detractors readily admitted that any new play by him was a major event.

Rattigan's creation of the Play of Ideas controversy was to have a profoundly damaging effect on his reputation and career. By his article he placed himself, in the minds of a new though as yet uninfluential set of young writers and critics, irretrievably among the ranks of the reactionary theatrical establishment. The shape of things to come was discernible among the responses to Rattigan's original article. Ted Willis, who a year previously had devoted an article to a discussion of the conscience or lack of it in Rattigan's work, weighed in with a piece in which he looked forward to the day when the British theatre would find a new generation of dramatists uninhibited by present standards or examples, who would give the theatre the shot in the arm it so badly needed; it would only climb out of its soggy inertia if dramatists started dealing in 'ideas instead of trivialities'.[4] Most significant of all perhaps was an article by a young writer, Robert Muller, in *Theatre News Letter* on 25 March 1950. Muller said only haste could excuse, or persecution mania justify, Rattigan's article; what Rattigan had written was violently political: 'It makes a nonsense of the old adage that plays like *While the Sun Shines* and *French Without Tears* are non-political. The article proves them to be otherwise.' Muller, who knew that the article was no whim and had been a long time in preparation, went on to ask:

Who are these Playwrights of Ideas that make Mr Rattigan foam at the mouth, these spoilers of the drama who splutter ideas only because they cannot create character? Mr R. mentions Shaw and Ibsen in his lines, and between them we read the names of every other writer for the theatre who possessed that dangerous thing—a social conscience. It is all very transparent. Mr Rattigan condemns the writer of ideas whose ideas are not identical to his own. He does not condemn Mr Noël Coward's adventure into ideas, *This Happy Breed*, because it drew no bothersome conclusions. Only the Shavian penslavers who dare to plumb the lower depths and come up with an idea are the ones that rouse his fury and get his goat ... Equate character with Right thinking and Idea with Subversive thinking, and you begin to appreciate what Mr Rattigan is trying to say.

In hitting out at Rattigan, Muller and Willis were hitting out at the theatrical establishment. In the West End of London by 1950 this meant H. M. Tennent and the companies controlled by Hugh 'Binkie' Beaumont (John Perry, Rattigan's friend since Oxford, was one of Beaumont's advisers and a co-director). Beaumont, a brilliant entrepreneur, established such a strong personal influence over the London theatre that people were frightened to oppose him. Matters reached such a point that early in 1954 a Private Member's Bill—The Theatrical Monopolies Bill—was laid before parliament, partly intended to put a curb on Beaumont's power. The objection to Beaumont was that, although he staged many brilliant productions, the domination of his taste to the growing exclusion of all others was unhealthy. In the parliamentary debate Woodrow Wyatt, the sponsor of the Bill, talked about Hugh Beaumont's monopolistic power and of actors and actresses who offended him being told they would never get a West End part again. It was explained that other managements and agents were afraid of employing anyone condemned by Beaumont because his interests were so extensive that he could squeeze out of business those who challenged his authority. Beaumont was suave, homosexual and charming; the smile was said never to leave his face, even at his most ruthless. Tyrone Guthrie, one of the few people with both the reputation and the courage to risk offending him, talked openly about Beaumont's disproportionate accumulation of power. He confirmed that more than any other single individual Beaumont could make or break the career of anyone in the theatre, adding that 'the iron fist was wrapped in fifteen pastel-shaded velvet gloves, but no one who has known Binkie can for a moment fail to realize that there is an iron fist.'

It is hardly surprising that many of the young people entering the theatre at this time, increasingly from working-class back-grounds, found the Beaumont style objectionable. His taste extended beyond what was seen on the stage into the private lives of those who worked for him. His preference for working with fellow homosexuals became notorious, especially among those who were not homosexual and often felt they were excluded for this reason alone. These charges were doubtless exaggerated but they were not groundless, as one young actor in the production of a Rattigan play discovered when, in outraged innocence, he complained that the designer of the production was making particularly crude homosexual advances to him. The actor, who had been in successive productions of Rattigan plays, did not work for Beaumont again for a long while. It is worth pointing out that although the actor was a very attractive young man, who had been personally recommended for the productions by Rattigan himself, Rattigan respected his sexual preferences and never made a pass at him or expected any favours from him in return for doing a great deal to help him personally and promoting his career. The designer involved was also an intimate friend of Rattigan's and it was typical of the writer that he remained friends with both men.

Rattigan, of course, fitted naturally into the Beaumont stereotype—well-spoken, immaculately turned out and with a public school background. By 1950 he had enough of a reputation to stand on his own, as he had demonstrated by taking *The Browning Version* to Stephen Mitchell after Beaumont had turned it down. However, it would have been dangerous for even Rattigan to defy Beaumont. As it happened, he did not want to. It is, though, open to question whether Beaumont was really the best manager for Rattigan's long-term interests. He had poured cold water on Rattigan's finest work, *The Browning Version*, but had encouraged the overblown pretensions of *Adventure Story*. He was not the sound adviser Rattigan needed, and one of Rattigan's problems was that he was becoming increasingly cut off from sound advice. Since the war, and particularly the death of Anthony Goldschmidt, Rattigan had become detached from the intellectual stimulus of his Oxford friends. Although he still worked with many of the most talented people in the theatre and the cinema, in his private life Rattigan increasingly surrounded himself with people who were no match for him intellectually, often actors and designers who behaved in a subservient way to him. Although he was not yet plagued by the swarm of sycophants who would later have such a deleterious effect on him, his intimate friends, with the exception of Anthony Asquith, were not people who challenged him creatively or intellectually. Because of his very success, it was inevitable that Rattigan would be identified with Beaumont and the theatrical establishment, but with the Play of Ideas controversy he had branded himself as their leading apologist. He never lived it down.

Notes

1 *Daily Herald*, 29 April 1949. Rattigan had first defended his methods in broadly these terms as long ago as 1937, at the time of the New York production of *French Without Tears*. It seems to have been a defensive posture he took up whenever he felt threatened by critical attacks on him for failing to be sufficiently serious.

2 Max Parrish, London, 1950.

3 *New Statesman and Nation*, 14 March 1950.

4 *New Statesman and Nation*, 15 April 1950.

11
Plays for Father

'To my father, with love, with gratitude and in apology.' Thus
ran the dedication to the published version of *Who Is Sylvia?* This
was the play Rattigan had had trouble getting down to in the
spring and summer of 1949. 'It was, if you like, the play that led
me to break with my previous dramatic writing. For it is based on
the lives of two real people. A married couple ...', Rattigan told a
Danish journalist before the Copenhagen production of the play
in 1959.[1] Rattigan explained that the couple had stayed together
through thick and thin, in spite of the fact that the man had
chased a succession of almost identical-looking young women. The
couple, he said, were now both dead, but they had been 'very good
friends of mine'. They had indeed—they were his own parents.
Rattigan made no secret of the true identity of the protagonists to
his closest friends. Nor did he disguise his intentions. He blamed
his homosexuality, which he still found a source of shame and
regret, on his father, on the pain Frank Rattigan had inflicted on
his mother with his cohort of mistresses and the rows Rattigan
had witnessed between them as a child. If *Adventure Story* was to
some extent an attempt to place on record his love for his mother,
Who Is Sylvia? was intended to express his very different feelings
for his father.

In addition to the turmoil of his own feelings after the death of
Ken Morgan and the failure of *Adventure Story*, the problem

Rattigan had faced when he first sat down to write *Who Is Sylvia?* in the summer of 1949 was that although it was a subject of such intense seriousness to him, he realized that he would have to keep it light. Worse than the danger of self-indulgence was the fact that he did not really want to hurt his parents' feelings. In 1950 Frank Rattigan was seventy and was, at last, becoming infirm. How could Rattigan hold him up to public obloquy or even ridicule? If he did, his mother, who had stuck to him in spite of everything, would be almost as hurt as Frank himself. From these conflicting intentions, the essential weaknesses of *Who Is Sylvia?* grew. When it was completed Rattigan, as he proudly told journalists, was able to read it to 'the elderly couple' on whom it was based: 'They laughed until the tears ran down their faces and they gave me their blessing to use the material in this way.'

Rattigan had continued in the habit, begun during the two-year trial period when he lived at home on an allowance, of reading each new play to his parents. Although his father was no longer able to keep up his pretence of interest and often nodded off during the reading, Vera Rattigan still listened intently to every word and was forthright in her opinions. Rattigan still valued her reactions and often made changes as a result of them. Had *Who Is Sylvia?* remained 'the serious comedy' he had intended, ending with the character identified with his father being made to look both cruel and ridiculous, the customary domestic reading would have been a very painful occasion. In the event, both parents were able to laugh uproariously at *Who Is Sylvia?* as a gentle comedy on human folly—close enough to themselves for them to enjoy some sharpness in the humour, but not so close as to really hurt them.

The play opens in 1917 and covers three decades in the life of a philanderer. At the outset, Mark is thirty-two and a rising diplomat. Embarking upon his career as an amorist, which he takes pains to keep secret from his wife, he is at first dependent on the help and advice of his best friend, Oscar, an army officer.

Mark has pursued an unattainable ideal of womanhood ever since he was seventeen and met a girl called Sylvia at a garden party. He kissed her only once, after playing tennis with her; then she returned to South Africa and married someone else. As the play progresses and he becomes older, his amorous encounters are all with girls physically identical to Sylvia (they are all played by the same actress). Oscar, who knows of Mark's obsession with Sylvia, accuses him of being 'an emotional Peter Pan', to which Mark replies that he prefers to keep his emotions adolescent —'they're far more enjoyable that way'. Although this exchange looks remarkably like a piece of self-projection on Rattigan's part, those who knew enough of the Rattigan family background to recognize biographical elements in the plot clearly identified Mark with Frank Rattigan. By likening him to Peter Pan and making him essentially an innocent, even a romantic idealist, Rattigan took the curse off Frank's real-life philandering, seeming to say it had done no real harm. Further evidence for identifying Mark with Frank Rattigan is provided by the fact that he has a son, Denis, who is sent to a crammer in France but flies home at a moment's notice because he has fallen in love with an actress and intends, against his father's wishes, to go into the theatre. But Rattigan turns the actual relationship between himself and his father gloriously on its head when he has Denis discover his father's intention to leave the Diplomatic Service for one of his girl friends. Denis says to Mark reproachfully: 'Oh, Father! You're not giving up the Diplomatic, are you? ... I know exactly how you feel and I do sympathize with you—really I do. But you've had such a brilliant career up to now, haven't you? I do think it would be an awful waste to throw it all away now.' Advice which Mark accepts.

The play ends in 1950 with Oscar, now a general, and Mark, Ambassador in Paris, both elderly gentlemen. The amorousness now goes no further than a polite pretence—Mark is past it. His wife appears and reveals that she has known all along about her husband's 'Sylvias'. The only person who has been deceived is Mark himself. She explains that as she wanted to remain his wife more than anything else in the world she had to accept that, if there were things he needed which she couldn't give him, she would just have to accept his going elsewhere for them.

For most of its length *Who Is Sylvia?* is a pleasant enough little romantic fantasy. However, there is an unevenness of tone and a lurking sense of something darker buried beneath the surface. Although the audience's attention is skilfully drawn towards Mark as the principal character, a more careful look at the drawing of Oscar reveals Rattigan's originally harsher intentions for the play. Rattigan had hoped that Rex Harrison would play Mark, but Harrison spotted that although he had been offered the lead, Oscar was a much better-written part than Mark. Although Oscar has none of the external trappings of Rattigan's father, except significantly the *nom de guerre* ('The Major') by which he likes to be known during his own amorous adventures, he comes much closer to being a portrait of Rattigan's father than Mark. More callous and calculating, in the last act Oscar is shown up as the ridiculous figure he has been all along. Fat, breathless and loveless, in old age he clings to the idea of himself as a gay dog, oblivious of the fact that in doing so he only succeeds in making a fool of himself.

When *Who Is Sylvia?* opened at the Criterion on 24 October 1950, everyone was very much aware that it was at this theatre fourteen years before that Rattigan had first shot to success with *French Without Tears*. Although Rex Harrison had turned down the part of Mark, two other members of the original cast of the earlier success starred together as Mark and Oscar—Robert Flemyng and Roland Culver. Rattigan had written the play intending that Glynis Johns should play the succession of 'Sylvias', but owing to film commitments she was unable to appear and Diane Hart had been engaged. Rattigan made little secret of his disappointment; in fact, he was angry about the whole production. Robert Flemyng generously put down its failure to his own playing, believing that perhaps he should have gone more for the farcical elements of the play, and resisted bringing out the sympathetic elements in Mark's character. But the press found little to fault in the playing and were almost unanimous in detecting a more serious play lurking underneath. They regretted that Rattigan had not chosen to write it and blamed him for wasting an interesting idea on a frivolity. The general feeling was summed up by the thundering headline to Beverly Baxter's review in the *Evening Standard*: 'This Will Not Do, Mr Rattigan.'

Just as *Who Is Sylvia?* was going into rehearsal, Frank Rattigan went into hospital. Even if *Who Is Sylvia?* gave him offence, Rattigan already had another play on the stocks that would more than make up for it. This was the commission he had received from the BBC in the summer of 1949 to write a television play for the Festival of Britain in 1951. Its production was planned as a major television event (although Rattigan's fee was only £300!)—the first television play by Britain's most successful playwright. He was guaranteed the widest possible audience for what he intended, in part, as a public eulogy to his ailing father. Rattigan had never written for television before, and had only a hazy idea of television technique. But he had become a keen, though sometimes critical, viewer; and he decided that something other than either a watered-down film script or a rather more mobile stage play was needed. He saw the potential strengths of television drama as its flexibility, its immediacy and its intimacy. The medium was best at bringing events into the home as they happened. Early on Rattigan decided he would build his play around one 'topical feature'.

For a long time he could not decide what this 'topical feature' should be, but eventually he opted for a Test Match between England and Australia. Cricket was still Rattigan's favourite sport; although he no longer played very often, he still spent hours watching it. He confessed to a secret Walter Mitty dream in which he was a professional cricketer, dropped from the England team. After a disastrous second Test in Australia, a cable arrives imploring him to fly out at once. He dashes for a plane and arrives just in time to help England win by the narrowest of margins. In 1950, cricket was a sport which television brought most effectively into the home, not only allowing many more people to see important matches, but allowing them to see what was happening much more clearly than they could by going to the ground.

Rattigan determined to mix drama and reality in a novel way. His story would concern Sam Palmer, a much-loved England batsman playing in his last Test, and the clash between his values and those of his son, an aspiring poet. The Test Match shown would be a real one; Sam Palmer, his son Reggie and the other principal characters would be played by actors, but members of the England team would appear as themselves. It was a challenging idea. The action cut between the Palmers' house, the home of a successful poet, a pub near the ground, and the Oval—showing scenes from the match itself, the pavilion, the dressing-rooms and the players' balcony.

The son, although expected to be a good cricketer because of his father, is not really interested in the game. Reggie struggles to complete a poem rather than go to watch his father play in his last

Test Match. On the day of his father's last innings for England, Reggie arranges to go and see a famous verse playwright who has shown an interest in his work. Sam, deeply hurt by this, nevertheless tries to show an interest in Reggie's work, though he doesn't understand it, and even gives him the money for his fare to visit the poet. Sam prepares to bat, with the match in a critical position, and an added weight of personal disappointment heavy on his shoulders.

When Reggie meets the playwright, he finds he is a cricket enthusiast and cannot understand why Reggie is not at the match. Together, they race by car to the Oval. But on the third ball Sam is out for a duck. Nevertheless, the crowd rises to him as he returns to the pavilion, cheering and clapping in appreciation of a great career. The play ends with the playwright having dinner at the Palmers' house, both men comically in awe of each other, and Rattigan is able to work in some sincerely meant statements on the fallacy of the creative artist's work being superior to that of the performer or the sportsman.

The play is of course replete with autobiographical detail, personally significant nuances and private jokes. It is, however, patchy. The disappointment is the sharper because its central idea reveals that Rattigan had thought about the new medium and came up with a form that suited its special character at a time when most writers and producers still thought of television only as a medium for relaying stage plays.

Note

1   *Politiken*, Copenhagen, 20 December 1959.

12
The Deep Blue Sea

One of the probable reasons that *The Final Test* did not have the energy expended on it which it needed was that at the time of its composition Rattigan was deeply involved in writing the major play which had been forming in his mind almost from the moment that he heard of Ken Morgan's suicide. It had proved immensely difficult to write but at last, in the summer of 1951, *The Deep Blue Sea* was finished. One of the first people to receive a copy was Margaret Sullavan, the American star who had not appeared on Broadway for seven years and was looking for a vehicle in which to make a comeback. Rattigan's agent tore the fly-sheet out before sending it to her so that she should not know who wrote it. She read it and wanted to do it, so Rattigan flew over to New York to discuss it with her. After the failure of so many of his plays in America, he was reluctant to have it done there before London. He decided to postpone the New York production until he saw what the prospects were in London. Much would depend on Binkie Beaumont's reaction.

At this moment Alexander Korda approached him to ask if he would write an original screenplay for a film David Lean wanted to make about the new generation of jet aircraft and the breaking of the sound barrier. Lean had been impressed by a visit to the Farnborough Air Display a year before. He had the idea that the testing of a new high-speed jet would make a better basis for a film than the science-fiction stories which were being made about the possibility of flying to the moon. He spent a year touring aircraft factories and talking to test pilots and designers; at the end of it he had a mass of background material, plenty of enthusiasm and the absolute conviction that he had a dramatic story to tell. He managed to enthuse Korda also, but he still had no actual plot. To Rattigan, it sounded dangerously like a film of ideas rather than character. He turned it down; he knew nothing about jets. But Korda and Lean were not to be put off so easily. A few days later, they approached Rattigan again; would he at least spend a day at Farnborough with them? Rattigan agreed. 'It was a wet day. One of these very fast aircraft—a Canberra, I think it was—flew in low.' His interest was aroused. 'Then, meeting the characters involved—test pilots, quiet young men absolutely unlike the types I had known during the war—suggested new writing possibilities.'[1] Before the end of the day he had agreed to do the script.

Out of this rather unpromising beginning was born one of Rattigan's most philosophical and wide-ranging pieces of writing. The central question posed, as relevant today as it was then, is about the justification for pressing on with experiments into the unknown, at great expense in money, skill and men's lives, for uncertain scientific and social results. Again Rattigan interpolated real people and real events into his fictional story. Thus John Cunningham was the pilot who gave the film's hero a lift during the De Havilland Comet's test flight programme, and the actual death of Geoffrey de Havilland when testing a prototype supersonic fighter becomes a turning point in the development of Rattigan's fictional story.

The plot of *The Sound Barrier* centres on Sir John Ridgefield, the self-made owner of an aircraft manufacturing company, and his determination to build an aircraft that will fly faster than sound. Ridgefield is a domineering father who is finally revealed as a man frightened of being alone, craving human love but unable to show his feelings. His son, determined to prove to his father that he doesn't lack guts, is killed undertaking his first solo flight when he has no real aptitude for flying. Ridgefield's daughter Susan blames her father for her brother's death, and fears that his determination to build a supersonic plane may also result in the death of her husband Tony, a wartime fighter pilot

195

and her father's chief test pilot. Susan questions the value of her father's vision of supersonic flight. 'There are evil visions as well as good ones, you know, father ... All this so that a few people who have the money can spend a weekend in New York.' Is breaking the sound barrier and entering what her father has called a 'new world with speeds up to 1,500 to 2,000 miles per hour' really going to be of benefit to the human race, she asks. 'That depends on the human race!' he replies. 'What purpose did Scott have in going to the South Pole?' Susan retorts, 'I wish I knew. I really wish I knew.' The male characters in the film attach shame to being weak or womanly, but it is the women who are more far-sighted and have a proper sense of proportion and real values. At the same time, the men are frightened of them: Tony, the fearless test pilot, has not the courage to ask Susan to marry him, and she has to propose for him.

At the end of the film, with the sound barrier successfully broken, but at the loss of Tony's life, Susan remarks that she sees the world as a pretty hostile place. Her father replies that we live in a hostile universe and that is why mankind has been given so many weapons with which to fight it: brains and imagination, which together equal vision. By allying courage to this vision, man can reach success. In this scene, Rattigan makes one of his clearest statements of his own humanist beliefs. *The Sound Barrier* was a prophetic film which raised issues of ecology, pollution and the debate we have seen over Concorde, long before its time. Rattigan was nominated for an Oscar for the screenplay.

By the time Rattigan had finished writing the screenplay of *The Sound Barrier*, Binkie Beaumont had agreed to put on *The Deep Blue Sea*. Rattigan admitted that it had been 'the hardest of my plays to write because of the emotional angle', although he was understandably unwilling at that time to go into any more detail. The play had occupied him on and off for over two years. In an early version, probably the first, written within a year of Ken Morgan's death, it had been the story of a disastrous homosexual love affair. By December 1950, a completely new version had been written which fairly closely resembled the story as it was put into production.[2] This was still not the final version, however, and further work was done during 1951 and continued during rehearsals.

Rattigan himself approached Peggy Ashcroft, whom he considered, with good reason, the finest actress working in the British theatre, to play the lead. Fortunately for Rattigan, perhaps, she had forgotten all about the previous time they had worked on a production together—in Gielgud's Oxford *Romeo and Juliet*. Rattigan invited her to lunch. She imagined he wanted her for a comedy and was rather pleased at the thought. Looking forward to hearing about a role that would contrast with the heavy parts she had been playing for so long in the West End, she dressed accordingly. Her heart sank when Rattigan explained that the play opened with the woman he wanted her to play, Hester Collyer, apparently dead in front of a gas fire after a suicide attempt. By the end of the lunch she was less than enthusiastic, but agreed to take the play home to read. Although she found the play absorbing, by the time she had finished reading it she was convinced she did not want to do it. She found the woman she was to play selfish and unsympathetic. If she didn't sympathize with Hester, neither would the audience, and the play would fail. She turned it down. But Binkie Beaumont would not take 'no' for an answer. He called her in for discussions and tried to persuade her that her judgement was wrong. After much heart-searching, she reluctantly agreed to take the part.

Frith Banbury was hired to direct and Roland Culver was engaged to play Hester's husband. The major casting problem now was to find a young actor to play Freddie Page, an ex-Battle-of-Britain pilot for whom Hester has left her husband. Frith Banbury favoured a tall, fair-haired ex-Commando called Jimmy Hanley. But playing golf one day with a rising, little-known actor called Kenneth More, Roland Culver suddenly had the idea that he might fit the bill. He suggested him to Rattigan, who remembered seeing him a year earlier giving a promising performance in a Lonsdale play, *The Way Things Go*, in Brighton. Rattigan suggested him to Binkie Beaumont, who in turn agreed to audition him. The audition was held at the Globe Theatre. The only people in the darkened auditorium were Beaumont, Peggy Ashcroft, Roland Culver and Rattigan. As Kenneth More walked on to the stage, Frith Banbury handed him a script and said, 'Here you are. You're Freddie Page. He's a sexy young man. This woman is mad about him, not because of his looks or his background, but because of his sex. Now go ahead: read.'[3]

More began at Freddie's first entrance, when he returns to the North London flat he is sharing with Hester after a golfing weekend at Sunningdale, cheerfully oblivious of the fact that he has forgotten Hester's birthday and thereby pushed her into attempted suicide. Nervous and in the dark about the plot, More's reading lacked the breezy self-confidence of the character. After a few lines Beaumont interrupted and called up to More, 'Can't you make it gayer?' Banbury also asked him to make it lighter. More's nerves were now thoroughly on edge, and he only succeeded in making his reading heavier. 'Thank you, Mr More. We'll write,' said Banbury. He was still convinced Jimmy Hanley was the actor for the part. However, Rattigan was now certain that, in spite of his clumsy reading, More had the right personality for the part. Beaumont was inclined to agree with him. A fortnight later, a second reading was held to decide the issue. It took place in the more relaxed surroundings of Rattigan's Albany chambers. Although More had now had a chance to read the script, Rattigan knew he would still be nervous, so when he arrived he took him on one side, asked him if he would like a drink, and poured him a stiff whisky. He watched him gulp it down, then said, 'And another?' More accepted with alacrity. This time, More read with much more confidence. At the end he turned to Rattigan with triumph written all over his face and asked: 'Howzat?' There was no need to reply; the part fitted him like a glove.

From the start rehearsals went well and Peggy Ashcroft recalls how surprised she was at Rattigan's relaxed attitude. He made it clear immediately that he did not regard the text as sacrosanct: if the cast wanted to change the odd word here or there he would not mind in the least. If they needed help he would be on hand when required. Apart from that, he said, he didn't think it was the author's place to interfere: 'Once I've made any corrections to the script that I think are right and are agreed on, I wash my hands of the play. It's in the hands of the director and the actors.' No one was entirely happy with the third act and he had to do quite a lot of rewriting. He calculated that by the time the play opened he had rewritten that act seven times since the first draft. Even after the play opened, Act Three remained a bone of contention.

The Deep Blue Sea had a brief pre-West End try-out at Brighton in February 1952, and opened in London at the Duchess

Theatre on Thursday 6 March. The audience in the small theatre were held in hushed silence from the beginning. From his own intense feelings over the tragedy of Ken Morgan, Rattigan had developed a play of extraordinary tension as well as of deep feeling. He had drawn material from other experiences. The characters of both Hester and Freddie owed things to people he had met playing golf at Sunningdale and acquaintances from his RAF days. Although the play had its roots in a homosexual relationship, Rattigan's long creative process of assimilation and distillation had recreated this emotional experience into a play with a life and characters of its own. Recently, a few people have suggested that in the character of Hester in particular the play betrays its homosexual origins.[4] This seems to us a case of hindsight. At the time of the play's first appearance none of the critics detected a homosexual connotation. Peggy Ashcroft never thought of Hester as anything other than a convincing woman. Her initial antipathy to Hester did not result from any doubt about the authenticity of the character but from a lack of sympathy for the attitudes of a woman who was all too recognizable. Once she had started working on the role, Dame Peggy's antipathy turned to strong sympathy and she defended Hester's actions fiercely against all who criticized her. Rather than looking for the homosexual residue in Rattigan's character-ization of Hester Collyer, it is surely more to the point to see in Rattigan's creation both a remarkable insight into women and an ability, rare among contemporary playwrights, to create credible female characters. Hester Collyer is that rarity in post-war drama—a cracking good female lead. In *The Deep Blue Sea*, and through the character of Hester Collyer, Rattigan can be seen, far ahead of his time, exploring the dilemmas of women who feel that they have lost or never found themselves as individuals because they have been conditioned to shape their whole lives through their menfolk, their marriages and their love affairs. Rattigan was in a sense echoing Ibsen in *The Doll's House*, whose heroine also discovered that she could not live through the men in her life. *The Deep Blue Sea* was culturally prophetic. It appeared more than a decade before the general awakening to the specific issues confronting women and the emergence of the Women's Liberation movement.[5]

The plot of *The Deep Blue Sea* is fairly simple. Its skill lies in the way in which tension is maintained, its value in the creation and exploration of the emotional relationships. The play is set in a dingy furnished flat in North-west London, where Hester has been living with Freddie Page for about a year since leaving her husband, Sir William Collyer, a judge. The action all takes place in one day, starting in the morning when Hester is discovered by other residents of the house in front of the gas fire after a suicide attempt (unsuccessful because not enough coins had been put in the gas meter), and ending late that evening when, now firmly separated from her lover, Hester again turns on the gas fire, but this time lights it, having apparently made up her mind to try to face the reality of life on her own. Rattigan called the play 'a study of obsession and of the shame that a sensitive, clear-minded and strong-willed woman must feel when she discovers she has inside her a compulsion that seems too strong for her to resist'.[6]

Slowly the reasons for Hester's attempted suicide, her feelings for Freddie and for her husband, are revealed. Questioned by the landlady about why she did such a wicked thing, she says only that she supposes it was the devil: 'When you're between any kind of devil and the deep blue sea, the deep blue sea sometimes looks very inviting.' Cross-examined by her husband, an amiable man who still loves her despite all that has happened, and wants her to come back to their comfortable life together, she explains further: 'Anger, hatred and shame, in about equal parts I think.' Anger at Freddie, hatred of herself and shame at being alive. Freddie still loves her as much as he did at the outset, she says, but his love compared to hers has always been zero. Nevertheless, he can still sometimes give her something that her husband cannot give her—himself.

Freddie, who has been unable to adjust to life since the war, complains about the unfairness of what Hester has done—if she had managed to kill herself it would be him who would have been blamed, first for breaking up a marriage and then for driving her to suicide. He complains that he is out of his depth. All his life he has tried to avoid getting tangled up in people's emotions, yet it always seems to be happening to him: 'Too many emotions. Far too ruddy many. I loath 'em ... She says I've got no feelings and perhaps she's right, but anyway I've got something inside that can get hurt—the way it's hurt now. I don't enjoy causing other people misery. I'm not a ruddy sadist. My sort never gets a hearing. We're called a lot of rude names, and nobody ever thinks we have a case ...' Later, Hester tries again to explain to her uncomprehending husband the quality of her feelings for Freddie: 'Neither you nor anyone else can explain what I feel for Freddie. It's all far too big and confusing to be tied up in such a neat little parcel and labelled lust. Lust isn't the whole of life—and Freddie is, you see, to me. The whole of life—and of death too, it seems ...' Freddie makes up his mind to leave Hester. He tells her it is the only chance for either of them. They are literally death to each other. He will stop drinking—something he only started in the search for oblivion since he met her—and try to make a come-back as a test pilot, although he knows that he is really too old. It is another lodger, Miller, a doctor who has been disqualified as a result of some mysterious public scandal, who finally gives her the courage to go on living. An outcast who has himself faced despair, he reminds her that most people manage to face life, and when she asks how anyone can face life without hope he replies that to face life without hope can mean to live without despair. To get beyond hope is her only chance: beyond hope lies life. 'Listen to me,' says Miller. 'To see yourself as the world sees you may be very brave, but it can also be very foolish. Why should you accept the world's view of you as a weak-willed neurotic—better dead than alive? What right have they to judge? To judge you they must have the capacity to feel as you feel. And who has? One in a thousand. You alone know how you have felt. And you alone know how unequal the battle has always been that your will has had to fight.'

The Deep Blue Sea is undoubtedly Rattigan's finest full-length serious play, an opinion the first-night audience showed that they shared by breaking into prolonged cheering after the final curtain. It turned Kenneth More into a star and re-established Rattigan as Britain's most important practising playwright. The reviews were virtually unanimous in their praise. The only serious matter of contention was the ending. A number of critics argued that Rattigan should have allowed Hester to kill herself. Kenneth Tynan, hailing the play as 'the most absorbing new English play for many seasons', recorded how he had gone out at the second interval exulting that 'I was seeing the most striking new play I could remember'. But, he continued: 'I shall never forgive Mr Rattigan for his last act. It is intolerable: his brilliance lays an ambush for itself, and walks straight into it. If his heroine kills herself, he will merely be repeating the pattern, so he decides to let her live. But he has stated the case for her death so pungently that he cannot argue her out of the impasse without forfeiting our respect ... Dishonestly, he makes her insist that she does not *deserve* to live, thus hauling in all kinds of moral implications which are totally irrelevant, since her point was purely that she could not *bear* to live. When, finally, she chooses survival, it is for all the wrong reasons.'[7] Rattigan argued strenuously for the rest of his life against Tynan and all those who agreed with him over the ending: a suicide would have been too pat; it would have been the sentimental ending, the one the audience wanted, the one he would have been unable to resist as a schoolboy dramatist when his heroines still 'measured their lengths' at suitably dramatic moments. However, the whole conscious intent of his adult writing had been to show the necessity, difficulty and courage of facing oneself and one's life as it really is. Hester had to live, but to live in the knowledge that she was living for nothing.

The problem here is that Rattigan's conscious purpose, his philosophical intention, is in conflict with the emotional direction in which his characters have instinctively taken him. Rattigan's play of ideas lets down his play of character. However morally right his ending may be, it fails to carry conviction because it feels contrived. Similarly, most of the subsidiary characters are unconvincing because they have to fulfil representative functions in Rattigan's conscious design. Least convincing of all is Miller, the outcast who argues Hester out of her death. In early drafts of the play Miller's offence, the reason for his being struck off the medical register, was that he was a homosexual. (An early draft had Miller saying: 'Some people are born different to others and it's no good pretending that that makes them wicked and striking them off registers just because of it.') By the third draft, his offence had become unclear, to meet possible objections by the Lord Chamberlain, and to make him a more universal figure. A potentially interesting character, he became a device.

Some reactions to the play underlined the need for the plea for tolerance that Rattigan had embodied in it. Ivor Brown, in the *Observer*, suggested that all Hester needed was a good slap and a chat to a marriage guidance counsellor. When the play was shown on television, journalists wondered whether it was suitable for family entertainment, fearing that the public were bound to find such 'worthless characters' and such honest emotion distasteful.

The play struck a deep chord with British audiences. Once again Rattigan had demonstrated his uncanny knack for being in touch with the feelings of his contemporaries. In Freddie Page, people found more than an understanding portrait of a familiar type of Englishman. He was also something of an allegorical figure for the time—a war hero, living in the past and unable to come to terms with the present; beginning to age, his talents no longer in demand, he finds it difficult to make a satisfactory life or to find a job; his good intentions rebound on him. He could have been a symbol for Britain itself in 1952.

The play's special potency for the post-war British audience was underlined by its abject failure in New York. It was fortunate that Rattigan had not allowed the Broadway production to precede the London opening. Despite the fact that it brought Margaret Sullavan back to Broadway, the play was dismissed there as cleverly crafted soap-opera. Remarking that 'a romantic play which is not a comedy is the hardest thing in the world to put over on a New York critic', Kenneth Tynan wrote a long article in *Harper's Bazaar* of November 1952 about Rattigan, trying to prepare the American public for *The Deep Blue Sea*. He started by saying how tired he was of the way in which Rattigan was put down by people because of his success. Such people would say: ' "Good commercial stuff—good theatre too" ... "but he's not really a *dramatist*" ... "Good theatre": the phrase smacks of condescension, of giving the poor fellow his due; there is an unspoken "but"—which must some day be demolished. It implies that there is something improper in writing deliberately for your chosen medium—not print, or pure sound, but an upturned host of faces in a darkened hall.' Tynan went on to explain why he too had once dismissed him: 'I remember exactly when I gave Rattigan up for lost: it was in the autumn of 1950, when I saw *Who Is Sylvia? ...* We had, I concluded, a competent, but minor playwright.' But Tynan, in a dramatic about-face, immediately recants: 'I was quite wrong, which is why I am writing this. I had missed a clue, a vital signpost: it occurs in *The Browning Version*, during the long speech in which the schoolmaster ... speaks of himself, with arid desperation, as a traditional hen-pecked husband. "It is usually, I believe, a subject for farce." Enlarging on his relationship with his wife, he uses the crucial phrase: "The love she required, and which I was unable to give her".' Tynan goes on to explain how this clue—'the conflict of two quite incompatible kinds of passion'—has become the germ of *The Deep Blue Sea*, by far the best thing Rattigan has written. 'I do not say Rattigan has taken on gianthood as a dramatist. His characters still think in terms of "niceness" and "unpleasantness", not of "goodness" and "evil", but they are less evasive than they ever were. They are talking about realities, probing past appearances, and scarring each other.'

Repeating that *The Deep Blue Sea* was the most striking new English play of the decade, Tynan looked hopefully towards Rattigan's future: 'There, to date, stands Rattigan, partially fulfilled, tall and softly smiling, crisp of speech and wise of eye. What next? Not, I am sure, a novel. He is scared of the freedom it implies; those infinite spaces of time and place terrify him; he prefers the limits of the stage, the specific actor and the deadline. He may now club us with a masterpiece. Or perhaps his so acute ear for dialogue will betray him with ditchwater fluency again ...' But, Tynan concluded: 'One distinction will probably never be wrested from him: I support it with a completely unauthenticated story. It was told me by a friend who arrived at a Knightsbridge party and was ushered upstairs to doff hat and coat. Pausing on the cloakroom threshold and peering through the crack of the door, he saw someone talking to the mirror. Rattigan had stopped in the middle of combing his hair to muse, with a little groan, "If you're not very careful, Terry Rattigan, you won't be the prettiest playwright in London".'

The prettiest; the wittiest; now the best ...

Notes

1   Based on an interview with Charles Hamblett in *John Bull*, 6 December 1952.

2   The earlier, homosexual version was later completely suppressed and does not now seem to survive even among Rattigan's carefully preserved collection of papers. However, if it was destroyed by Rattigan or someone else for whatever reason, this did not happen until some years after its completion, since Rattigan showed the homosexual version to the director Alvin Rakoff in the early 1960s.

3   In describing the casting and production of *The Deep Blue Sea*, we have made considerable use of Kenneth More's own description of the

events in his book *Happy Go Lucky—My Life*, published by Robert Hale Ltd, London, 1959.

4   See Anne Edwards' biography of Vivien Leigh, for instance.

5   Holly Hill was probably the first critic to point out that Rattigan was ahead of his time in his awareness of the specific problems of women, as she was in pointing to the importance of his indefinite, as opposed to happy, endings. In these matters, as in many others, we acknowledge our indebtedness to her.

6   New York *Herald Tribune*, 2 November 1952.

7   *Curtains*, by Kenneth Tynan, Longmans, London, 1961.

13
The Sleeping Prince

Rattigan was forty when *The Deep Blue Sea* opened in London.
His father died during the rehearsals. His brother Brian too was
dying of lung cancer. Rattigan's mother gave up what she called
'the coldest house in Bedfordshire' and moved back to London, so
that she would be able to see more of her sons. The top-floor flat
where the family had lived during Rattigan's childhood no longer
existed. The house, together with about a dozen others in the
terrace on the east side of the square, had been flattened during
the war, and in their place stood a nondescript modern block. On
the opposite side of the square, a number of old houses had been
joined together to form a residential hotel, the Stanhope Court.
Vera Rattigan moved in. The majority of the other residents were,
like herself, elderly gentlefolk, mostly living alone in polite,
slightly reduced circumstances. Although their lives were
occasionally enlivened by casual guests, the atmosphere in the
hotel was tranquil. Vera, although now in her sixties, was still a
spirited and strikingly handsome woman. She affected the style of
the grand lady, attending the theatre regularly and taking a great
interest and pride in all Terence's doings. Her famous son was a
frequent visitor at the Stanhope Court, calling to pick her up or
return her from an outing to the theatre or a party, and dropping
in for a quiet dinner or tea with his mother.

At the same time as his mother came to live in London,

Rattigan moved out of his chambers in Albany, and into a penthouse flat in Eaton Square. The sliding plate-glass windows of his sixty-foot lounge opened on to a balcony, fronted with well-stocked window boxes and looking out on to the mature trees in the Square. To enhance the impression of an open-air atmosphere, he had the largest uninterrupted expanse of wall in the lounge covered with a black and white photomural blown up from an old French engraving of a forest scene. The dining room had photomurals on all four walls, comprising a complete panorama of old London. Simultaneously, he took a country house backing on to his favourite golf course at the club where Hester and Freddie were supposed to have first met in *The Deep Blue Sea*, Sunningdale.

Rattigan now had quite an army of professional advisers, housekeepers and others attending him. The most prominent was his fiercely loyal secretary Mary Herring, another in the line of tough women in Rattigan's life who tried to protect him from the distractions and depredations of an ever increasing swarm of hangers-on. She normally worked from a small study in the Eaton Square flat. In addition to doing his letters, keeping his appointments book and organizing his life—which still needed a lot of organizing—she typed up his manuscripts. He still normally wrote everything in long-hand in exercise books. Over the years the background music had changed from jazz to Puccini and he now seldom wrote at a desk. Dressed in an immaculate silk dressing-gown, he usually wrote on a writing board purchased for him by his mother when he was a young man. This he rested on his knee while stretched out on a sofa. At Sunningdale he had a board specially made to rest on a comfortable armchair.

His normal writing routine had varied little with the years. Starting at about 10.30 in the morning, he would work until about 3.00 in the afternoon, barely stopping for a light lunch brought to him on a tray by a housekeeper. Then a walk for two hours, or a round of golf or a game of tennis. In London, the walk often consisted of exploring obscure back streets. He would be back at work by five, and continued until eight or nine. He seldom worked later unless he was very behind schedule, since it prevented him from sleeping. He reckoned that once he had prepared himself and was ready to start writing, he could complete a play, including final polishing, in about eight weeks.

Film scripts were even quicker. However, as we have seen, he would sometimes run into difficulties, in which case he might drop a play for months at a time before returning to it. While he was engaged in the actual writing, he would not go to the theatre and avoided reading novels, for fear of absorbing any of their style of dialogue. Film producers in particular were appreciative, not only of the speed with which he could work, but of the dispassionate view he took of his finished scripts. He was always open to suggestions for the changes which are part and parcel of the film-making process.

Apart from his secretary and his agent, the other main organizer of Rattigan's life was his accountant, Bill Forsyth. Rattigan had been earning £30,000 a year or more for a decade. The hole made in his finances by the gambling spree after *French Without Tears* had been more than repaired, but only by Rattigan subjecting himself to tough management by others. Left to himself, he still remained hopelessly extravagant, spending lavishly on Rolls-Royces, restaurants, furniture and Savile Row tailoring. Although he jokingly wondered if people would take him more seriously if he wore pyjamas and tousled hair, he still featured in the *Tailor and Cutter*'s First Eleven of Best Dressed Men.

He was generous to a fault, entertaining without stint and distributing expensive gifts. Yet he could boast that he did not owe a penny in income tax. This was achieved by Bill Forsyth who had instituted two accounts for his income. Into one went all his earnings, which Rattigan was not allowed to touch without Forsyth's express permission; the demands of the Inland Revenue were met from this account. Forsyth arranged for the payment of just £5,000 a year into a second account. This was Rattigan's spending money. Forsyth found that Rattigan soon used this up, so he got him to agree to a further restriction: all cheques above £10 had to be countersigned by Forsyth. A journalist recorded going out to lunch with Rattigan and, finding him moody, asked what was wrong. 'Money,' Rattigan replied. The previous evening, a friend had come to him with a hard-luck story and, much though he wanted to help financially, he knew Forsyth would never sanction the expenditure. Rattigan was wondering, not for the first time, how he could get his hands on some of his own money behind his accountant's back. 'They treat me like a child,' he complained, adding, 'and quite right too!'[2] The truth was that, although reassured by the success that large sums of money represented, and by no means above a little discreet showing-off (driving Noël Coward down to Brighton one day in his Rolls-Royce, he could not resist pointing out that his was a more expensive Rolls than the one owned by Coward), Rattigan did not really care about money. It was important to him as a symbol only—as a means to purchase those outward tokens of success that bolstered his self-esteem—but not in itself.

Rattigan's lackadaisical attitude showed up in the trouble he was always having with servants. While his vagueness sometimes made it difficult for them—summoning his housekeeper to lay on the food for a party, he often seemed incapable of being precise about what he actually wanted prepared, asking only for the inclusion of 'some of those nice little savoury things you made the other day' without any further description that might give a clue as to what they actually were—it also laid him open to being cheated. Here an onus of responsibility was laid on Mary Herring and the later secretaries, particularly as Rattigan turned a wilfully blind eye to successive cases of petty pilfering. But Rattigan seemed not so much to tolerate as positively to enjoy the human frailties of the people who worked for him. His inclination was to note their oddities for future use, rather than to correct them. One of many such couples, a husband and wife, who acted as butler and cook at the house in Sunningdale, became quite famous among those in theatrical circles privileged enough to be invited there. Arthur Abeles, a film-producer friend, was convinced that the woman was positively the worst cook in the world, while her husband was the most inept butler. The pair were over-chummy and surly by turns with guests. A famous actress, pausing to consider how many courgettes to scoop on to her plate from the proffered vegetable dish, was prompted to ''urry up dear, I haven't got all day', while a well-known mannequin had a large dollop of unwanted mashed potato slapped brusquely on to her plate with 'munch it up, dear, you're all skin and bone'.[3] The thieving of this couple became so blatant, and the amount of the housekeeping money they were spending on themselves so great, that some of Rattigan's friends decided they could no longer smile and ignore it. They remonstrated with him. 'Oh,' he said mildly when they pointed out the extent of the couple's depredations, 'I thought my housekeeping allowance wasn't going as far as it should.' It was clear that they would have to be dismissed, but Rattigan could not face the prospect of a scene with them. So he went off on holiday to the South of France and left one of his friends to deal with them.

This pathological desire to avoid unpleasant confrontations frequently landed Rattigan in awkward situations. Face to face with a supplicant, he would agree to lend his name to an enterprise, write something or contribute money, because he could not say no. Later, someone else would counsel against it and Rattigan would reverse his decision. The result was frequent changes of mind and someone being delegated to convey his final decision and clear up the mess—his secretary, agent, solicitor, accountant or a friend. In contrast, over things that affected his work he was decisive and often quite stony-hearted. No one was more loyal to the actors who appeared in his plays, but if one offended by giving a performance that disappointed him, then he would have to wait a long time before appearing in another Rattigan play. Robert Flemyng, who had almost reached the position of a one-man Rattigan industry by the time of his appearance in *Who Is Sylvia?*, never again appeared in a Rattigan première. An even more loyal ally, A. D. Peters, his agent, backer and champion since the days before his success, nodded off at lunch while discussing with Rattigan the manuscript of *The Sleeping Prince*. Shortly afterwards, Rattigan found himself another agent. Yet even his closest friends never saw him angry, though they knew that often he must be seething inwardly. Forced into a corner, Rattigan remained scrupulously polite. On one occasion, a man who had been involved in a situation which Rattigan had used in a play tried to blackmail him. Rattigan invited the man out to a good restaurant for lunch. During the meal he was the perfect host, polite and smiling, never alluding to the matter he had come to discuss. Then, after coffee and brandy had been served, he said, 'Oh, by the way, what an extraordinary letter you sent me. I hope you won't send me another one, because if you do I shall send it to my solicitor. Would you like some more brandy?' Needless to say, Rattigan was not bothered by the man again.

Although he was by no means tired of London, he loved the country. The reason for choosing a house at Sunningdale was almost entirely due to his enthusiasm for golf and his liking for that course in particular. He had been playing there regularly for a good many years before being able to get the house, which had a large garden with a gate leading directly on to the course. Rattigan had taken up golf during his first term at Oxford. After being dropped from the Harrow cricket eleven in his last term, he had realized that he was unlikely to get a cricket blue and had taken three perfunctory golf lessons, bought a few clubs and taken to playing by himself at the North Oxford course. In the last few years he had played with increasing dedication, steadily working his handicap down to nine, making him an averagely good golfer. His form was erratic; he had a good drive but putted badly. He found it an ideal game because it demanded such complete concentration on the actual shots that it effectively took his mind off his writing and allowed him to relax.

Rattigan's favourite golfing partners were Stephen Mitchell, the impresario who had put on the two one-act plays in *Playbill*, and a young film producer, Tony Darnborough. Other regular golfing friends were Arthur Abeles and Harold French. They never put less than ten shillings each on a round and never more than ten pounds.

In the afternoons, after a round of golf, Rattigan and his friends would repair either to the bar or to his home for a drink. If he wanted to carry on writing on these occasions he would sit in the lounge window while his friends played the record player and talked. Putting his feet up on a footstool, he scribbled in a notebook, apparently oblivious of the noise around him. If his friends volunteered to go away and leave him in peace he would say, 'Oh no, old boy, don't bother.' His style as a host remained very much that of the gallant head-boy. He drank a lot, but never seemed drunk. Since watching Puffin Asquith struggle with drink, he was cautious; after a string of hangovers he would con-scientiously cut down his consumption. Under the charm, tinged with engaging, shy modesty, the cold detachment of a natural observer had never disappeared. 'The man is a fish, a hard, cold-blooded, supercilious ... fish', Catherine had said of Sir Robert Morton in *The Winslow Boy*. Rattigan saw the same quality in himself, and thought it a fault as well as a necessary attribute of the playwright. Sometimes it did come dangerously near to seeming a fault to others, too. On one occasion some guests discovered he had recorded their conversation at dinner, when he played back a particularly foolish argument they had been having to reinforce his own assertion that they were being stupid. It was all taken as good fun, but at least one guest did wonder how many other times they had been recorded in order to supply raw material for a script.

Once Rattigan had got his Sunningdale house, he had no further need of his rooms at the Stag and Hounds, and so he bequeathed them to Arthur Abeles and Tony Darnborough, an act which was consistent with Rattigan's concern to be a considerate host. It spared his friends any embarrassment they might have felt over the changing assortment of young men he entertained together with other homosexual friends at his Sunningdale home, which was, in any case, not over-furnished with bedrooms. Although he made no show of his homosexuality to his heterosexual friends in the 'Sunningdale set' he still liked, as far as possible, to maintain a strict segregation between that compartment of his life and the rest. In any case the 'gay' young men would hardly have mixed with his more conventional heterosexual companions. Inevitably they came into contact sometimes; then Darnborough and Abeles and company would shake their heads tolerantly at 'Terry's little weakness', mildly regretting that so many of the young men seemed 'pretty rough trade', and dismiss them as 'purely medicinal'.

At this period Rattigan met a young man who would come to mean a great deal to him and was destined to play an important role in his life. Michael Franklin, a pretty young man with neat features and an almost retroussé nose. He bore a striking physical resemblance to other young men with whom Rattigan had affairs. Like his father and the hero of *Who Is Sylvia?*, Rattigan favoured an identifiable physical type. Michael Franklin was ambitious and not without ability as an interior designer. He became responsible for the decoration of Rattigan's homes.

The segregation between the sexual 'compartment' of Rattigan's life and the rest had been one of its more striking features ever since he left Oxford, but it was probably never more marked than at this period. Unlike Mark in *Who Is Sylvia?*, who boasted just before his final unmasking that by dividing the illicit and romantic from the domestic and secure he had found the secret of successful living—'to divide them into two worlds and then to have the best of both of them'—Rattigan feared their collision. This was largely due to the intolerant and narrow-minded legal and social strictures that still applied to male homosexuals. Yet his almost flamboyantly conventional, conservative life-style sometimes seemed not so much camouflage as over-compensation. He still felt regret, even self-disgust, over his homosexuality. Friends have testified that as he entered his forties and his looks started to fade, he thought again about marriage and regretted not having children. He had for a long time enjoyed the company of women at least as much, if not more, than that of men. He said he had made further sexual experiments with women after the abortive encounter with a prostitute in his youth, but never with any success or enjoyment. In such circumstances he was much too realistic seriously to contemplate marriage.

This division of Rattigan's life led to some pretty close shaves when the two worlds threatened to collide, circumstances which were not quite as funny in real life as they might have been on the stage. The young men who were his sexual partners did not like being bundled out through the back door when 'straight' guests were coming. They were resentful of the implication that they were not good enough to meet the celebrities with whom Rattigan consorted in his 'other world'. Rattigan seems to have gone to particular lengths to avoid them meeting his mother—not always an easy task, especially as she lived with him at Sunningdale for quite extended periods. Although her suspicions may have been aroused, Vera seems still not to have known of her son's homosexuality; or if she did, she refused to admit it. She continued to cherish hopes that he would marry. Stephen Mitchell recalls sitting beside Vera at a Rattigan party when she said quizzically, 'Why are there always so many young men and so few girls at Terence's parties?'

Some of his parties amounted almost to theatrical state occasions. Typical were Rattigan's house parties at Sunningdale for Royal Ascot Week, at which there was no suggestion of there being too many young men present. The most famous of these occasions was during June 1953, Coronation year, when house-guests included Sir Laurence Olivier and his wife, Vivien Leigh, the ruling monarchs of the British Theatre. Rattigan's hostess for the week was Jean Dawnay, one of Britain's top fashion models and the girl Vera Rattigan currently seemed to hope her son might marry. She had been his closest woman friend for some years.

The Oliviers were, so to speak, the guests of honour at Rattigan's Royal Ascot house-party in 1953 because they were due to appear in his new play, *The Sleeping Prince*. This was a very slight piece, which he called 'an occasional fairy tale'—the occasion being the Coronation. Rattigan claimed that on 1 January 1953 he had woken up with the customary blinding hangover and, later in the day, to the equally blinding thought that this was Coronation year and that he ought to do something about it, since everyone else seemed to be doing something for the occasion. But what? His mind was blank. By the beginning of February he had an idea and had started writing. Largely at the prompting of his mother, he had decided to set his play at a Coronation, that of King George V and Queen Mary, which had coincided with his birth. He later claimed that as his birth had deprived his mother of the opportunity of being present at the ceremony, he was making it up to her through the play. The idea was also prompted by some memoirs of the period he had been reading, and the background was further filled out by details of his father's experiences as official host to the Grand Vizier, the most colourful of which had been diplomatically excluded from his book of autobiographical memories. More routine details came from some little books marked 'Strictly Confidential' proffered by his publisher and school-friend, Roger Machell. These, preserved by members of his family, had been issued to visiting royalty and officials during the 1911 Coronation and contained notes on procedure, useful private addresses and telephone numbers, etc.

Rattigan knew that if he was to get the play on in time for the Coronation in June, he would have to work very fast, even by his standards. On one thing he was quite positive from the outset: his play was to be a very light comedy of the sort that he was supposed to have grown out of. He knew that in this he risked a panning from the critics, but he intended to offset their rage by making it clear that this was not meant to be a serious offering to follow *The Deep Blue Sea*, but simply a little nonsense for a great occasion. He planned to make his strictly limited intentions clear by having a small-scale production, with a short run of three months and a non-star cast.

His aim was to stand a familiar romantic cliché on its head and

214

play the results for laughs. The setting was the Carpathian Legation in London on the eve of the Coronation. The Regent of Carpathia, deliberately depicted to be as far as possible from the romantic idea of the Ruritanian prince conjured up by his title, treats love as 'purely medicinal', a favourite sport so long as it does not interrupt State routine and can be scheduled to fit into an hour at the end of a busy day. In his four-day visit to London he has only one such available hour. An American chorus girl, appearing in London, Mary Morgan (the name Morgan is undoubtedly deliberate), is hastily acquired. To the Regent's dismay she proves reluctant to be seduced. If she is going to succumb at all, it will only be to the accompaniment of tzigane music, high-flown speeches and the full paraphernalia of a traditional royal seduction, as in romantic fiction. Since there is no time to acquire a more compliant girl, the Regent reluctantly turns on the standard romantic accompaniment for a seduction, but with too much success. Mary takes the empty endearments seriously and by next morning has decided to stay with him for life.

The Sleeping Prince, the lightest soufflé, nevertheless clearly depends on familiar strands of the Rattigan *leitmotif*. Writing of *The Deep Blue Sea*, Kenneth Tynan had said that its keynote was 'the failure of two people to agree on a definition of love'. This, too, is the keynote of *The Sleeping Prince*, but with completely different consequences. In the same article, Tynan had reflected on *Adventure Story* and the way in which Alexander and Rattigan had both seemed to spend their whole careers repeatedly killing their fathers.[5] It is significant that in even such an inconsequential piece as *The Sleeping Prince* the principal sub-plot centres on the young heir apparent, who tries to start a revolution in defiance of the Regent, the father figure. The play abounds in biographical references. In the first scene, the Regent confers on the telephone about a crisis involving the Entente Powers and their ambitions in Morocco, an echo of one of Frank Rattigan's diplomatic involvements. Mary and the young heir apparent provoke an incident at a state ball when Mary, like Frank Rattigan, 'alters the tempo' of one of the rather staid dances. One character refers to 'dear, witty Mrs Asquith', and Mary reproaches two characters for talking as if they were George Bernard Shaw.

Taken purely at the level at which Rattigan said he intended it, as a light fantasy with which to celebrate the Coronation, *The Sleeping Prince* is on the whole admirable. However, as a vehicle for the comeback of Sir Laurence Olivier and Vivien Leigh after a two-year absence from the London stage it was altogether inadequate. Their last appearance together had been in a season in which they played opposite each other in *Antony and Cleopatra* and *Caesar and Cleopatra*.

Rattigan has recorded how the Oliviers' involvement in *The Sleeping Prince* came about. In mid-February 1953, when he was about halfway through writing the play, the telephone rang in his Sunningdale study, a little after midnight. As Rattigan put it, he did not suppose that a call from Olivier after midnight was going to be about the weather, and immediately suspected that 'something was afoot'.[6] 'After only the minimal exchange of "darling old boys" and "loveys", the voice changed into that quietly imperious register. "I hear you're writing a play for the Coronation that might suit Vivien and me." ' Rattigan recalled that there seemed only one answer to this—'No'—and that he gave it. He was not writing a play that would suit the Oliviers. 'Bold stuff,' Rattigan reflected, but it would have been even bolder if he hadn't consented, at the end of about half an hour, to 'let him have a glance at it, old ducky, when it was finished, so that he could judge all that for himself'. Rattigan had given Olivier all the compelling reasons why he thought such casting would be utterly fatal for the Oliviers and himself. His 'occasional fairy tale' could not contain one, let alone both those gigantic talents; how could Olivier persuade an audience that he was 'Prince Uncharming' when he had made Richard III into one of the most sexually attractive characters ever to disgrace a stage? How could Vivien Leigh, 'one of nature's grand-duchesses if ever I saw one, walk on to a stage as a chorus girl thrilled to her Brooklynese death at the prospect of meeting a real grand duke in the flesh'? What would the critics say?

Rattigan supposed that from the moment he received that telephone call it was almost inevitable that he would eventually give way if Olivier finally did want to do the play. Was it the Lunts and *Love in Idleness* all over again? Regrettably, the parallels are all too familiar. Just as we had to cast doubt on Rattigan's later protestations about the Lunts changing the intentions of that play against his will, we are bound to ask whether Rattigan was really so reluctant to have the Oliviers do *The Sleeping Prince* and whether his later version of the story was an exaggeration, a partial self-defence against unfavourable critical opinion. Olivier has never confirmed that Rattigan protested particularly strongly. In an article written in 1957, Rattigan confessed that although he had believed the Oliviers were otherwise committed during the summer of 1953, he had nurtured hopes of them doing his play and that he had actually refused to give a firm undertaking for anyone else to do the play until he knew whether the Oliviers would do it.[7] This article suggests the reverse of reluctance at the prospect of the Oliviers doing the play. But regardless of the Oliviers, Rattigan was surely being uncharacteristically naïve to assume that anything he now wrote would simply be passed over by the critics. He had had the experience of *Who Is Sylvia?* to teach him about critical expectations. With *The Deep Blue Sea* still running, there was no chance of *The Sleeping Prince* sneaking past as a *pièce d'occasion*.

Owing to other commitments and the fact that Vivien Leigh was only just recovering from a mental collapse, rehearsals did not begin until September 1953, long after the Coronation itself was over. Although he paid gallant tributes to Viven Leigh's efforts, Rattigan continued to think her miscast. He attended rehearsals more than was his wont, largely for the simple joy of watching Olivier work on the part. He was fascinated by the amount of trouble he took, building up his performance from a mass of tiny details, discarding some, retaining others, continually experimenting. Sometimes proceedings would come to a halt because Vivien Leigh could not help giggling at some piece of business her husband had put in or the way he played a line. 'Is it as funny as that?' Olivier would ask anxiously. 'Terry, what do you think?' In paroxysms of laughter Rattigan would reply, 'Yes, marvellous.' Quite often Olivier would then say, 'No, I think it's too much. It's out.' Olivier was very faithful to Rattigan's text and even to the stage directions. Rattigan commented ruefully, 'Most directors don't even read them.' He had not expected Olivier to be such a perfect light comedian and was bowled over with admiration.

His last remaining fear, that Olivier would still prove 'Prince Utterly Irresistible' rather than 'Prince Uncharming', was laid to rest at the dress rehearsal before the opening in Manchester.

Going to Olivier's dressing-room just before the curtain rose, he was confronted by a monocled, dull-looking little man with an anaemic complexion, a thin, prissy, humourless mouth and centre-parted hair plastered repulsively down over his ears. Rattigan claimed that it was only when he noticed the Edwardian costume and the Order round his neck that he recognized him as Olivier—his own, true, living, breathing, Sleeping Prince.[8]

The play opened in London at the Phoenix Theatre on 5 November 1953. People had by now had rather too much of the Coronation, and the play threatened to be a damp squib. Whatever Rattigan's private fears about the play's reception that evening, he kept up his usual self-confident appearance. In the afternoon, he played a round of golf with Tony Darnborough. He was in winning form. In desperation Darnborough tried a little gamesmanship. Each time Rattigan addressed the ball he would remind him of the approaching first night, saying something like, 'I think we're going to be late for the curtain.' Each time, Rattigan drove or putted with more confidence. At the first night itself he maintained the same self-confidence. Reactions to the first act were by no means clear-cut and when he went round to Olivier's dressing-room in the interval, Sir Laurence asked, 'How's it going out there?' 'Pretty good,' said Rattigan. 'But I must say I think you are a little down. Are you sure you're feeling all right?' 'Perfectly,' replied Olivier. 'Tell me, Terry, how are they liking Puss?' (This was his nickname for Vivien Leigh.) 'Very much indeed,' Rattigan replied. Olivier shook his head. 'I don't think so. I don't think so at all. I don't think she's going over as well as she should be.'

During the next act Rattigan noticed that Olivier had lowered his performance even more. The impression from the front was that Olivier was way below par. As the run continued, that impression was maintained, and both critics and public were disappointed. Although a number of critics conceded that a *pièce d'occasion* was not to be judged by the same standards as would apply to works written without any conditions attached, the prevailing view was summed up by Milton Shulman in the *Evening Standard*: 'It seems a pity that in these spare times so much talent should have gone into so little.'[9] Although Rattigan had anticipated such attacks, he was still very bitter when they materialized. But with such names the play could hardly fail to draw audiences and it ran for 274 performances, and would have run longer if the Oliviers' commitments had allowed.

Three years later, Rattigan consented to allow the play to be done on Broadway, where it could in no sense be expected to be taken as a *pièce d'occasion*. With Michael Redgrave and Barbara Bel Geddes starring, it ran for only 52 performances. Rattigan had only himself to blame when the critics slaughtered it. *The Sleeping Prince* was a sleeping pill: 'Playwright Rattigan here blindly scattereth poppyseed while contriving poppycock', said *Time* magazine.[10]

Notes

1   *Tailor and Cutter*, 15 February 1952.
2   *Picture Post*, 5 April 1952.
3   The story was recalled by Arthur Marshall in the *New Statesman*, 9 December 1977.
4   *Sunday Times*, 25 June 1950.
5   *Harper's Bazaar*, November 1952.
6   This account is taken from Rattigan's contribution to *Olivier*, edited by Logan Gourlay, Weidenfeld and Nicolson, 1973.
7   *Daily Express*, 25 June 1957.
8   *Olivier*, edited by Logan Gourlay.
9   *Evening Standard*, 6 November 1953.
10 *Time*, 12 November 1956.

14
Aunt Édna

Almost simultaneously with the opening of *The Sleeping Prince*, Hamish Hamilton published Rattigan's *Collected Plays* in two volumes, each with a Preface by the author. They contained all the produced plays which Rattigan had written on his own, except one—*After the Dance*. It was surely a mistake to have excluded that fine, too little known play, while including *Who Is Sylvia?* It could only do harm to Rattigan's reputation as a serious playwright. But the inclusion of *After the Dance* would have weakened Rattigan's argument in his Prefaces—that the popularity of his plays was no disqualification for taking them or their author seriously.

He began his first Preface by saying he found himself at something of a disadvantage when it came to being presented to the discriminating public as a serious dramatist because all the plays in the first volume had been successes and he could not therefore commend them on the grounds that undiscriminating audiences had rejected them. He intended to argue, therefore, that the fact that they had been uniquely successful with West End audiences might imply positive virtues. This was a difficult, even a dangerous, argument for Rattigan to pursue but, as we have seen, it was a matter of intense importance to him. He covered himself by adopting a characteristically mock-modest, banteringly apologetic, schoolboy tone. Unfortunately, it was a line of argument which was inimicable to the public schoolboy ethos and gentlemanly self-effacement. The result was simultaneously to weaken his case and hand a lot of ammunition to his critical enemies. In the Preface to Volume One, having cited the repertory manager who told him: 'What's so nice about doing your plays in my theatre is that their profits pay for the good ones'—and called in aid Lady Bracknell's reproof to her nephew: 'Never speak disrespectfully of society, Algernon. Only people who can't get into it do that'—to deal with highbrow playwrights who sneered at his lowbrow success, Rattigan went on to suggest that down the ages popular taste had not been so bad as snobs have supposed. That the plays in the volume scored five successes out of five must indicate not just luck but a common denominator that made them appeal to audiences. This Rattigan described as a 'sense of theatre', a vague concept allied to the ability to thrill an audience through the power of suggestion; to move it to tears or laughter through the implicit rather than the explicit. This instinct—for he claimed it was a creative gift rather than a craft to be learned—entailed being able to act simultaneously as one's own audience while in the actual process of writing a play. This gift manifested itself in the negative virtue of knowing what not to have your actors say rather than in anything more recognizably positive. While it was not a quality which would on its own ensure great drama, it was a quality shared by all great dramatists. It was the quality which Rattigan knew he possessed, and without which he knew he would have had no hope of achieving his one great ambition: 'to write, before I die, one great play'.

To press this bold argument further, in the Preface to Volume Two Rattigan sought shelter behind the creation of a comic figure to personify his idea of the audience which down the ages had not been bamboozled by changing fashions or pretensions, who ultimately sifted the dramatic wheat from the theatrical chaff. This was Aunt Edna. Today her views bear alarming similarity to those of Mary Whitehouse; in 1953 she bore a striking resemblance to Vera Rattigan.

She is, we are told, a nice, respectable, middle-class, middle-aged, maiden lady, with time on her hands and money to help her pass it, who resides in a West Kensington hotel. There she dispenses opinions on the arts over the teacups with her cronies.

She enjoys pictures, books, music and the theatre, and although she does not bring much discernment to any of them she 'does know what she likes'. Rattigan tells us she does not appreciate Kafka: 'so obscure, my dear, and why always look on the dark side of things?' She is upset by Picasso: 'those dreadful reds, my dear, and why three noses?', and she is against Walton: 'such appalling discords, my dear, and no melody at all'. She is, in short, 'a hopeless lowbrow'. But no playwright dare ignore her or his play will fail. She will broadcast her disapproval of a play that has displeased her at a matinée to the other potential members of the audience in her hotel and beyond that same evening: 'Oh, it was so dull, my dears, don't think of going to it. So much talk, so little action, so difficult to see the actors' faces, and even the tea was cold.' She is immortal and international, her voice as powerful in Moscow as in London; she sat on the hard stone seats of the theatre in Athens, clutching her neighbour's arm and whispering: 'My dear, do look at that blood on the actor's mask. He's supposed to have blinded himself. I'm so glad it didn't happen on stage, though. I always say you can rely on Sophocles.' She was shocked and intrigued by Euripides and dissolved into laughter at Aristophanes. At the Elizabethan Globe she took on the aspect of Queen Elizabeth and held sway over Shakespeare and his contemporaries. In Restoration times she assumed the attributes of one of Charles II's naughtier mistresses, and in the Victorian era took on the image of the queen herself. Although Aunt Edna may sometimes enjoy the trivial she will always appreciate the best. What Aunt Edna does not like, no one will ever like. While she enjoys a little teasing and even some bullying, a dramatist must never go so far as to incur her displeasure. Rattigan said that in his attempts to grow from a playwright into a dramatist he tried to distance himself from Aunt Edna just enough to overcome his tendency too consciously to please the audience, but at the same time he tried not to go too far for Aunt Edna. He said: 'A play does not fail because it is too good: it fails because it is not good enough,' and applied the same harsh logic to his own isolated failure, *Adventure Story*.

Rattigan wrote this Preface in a hurry, between commitments in the summer of 1953, in order to meet his publisher's deadline. At the time he and his editor at Hamish Hamilton, Roger Machell, were blissfully unaware of the harm the second Preface would do Rattigan. Machell later recalled that he and his colleagues had found Aunt Edna 'awfully amusing, written slightly tongue-in-cheek. I couldn't imagine anyone taking it completely seriously. I never thought for a moment that it would be used as a stick to beat him with. I've kicked myself ever since.'[1]

The conflict between popularity and quality had dogged Rattigan in his dealings with the critics ever since James Agate attacked *French Without Tears*. With his Prefaces, Rattigan had laid himself wide open and the attacks began the moment the books were published. In the *Daily Express*, John Barber told him in no uncertain terms to 'come off it, Mr Rattigan'. He said he knew why Rattigan was cross—it was because the critics had not liked his later comedies and had stopped praising him: 'That is what hurts.' But he warned that he would go on nagging him to write his best: 'You say you do not want to pander to Aunt Edna in the stalls. Then don't ... Sad isn't it? To be so prosperous, so gifted—and so spoiled. For that is what it comes to—to be so avid for more success and more success that it gets harder every morning to sit down in humble obedience to your own finest instincts.'

Still more significant for what it portended for the future was an article by Kenneth Tynan, newly installed as drama critic of the *Observer*. Tynan still regarded Rattigan as the most promising British dramatist, but the conjunction of the Prefaces with the production of *The Sleeping Prince* confirmed his worst suspicions. He pointed out that Rattigan was wrong to say that plays which failed did so because they were not good enough for Aunt Edna—they failed because they were not bad enough for her. Rattigan was blind to her failings; she went to *Hamlet*, for instance, not because she recognized its quality but because generations of highbrows had told her to. She follows, never leads, intelligent taste. Rattigan's output was marked by the negative virtues associated with pleasing her: 'that marketable quality known to cynics as ingratiation and to romantics as charm ... tact, understatement, avoidance of cliché—the hallmarks, in fact, of the "gentleman code" which holds so much of West End playwriting in curious thrall'.

By November 1953, when the Collected Plays were published, Rattigan's next play, or more correctly, pair of one-act plays, *Separate Tables*, was well advanced. In these, too, the residence of

Vera Rattigan in the Stanhope Court Hotel was an important element of the inspiration. Rattigan in fact dedicated them to his mother. 'The inspiration there was that my mother was in a hotel for old people in Kensington and I used to go and have dinner with her, and I used to observe the people sitting at these tables all around, occasionally visited by their sons, and their nephews and their grandsons, and I wondered about them. I wasn't told much about them, I just tried to imagine what they would be like, what their lives would be like. I stuck it in Bournemouth just in case I was sued by the hoteliers.'[2]

The distance the characters in the plays travelled from their real-life origins in the course of the working of Rattigan's creative mind is even greater than the distance between Kensington and Bournemouth. Nevertheless those origins can still be detected in the finished plays. There is ample evidence in the way Rattigan's creative mind worked throughout his career for seeing in the relationship between the domineering Mrs Railton-Bell and her sexually repressed daughter Sibyl an extreme reshaping of Rattigan's relationship with his own mother. The very fact that the bogus major calls himself 'the Major' is a signpost directing us to look to Rattigan's own family background for clues to the character's genesis. In the first play the quality of the lovers' quarrels, indeed of their relationship in general, draws directly on Rattigan's own experience. It may be worth noting in this connection that this is a play in which, as we know from our own experience, casts have found it helpful at times in rehearsal to think of both characters as men and have thus uncovered nuances in the dialogue which have enriched the texture of the whole.

The origins of both plays in *Separate Tables* lay in events in the lives of two people who mattered a great deal to Rattigan. We have already mentioned Jean Dawnay, his fashion model hostess at the house party at which the Oliviers were guests of honour during Royal Ascot Week in 1953. As well as being beautiful, Jean Dawnay was a very interesting woman. Brought up without a mother, she had during the war worked in a parachute factory and been the youngest WAAF. By late 1947 she had graduated to being a hard-up air-hostess with a struggling private charter airline, but had had to give up flying because of ill health. Despite a difficult start in life she was ambitious. But the opportunities open to a girl at that time were strictly limited. Her looks were

224

likely to be her most marketable asset, so she had her teeth fixed on an instalment plan and set about learning to be a fashion model. Within three years she was, with Barbara Goalen, perhaps Britain's best-known model. She worked for Dior, Beaton and Armstrong-Jones; had 'shown' before the Queen; and was, as the gossip columns never ceased to remind their readers, the friend of Aly Khan and Bill Astor. It was inevitable that in the course of the social round she would meet Rattigan; what was not so easy to forecast was that they would become such close friends that Vera Rattigan would entertain hopes (or, as one person we talked to suggested, fears) that she and her son would marry.

What intrigued Rattigan was that behind the confident worldly exterior he found a vulnerable, inexperienced girl. She had catapulted herself so far and so fast that she had arrived quite unprepared in an alien social world, which was often as frightening as it was exciting. She was also refreshingly direct. When she met him, about 1950, she was unaware who he was; she knew nothing about the theatre or his reputation as 'the great playwright'. She was totally unimpressed by the sycophants and hangers-on who surrounded him. She found Rattigan's homosexuality a relief; it meant that in a circle of men there was for once 'no question of what happened at night'. It helped the development of a mutually confessional relationship, in which there was affection without sex. She talked candidly about her problems and love affairs; Rattigan talked candidly about his. What she could not understand about Rattigan and his friends was that none of them had any comprehension of permanent relationships.

Jean Dawnay was at this time continually falling in and out of love, but she knew that none of the men was really 'right'. Rattigan became a refuge, a father figure, a concerned and charming listener, who took her out to the theatre, cheered her up and demanded nothing in return. One story she told Rattigan seemed to affect him particularly and he asked her to repeat it. She had been attacked by a boy friend, badly enough for her screams to have led to the police being called. She had told the man that their relationship would have to be broken off. What appeared to have particularly annoyed the man was the calm way in which she broke the news to him and continued to appear unruffled when he argued with her.

The first play in *Separate Tables—Table by the Window*—concerns a fashion model, Anne Shankland, and her stormy relationship with her ex-husband John, a former Labour politician turned journalist. When the play opens she is forty and her looks are fading. Her inability or unwillingness to gratify his overpowering sexual needs during their marriage resulted in his attacking her, his imprisonment and disgrace for attempted murder, and their divorce. Lonely and frightened for her future, divorced from a second husband, also on grounds of cruelty, Anne has sought John out in the quiet hotel where he has secluded himself since his release from prison, in the hope of effecting a reconciliation. Again, Rattigan is delving into the conflicts between different kinds of need and the clash between incompatible types of love. 'Girls,' John asks rhetorically, 'which husband would you choose? One who loves you too little or one who loves you too much?'

John married Anne because his love, his craving for her, was so violent he could refuse her nothing—not even a marriage he knew was bound to be disastrous because of the gulf between his rough working-class background and her Kensington upbringing. She, he claims, married him rather than any of her other, wealthier suitors because she wanted the enjoyment of enslaving someone as wild and brutal as himself. She now needs him as the only person she has ever been fond of. She is losing the art of making people fall in love with her and fears loneliness—the hotel, full of lonely old people, she says, gives her the creeps. John needs her in the same way as he always did, and against reason. He has started a nice, sensible little affair with the hotel manageress which had seemed to be leading to marriage, but seeing Anne again confirms for him that he can only really love one type of person—the prototype—Anne. Later realizing that Anne has staged the whole meeting, that it wasn't the hand of fate which brought them together again, John becomes very angry and is on the point of trying to strangle her again. Eventually, with help from Miss Cooper, the hotel manageress, who renounces her own claims on John, they are reconciled. They have little hope together, but none apart. In this play, like *The Deep Blue Sea*, love is seen as a disaster. The principal characters are like addicts; once they have tasted each other they cannot overcome their dependence, even though they know that they will destroy each other.

226

When Rattigan showed the play to Jean Dawnay she was horrified, not simply because some of the details made it seem likely that people in the story might recognize themselves (Rattigan readily agreed to make changes which protected their anonymity) but because the model appeared such a hard bitchy character. Jean overlooked the vulnerability of Anne and the skill with which Rattigan had projected her into an imaginary future; a future which he was beginning to understand and fear for himself, in which his saving vitality had been exhausted, leaving only a creaking husk. (In fact, Jean Dawnay escaped the fate that Rattigan had imagined for somebody blessed with her fatal attractiveness; not many years after the production of *Separate Tables* she married and is today the charming and attractive mother of a daughter who looks set to be as beautiful as she.)

A striking example of courage in the face of painful publicity, which occurred during the preparations for the production of *The Sleeping Prince*, inspired the second play in *Separate Tables*, *Table Number Seven*. This centred round the hero of Rattigan's youth, John Gielgud. During the autumn of 1953, Gielgud was charged with a homosexual offence. He was fined £10 for being drunk and disorderly and told by the magistrate to see a doctor. It was a matter of little real significance and indeed it looked as if the press was content to ignore it. However, a day or two before Gielgud was due to open in N. C. Hunter's *A Day by the Sea* in Liverpool, the *Daily Express* picked up the story and plastered it, together with a photograph of Gielgud, across their pages. The manager of the theatre in Liverpool received a number of ominous telephone calls, and it began to seem that if Gielgud appeared on stage there would be some sort of demonstration against him.

Gielgud, with moral support from Binkie Beaumont, John Perry and his co-star in the play, Sybil Thorndike, was not to be intimidated. When the opening night arrived, the backstage atmosphere was understandably tense, but as Gielgud made his entrance there was no demonstration; the audience in the packed house seemed somehow just to sigh and the performance continued as if nothing untoward had happened. Rattigan was very moved: 'He had enough courage to go on and the audience had enough grace and sympathy to accept him purely as an actor. Everyone reacted with dignity rather than hysteria, as might have been expected. The acceptance by these very ordinary people of something about which they had little understanding was very moving. In these people there was a strong feeling of humanity.'[3]

The laws relating to homosexual offences had in no way been relaxed in the years since Rattigan's youth. The prosecution and blackmail of adult homosexuals continued. The usual sequel to the public revelation of 'abnormal sexual practices' was still disgrace and banishment from public life. When the news of Gielgud's arrest broke, Rattigan said to his friends, only half-jokingly, 'There'll be no Sir Terry now.' He, like many another homosexual, was genuinely alarmed. The humanity he applauded in that Liverpool audience was far from universal. Public hounding of homosexuals seemed to have become a minor blood sport among illiberal journalists and their editors that autumn. The popular press became fond of running leaders on 'evil men' in high places. One case, involving a peer of the realm, seemed to be blazoned across the pages of the best-selling Sundays every week between August Bank Holiday and Christmas that year.[4] When one of the other defendants in the case sought refuge from the hounding of the press in Rattigan's London flat, Rattigan turned him away. He dared not risk becoming publicly associated with anyone in the case or with homosexuality. Above all, he told the man, he was frightened of doing anything that might lead to his mother finding out he was himself homosexual.

Even if Rattigan had wanted to make the principal character—the Major—in the second play of *Separate Tables* a homosexual, the Lord Chamberlain's office would almost certainly have banned it. The subject was still taboo in the theatre. But the need to make the Major's offence the 'lesser' one of touching-up women in a cinema had important compensatory virtues for Rattigan: 'If I had written the man as a homosexual, the play might have been construed as a thesis drama begging for tolerance specifically of the homosexual. Instead it is a plea for the understanding of everyone.'[5] In fact when the play was presented in New York two years after its London production Rattigan was persuaded to rewrite it with the Major as a homosexual. It didn't work: 'the reconception had become so real that it could not be bent back,' Rattigan explained.[6] That version was abandoned without the director, Peter Glenville, even being informed.

The second play in *Separate Tables* makes a perfect contrast to the first and gains considerably thereby. Its effectiveness is heightened by Rattigan's idea of having the two leading parts played by the same two stars. So the glamorous fading ex-model becomes a dowdy young spinster, Sibyl, suffering extreme emotional repression at the hands of a selfish and domineering battle-axe mother, Mrs Railton-Bell. John, the rough, working-class ex-politician, becomes the bogus 'Major' Pollock, affecting a public-school background, a pukka accent, a distinguished career and perfect social conformity. The only grounds for suspicion of him are, as Rattigan directs, that he seems almost too exact a replica of the traditional retired Major figure to be entirely true.

When the play opens, the Major appears to have got away with his offence, until Mrs Railton-Bell finds 'the story'—his minor sexual misdemeanour—tucked away on an inside page of a local newspaper. She calls a meeting of the other residents with the intention of getting them to allow her to go to the manageress on their behalf and ask for 'the Major' to be expelled from the hotel. 'The Major' is, in effect, tried in his absence by his fellow guests, each of whom strikes a different moral attitude. The only person to side with 'the Major', a young doctor, accuses Mrs Railton-Bell of conducting the meeting in a manner worthy of Senator McCarthy. His defence of the Major is the rational one: 'The Major presumably understands my form of lovemaking. I *should* therefore understand his. But I don't. So I am plainly in a state of prejudice against him.' He asks what actual harm the Major has done from the standpoint of Christian ethics and concludes: '... apart from possibly slightly bruising the arm of a certain lady and telling a few rather pathetic lies about himself, which most of us do anyway, he has done nothing to justify throwing him out of the hotel.'

Another guest, a retired schoolmaster, cites the wave of vice and sexual excess which has swept the country since the war as evidence of the adage that tolerance of evil may itself be an evil. He is, however, unhappy about siding with someone whose motives are as doubtful as Mrs Railton-Bell's. He says, in a comment all too reminiscent of the situation Rattigan had found himself in during the previous ten years: 'The trouble about being on the side of right, as one sees it, is that one sometimes finds oneself in the company of such very questionable allies.' When Mrs Railton-Bell's deeply repressed daughter is asked to express her opinion, the girl becomes hysterical and the meeting breaks up. The young doctor comments that if she could only once publicly stand up to her mother it might save her soul.

In the play's most touching scene, which is written with such mastery as to banish the basic implausibility of the situation, Sibyl encounters the Major and asks him why he did it. 'Why does anyone do anything they shouldn't—like drink or smoke?' he asks. Since the newspaper report has exposed his pretensions to being an ex-war hero, and revealed that he was nothing more than a lieutenant in charge of a small supply depot, the Major drops his façade, and in a moving confession, which Rattigan clearly invested with many of his own deepest feelings, tries to explain how he reached his pathetic state:

> 'You wouldn't guess, I know, but ever since school I've always been scared to death of women. Of everyone, in a way, I suppose, but mostly of women, I had a bad time at school—which wasn't Wellington, of course—just a council school. Boys hate other boys to be timid and shy, and they gave it to me good and proper. My father despised me, too. He was a sergeant-major in the Black Watch. He made me join the Army, but I was always a bitter disappointment to him ...'
> [Getting his commission during the war was the one success of his life:] 'It meant everything to me ... Being saluted, being called sir—I thought I'm someone now, a real person. Perhaps some woman might even—(He stops.) But it didn't work. It never has worked. I'm made in a certain way, and I can't change it ...'

Sibyl is the first person he has ever talked to in this way. He supposes they have drifted together in the hotel because they are fundamentally alike: '... We're both of us frightened of people, and yet we've somehow managed to forget our fright when we've been in each other's company.' He has told lies about himself because he doesn't like himself as he is and so has had to invent a new person.

The Major is eventually encouraged to overcome his fear, risk the hostility of his fellow guests and stay on in the hotel. His possible salvation lies in the fact that his façade is now exposed and he will have to live among his fellow guests as himself. Finally the Major takes his place in the dining room with the other residents at dinner. His entrance is greeted with a shocked silence. Slowly, one by one, each guest acknowledges him. Finally, Mrs Railton-Bell, who has been glorying in her 'victory', is isolated. Standing up, she orders her daughter to leave the dining room with her, but Sibyl[7] also acknowledges the Major and refuses to leave. This tiny public gesture of defiance brings the curtain down on a note of triumph for humanity over repression and prejudice.

After a short provincial tour, *Separate Tables* opened at the St James's Theatre on 22 September 1954. It was presented by Rattigan's friend Stephen Mitchell, who had put on *Playbill*. Like *Playbill*, *Separate Tables* was directed by Peter Glenville and starred Eric Portman and Margaret Leighton. After the first night, Rattigan took Jean Dawnay backstage to meet her, and introduced her to Margaret Leighton by saying that she was the original for the character of Anne Shankland. As Jean Dawnay dropped out of Rattigan's life during the next few years, it was Margaret Leighton who took her place.

Separate Tables was an enormous success. 726 performances in London were followed by 322 when the same production was transferred to New York in 1956. The glowing London reviews, which were liberally sprinkled with words like 'dazzling', 'masterly' and 'triumph', were, for once, matched by those in New York. But even though *Separate Tables* was a success, Rattigan's own creation of Aunt Edna was called forth by reviewers to chastise him. The critic of *The Times* blamed his subservience to her for the 'faint streak of falsity' he found, particularly in the play's ending. Kenneth Tynan wrote his review in the *Observer* as an imaginary conversation between Aunt Edna and a Young Perfectionist. After the Young Perfectionist has explained the plots, Aunt Edna comments:

'I knew I was wrong when I applauded *The Deep Blue Sea*. And what conclusion does Mr Rattigan draw from these squalid anecdotes?'

YOUNG PERFECTIONIST: From the first that love unbridled is a destroyer. From the second that love bridled is a destroyer. You will enjoy yourself.

AUNT EDNA: But I go to the theatre to be taken out of myself!

Aunt Edna suspects that the Young Perfectionist is a bit 'peeky' and asks what is biting him:

Y.P.:   Since you ask, I regretted the Major's crime was not something more cathartic than a mere cinema flirtation. Yet I suppose the play is as good a handling of sexual abnormality as English playgoers will tolerate.

A.E.:   For my part, I am glad it is no better.

Y.P.:   I guessed you would be; and so did Mr Rattigan. Will you accompany me on a second visit tomorrow?

A.E.:   With great pleasure. Clearly, there is something here for both of us.

Y.P.:   Yes. But not quite enough for either of us.

Notes

1   Roger Machell in interview with Holly Hill, August 1975.

2   Rattigan in a BBC Radio Four interview with Derek Hart, recorded on 26 November 1969.

3   Rattigan, in an interview with Arthur Gelb, *New York Times*, 21 October 1956.

4   It took the best-known defendant in the case years to live it down, but happily he has now returned to public life and the scandal is completely forgotten.

5   Interview with Arthur Gelb, *New York Times*, 21 October 1956.

6   'Rattigan talks to John Simon', *Theatre Arts*, April 1962.

7   Rattigan's choice of the name Sibyl, despite the spelling, was almost certainly intended as a compliment to Sybil Thorndike for her role in the incident which originally inspired the play.

15
Variations on a Theme

Writing of the dangers of early success a few months after the opening of *Separate Tables*, Harold Hobson in the *Sunday Times* said that only in exceptional cases was it not damaging. 'One of them, the most illustrious, is Mr Rattigan. Mr Rattigan began with a huge popular success. This success made my predecessor [James Agate] gravely uneasy. It need not have done. Mr Rattigan could hardly have developed finer qualities if, in his early days, he had been as viciously attacked as Ibsen.'[1] Perhaps Hobson spoke too soon. Nineteen years were to elapse between the production of *Separate Tables* and the London presentation of a new Rattigan play of comparable quality.

The reasons for this are complex—partly the result of the position Rattigan had worked himself into personally and professionally by the mid 1950s, and partly the result of changes which were going on in the outside world and the theatre alike. What happened in the theatre between 1955 and 1958 was in one sense a reaction to Rattigan's run of uninterrupted success. Starting with *Flare Path* in 1942, Rattigan had had ten new plays produced in twelve years. All but two of these had been big commercial successes, and six of them had been greeted with reviews that ranged from favourable to ecstatic. A reaction was inevitable. But Rattigan, whose fulfilment was so dependent on theatrical success that he was one of the writers least able to withstand critical disapproval, was almost totally unprepared for a critical onslaught. Worse, he had armed his future attackers, and aligned himself with their enemies, by his articles on the Play of Ideas and the creation of Aunt Edna. Worst of all, the creative and personal consequences of his years of crisis had led him to court fashionable society and surround himself with sexually congenial but intellectually inferior sycophants, and in the process had cut himself off from intellectually rigorous companionship and the vital forces at work in the arts. Rattigan had once been a radical; he was still a liberal humanist, but very soon no one under forty would believe it. In 1955, in 'The Lost Art of Bad Drama', Kenneth Tynan wrote that 'Mr Rattigan is the Formosa of the contemporary theatre, occupied by the old guard, but geographically inclined towards the progressives.' Like Formosa, he was about to become completely isolated; an embarrassing reminder of an old regime whose previous services were forgotten or derided in a world of changed alliances.

In 1955 the straws were already in the wind. The verse revival had started to wilt as quickly as it had bloomed. T. S. Eliot and John Whiting were seen as at best minority playwrights, and the view that verse drama was nothing more than a new way of disguising old trivialities had gained ground; 'the era of Fry' was short-lived. Coward seemed finished. Of the younger men, Ustinov was clever but so far little more; Dennis Cannan looked interesting rather than revolutionary, and had in any case not produced enough work for any conclusions to be drawn; in meagre times N. C. Hunter was over-encouraged on the evidence of some subfusc Chekhovian imitation. Alan Melville, Wynyard Browne and Warren Chetham Strode were workmanlike but no more. Hope for the serious theatre rested with Rattigan. Looking back three years later, Kenneth Tynan recalled: 'The climate on the whole was listless. We quarrelled among ourselves over Brecht and the future of poetic drama; in debate with foreign visitors we crossed our fingers, swallowed hard and talked of Terence Rattigan; but if we were critics, we must quite often have felt that we were practising our art in a vacuum.'[2] Tynan was not alone in crossing his fingers over Rattigan. Increasingly, commentators on the theatre asked what he would do next. They noted that he was now in his forties; it was the next decade that would decide whether he was more than a supremely competent craftsman.

After the output of the previous twelve years Rattigan needed a mental breather. His energies were diverted into less worthwhile—but better-paid—film work, partly because of the need to keep himself and his increasingly demanding entourage in the style to which they had become accustomed.

Despite his long run of successes Rattigan was still pathetically insecure. He told friends of an elaborate fantasy of his in which he is dying in poverty in a single London room. Summoned to the home in Brighton of Sir Jeremy Spencer, the director of the National Theatre (Jeremy Spenser was the young actor who played the boy-king in *The Sleeping Prince*) to discuss the possible revival of one of his plays, Rattigan spends his last few shillings on the rail fare to Brighton. He arrives at Sir Jeremy's house only to discover that Sir Jeremy has forgotten all about their meeting. Rattigan is left destitute in the streets of Brighton, not having even the money to get himself back to his London attic.

Immediately after the London opening of *Separate Tables* Rattigan went to Paris to work with Anatole Litvak on the film version of *The Deep Blue Sea*. Litvak was an intense, determined man and the working relationship was not at all like the relaxed days Rattigan spent with Puffin Asquith. Worse, the film was to be the first made in Britain in Cinemascope, a wholly unsuitable format for a claustrophobic drama played out in a dingy flat. And almost every change that Litvak wanted weakened the original play.

One evening, Rattigan was sitting alone drinking in the Boeuf sur le Toit, off the Champs Elysées—a favoured meeting place of Paris intellectuals as well as a stylish rendezvous for homosexuals—when a fair-haired young Englishman approached him: 'You're Terence Rattigan, aren't you?' Lonely and dispirited, Rattigan was glad of someone to talk to and invited him to sit down. Although he didn't recognize him, Rattigan had met Adrian Brown two years previously when he had sat next to him at an Oxford 'smoker'; Brown had since joined the Marquis de Cuevas Ballet Company, which was appearing in Paris. Although Brown was a lot brighter than many of Rattigan's young men he conformed physically to the Rattigan type: small, neat, fair and bright-eyed. Rattigan told him he was very pretty and Brown replied that so was he. Rattigan asked Adrian Brown which of his plays he liked best. When Brown replied, '*Adventure*

Story', Rattigan was very pleased. In spite of the tie with Michael Franklin, a relationship now started which lasted on and off for four years.

When he returned to London from 'being Litvak'd' in Paris, Rattigan faced a crisis on the film of *The Deep Blue Sea*. At a pre-shooting conference with Alexander Korda, Litvak and Vivien Leigh (who was playing Hester), Kenneth More blew up and said, 'Gentlemen, we can't start this film. The script is no good.' Litvak seemed astonished, but before anyone could intervene More pressed on, and with some justification. 'Frankly the trouble with the script is that there's too much Litvak in it and not enough Rattigan.'[3] Rattigan tried to calm him down, but More wasn't going to be silenced: 'I'd almost go so far as to say that all Rattigan has come out and all Litvak has gone in.' 'Oh, that's not true!' lied Rattigan loyally. 'Litvak and I spent months in Paris preparing this script. I was leaning over his shoulder the whole time.'

Once Korda had cooled things down, he took More on one side and told him not to make any further trouble. Litvak was able to go ahead shooting his version of *The Deep Blue Sea*, but it remained, in spite of valiant performances from More and Vivien Leigh, a grotesque exaggeration of the original play. With the film under way Rattigan flew off on a triumphal tour of Australia, giving interviews, attending packed gala performances of his plays and cheered by audiences calling 'Author'. Rattigan then flew on in mid-April for a few days' recuperation in Singapore, before returning to London via the Middle East, where he announced he would do some background work for a film he wanted to script about Lawrence of Arabia. Rattigan's interest in T. E. Lawrence went back to his early childhood, the time his family spent in Cairo before the First World War and his father's stories about his friendship with Ronald Storrs. His interest was quickened by the publication that year of Lawrence's long-suppressed reminiscences of his life in the RAF called *The Mint*. These were a frank account of life among the other ranks during the time he spent trying to hide his identity as an ordinary aircraftman under the assumed name of Ross. They raised again the never satisfactorily resolved enigma of why Lawrence, having achieved legendary fame during his leadership of the Arab Revolt, should after the war have sought anonymity. It was a question that fascinated Rattigan. He and Puffin Asquith wanted to set up an epic film which would tell Lawrence's story and throw light on the mystery. Work on the film script continued slowly over the next two years.

That autumn, while Rattigan himself still had no new play of his own on the stocks, a new play by Samuel Beckett opened at the Arts Theatre, directed by a young man recently down from Cambridge, Peter Hall. The play, *Waiting for Godot*, immediately became the subject of heated debate and soon transferred to the Criterion, where Rattigan had enjoyed his own first success. Its stark allegorical quality, posing fundamental philosophical questions of meaning, life and death, pain and purpose, destiny and God, without any conventional plot, divided critical opinion. To many, especially the younger generation, it seemed to offer hope of a new, more adult theatre. Many of the old guard dismissed it as rubbish. One of these was Rattigan's friend John Gielgud, who said simply that he didn't understand it and couldn't see therefore that it was important. Rattigan himself hurried along to see it.

Shortly afterwards, an article by Rattigan was published in the *New Statesman*, headed 'The Arts and Entertainment. Aunt Edna Waits for Godot'.[4] It took the form of a conversation between Aunt Edna and her nephew immediately after they have seen a performance of the play. Although the quality was essentially light (it is a good deal wittier than the original Preface in which he had introduced Aunt Edna), Rattigan took the opportunity to correct misapprehensions about Aunt Edna's tastes and to modify some of the more extreme views he expressed about the dominance of popular taste in the Prefaces. He represented Aunt Edna as very cross because the critics had told her she wouldn't like the play. To her nephew's surprise she tells him she has enjoyed her evening very much—not the play, but

'the evening. There's a big difference. How could I like the play, seeing that Mr Samuel Beckett plainly hates me so much that he's refused point blank to give me a play at all?' [But, she says, Mr Beckett is making a great mistake to hate her:] 'If he didn't he might have written a very good play indeed. I suppose he's a highbrow but even a middlebrow like myself could have told him that a really good play had to be on two levels, an upper one, which I suppose you'd call symbolical, and a lower one, which is based on story and character. By writing on the upper level alone, all Mr Beckett has done is to produce one of those things that thirty years ago we used to call Experimental Drama—you wouldn't remember that, of course, and that's a movement which led absolutely nowhere ...'

One of the reasons that Rattigan had time enough to advise Samuel Beckett on how to write his plays but no time to get down to a new one of his own was that he had become involved in an extraordinary series of events which would lead eventually to his scripting a film starring Marilyn Monroe and Laurence Olivier, from his play *The Sleeping Prince*. One afternoon in September 1955, the telephone had rung in his Sunningdale home just as he was about to go out for a round of golf. It was a call from William Wyler in Hollywood. 'Terry, we'd like you to come over here to discuss making a film of your play *The Sleeping Prince*. We're planning to star Marilyn Monroe. Laurence Olivier would probably take the part he played in the theatre. When could you fly here to have a word about all this?' 'How long would I have to stay?' 'Oh, we could tie up most of the loose ends in a couple of days.'[5] At this time, although Rattigan had of course heard of her, he had never seen Marilyn Monroe act. Although a number of his friends had suggested that Monroe was a much better comedienne than she was generally given credit for, the idea of Olivier agreeing to team up with the screen's biggest sex symbol seemed bizarre. Rattigan was fairly certain that Olivier had not yet been approached and he thought it unlikely that he would agree. However, he agreed to fly out the following Thursday. The thing that really persuaded him was that he knew the Ryder Cup golf match was due to be played the following weekend at Palm Springs, and an all-expenses-paid trip to Hollywood would give him the chance of going to it.

Arriving in New York on the first leg of the journey, he had a ten-hour wait at Idlewild Airport. As he followed a stewardess into the International Transit Lounge, a man approached him. 'Are you Mr Rattigan, sir?' he asked. Rattigan acknowledged that he was. 'I have a message from Miss Marilyn Monroe. She'd be happy if you'd take cocktails with her in the Barberry Room at 4.30 this afternoon.' Rattigan recalled: 'I imagine that to most people that news would have been electrifying. I'm afraid it wasn't to me.' After keeping him waiting for an hour in the Barberry Room, Monroe swept in, wearing dark glasses, followed by a posse of agents, lawyers and advisers. She bought him a stiff cocktail, his fourth, and after the formalities got down to business. This was made difficult by the fact that Monroe's quiet, shy manner meant he only understood about every third word she said, while she appeared to understand nothing at all that he said. However, he grasped the central points—if no definite offer materialized from Wyler's company she would buy the rights. The terms she was talking were in multiples of hundreds of thousands of dollars rather than tens of thousands. She was prepared to write out a contract on the bar table there and then. She had by now removed her dark glasses. She gazed straight into Rattigan's eyes and asked with that distinctive quality of knowing innocence: 'Do you think there's a chance that Sir Larry would do it with me?' Rattigan felt unable to say anything other than that he was sure he would. Indeed, he went so far as to assure her that he would leave no stone unturned to see that he did. Rattigan went on to Hollywood, saw Wyler and the Ryder Cup, then, returning, saw Wyler's producers and found there was still no definite offer forthcoming. On the way back through New York he phoned Marilyn Monroe and told her the rights were hers.

For the next few months Rattigan boasted that he was employed by Marilyn Monroe, but such large sums of money, as Rattigan must by now have known, do not come without problems. Any new work had to be put off indefinitely. There were endless problems over the screenplay. Arthur Miller, Marilyn Monroe's husband, thought it excellent, but Milton Greene, her business partner, wanted extensive changes. Olivier had views of his own, too. The film was announced to the public at a press conference in New York on 9 February 1956, at which Rattigan appeared on the platform to pose for the photographers with Olivier, Greene and Marilyn. When she appeared she was wearing a very low-cut black sheath dress. She left no one in any doubt about who was the centre of attention. At a strategic moment one of the dress's shoulder straps obligingly broke and a journalist was called upon to supply a safety pin to save the dignity of the occasion. During the rest of the conference, Monroe made it clear who was the boss, although Olivier was billed as the film's director. She said a number of times that she 'owned' the play. From this point Rattigan seems to have been left out of any discussions on the script, but to have written scenes to order as required.

In July, Marilyn Monroe arrived in England with Arthur Miller amid much hullabaloo. They went to stay in supposedly quiet seclusion in a house only a few miles from Rattigan's at Sunningdale. Rattigan threw perhaps the grandest of all his grand parties to welcome them. At the start everyone lined up to meet Marilyn, who was dressed in an Edwardian costume she had worn for the tests for the film. She and her husband more or less held court in an arbour in the garden while all the great names of the theatre waited patiently to be introduced. As the guests started to drift away at the end of the long evening, Rattigan and Marilyn were still waltzing exquisitely in the room which had been turned into a ballroom. It had been a party worthy of his great mentor, Chips Channon. This was the public image of Rattigan at the height of his wealth and fame, exquisitely turned out, host to the great and the beautiful, doing everything he attempted with seemingly effortless grace.

It was, however, an illusion, and one that was on the point of being rudely shattered. The filming of *The Prince and the Showgirl*, as the play was retitled, dragged on through months of widely publicized disputes and acrimony. When it was released a year later it was less than a success, in spite of the column yards of publicity that it received around the world. But by then an event of more significance for Rattigan's future had occurred.

On 8 May 1956, while he was still preoccupied with Marilyn Monroe's script, a new play had opened almost unheralded at the Royal Court Theatre, recently taken over by the English Stage Company and run by George Devine, Mercutio in the Gielgud production of *Romeo and Juliet* at Oxford. Rattigan was at the first night of *Look Back in Anger*, by a then unknown young actor, John Osborne. He had gone with Binkie Beaumont. In the first interval he bumped into his friend, the critic T. C. Worsley, in the bar. 'Marvellous, isn't it?' said Worsley. Rattigan and Beaumont clearly didn't think so; they were planning to leave. Worsley persuaded Rattigan to stay to the end, but Beaumont left. Afterwards he and Worsley had a violent row about the merits of the play, Worsley arguing that this play would be seen as one of the great events of the period, Rattigan conceding only that it was quite well written; it was badly constructed and he couldn't see what there was for Jimmy Porter to look back in anger about. At the end of the performance a *Daily Express* reporter had asked him what he thought of the play, and Rattigan had said that this young man, Osborne, was simply sitting there saying 'Look, Ma, I'm not Terence Rattigan.' This remark was duly reported and, as interest in the play mounted, the press started to create a largely false, but very damaging, contrast, first between Rattigan and Osborne and then between Rattigan and all the 'New Wave' playwrights who followed in Osborne's wake. Journalists seem to report all news, even developments in the theatre, in terms of personal conflict—so Rattigan *v.* Osborne and the New Wave came to be believed in, even though the battle scarcely existed in the minds of the supposed combatants, and in spite of Rattigan's repeated corrections of that hasty first-night statement. Although he disagreed with much of what Osborne was saying and his way of saying it, Rattigan much admired his use of language and had sympathy for much of what he stood for. Rattigan had not completely forgotten that he too had once been an angry young man. As for Osborne, Rattigan was never a specific target. He represented what he called 'the pale side of the establishment'; if they were going to sweep the establishment away, then he would be one of the casualties. Osborne and his friends resented much more someone like Noël Coward, who they saw as a decadent show-business butterfly, the epitome of the vulgarity and conservative narrow-mindedness they associated with Binkie Beaumont and the West End.

The important point about *Look Back in Anger* was that, as Kenneth Tynan said, it lanced a boil which had been coming to a head for some years. The post-war generation had at last burst triumphantly on to the stage, and, through Jimmy Porter, John Osborne articulated their long-pent-up attitudes. It was invigorating to go into a theatre and hear not the decorously modulated tones of yet another damp young man from RADA, but the vigorous rough-edged roar of Kenneth Haigh, as Jimmy, spitting out with uncompromising and nerve-tingling venom the thoughts the new generation had long nursed but could never hope to express with such élan.

But the revolution did not come about all at once. It took time to gather momentum, and four months later Rattigan was apparently still completely unaware of the threat to him. That autumn he wrote an appreciation of Noël Coward, making ample amends for his dismissive undergraduate criticism of *Cavalcade*. Hitherto he had been careful to dissociate himself from Coward, pointing to the differences in their style and subject matter, and reminding people that Coward belonged to the generation before his. Rattigan's foreword to *The Theatrical Companion to Noël Coward* helped prompt the indiscriminate coupling of their names in the attacks of the ensuing years. In an article in the *New York Times*, Rattigan again attacked Shaw, adding the name of Brecht, whose work had just been presented in London for the first time by the Berliner Ensemble.[6]

That autumn, which split Britain over the Suez crisis and offered a sight he would once have welcomed, that of crowds demonstrating in their thousands against a British government's use of armed force, Rattigan was in America. *Separate Tables* and *The Sleeping Prince* were due to open almost simultaneously on Broadway at the end of October. He took his secretary, Mary Herring, with him to help deal with the flood of offers, press interviews and complex hotel and travel arrangements involved in trying to keep track of two productions which were 'on the road' to Broadway at the same time. Basing himself and his mother, whom he showed off proudly to American journalists, in a plush suite at the Ambassador in New York, he shuttled back and forth between Philadelphia, Princeton, Boston and New York, often uncertain which town he was supposed to be in, when, or for which play. He explained to Emory Lewis of *Cue* magazine: 'I'm never quite sure which I'm working on. I think I've changed the second act of one of them in Boston and it turns out to be the other play. I ask my faithful secretary, Miss Herring, where we are to go each morning—north or south. I'll never open with two efforts again. We had to bring over *The Sleeping Prince* now, because of contractual arrangements with Miss Marilyn Monroe ...'[7]

After returning briefly to London for Christmas, Rattigan flew out again to Hollywood to write scripts for *Separate Tables* and a projected screen version of *Love in Idleness*. In Beverley Hills, he shared a house with Rex Harrison. This was shortly after Harrison had heard that Kay Kendall had terminal leukaemia,

242

but was still desperately trying to conceal from her the seriousness of her condition. Rattigan gave Harrison a lot of sympathetic support over the ensuing months as Kay Kendall grew progressively weaker.[8]

This was Rattigan's first sustained dose of Hollywood and he hated what he called 'the swimming pool and star-value protocol general hysteria'—the way in which people were valued by the size, shape and depth of their swimming pool, the size of their contract and whether they were judged to be going up or down. The continuous parties, not something he normally objected to, irritated him too, because the guest lists were always drawn up on the basis of the same star protocol. 'They started at 7.30 but there was never any food before 10', by which time, he objected, everyone was 'fried' with highballs. Domestic arrangements were another problem. Harrison hired them a temporary cook. Before she arrived, she phoned to say that she had just bought a Cadillac and was worried about driving it up the steep hill to their house, so could they send their chauffeur to drive it up for her. Harrison went down and drove it up himself—he had no chauffeur. Next day the girl packed the job in. Finally, they found two other servants, both black girls: a cook called Hester and a housemaid called Patsy. But what upset Rattigan most was the way in which he was expected to work. The interminable story conferences and general hysteria had depressed him, he told a reporter when he arrived back in Europe. 'The first thing they always do is hand out tranquillizers—little pills that keep you working and keep your temper. The desks are piled with them—all colours, sizes, shapes. The consumption is fantastic.'[9]

In six weeks he had written only forty-five pages. In spite of offers to stay in Hollywood, totalling more than £200,000 for four scripts over seven years, he sailed home on the *Queen Mary* in disgust. He was not going to do hack work in front of a heated swimming pool, even at that price. In future he would work from the calm of his own home. Nor was he going to move out of England to a tax haven, as Noël Coward and some British film stars had done. He announced repeatedly that living in England mattered to him and if the privilege of doing so was expensive, so be it.

Work on his scripts for the films of *Separate Tables* and the Lawrence story took several more months, but by the summer of

1957 Rattigan had settled down to writing a new play. He had earned £100,000 in the preceding year, most of it from films, but he told his friends that he hated the cinema and intended to do no more for at least three years. After toying with a play based on issues raised by the Christie murder case (tentatively called *Man and Boy*, it seems) he opted for a modern reworking, based on recent episodes from his own life, of Dumas' *La Dame aux Camélias*. *Variation on a Theme*, the title Rattigan gave the play, was dedicated to Margaret Leighton and written with her in mind as its star. In fact, the play comes very close in places to paralleling events in Margaret Leighton's own recent life. Rattigan and she had become very close as a result of *Separate Tables*. Many people who knew them both said that she would have gladly married him if he had asked her, at least after she had got over Laurence Harvey. Rattigan's mother certainly seems to have entertained hopes of a match.

In *Variation on a Theme*, Rattigan's Marguerite Gautier is Rose Fish, who unlike Marguerite has married her men rather than merely being kept by them. Already wealthy as a result of three good marriages, she is about to marry a rich German banker, but falls for Ron, a young ballet dancer even more unscrupulous than herself. Ron bends his sexual tastes to suit his needs. When Rose meets him he is living with a homosexual choreographer, who is keeping him; seeing the prospect of an easier and even more luxurious life as Rose's lover, he makes a successful pass at her. Problems arise when they realize that they have really fallen for each other and cannot bear to live apart, no matter what it may cost them in wealth, health or even happiness. Like so many Rattigan lovers, they are a bad match, quarrelling and hurting each other despite being drawn irrevocably together. By leaving the choreographer for Rose, Ron forfeits advancement in his career. By taking Ron as her lover, Rose loses both her German banker and eventually her life, since she is, like Marguerite Gautier, a consumptive and has been told by her doctors that she must live in an expensive Swiss sanatorium.

Rose Fish's experience paralleled Margaret Leighton's in that when she fell for Laurence Harvey he was being kept by a film producer, who had been responsible for making him a film star. Much about Harvey's courtship of Margaret Leighton, which had started when he was a young actor at Stratford and she was already a star, is reminiscent of the cheeky, calculating way in which Ron thrusts himself on the attention of Rose. Ron, having fallen in love with Rose in spite of himself, hesitates before leaving the choreographer for her. Harvey hesitated before leaving the protection of the film producer and marrying Margaret Leighton. When they did marry, it was a short-lived disaster, as Rattigan and many other friends had predicted. Rattigan hated Harvey for the way he treated Margaret Leighton, although he probably also pitied him for the weaknesses that led to his vanity and posturing. He thought little of Harvey's talent either, and Ron is depicted as self-centred and worthless, confusing money with talent, a second-rank dancer whose success was not due to ability or real love of ballet, but to being kept at it by the hard-working and devoted choreographer who had promoted him. Like Laurence Harvey, Ron Vale has changed his name (he dances as Anton Valov) and romanticized his origins.

Much though the plot and characters owe to Dumas and the Harvey-Leighton affair, *Variation on a Theme* owes still more to Rattigan's own experience. He said while he was writing it that he intended to 'blow up the Establishment', and that he expected to have trouble with the censor because of the frankness of his material. In the autumn of 1957, the Wolfenden Committee made its eagerly awaited report, advocating reform of the law relating to homosexuals and the abolition of penalties for sexual acts in private between consenting adult males. The Report is actually alluded to in the text and it seems probable that Rattigan hoped, in keeping with the mood of liberal optimism which briefly prevailed, that he might be able to write a frankly homosexual play which would perform some of the functions of a confession. In the event, neither the public climate nor the cast of his own creative mind permitted such a thing.

Adrian Brown who, it will be remembered, had begun a relationship with Rattigan late in 1954, is in no doubt that Rose Fish is to be taken as a self-portrait of Rattigan and that Ron Vale is an amalgam of himself and others. Kurt Mast, the German banker, can be taken both as representative of the wealthy protectors in Rattigan's own past, particularly Chips Channon, and of the wealthy employers, particularly in the film industry, for whose ample cheques Rattigan often felt he prostituted his talent. When Rose finally deserts Kurt for a life of poverty and discomfort with Ron—significantly they will have to live off his comparatively meagre earnings from the theatre—one senses that Rattigan is not only following the dictates of Dumas' story, but symbolizing his own desire to turn his back on Hollywood and devote himself to the theatre.

Rattigan's choice of names for characters is often significant, but nowhere more so than in *Variation on a Theme*. There is actually a minor character called Adrian, a gigolo whose wealthy lady patron is pointedly called Mona. Rattigan's friends would undoubtedly have enjoyed the joke. They would also have recognized his self-projection in Rose Fish. 'Fish' has allusive undertones in Rattigan.[10] Sir Robert Morton, the defence lawyer in *The Winslow Boy*, who seemed incapable of the personal feeling that Rattigan identified with himself, was described as 'a fish' and as 'fishy hearted'. Rose too seems unfeeling, keeping herself above emotional involvement in single-minded pursuit of the main chance. When she meets Ron, it is only slowly revealed that what she really craves is real love. Much of the play charts her struggle with her desire to abandon herself to her feelings. Adrian Brown had found Rattigan like Rose, in that he had a strong desire to be loved, both emotionally and physically, but found difficulty in reciprocating. The idea of himself romanticized into a latter-day Marguerite Gautier was both appropriate and pathetic: appropriate because of his increasingly pity-seeking hypochondria, which made him prone to striking attitudes in private which were in keeping with the nineteenth-century dying heroine; pathetic because of the implied self-disgust. Like Rose, Rattigan was drawn to, though not of course exclusively, 'the bad boys'—the ones he knew were worthless, who he knew would use him, were likely to behave embarrassingly, make scenes and demand money.

When Adrian Brown (not one of Rattigan's 'bad boys') first met Rattigan he was a minor ballet dancer, who had directed while at Oxford and had ambitions to get back into the legitimate theatre as a director. Subsequently, Rattigan made him an allowance to go back to London and start making his way as a director. Within a few years he was directing plays in the West End, and is now a respected television and opera director. But when he was first taken up by Rattigan as a young man, he was dazzled by the circle he suddenly entered—dinner with Gielgud, lunch with Robert Graves, names he had hitherto only admired from afar. In such superficial respects—being a ballet dancer and his obvious wonder at Rose's life and friends—Ron Vale is very like Adrian Brown. Also, known to Rattigan but almost no one else, Adrian Brown's actual first name was Ron. However, in other respects Ron Vale and Adrian Brown are different. The feeling between Adrian Brown and Rattigan was never very intense; there were not the scenes and recriminations of the play. Here Rattigan is drawing on other relationships, those with Ken Morgan and others. At one point Ron Vale threatens to go off with another, wealthier woman in order to make Rose jealous. One of Rattigan's young men had calculatingly played him off against Ivor Novello by moving back and forth between the two. Ken Morgan had led Rattigan a painful dance by his infidelities.

Michael Franklin, who was known somewhat disparagingly as 'The Midget' by people around Rattigan, became almost universally disliked among those friends because, they alleged, he repaid generosity and affection with ingratitude. Yet Rattigan persisted in the relationship. Franklin must have been jealous because of Adrian Brown's arrival on the scene, and Rattigan probably made more allowances for this than some of his friends. Adrian Brown is not alone in claiming that Franklin turned up on numerous occasions to throw tantrums. In Ron Vale, Rattigan fashioned a character who was an amalgam of many people he had known, and who perhaps even owed something to his own treatment of Chips Channon. In the play, the worse Ron behaves, the more Rose feels for him. However much he may hurt or embarrass her, she recognizes in his jealousy the love that she so desperately craves. In his own relationships Rattigan had felt the same. His relationship with Michael Franklin, despite the massive and vocal disapproval of his friends, lasted for the rest of his life. Rattigan himself was disparaging about Franklin but, although he often didn't see him for long intervals, he never deserted him. Ken Morgan's suicide had bitten deep. Rattigan also created two people who loved Ron—Rose, and Sam Duveen, his homosexual choreographer patron, who before he leaves him describes what it has been like loving someone who needs people but is himself incapable of real love: 'You don't seem to understand that the Rons of this world always end by hating the people they need. They can't help it. It's compulsive. Of course it probably isn't

plain hate. It's love-hate, or hate-love, or some other Freudian jargon—but it's still a pretty good imitation of the real thing ...'
In the play Sam learns from his experience with Ron not to make too heavy an emotional investment in one person, as Rattigan had with Ken Morgan.

In his turn Ron spits out his resentment at the way Rose keeps him in a separate compartment, divided off from the rest of her life and her high-society friends, just as Rattigan tried to keep his boys away from his 'straight' friends: 'I wonder. Have you ever thought what it's been like for me, asked over here a couple of odd evenings a week whenever there's no important people around—because common Ron mustn't meet important people—oh dear no, that'd never do ...' However unscrupulous, ungrateful or difficult his boy friends, Rattigan could still feel sympathy for them—a fact his straight friends found incomprehensible. Ron says: 'You all think I'm a proper bastard, I know, and just out for what I can get, and I dare say you may be right. But that's how I was told when I was a kid—in this world, Ron boy, they said, you got to work it so it's "F.U., Jack, I'm all right", or you go under—and Christ, Rose, that's true. Look at the people who do go under—even in this bloody Welfare world. What's so wrong in looking after oneself? You've done it all your life, haven't you? ...'

Variation on a Theme was completed in December 1957, and Rattigan dispatched a copy to Margaret Leighton, who had been playing in *Separate Tables* in New York, inviting her to play Rose Fish. She accepted with alacrity. At last, after twenty years of trying, Rattigan got Gielgud involved in the production of one of his plays by persuading him to direct it. Rehearsals began in March 1958.

The play opened at the Globe Theatre, London, to generally disastrous notices. It was not helped by what the critics agreed was a downright bad production. Far from being an iconoclastic demolition of the Establishment, as Rattigan had promised, *Variation on a Theme* seemed a pallid star-vehicle. On this occasion his usual mastery of understatement and the oblique approach had betrayed him into downright evasion. In the new climate of forthright committed theatre, the play received an even harsher handling than it merited. It seemed to epitomize the worst of the old vices. For Rattigan's reputation as a serious playwright, the timing of its appearance could not have been worse.

Tynan accused Rattigan of clumsily disguising a blatantly homosexual theme in an attempt to please both the Lord Chamberlain and Aunt Edna. Harold Hobson slaughtered both play and production under a headline which asked 'Are Things What They Seem?'[11] He had felt he was watching a play which was really about something which was not its ostensible subject. The *Manchester Guardian* said that by sliding the play's homosexual subject past the Lord Chamberlain all Rattigan had done was to emphasize its vulgarity. Only T. C. Worsley carried on a spirited defence of the play, in the *New Statesman* and the *London Magazine*. He seems on this occasion, however, to have slipped below his normally high standards as a disinterested critic. Claiming to know the lady upon whom the story was based, he accused the critics who had said it had a covert homosexual theme of 'a seamy line of personal smear'. Worsley, a close personal friend of Rattigan's who frequently travelled with him and benefited from his hospitality, certainly did know that the 'case' the play was based on was that of Margaret Leighton, although he tactfully did not reveal her name. Nor, however, did he admit to his own equally good knowledge of and involvement with the other elements of the play's background. By attacking his fellow critics in this way, while not declaring his own hand, he brought his own critical reputation and, by association, Rattigan's into unnecessary disrepute.

Immediately after the opening, Rattigan retired to Cannes to nurse his wounds among the gambling set that he had said he despised. 'I don't mind the criticisms,' he said, 'but I do wish somebody had given me credit for kicking Aunt Edna down the stairs. It would have been so easy for me to make it an Aunt Edna play, to have given the woman a heart of gold. But I purposely took the most Aunt Edna play of all time, *La Dame aux Camélias*, and showed up the characters for what they really are.'[12]

Meanwhile, back at home, even more damage was being done to his reputation by a story spread around about a schoolgirl playwright called Shelagh Delaney. It seemed that she had attended *Variation on a Theme* during the first week of its try-out in Manchester, and was so maddened by seeing her favourite actress Margaret Leighton wasting her time traipsing about in rubbish that she had gone home and written a play in a fortnight. This, *A Taste of Honey*, she sent to Joan Littlewood at Theatre Workshop, a radical theatre group in London's East End which was just gaining overdue recognition. It had gone into immediate production and opened only two weeks after *Variation on a Theme*. Rattigan's detractors could claim, with some justification, that the schoolgirl's play had the virtues that his lacked: it had honesty in place of evasion and vigour in place of tired technique. *A Taste of Honey* was a huge success and transferred to the scene of Rattigan's first triumph, the Criterion.

Rattigan was awarded the CBE in the Birthday Honours List in June, and subsequently invited to a private lunch with the Queen. But in July another blow fell. Filming of the script about T. E. Lawrence was at last about to start, after many delays. Against Rattigan's wishes, Asquith had cast Dirk Bogarde as Lawrence; Rattigan conceded that he was a good actor, but hardly right for Lawrence. In spite of repeated remarks about hating the cinema, Rattigan had always excepted his work with Asquith and he had invested a lot of effort in the script. Returning from Iraq, where they had been hunting for locations, Asquith and Anatole de Grunwald were passing through Immigration Control at London Airport when they were given a message from Rank, the production company, that the film had been abandoned. Another crisis had hit the British film industry and the £700,000 budget for the film was simply too much. Three years' work, albeit intermittent, was to be thrown away.[13] Asquith, Bogarde and Rattigan were desolate over the death of their project. It was not, however, in character for Rattigan to mope over a setback where the production of something he had written was concerned. He settled down to rewrite his film into a free-wheeling play. Like *Adventure Story*, it was an epic, covering the rise and fall of a legendary hero in a series of short scenes, but the flow was more supple and the style more appropriate to its subject. The play, *Ross*, was almost certainly better for having started life as a film.

Rattigan finished the play at 6 a.m. on 13 February 1959, the morning of the British première of the much messed-around Hollywood film of *Separate Tables*. Immediately afterwards he left on a three-month world tour, combining work and relaxation. On his way home through America he saw the CBS television broadcast of *The Browning Version* directed by John Frankenheimer, in which Gielgud had at last played the part written for him and for which he received glowing notices. In Hollywood, he turned down a lucrative offer to script a film from Nabokov's novel *Lolita*. He was sticking to his resolution to reject easy film money and honour his vocation to the theatre. He returned home aboard the *Queen Elizabeth* with Margaret Leighton, whose marriage to Laurence Harvey was by then in trouble.

Back at home, he threw himself into the work of revising and preparing *Ross* for production. Alec Guinness was to star as Lawrence and Glen Byam Shaw, who had done *The Winslow Boy*, was to direct. Extravagant scenes left over from the film version had to be cut, such as one which involved Ronald Storrs and twenty airmen in a billet with twenty beds, singing at a piano. There was trouble too with film producer Sam Spiegel who, since the dropping of the Asquith film, planned to make his own epic version of the Lawrence story and seemed to be set on preventing the production of Rattigan's play, lest it steal some of his thunder. Lawrence's brother had sold the film rights of *Seven Pillars of Wisdom* to Spiegel and would not give his permission for the representation of his brother on stage—one of the more arcane requirements of the Lord Chamberlain's office. Rattigan assured the Lord Chamberlain, however, that if he did not give his permission he would have the play done on television, over which the Lord Chamberlain had no jurisdiction. That disposed of those objections. Any possible infringement of Spiegel's copyright was circumvented when Rattigan and his lawyer approached Liddell Hart, Lawrence's biographer, and credited his 'advice' in the preparation of the play. His biography became their 'official source'. Work on the production went ahead uninterrupted.

Rattigan talked about writing a new play stemming from the death by leukaemia of Kay Kendall. He had seen a lot of Rex Harrison during the two years that Harrison had tried to keep her life as normal as possible so that she should not know she was dying. After living with Harrison in Hollywood, he had stayed with the couple in St Moritz during one of Kay's temporary rallies. Now that Kay had died, Harrison had gone to stay with Rattigan at Sunningdale. There, with the help of Harold French and his wife Peggy, Rattigan tried to help Harrison recover from his grief and two years of intense physical and emotional strain. When the press got wind of the possibility that Rattigan might write a play about Harrison and Kendall, he put out a strongly-worded denial, saying that he was not at the moment, nor would be in the foreseeable future, engaged on such a project. The idea lingered, however, and eventually did form part of the basis of one of his last and, in our view, greatest plays.

Following the failure of *Variation on a Theme* and the collapse of the Lawrence film, there had been a renewed resolution about Rattigan, a determination to tackle more difficult subjects and extend his range in the theatre. In an extraordinarily frank interview with Robert Muller, one of his fiercest critics in the Play of Ideas debate, he said that although he had made a mess of his personal life he had done what he could with his talent. His aim was what it had always been—to write a masterpiece: 'The two greatest dangers to the middle-aged playwright are sentimentality and disenchantment.' He did not intend to succumb to either. He renewed his defence of the well-made play and attacked some of the new playwrights: 'I may be old-fashioned about some of these new playwrights, but they've just got to learn their job. It's not really a help to a writer to be called a genius with his first play.' Slipping into the theatre with a farcical comedy, he could now see, had been an advantage; no one had expected anything of him and he had had a chance to learn his craft. 'If I'd started off with an angry political play I might have been called a genius, and that could have finished me.' He recalled his own political anger and being charged by the police when protesting about the Spanish Civil War. 'In the late thirties we had things to be indignant about ... Because I've always put character before ideas in my plays, people think I have no political views ... People just never think of me in that sort of way. I suppose I wear the wrong kind of clothes.' But, he pointed out, a rich writer suffered the same frustrations as a poor one and the same compulsions: 'Every playwright is compelled to write the same play over and over again. He would be dishonest if he didn't.'[14]

The interview with Muller disclosed one disquieting fact, which cast doubt on just how easy Rattigan was finding it to settle down and concentrate solely on new work for the theatre. He had agreed to collaborate with Robert Stolz, the composer of *White Horse Inn*, and Paul Dehn on a musical re-write of *French*

Without Tears. This disastrous-sounding notion seems to have been the brainchild of the all-powerful Binkie Beaumont. Muller suspected he was doing it to please Aunt Edna and concluded that 'the pull of public approbation is irresistible ...', though it seems more likely that Rattigan thought it might be an amusing and harmless way of making some money; despite his new-found resolution there was no new play he was ready to start on. Finding subjects that he believed in was becoming a problem. In the twenty years between *Variation on a Theme* and his death, he wrote only one complete stage play which was not an adaptation or reinterpretation of a well-known story.

In the spring of 1960, as the openings of both the musical (for which Rattigan had resurrected an earlier, discarded title for *French Without Tears, Joie de Vivre*) and *Ross* approached, the press seemed on the point of making a fresh and more serious evaluation of Rattigan's accomplishments as a dramatist. Articles in the *Daily Express, Daily Mail, Evening Standard* and *Manchester Guardian* all conceded that he had been too readily dismissed, and saluted the way in which, while sticking courageously to his belief in the well-made play, he had deepened his art and extended his range. The *Manchester Guardian* likened him to Molière as a dramatist who alternated between serious plays and 'occasional entertainments'. His generally left-of-centre sympathies were recognized, and it was suggested that the Royal Court would do well to respond to his stated desire to write something for them. No such invitation was forthcoming.

Rattigan said a great deal, far more than was his custom, both before and after its production, about his intentions in *Ross*. Some of it was inevitably contradictory, but the most important elements are clear. Just as he had set out in *Adventure Story* to answer the question 'Where did it first go wrong?' in respect of Alexander, so in *Ross* he searches for the 'flaw' in Lawrence which caused him, at the height of his success, to feel driven to seek anonymity in the ranks of the RAF under the name of Ross. 'Oh Ross, how did I become you?' Lawrence asks. Opening his play after the war with Lawrence masquerading as Ross, he 'flashes back' to chart his victorious progress as leader of the Arab revolt and discover the 'truth' that led his hero, who seemed so much to enjoy success, limelight and subtle showing-off, to hide himself away out of his own sense of self-disgust. The essence of Lawrence's inner life,

253

Rattigan pointed out, was contained in the *Seven Pillars of Wisdom* and consisted of persistent self-defeat throughout the crucial and outwardly victorious years. When Robert Muller had interviewed him for the *Daily Mail*, Rattigan would not reveal what had happened to change the carefree young Rattigan into the sad, disenchanted middle-aged Mr Rattigan who, while having everything he could want materially, was clearly so desolate spiritually. 'I may be a success as a writer, but as a person I am not.' All he would say was that he had put more of himself into *Ross* than he had dared in any previous play. Rattigan had settled on one incident in particular as the turning point in Lawrence's life: his capture by the Turks at Deraa, where, according to Rattigan in *Ross*, but not to Lawrence in *Seven Pillars of Wisdom* (nor to Liddell Hart), he had found sexual gratification when being beaten and homosexually assaulted. Rattigan said that anyone reading *Seven Pillars of Wisdom* would see that the man was devastated by the revelation that he had homosexual and masochistic tendencies. 'This was before Freud, you remember,' he told Frances Herridge of the *New York Post* just after the Broadway opening. 'To him it was shattering to suspect what was in the back of his tremendous will power. He couldn't live with himself. You might say he committed mind suicide, wanting to be a number in the Air Force.'[15]

Peter Glenville, Rattigan's friend from their days together at Oxford and often his director, has claimed that from his student days onwards Rattigan's major deficiency both as a playwright and as a man had been a lack of a spiritual quest or desire to confront life's higher mysteries. Defenders of *Ross* may say that to avoid the 'mysteries' in dealing with T. E. Lawrence is to avoid the cant, but surely it is a deficiency in any play which claims to be based on either Liddell Hart's biography,[16] or *Seven Pillars of Wisdom*[17] so completely to subdue the spiritual and wider philosophical questions posed by Lawrence's career, character and writing. Liddell Hart, pointing out that what most astonished the public was Lawrence's disregard of the pleasures that ordinary men pursue, found no great mystery in self-immolation in the RAF, which he likened to medieval man's choice of the monastic life. 'The drab mind instinctively seeks a colourful explanation of the simple,' he said.

After a short pre-West End tour the play opened at the

Theatre Royal, Haymarket. This was a large theatre, but the play enjoyed a longer run than any of Rattigan's serious plays.[18] The critics praised the play as more than a magnificent piece of story-telling and economic stagecraft. 'It is long since I remember a new play that has been more enthralling in the theatre, or that is likely to start more discussion outside,' wrote J. C. Trewin in *The Lady* of 26 May 1960. Kenneth Tynan did not catch up with the play until Sir Alec Guinness had left the show and the part of Lawrence was taken over by Michael Bryant. He then wrote a scathing review: 'For the second time in his career (*Adventure Story* was the first), Mr Rattigan shows us a conquering hero who is stopped dead in his tracks by a revelation of sexual abnormality somewhere east of Suez.' He continued: 'But my main objection to *Ross* is not that its view of history is petty and blinkered; so, it might be urged, is Shakespeare's in *Henry V*. What clinches my distaste is its verbal aridity, its flatness of phrase, and above all—its pat reliance on the same antithetical device in moments of crisis.' Tynan went on to list examples of a device Rattigan had used from the start of his career. To take just two examples from Tynan's eight: ' "And is this only the beginning?" "It may be the ending too." ' and: ' "There's nothing in the world worse than self-pity." "Oh, yes there is. Self-knowledge." '[19] While the first is certainly pat, it could be argued that the second is not only an effective reply but an economical way of developing the dialogue.

In contrast to Tynan, Harold Hobson called Rattigan 'the brightest and wittiest of our dramatists', and said that by posing the central question of why Lawrence recoiled from his success he had made him into '... the uneasy spectacular symbol of the conscience of the West in the twentieth century. After both the great wars of our time the victorious powers have been assailed by feelings of guilt ...'[20]

Immediately before the West End opening of *Ross*, Rattigan had been ill. As rehearsals started he was recovering from 'flu' but was determined to be available if required. He got up too soon and, by April, with both *Ross* and *Joie de Vivre* in rehearsal, was walking between the two rehearsals at the YMCA in Tottenham Court Road and the Theatre Royal, Drury Lane. He collapsed and spent the first two weeks in May in a London clinic with virus pneumonia. His doctor ordered a complete rest and he went off to Brighton to recuperate. He fell for Brighton, and by the time *Joie de Vivre* was ready to open in London on 14 July he had taken a three-year lease on a seventh-floor flat in a block called Embassy Court. As a result of his illness he had seen little of the pre-West End tour. If he had, he might have done more to improve the play and the production. After all it was an expensive show to mount, with a cast of thirty, complicated settings, an orchestra and dancers, and he had invested quite a lot of his own money in it. Yet it was not Rattigan's way to interfere in productions, even one as inept as this was turning out to be; in any case, the director was an ex-designer friend of his, William Chappell. The reactions of provincial audiences and those at the London preview had been favourable. If Rattigan was worried at all he concealed it pretty well. That morning the papers carried splash stories, asking if Rattigan could repeat the success of the original production of *French Without Tears* with this musical reincarnation. Rattigan himself, always nervous and superstitious before a first night, was a little reluctant to say too much about the production, preferring to talk about the success of *Ross*.

The Queen's Theatre was packed with an expectant audience. Rattigan stood, outwardly relaxed and confident, looking surprisingly little aged by the twenty-four years that had elapsed since that first, much less auspicious first night. Strategically placed in the Upper Circle was Mary Herring, his secretary. The curtain went up on Monsieur Maingot's French crammer, set this time not in a small French west coast town in 1936, but in a Mediterranean sun spot in 1960. Rattigan had told Robert Muller that he was trying to 'project the middle-aged me into the youthful me', but, as Harold Hobson pointed out to him in his review, in attempting to modernize his youthful success by dragging in references to the H-bomb, swear words and references to the Royal Court's playwrights 'as if they were a compulsory allusion in an examination paper', he only achieved 'a sort of political hypocrisy, a sad effort to appear up to date'.[21]

Nevertheless, at the interval it seemed to be going quite well. W. A. Darlington, the critic of the *Daily Telegraph* and a very experienced first-nighter, was preparing to write a tolerant review saying that, although nothing like as funny as the original, the show had kept its audience reasonably well entertained.[22] But before the interval ended Mary Herring had made her way down from the Upper Circle and sought Rattigan out. 'Bad news,' she told him. 'I've heard a whisper that it's going to get the bird.' Rattigan didn't believe it. But as the show got under way again there was an indefinable, but tangible, air of tension in the theatre. Then it happened. The line 'It isn't funny—it's a bloody tragedy' was greeted with roars of agreement. The unkind laughs and the rhythmic rounds of applause mounted. The curtain calls were clearly going to be a disaster. Darlington, who had been to many disastrous first nights, was convinced that this wasn't a prearranged demonstration but a spontaneous reaction from the audience. In the view of Harold Hobson, one of Rattigan's most consistent advocates, their disapproval was well merited—there was something both 'peculiarly revolting' and 'pathetic' about the show. Rattigan's first reaction was to feel terribly sorry. As the jeering continued, his surprise quickly turned to resignation. He looked at William Chappell beside him, and then walked out of the theatre and round to the stage door. Behind the set he called together the stage management and those members of the cast who were waiting for their cues and said firmly, 'They're going to give it to us, so no special calls. Bring the curtain down and keep it down.' The final curtain was almost on them. When it fell, there was a storm of booing. It did not rise again, and when the house lights went up the audience slowly picked their way out of the theatre in a disordered daze.

Next morning, Rattigan sat among the debris of the grim first-night party in his Eaton Square flat and faced a reporter from a London evening paper, who was eager to know how the man who had known nothing but success was taking failure. He was not believed when he said he had known worse moments. His main concern was for the cast: 'Poor darlings. I felt so sorry for them.'[23] That afternoon, putting a brave face on what had happened, he climbed into his Rolls-Royce and was driven to Ascot Races. There, no one mentioned the play at all: 'It's odd,' he mused, 'they all behaved as though my mother had just died. Most peculiar.' That afternoon he backed more losers than winners.

On Saturday night, after four performances, *Joie de Vivre* closed. In his scathing notice next day, Harold Hobson nevertheless concluded by saying that though bruised in spirit and flushed with embarrassment, he was left 'brooding over the extraordinary talent of Mr Rattigan. Here is a man who has a greater sense of the theatre than any of his contemporaries except Jean Anouilh, a man who, lacking only the fertilising flood of words, can be witty or touching, or, as in *Ross*, delicately and penetratingly perceptive in dangerous quarters of the human spirit. In the thirties several dramatists of promise appeared, Ronald Mackenzie, J. B. Priestley, W. H. Auden, and Mr Rattigan himself. What has become of them? Mackenzie died. At some time in his career Mr Priestley became a politician and Auden a professor. Only Rattigan remains ...'[24]

Notes

1 *Sunday Times*, 2 January 1955.

2 *Curtains*, by Kenneth Tynan, Longmans, 1961.

3 *Happy Go Lucky*, by Kenneth More, Robert Hale Ltd, London, 1959.

4 *New Statesman*, 15 October 1955.

5 Sources: *Woman*, 20 December 1960; *Daily Express*, 25 June 1957; and *Marilyn Monroe*, by Maurice Zolotow, W. H. Allen, 1961.

6 *New York Times*, 23 September 1956.

7 *Cue* Magazine, New York, 25 October 1956.

8 *Rex—an Autobiography*, by Rex Harrison, Macmillan, London, 1974.

9 *Daily Express*, 3 April 1957.

10 Rattigan also said later that he may have chosen the name Fish out of some subconscious association with Mary Herring. Rose Fish in the play started her career as a very efficient secretary.

11 *Sunday Times*, 11 May 1958.

12 *Evening Standard*, 17 May 1958.

13 It is worth comparing Rattigan's script with that by Robert Bolt for the film eventually directed by David Lean. A direct comparison can be made, for instance, between the way Bolt and Rattigan handle the scene where Lawrence meets General Allenby for the first time. In both screenplays it is a crucial moment which sets the tone for their relationship and establishes important facts for the development of the plot. Both writers allot about the same length of time to the scene, but Rattigan achieves a more interesting relationship while getting across his complex plot information in an unobtrusive way and creating tension and anticipation. His economy has a recognizable style without rupturing the illusion of naturalism. One of the reasons for Rattigan's lack of proper recognition as a writer is that such opportunities for direct comparison with other acknowledged writers so rarely occur.

14 *Daily Mail*, 23 September 1959.

15 *Theatre Arts*, New York, April 1962. Interview given in December 1961.

16 *T. E. Lawrence: In Arabia and After*, Jonathan Cape, 1935.

17 *Seven Pillars of Wisdom*, by T. E. Lawrence, Jonathan Cape, 1935.

18 The possibility of a film based on Rattigan's script was again briefly mooted and he received £10,000 from the producer, Herbert Wilcox, for the rights, but the plan soon evaporated, leaving Spiegel alone in the field.

19 *Observer*, 5 February 1961.

20 *Sunday Times*, 15 May 1960.

21 *Sunday Times*, 17 July 1960.

22 *Daily Telegraph*, 15 July 1960.

23 *Evening News*, 15 July 1960.

24 *Sunday Times*, 17 July 1960.

16
Not for Fun

'It's not for fun, it's for money,' a character in *The VIPs* says, explaining why she is going to America. Rattigan was probably more hurt by the disaster that had befallen *Joie de Vivre* than he ever admitted. He returned to the flat he had taken in Brighton and tried to concentrate on shaping the play he had been talking about writing for Rex Harrison. Already his resolution not to waste his time on films was weakening. Anatole de Grunwald, who had recently signed a contract to produce films for MGM, approached him and asked if he would submit an original script.

In October, Rattigan left for America to discuss the Broadway production of *Ross* and the staging of a musical version of *The Sleeping Prince*, with lyrics by Noël Coward, under the title *The Girl Who Came to Supper*. Checking in at London Airport he was, as usual, shown into the lounge reserved for VIPs. As he sat idly wondering who the other passengers in the room with him might be—presuming them to be generals, civil servants and business magnates—a fog came down 'like the curtain at the Queen's Theatre', he commented ruefully later. As flights began to be delayed, the calm of the room was slowly broken, executives and government officals began to fume. Alternative travel arrangements were discussed, then cancelled, then reconsidered. The day wasted away in growing bad temper. The airport remained closed for forty-eight hours. With nothing else to do,

Rattigan began to imagine the drama behind the anxious enquiries to flustered stewardesses and the furious explosions about cancelled meetings and lost contracts. By the time he arrived in New York he had an idea, which he thought might suit de Grunwald, for a 'compendium movie' set in a VIP lounge and revealing the dramas of an assortment of people trapped there by a sudden fog. He flew on to Hollywood and sold the idea to de Grunwald for a fee somewhere in the region of £40,000.

Rattigan seemed unable to settle for the next few years. Bouts of energy were followed by heavy drinking and listless moving from place to place. This was the beginning of a new phase of his life, the most restless period of an already restless existence. Returning to England, he decided to sell the acres in Sunningdale. His absorption in golf was waning. He looked for a house in Brighton and soon found one: Bedford House, a Regency building with a view of the sea, costing £20,000. One of its features was to be a Margaret Leighton bedroom, kept exclusively for her use whenever she wanted it. Her marriage to Laurence Harvey was ending in the predicted divorce. Rattigan's feelings about Harvey became crystal clear when an American impresario, David Merrick, invited Harvey to star in the Broadway production of *Ross*. Rattigan, who had right of veto on casting, quietly but firmly refused to allow Harvey to play Lawrence, thus denying him the chance of taking an important step forward in his career.

By April he had completed the purchase of his Brighton house and was off to stay in a villa in Ischia rented from Sir William Walton. There he intended to finish his double bill of plays for Rex Harrison, called provisionally *Like Father, Like Son*. The first play, *Like Father*, was finished. It was, he said, a political comedy about the present plight of the Labour Party, personified by a 1930s rebel who has become a very successful painter. He is confronted by his terribly conformist son—'It's rather what's happening to England, isn't it?' Rattigan told a reporter.[1] *Like Son*, he said, would be a serious play, about a scandal or a resignation in a politician's family, inspired by the rows and resignations in both Macmillan's government and the Labour Party. It would contain a part for Rachel Roberts, with whom Rex Harrison was at that time having a much publicized affair.

In May, Rattigan turned up at the Cannes Film Festival, where the press stage-managed a meeting between him and some

261

marijuana-smoking 'beat' poets, headed by Allen Ginsberg. Rattigan announced that he had gone to Cannes in order to write a preface to the third volume of his *Collected Plays*, in which he intended to kill off Aunt Edna. The book did not in fact appear for another three years, and then he only tried to modify the image of Aunt Edna by writing his Preface as a mock trial in which Rattigan is being sued for libel by Aunt Edna for trumpeting abroad a distorted and perverted image of her. He knew he could not kill off Aunt Edna without it seeming an insincere gesture and without being accused, once again, of bending to popular demand. Like it not, she was his most famous character and he was stuck with her. In any case he had long said that by Aunt Edna he meant 'the great audience', not merely prurient, matinée-going old ladies. He still held the view that for a dramatist to deride or dismiss the audience was suicide, sacrilege to the god of drama, and that it was audiences rather than critics who, sooner or later, established what was or was not a masterpiece. The fact that since 1956 audiences had worn jeans rather than dinner jackets was to be welcomed, but did not alter his thesis about the dramatist's relationship with the public or the primacy of character and plot over ideological content. The only development that had surprised him was the continuing popularity of Samuel Beckett. Ionesco and the 'anti-dramatists' he loathed, but he remained confident that the public would soon see them for what they were and dismiss them.

By June, the second of the plays for Rex Harrison was lost to the stage for ever. It was being transformed into a television script. This was the result of an approach by the BBC who, with thirteen other European television networks, were trying to attract the best writers in each country to write for the medium. At that time television could only pay £750 to £1,000 for a play, and many highly-paid dramatists refused commissions. To overcome this, each of the television networks in the scheme undertook to commission a play from a leading author and guaranteed to produce all the plays commissioned. This would guarantee the authors a fee of about £10,000 and an audience of up to 80 million. Such an offer, while not commensurate with what Rattigan could get from Hollywood, contrasted with the fee of £300 he had received for his earlier television play, *The Final Test*. Rattigan had long brooded on a play about a scandal inside a Tory cabinet, and this seemed to offer a way of doing it. Two other recent happenings were also on his mind. One was the use of television in American politics, particularly the confrontations between Kennedy and Nixon during the 1960 Presidential election, which Rattigan had seen during his visit to America the previous autumn. It was Nixon who fascinated him. Although shown up by Kennedy in their confrontations, Rattigan remembered how some years earlier Nixon had pulled himself back from political extinction in California, after being accused of accepting bribes, by an emotional television appeal. Then Nixon had appeared, complete with his wife and the family dog, and tearfully told the electors that all he had done was to allow someone to pay for a family holiday which they all, particularly his wife, needed after the years of struggle in politics—from which they had never made money. He had not done anything that any other ordinary man who cared for his family would not have done under similar circumstances. It was powerful emotional stuff and banished the 'Dirty Dicky' image for long enough for him to become Eisenhower's Vice President.

The other happening which affected Rattigan's choice of format was the series of interviews done on British television by John Freeman with leading public figures, called 'Face to Face'. These had represented a breakthrough because Freeman had probed into the private lives behind the public faces, a thing previously unheard-of on television, which until then had treated public figures more as idols to be worshipped than as people to be examined. In one interview, Gilbert Harding, a radio and television personality noted for his gruff manner, had actually broken down in front of the cameras and wept.

Once again Rattigan found a way to write a television play that exploited the distinctive qualities and strengths of the medium. His plot centred on a television interviewer, David Mann, whose vastly popular series of 'Face to Face' type interviews is dedicated to bringing to the public 'the truths of the heart'. He is preparing an interview with Sir Stanley Johnson, a cabinet minister whose carefully fostered 'I'm an ordinary no-nonsense bloke like you' public image has put him in line of succession as a possible prime minister. During the course of his preparation for the interview, information comes into Mann's possession that Johnson accepted payments amounting to bribes while a junior minister, that he has

263

a mistress and is not the beer-drinking family man of the people he has made himself out to be. The play traces the various personal and professional pressures which are put on Mann not to use this information during the interview. Johnson, who seeks the advantages to his career that an appearance on a popular television programme will bring, uses his contacts in the Establishment in an attempt to tame David Mann and turn the interview from an inquisition into a showcase.

Rattigan's demonstration of the various ways in which pressures are brought by powerful people on supposedly impartial television organizations is, if anything, even more relevant today than when he wrote the play. Finally Johnson is panicked into making a direct appeal to the public on the air, emotionally confessing to accepting one small payment. He offers to resign, but asks the viewers if he has really done anything that each of them would not have done. Like Nixon, he claims that all he did was to accept a little help so that his poor wife could have a much-needed holiday. He even manages to bring in the family cat, which we already know he secretly hates. At the end of the interview, viewers' telephone calls start to come in. The overwhelming majority support Johnson and say he must not leave public life. But, suggests Rattigan, the few dissenters may one day swell into a large enough chorus to chase him from office. Prophetic, indeed.

The play was finished late in 1961 at Noël Coward's home in Jamaica. While it was being typed up and sent to the BBC, Rattigan dashed off to New York to preside over the opening of *Ross*. He already had another play in draft which he took with him to work on. This had been inspired by a book published earlier in the year about the demise of a fraudulent Swedish financier in the 1930s. The idea of public façades covering private corruption was much in his mind as a theme during 1961. This new play was the third he called *Man and Boy*.[2] With the smooth but steely-willed financier he hoped to provide Rex Harrison with the leading role he had now been promising him for two years. At a party in New York someone put the manuscript on a stand together with a score by William Walton and, as a joke, surrounded them with laurels and stood a candle in front of them. A quiet, greying man in his fifties, whom Rattigan did not recognize, picked up the manuscript and asked if he could take it

264

downstairs to read. When he returned he expressed an interest in doing it. While he had been out of the room, Rattigan had found out who he was: the veteran film star, Charles Boyer.

Early in the spring of 1962, the BBC started work on the production of *Heart to Heart*. Rattigan was staying at the Hotel Martinez in Cannes, and Alvin Rakoff, the man selected by the BBC to direct it, was despatched with a producer to meet him. On the night they arrived, Rattigan took them to dinner in the best restaurant in Cannes and then on to a night-club. The main feature of the club was a troupe of exceedingly beautiful girls who finished their act by stripping down to G-strings. The two BBC men were carried away by the exotic life Rattigan had introduced them to, and the producer seemed to want to sleep with one of the strippers. Rattigan, ever hospitable, approached the girl and offered a generous sum of money. When this was refused he approached the owner of the club with a still bigger sum. Even when it reached £500 for one girl for one night, the owner and girls still resolutely refused.

The next day the producer had to return to London, but Rattigan and Rakoff again visited the club. Still mystified by their unyielding rejection, Rattigan invited the owner, an American lady, to have a drink with them. After some time, because, she said, she could see they were 'men of the world' and she was in any case a fan of Rattigan's, she confided in them. Her strippers were in fact men who had had elaborate hormone treatment. She made it an absolute rule not to let her 'girls' meet British men as they became not just abusive, but violent, when they found out the truth. However, as she realized that Rattigan and Rakoff were 'not like the Englishmen who usually frequented the club' she offered them a 'girl' each for the night. It was now their turn to refuse. Rattigan said: 'I like men, not men dressed as women', Rakoff that he liked women.

Rakoff found Rattigan a strange mixture of confidence and diffidence. Flitting between the fleshpots of Europe, dashing off Hollywood scripts for *The VIPs* and *The Yellow Rolls Royce*, he nevertheless asked Rakoff more than once whether he wouldn't rather be working with Wesker or one of the new playwrights. He confided in Rakoff and his wife about his homosexuality, subscribing to the view expressed in a new book on the subject that its root was not overpowering mother-love but a failed relationship with his father. He asked anxiously about the Rakoffs' relationship, not its sexual but its emotional aspects. He was eager to hear about any other liaisons they might have. He was now turned fifty, but his mischievous energy was undiminished. His relish for gossip was unabated and he could still not resist setting up disputes between people and then sitting back to see the results. He loved making indiscreet remarks to journalists, about celebrities he knew, but then swearing them to secrecy, tantalizing them with information they could not use and watching them squirm. A regular companion at this time was Robin Maugham (Somerset Maugham's nephew and also a writer) who, like him, had a house in Brighton. Maugham was a frequent visitor to Ischia, where Rattigan now had two villas managed and let for him by the stage designer Michael Weight. A procession of the great and famous came to stay—Elizabeth Taylor, Richard Burton, Roddy McDowell. Rattigan's stays there were often what he termed 'very debauched'. On one holiday he and Robin Maugham sat up together with a bottle for fourteen nights in a row until sunrise. One evening Rattigan appeared in a very distraught state: he had lost the only script of *The Yellow Rolls Royce*. There was a frantic search of the villas, before Maugham eventually found it on top of a ladder propped up against the side of his house.

The Yellow Rolls Royce was another of Rattigan's pot-boiling compendium movie ideas. Tracing the career of an elderly Rolls from grace to disfavour, it has not stood the test of time and looks anaemic. He had managed to sell the script to Hollywood in the autumn of 1962; the idea had come to him as he sat in his own Rolls in a London traffic jam, speculating on the looks of hatred, compounded with envy, he received from the occupants of other cars in the jam. He remembered also the old Rolls-Royce found by Puffin Asquith and Anatole de Grunwald while looking for locations in Iraq for the abortive Lawrence film; the car was said to have been used by General Allenby when he was in command of armies in the Middle East during the First World War.

The least popular person in the 'Rattigan set' at this time was still Michael Franklin. Rattigan's other friends still thought he treated Rattigan badly. In *Variation on a Theme*, one of the characters had been given the line: 'Adrian ... He's hell, that one. He'll have to go ...' And sure enough, shortly after the pro-

266

duction of that play, Adrian Brown had gone, leaving the field clear for Franklin. Everyone who has talked to us has agreed that Rattigan seemed 'besotted' with Franklin in the early 1960s and 'gave him everything'.

Another regular visitor to Ischia was Vera Rattigan, still sprightly, even in her seventies. Rattigan had given up careful concealment of his homosexuality even in his mother's presence. She never made any comment, except occasionally to tick him off for his bad language. Although the law on homosexuality had still not been reformed, Rattigan was now more relaxed about seeing that no hint of it reached the public. As late as 1959, he had briskly put down a Danish reporter who asked too bold a question about his bachelor status. He still played the game for journalists, especially when they asked questions about him and Margaret Leighton. But his plays themselves, and particularly his statements about *Ross*, left no one in any real doubt about where he stood. Rattigan was instrumental in persuading Robin Maugham to publish a novel called *The Wrong People*, which had a homosexual theme. It appeared in America under a pseudonym and flopped, but Rattigan pressed him to publish under his own name in England. The result was a bestseller. Maugham was very touched to receive a telegram from Rattigan on his sixtieth birthday: 'Dearest Robin, your uncle thought you would never make a writer and I thought you would never make sixty. I am delighted we have both been proved so triumphantly wrong. Great love, Terry.' It was, however, typical of Rattigan that at about the same time he said to another friend: 'Maugham! He couldn't write bum on a wall; and if he could, he'd spell it Baugham.'

While they were working on *Heart to Heart*, Rattigan took Alvin Rakoff to meet Elizabeth Taylor and Richard Burton, who were in Rome making *Cleopatra*. After making a series of lunch dates with her, each of which was cancelled, Rattigan and Rakoff were finally invited to meet her at the studios. They were shown into a very long room where Miss Taylor was sitting at the far end. As they approached, Rattigan muttered to Rakoff, 'Nobody could live up to this entrance!' After the meeting with Taylor and Burton, Rattigan returned triumphantly to England brandishing Richard Burton's signature on an agreement to play David Mann in *Heart to Heart* opposite Ralph Richardson as Sir Stanley

Johnson. Elizabeth Taylor and Richard Burton were not yet married, and Rattigan was one of the great champions of their relationship. If they really loved each other, he kept telling them, then they must allow nothing and nobody to stand between them. He told Rakoff one day that he would probably write a Burton-Taylor story. In fact he included a pair of tempestuous lovers in *The VIPs* who might well have been based on them and who were eventually played by them.

Filming of *Cleopatra* dragged on, and so Burton was unable to play David Mann in *Heart to Heart*. The recording was made at the BBC Television Centre in November 1962, with Kenneth More in the part. Press reactions were very favourable. In the *Daily Express*, Herbert Kretzmer said that *Heart to Heart* was a savage exercise in Establishment-debunking which brought Rattigan into common alliance with Osborne and Wesker.[3] The only notable person who seemed not to like it was John Freeman.

As the week of previews and press conferences leading up to the transmission drew on, Rattigan went down yet again with a virus infection. By the transmission date, Thursday 5 December, he was in the London Clinic with jaundice. He watched the play from his hospital bed. A few weeks later, although still not fully recovered, he was strong enough to embark on a ship bound for Hong Kong. There were by now serious fears about the state of his health, but it was hoped that the cruise would give him the relaxation he needed for a full recovery. He tried to avoid the other passengers, but inevitably it became known that the famous playwright was on board. His fellow passengers became inquisitive and wanted to know what he was doing. 'Oh,' he assured them, 'I'm travelling with my secretary and writing a play.' So that explained it, the passengers told one another, and it accounted for the little old lady they had noticed going into his cabin every morning: an embellishment that so delighted Rattigan that he gleefully passed the story round among his friends in Ischia on his return. The person the passengers had mistaken for an old lady was Michael Weight.

Rattigan seemed completely recovered and by March he was in New York. There he completed arrangements for the production of *Man and Boy*, which was to star Charles Boyer and play a short autumn season in London before transferring to Broadway. He sailed back to England on the *Queen Mary* at the beginning of April and then went on to Ischia. There he complained to his early summer guests, who included Robin Maugham, of headaches and a sore throat. Every night his temperature shot up, but no one suspected there was anything seriously wrong with him. Because he had always been something of a hypochondriac, they tended to dismiss his illness; it was just 'Terry being unwell again and drawing attention to himself'. Some suspected that the jaundice that winter had really been incipient cirrhosis of the liver from the years of hard drinking. However, the tally of mysterious 'virus' infections since his illness three years earlier, just before the opening of *Ross*, was mounting. The up-and-down pattern of his health was in itself a cause for concern, and a specialist had been called in. That spring the specialist made a firm diagnosis: leukaemia. Ever since Kay Kendall's death, Rattigan had had a particular dread of leukaemia.

'At first I had to get over the alarming discovery that I am mortal. That not only would I die, but I was likely to do so in a short while.'[4] While still getting over the initial shock, he had to take steps to stop the news being trumpeted in all the papers. Above all, he didn't want his mother, who was due to come out to Ischia on holiday, to find out. He wrote to Robin Maugham, who had returned to England a few days earlier, telling him about the leukaemia but swearing him to secrecy. He wanted no one else to know. When his mother arrived, he got up from his bed and put on a brave show. He got through the holiday without her discovering the truth, although she must have suspected something, if only because he was now visibly losing weight. Having watched Rex Harrison nurse Kay Kendall, Rattigan had no illusions about the course it would take. Despite periods of remission, he would dwindle to an inevitable end. This, he was told, would be in about six months. He ordered his Brighton house to be put on the market and himself prepared to stay in Ischia, concentrating the rest of his time on the thing that mattered most to him: his writing. Rather than trying to complete one last 'great work', he got on with the commissions already in hand, the film script of *The Yellow Rolls Royce*, the outline of a film in which Rex Harrison was to play Edward VII, and some final corrections to *Man and Boy*. In his condition, the heat of the southern Italian summer was debilitating, and he was relieved when a message arrived from Binkie Beaumont summoning him back to London for urgent consultations about the play. In view of his determination not to let anyone know how ill he was, he could not in any case refuse to go.

In fact, the summons to return was not what it seemed. Robin Maugham, who knew enough about leukaemia to know that the heat of an Italian summer would be bad for Rattigan, had let Binkie Beaumont into the secret and together they had concocted the excuse to get him back to England. Once back in London there would be medical rather than theatrical consultations. Rattigan returned, and by midsummer he was undergoing another round of tests and blood counts. Inevitably the news of his illness did leak out and before long a newspaper approached him with an offer to buy his story. He refused. But the whisper grew in theatrical circles. Then at a party an actor came up to him and said he was terribly sorry to hear that he was going to die. This brought matters to a head. Rattigan told his doctor he must go back to the specialist—'my executioner'—and force him to give an estimate of how long he had got. Rattigan claimed, unlikely though it may seem, that he was eventually given an exact date in September by which he would be dead. It was just after *Man and Boy* was due to open in London.

'A crash course in how to live' was what Rattigan later called those weeks. 'My priorities changed; time became the most precious commodity in the world. The most commonplace event was an occasion.'[5] He pared down his friendships, spent time only with those people he really liked and worked harder than ever before. He completed his film scripts and started to map out a serious play he had been intending to write about the law and insanity. He contributed an article about Aunt Edna to a new debate raging in the *Daily Telegraph*, and started to give confident interviews to journalists about *Man and Boy* and his film, *The VIPs*, which were due to open almost simultaneously. Although he was cutting out the dinner dates with insistent, but boring, London hostesses, and avoiding dull night-clubs, he still continued to go to parties. When he heard the smug, pretentious conversations of his friends he was apt to crash in with remarks like, 'You people are all fools. Don't you know you won't live for ever.' When his friends objected that his conversation was hardly calculated to brighten up a party, he would reply that if a man couldn't live to enjoy his own death what could he do?[6]

The appointed day was less than two months away when Stephen Mitchell prevailed upon him to seek yet another medical opinion, this time from the specialist, Sir Horace Evans. After more tests showing that the red corpuscle counts were not as low as expected, Evans told him he had not got leukaemia; he had had a series of virus infections which together made up a pattern that looked suspiciously like leukaemia. Evans is reported to have concluded by telling him, 'We haven't met before, but in view of the life I understand you have led you are a remarkable specimen.'

When *Man and Boy* opened in Brighton for two weeks on Monday 19 August 1963, prior to going on to London, Rattigan triumphantly announced to local journalists that he was taking his house in Brighton off the market. He confessed that he had not been too well since the winter, but that he had really started to feel better since he returned to Brighton a few weeks ago: 'the view might not be as good as Ischia, but the air is a damn sight better. Now I am taking walks along the seafront every day and I am taking up golf again.' In fact, blood tests were still being made regularly and he still had only Sir Horace Evans' opinion to set against the diagnosis of the earlier specialist. He was by no means absolutely certain in his own mind that he was out of danger or that he would survive beyond the 'appointed day'.

Man and Boy opened in London on 4 September at the Queen's Theatre, the scene of the calamitous first night of *Joie de Vivre*. Rattigan, still half believing that this might be his last first-night, waited anxiously to see how the show would be received.

Although the programme credited Robert Shaplen's recent biography of the Swedish swindler/financier Kreuger for 'suggestions', the plot of the play was largely invention. It had been sparked off by Rattigan's discovery that Kreuger had had an illegitimate son. He wondered how such a boy would have reacted to the discovery that his father was an arch-criminal. *Man and Boy* is the first of a sequence of plays, continuing until Rattigan's death, which feature boys who have their illusions about their father-figures shattered. In this sequence of plays it is possible to detect Rattigan undertaking a gradual reassessment of his relationship with his own father and of his father's importance in his own development.

271

In the play, the financial wizard (whom Rattigan significantly gave a Romanian rather than a Swedish background and renamed Gregor Antonescu) is presented as a heartless villain who has built his empire on fraud. Regrettably Rattigan does not adequately explain the background to Antonescu's rejection of emotion and the underlying causes of his unscrupulous pursuit of power. At the very end of the play the voice of a radio announcer pronounces that 'to be absolutely powerful a man must first corrupt *himself* absolutely'. The man without feelings is an emotive figure for Rattigan, but in *Man and Boy* he does not probe his character's background, and Gregor Antonescu remains essentially a figure from melodrama. Antonescu's illegitimate son, Basil, is by contrast weak: a musician who has run away from his father and believes he hates him, but who discovers he really admires him. The boy is a socialist who believes that the collapse of capitalism must usher in a better alternative.

The play is set in Basil's Greenwich Village flat in 1934, to which Antonescu lures the chairman of a powerful business corporation to negotiate the deal upon which hangs the only chance of saving his own business empire from collapse and himself from exposure and ruin. Antonescu knows the man to be a homosexual, and so pretends to be one himself. He conceals his son's true identity, implying that he is a young lover whom he would be willing to share. The tension hangs on whether the corporation chairman will swallow the bait and thereby save Antonescu's fortunes or, once Basil has grasped the full implications of what his father is doing, will betray him. Antonescu ends the play facing a lonely death; suicide is his only way out. The final speech of the play, by a radio announcer speculating on Antonescu's whereabouts, was remarkably appropriate to Rattigan's own situation on the first night as he waited unrecognized at the back of the theatre for the audience's reaction: 'Wherever he may be tonight ... it is certain that this suave, cool, elegant and utterly charming personality is showing the same unruffled front that he has always shown to the world, through every crisis that has beset him ...'

The reactions when they came were more contradictory than for any play he had written. In the *Daily Mail*, while admitting that Rattigan might not have explained the psychology of great men who turn to crime, Bernard Levin spoke of his 'unfailing dramatic cunning; his narrative power, faultless in its patient unwinding; above all his restless imaginative curiosity about the springs of human activity; these fuse, hot and glowing, into his finest work and a play that outdistances all but a handful of authors writing in England today.'[7] In contrast, David Nathan in the *Daily Herald* started his review: 'The next time "disgusted" writes to complain that our young playwrights are obsessed with squalor and homosexuality and cites Terence Rattigan as the preserver of all the traditional values, I will recount the plot of *Man and Boy*,' and concludes: 'The whole play in fact, seems false and hollow with much profundity intended and none achieved ... The play is here for only eight and a half weeks before going to New York. New York is very welcome to it.'[8]

Regrettably for Rattigan, New York gave *Man and Boy* even less of a welcome than had London. American critics found it dull and it ran for only 54 performances. In the same week as *Man and Boy* opened at the Queen's Theatre, Rattigan's film *The VIPs* opened in London. This also received a critical drubbing. Rattigan was so incensed that he did something his pride would never had allowed him to do earlier in his career. He wrote a twenty-five-page letter to his most outspoken critic, Alexander Walker. Walker sought an interview with Rattigan. When they met, Rattigan confessed how much the critics had hurt him; how he now dreaded even the word 'craftsmanship' when applied to him, as it was usually intended as a term of abuse meaning 'insincere'; how he hated the insistence that he was 'glib', 'slick', that his work was 'unfelt'; how painful it was to be told he had 'a cliché-ridden mind'.[9]

Beset though Rattigan now felt, his health continued to improve. The predicted date of his death had passed, and he stayed on in New York after the première of *Man and Boy* for the opening of the musical adapted from *The Sleeping Prince, The Girl Who Came to Supper*. This was much better received, although a number of critics went out of their way to say how much Harry Kurnitz had improved on Rattigan's original script.

Early in 1964, Rattigan was back in England, commuting between the Brighton house and his Eaton Square flat. The old high-life had resumed and he seemed surrounded by friends, yet the inner loneliness which he had quietly endured all his life was now greater than ever. Bereft of the success which had been such an important element in his fulfilment, Rattigan needed friends, but by now many were dead or had grown apart from him. Too many of those who now surrounded him were sycophants rather than friends. The brunt of his loneliness and uncertainty fell increasingly on his staff—a long-suffering housekeeper and a secretary. Mary Herring had finally left him. When a new secretary proved inadequate, he consulted Binkie Beaumont, who suggested Sheila Dyatt; she had previously worked in Beaumont's office and, like Rattigan, lived in Brighton and also had a flat in London. She quickly found that Rattigan was not an easy person to work for. The disciplined hours of writing were now a thing of the past. He rose late, worked for perhaps an hour before lunch and then again for an hour later in the afternoon. He now often worked at night and even when he finally went to bed took a notebook with him. Everything was still written in longhand in exercise books, but he was continually running in and out of his secretary's room, changing a word here or a detail there. If she stayed on typing late in the evening, he would tell her he didn't pay her to stay until all hours, but if she didn't stay he complained that she wasn't interested.

One of the things which most shocked Sheila Dyatt was the number of people who simply sponged off him, especially when Rattigan was in Brighton. There was always a gang of people in the house, eating his food and downing his drink, who never seemed to reciprocate his hospitality. One Easter, when Sheila Dyatt had been with him only a short time, Rattigan collapsed with a fever in the Eaton Square flat. There was no one else to look after him, so Sheila Dyatt stayed and nursed him through the Bank Holiday. His mother telephoned him, but no one else came near him. It was then that she first realized the full extent of his loneliness. Here was this great and successful man, with 'lots of people who liked him, but no one who really cared for him', left alone in his sumptuous London flat to fight his illness, the only person with him a secretary he hardly knew. Yet there remained an oddly aloof quality about his attitude towards her. A few months afterwards he suddenly said out of the blue, 'I don't think you're really interested in the work. I'm sure you'd make a very good secretary to a businessman or something, but you're not right for me. I think you'd better go by Christmas.' She replied that if she was going she'd go quicker than that. Next day, when she told

Binkie Beaumont that she had been fired, he was very surprised; Rattigan had been singing her praises to him only a day or two before, and he advised her to ignore it. Rattigan, who had always rung people at all hours of the day and night, then telephoned Beaumont. As always with anything that might be remotely tricky or could lead to some sort of confrontation, he circled round the point before making it clear that he wanted Beaumont to patch things up for him with Sheila Dyatt. Beaumont, having already spoken to her, said nothing more. The only time Rattigan referred to the incident again was some time later when he told her he was glad she had not left.

One of those who availed themselves of Rattigan's generous hospitality in Brighton was T. C. Worsley. Unlike others, he did at least repay him with his pen. We have already noted his defence of *Variation on a Theme*; but when J. W. Lambert in the *Sunday Times* and Penelope Gilliat in the *Observer* raised doubts about the real subject of *Man and Boy,* suggesting it was about an older man and his boy lover thinly disguised to look like father and son, Worsley again raced to Rattigan's defence. In an article in the *London Magazine* he said: 'This seamy line of personal smear is not criticism; it is gossip journalism.'[10]

Shortly afterwards, Worsley devoted a full-length article to a critical reappraisal of Rattigan's work.[11] He pointed to the recurrent themes of humiliation and obsession, saying that, although their range may be narrow and their scale small, they are true and exact, persuading us to experience and sympathize with a corner of human weakness. Although, as early as 1957, C. P. Snow had raised objections to the way the critics under-rated Rattigan, Worsley's defence was long overdue. But it failed to provoke any further reappraisals. For Rattigan himself Worsley's efforts, though gratefully received, made little real difference. He was too honest with himself to be able to overlook the fact that Worsley was beholden to him, while the public pronouncement that the recurring themes of his work were humiliation and obsession preyed on his mind. His worst fear of critics was not so much their disapproval as that they might make him self-conscious as a dramatist. He remained more discouraged than he had ever been in his life. It says much for Rattigan that even at this low ebb he backed others in whom he saw ability. In

1964 he put up money for the London production of Joe Orton's first play, *Entertaining Mr Sloane*.

Another of those who made some return, beyond the obvious, for Rattigan's hospitality was Michael Franklin. He now arranged all the decor of Rattigan's homes. As well as the flat in London and the house in Brighton, Rattigan had bought a mansion in Scotland which he had little use for, but in which Franklin often lived when Rattigan was abroad.

The problem of loving someone who is widely disliked by one's friends, and continuing to love them despite being able to see their faults, was at the root of Rattigan's next play. In the spring of 1964, he concluded a deal with Associated Television. They were to transmit two or possibly three of his stage plays—*Variation on a Theme* and *The Browning Version* were the ones finally agreed on—and he was to write a new play specifically for television. 'The most important drama shows ever produced for television,' announced Lew Grade, boss of ATV, with characteristic ebullience. The new play was to be introduced by the Duke of Edinburgh, and some of the proceeds were to go to his Award Scheme and a fund with which he was associated to save the sailing clipper, the *Cutty Sark*. An appropriate subject was needed and Rattigan voiced a long-nurtured idea of trying a play about Nelson. Discussions were held at Buckingham Palace. Rattigan told the Duke of Edinburgh that after some consideration he didn't think he could do it. Nelson was too much of a success story. A further meeting was arranged but Rattigan still said he hadn't found a way into the subject: 'The man was too bloody successful. I can't be sorry for him, and I can't write about anybody for whom I can't feel compassion. I prefer failures.' (Sam Duveen, Ron's choreographer patron in *Variation on a Theme*, was also unable to like people unless he first felt sorry for them.) It was Prince Philip who got over Rattigan's block. He reminded him that Nelson did suffer one great defeat—he was unable to get the nation to accept his mistress, Emma Hamilton.

That fired Rattigan's imagination. Why had the nation, which honoured Nelson's wishes over so much else, refused to accept his bequest of Emma Hamilton? 'It wasn't meanness—they gave a lot of money to his brother. It wasn't snobbery—she was the wife of the British Ambassador to Naples and was perfectly acceptable as Lady Hamilton. And it wasn't prudishness—that age was as permissive as our own. Then I thought, isn't it just possible that no one liked her? That she was an absolute cow?'[12] That was the breakthrough. Researching into the history of the romance with Lady Hamilton, Rattigan came to the conclusion that it was probably Nelson's first real love affair. 'He was probably 40 when he met her. His wife was a cold woman. And though he'd probably spent a lot of time in brothels, this was the first time he'd done it with an expert.'[13]

The script which Rattigan finally came up with was set during Nelson's last brief visit to England just before the Battle of Trafalgar. Nelson, already a national hero, is cheered in the streets. The only blemish to his image is Lady Hamilton, who is no longer the beauty of Romney's portrait, but an over-blown, thick-trunked, coarse, hard-drinking forty-year-old. When she appears at his side, the cheering wavers and some people actually laugh or jeer. The conflict between Nelson's public and private life is exposed through a hero-worshipping teenage nephew, George Matcham. George cannot understand why Nelson, a compassionate man loved by both his family and his men, has treated his estranged wife with such cold cruelty. He is unable to believe any evil of Nelson and assumes that Lady Nelson must have done him some awful wrong. During the play he is steadily disillusioned about his hero (who is, of course, a father figure). He is shocked by Lady Hamilton's vulgarity, which so ill befits the woman beloved by his hero. Nelson confesses that he can see Lady Hamilton as the world sees her and dies 'a thousand deaths' each day he is with her. Yet he cannot bear to be apart from her. 'How can a love be so deep that begins and ends in the bed?' he asks rhetorically, answering that although a love which can overcome his disgust 'isn't perhaps the love most suited to a hero ... it is the one most suited to me'. Therefore, it is 'the greatest, the most enduring and the deepest of all.'[14] *Bequest to the Nation*, as the play was called when it was later adapted for the stage and published, was dedicated to the person whose love had been the underlying subject of its conception.

Shortly after the television transmission of *Nelson—a Portrait in Miniature*, Rattigan announced that he was selling up his homes in England and going to live abroad. 'Everything,' he explained, 'has happened together. This winter I've had three virus infections and, as I said to a member of the Test team,

"Unlike some of you, I catch everything that's going." '[15] His doctor had been pressing him for some time to live somewhere warmer in the winter. It was a decision he had resisted for years, and even now he didn't intend to leave Britain for good. However, he had signed contracts to write two Hollywood film scripts, and the tax advantages of staying out of the country for at least a year were enormous. On top of that his landlords in Eaton Square had just announced that they were going to double his rent. It seemed a good moment to go.

Inevitably, there were deeper reasons underlying his decision. As he told a BBC Radio interviewer only a few weeks before his death, he had kept his vow not to yield to the financial temptations of Hollywood until he discovered that any and every play he wrote was going to get 'smashed' by the critics. 'I had no chance with anything. They didn't give me reasons for it, they just said, "It must be bad; it's just the old effete theatre. It has nothing to do with the ongoing movement of the time." I thought the time has come. I'm not getting any younger and I haven't saved any money.'[16] Hollywood was still making him handsome offers of up to $150,000 per film and he decided he had better cash in while he still could. Even if it was not work he liked, it was easy.

He did not return to England for a year. Even when his mother fell ill the following Christmas he did not enter the country, although he flew back across the Atlantic to be near her. He got as close as Paris and from an apartment there telephoned her twice a day in the London Clinic where she was suffering from eye trouble. It had been pointed out to him that in previous cases people who had set foot in the country for whatever reason without completing a full year of non-residence had been made to pay tax in both Britain and their chosen country of residence. In his case, even a short visit to his mother might put up to £60,000 on his tax bill. For almost a year Rattigan shuttled restlessly about the world like some latter-day Flying Dutchman, moving uneasily between Hollywood, his villa in Ischia and a Paris apartment. Then he rented a house, somewhat unfortunately named 'Sitting Pretty', in Bermuda. As this was one of the few places in the world where there was no Income Tax, where the climate was suitable and which was still under British rule, he decided to look for a permanent home there.

By May 1967 he had established his non-residency in the

United Kingdom for tax purposes and was able to return for brief periods. His first priority was to visit his mother who was now seventy-nine. Next, he had to get his financial and domestic affairs into good order. The Brighton house and some of the furniture had gone, bringing in over £30,000, and the Eaton Square flat was no longer his. He had bought a house overlooking the Atlantic in Bermuda and was redistributing his remaining furniture and valuables between this house, Ischia and storage depots. Sheila Dyatt was kept on a retainer, but increasingly Peggy French, with her husband Harold, the director of the original production of *French Without Tears*, was taking over the administration of his daily routine. Michael Franklin continued to look after his possessions in Britain, and his agent, solicitor and other advisers took charge of documents, manuscripts and other matters. Rattigan, such a dedicated patriot, was a tax exile. It was a role he hated.

Although the dollars still rolled in, the late 1960s were an arid time for him. In the era of 'swinging Britain', anti-Vietnam demonstrations and the Rolling Stones, Rattigan seemed hopelessly out of date. As though to underline his irrelevance, someone revived *The Sleeping Prince* at the St Martin's Theatre. Reviewers recalled with astonishment that Laurence Olivier and Vivien Leigh had only fifteen years earlier wasted their talents in this flimsy bubble: 'Give it a whiff of flatulence and it shatters,' said the *Observer*.[17] The only faintly cheering event of that year, as far as Rattigan's survival as a serious playwright was concerned, was a fifteen-minute trifle written for Margaret Leighton to perform as a solo turn in a BBC2 Television slot called *All On Her Own*. In it she played a widow missing her booze- and rugby-loving husband, addressing the empty sofa where his body was found and trying to convince herself that his death was an accident, not suicide. It was a competent exercise, but little more.

By the time of its transmission in September 1968, Rattigan seemed once again to be on his death-bed. He had been in Pompeii for a musical re-make of *Goodbye, Mr Chips*, starring Peter O'Toole and Petula Clark. This was the script he had left England to write in Hollywood two years earlier. He had done a workmanlike job, bringing elements of Crocker Harris to the character of Mr Chipping. Nevertheless, it was a sad waste of his talent to have to rework material from his masterpiece *The Browning Version* in this way. On location he was seized with a violent pain and rushed to a Naples hospital to be operated on for a burst appendix. For two weeks he lay in a state of delirium, while he and all around him thought he was on the point of death. He found he was no longer afraid of dying; he had crossed that bridge during the leukaemia scare. Sheila Dyatt rushed to Naples when she heard the news. Again Rattigan had given instructions that his illness must be kept out of the papers for fear of upsetting his mother. By the time Sheila Dyatt arrived the appendix had gone gangrenous. The hospital was dirty and Rattigan's soiled bedclothing was left unchanged. He was hot in the day, but cold at night as he was only covered with a sheet. He suffered agonies of dehydration, yet the Italian doctors refused to give him water. Fortunately Rattigan's own doctor was holidaying in Italy and was found and called in. In the meantime, Sheila Dyatt had also informed the British Consul; she did not want to be accused by Rattigan's mother and friends of keeping the whole affair secret if he did die. At the climax of the infection, Sheila Dyatt and the doctor left the hospital for the night, convinced Rattigan would not survive till dawn. But when they returned the next morning they found him sitting up in bed. From then on he began to gain strength. Although the hospital was loath to lose such a famous patient, he was removed as soon as possible to Switzerland and then on to Baden Baden. There he finally recovered. The crisis had lasted some six weeks.

By the time *Bequest to the Nation* was ready for production in the West End in September 1970, there was an air of expectancy and a seeming willingness to welcome Rattigan's return. It was the first new play by him seen in the theatre for seven years, even if it was only the rewrite of the already flawed television script *Nelson—a Portrait in Miniature*. In turning it into a stage play, Rattigan had tried to heighten the contrasts between Nelson's blameless public image and the vulgarity of his mistress. The result was not only to make her coarser but to make the whole fabric of the play cruder. He also dragged in uneasy parallels and allusions to *Antony and Cleopatra* which, if anything, showed up the play's shortcomings rather than pointing an effective ironic contrast.

At the heart of both the television and stage versions of the play lies Nelson's sexual obsession with Emma. In the stage version the nature of Nelson's sexual love emerges in a frank, even raw, self-confession to Hardy. In answering the question 'How can any love be respected that begins and ends in bed?', Nelson sums up the feelings that had obsessed Rattigan's writing since the early 1950s and whose roots go back still further:

> ... in the release of the bed there lies an ecstasy so strong and a satisfaction so profound that it seems that it is everything that life can offer a man, the very purpose of his existence on earth ... You must remember, you see, that even at that age, I was still the rector's son who, from the cradle, had been preached the abomination of carnal love, and the ineffable joys of holy wedlock. But when at last I surrendered to Emma, I found—why should I be ashamed to say it?—that carnal love concerns the soul quite as much as it concerns the body. For the body *is* still the soul and the soul *is* still the body. At least they are for me ...

The conflict between carnal and spiritual love had always been a theme of Rattigan's writing, but starting with *Separate Tables* the two had become increasingly divorced. This can be traced both to events in his private life in the early 1950s—the growing sexual dependence on 'rough trade' deplored by his friends—and to the increasing freedom to write frankly about sex in the theatre which accompanied the more liberal atmosphere of the 1950s. Starting with *Separate Tables*, but particularly from *Variation on a Theme* onwards, sex had become something to be bartered, something to be ashamed of and finally an open obsession. Although a reflection of the experience of Rattigan the man, this did not help Rattigan the dramatist. A shy man, with a veneer of social ease but tortured by self-doubts, Rattigan made his art depend upon the oblique, the implicit, the struggle of frightened, damaged people to find self-expression and fulfilment in a society whose strict moral codes inhibited them. Once the moral codes had been relaxed in the theatre, Rattigan was not only out of fashion, he was stranded. Not only his technique as a writer but his background and lifetime's conditioning meant that however passionately he resented the old hypocrisies, he was not equipped to make do without them. The result was that when he tried to confront sex in his writing, however frankly and sincerely, in the permissive atmosphere of the post-Osborne theatre, he seemed evasive, insincere and sometimes actually embarrassing. In the nineteen years between the production of *Separate Tables* and the appearance of *In Praise of Love*, his best play was undoubtedly *Heart to Heart*. Perhaps because of the less permissive atmosphere of television, the play did not depend on sexual revelations; the drama was taut and controlled. It depended on implicit dishonesties, threats and conflicts in both the emotional and political relationships, culminating in a confrontation and a self-revelation whose power lay not in its frankness but in the realization of its full implications.

As though to provide an opportunity to rub salt into the wounds of Rattigan's rejection, a revival of *The Winslow Boy* opened six weeks after *Bequest to the Nation*. Time had shown up all the cumbersome craftsmanship of this exercise, while making suspect the ideals which had guaranteed its acceptance by the theatre-going audience of 1946. In *New Society*, Albert Hunt wrote a devastating denunciation of Rattigan headed 'Danger: craftsman at work'. Noting that the writer of the programme note had said that nostalgia was the 'in' thing that autumn, Hunt examined Rattigan's technique, concluding that the much-praised craftsmanship was overrated: 'It consists largely of setting up the obvious in a somewhat laborious way.' In dismissing *The Winslow Boy* he dismissed Rattigan's entire output: 'It's ... facile knowingness that's at the heart of Rattigan's theatre. For if he sacrifices everything to plausibility it's not because of some dramatic theory, it's because that's the way he responds to his material. Every complexity can be explained away, every facet of human experience reduced to a simple matter of manipulation. What *The Winslow Boy* says in the end is that there may be wrongs, but that in our good old British democracy, with its right thinking men of all parties, always ready to come together that right may triumph, we, the audience, live in a world in which everything can be solved by a little craftsmanship. It may be that smugness, not nostalgia, is really the "in" thing in the autumn of 1970.'[18]

In an article which asked the question which many critics had long given up posing, let alone trying to answer, Ronald Bryden used the revival to wonder why Rattigan had not turned into the playwright he promised to become twenty-five years earlier. In

The Winslow Boy, he said, he saw 'the weaknesses in his later work: the easy, sentimental, mechanical plotting, the flattering reassurance of the middle-class audience'. But Bryden was also one of the first to detect, or rather to rediscover, some of the real underlying significance of what Rattigan had been up to. Comparing his position in the conventional British theatre of the 1940s to that of dramatists working behind the Iron Curtain, he pointed out that Rattigan had been forced into 'hiding the play he wanted to write behind the one his audience would accept'. Lurking beneath the self-congratulatory glow of *The Winslow Boy*'s main plot Bryden noted the way Rattigan had kept running the apparently unimportant sub-plot about the Suffragette daughter's engagement to an army officer and the way in which he used this at the end of the play to explode the virtuous face of the Establishment. Here he showed the other face of traditional British 'decency', the one that is willing to ruin the girl's happiness in an attempt to stop the Winslows' 'anti-Establishment circus ... the face which frowns on breaking ranks, rocking the boat, wearing long hair, showing emotion, which would exclude foreigners, jail homosexuals, birch louts who won't stand up for the Queen'. This was the same Establishment which prided itself on its tolerance. Bryden noted that the 'new wave' of dramatists were now themselves part of the Establishment, but he concluded: 'There hasn't been much tolerance in, for instance, the treatment of Rattigan and his recent work.'[19] The revival of *The Winslow Boy* ran for more than six months, almost twice as long as the new play, *Bequest to the Nation*.

The bitterness of the attacks on Rattigan were compounded of more than a reaction against his years of success; they owed much to the disappointment of those who had hoped for so much from him and were disillusioned. Once the restrictions on what could be said in the theatre had been lifted, he had tried after 1956 to come out into the open, but he was not at ease there. He was the creature of his upbringing; his strength was implication, not rhetoric; he was better as a subversive in an occupied country than as a revolutionary at the barricades. Like many a resistance fighter he was not an effective leader after the liberation. However, by 1970 the liberators of the 'new wave' had themselves begun to look like a theatrical dictatorship. Perhaps Rattigan would find a new subversive role. Ronald Bryden had begun his article on *The Winslow Boy* with a statement: 'Against the gains our new theatrical freedoms have brought us should be set one major loss: Terence Rattigan.' He ended: 'The play stands up, a monument to the playwright we lost to permissiveness.'

Notes

1   *Daily Express*, 10 November 1960.

2   This play seems to have been a cut-down version of a previously completed three-act play called *Man and Boy* (a title Rattigan had used provisionally for his projected drama about Christie and Evans, and which he would use again for yet another play).

3   *Daily Express*, 1 December 1962.

4   To Sheila Duncan, *Daily Mirror*, 13 May 1964.

5   To Clive Hirschhorn, *Sunday Express*, 20 September 1970.

6   Interview with Sheila Duncan, *Daily Mirror*, 12 May 1964.

7   *Daily Mail*, 5 September 1963.

8   *Daily Herald*, 5 September 1963.

9   *Evening Standard*, 23 October 1963.

10 *London Magazine*, October 1963.

11 *London Magazine*, September 1964.

12 Rattigan to Howard Kissel in an interview in *Women's Wear Daily*, 17 April 1973.

13 *Ibid.*

14 ATV production script.

15 *Daily Mail*, March 1966.

16 Interviewed by Sheridan Morley, BBC Radio 4, July 1977.

17 *Observer*, 12 May 1968.

18 *New Society*, 12 November 1970.

19 *Observer*, 6 November 1970.

17
In Praise of Love

In June 1971 Rattigan was sixty. His best birthday present was undoubtedly the knighthood conferred on him in the Queen's Birthday Honours list. He was only the second playwright to be so honoured this century—the first being Noël Coward. Whether it was the knighthood or the fact that he was missing England and had in any case now saved enough money from film scripts to be able to afford to live in England again, is uncertain; but a few days before the publication of the Honours list the newspapers welcomed Rattigan's announcement that he had decided to resume living in England. When news of his knighthood broke, the *Sunday Express* commented: 'Many people must have been touched that in Mr Rattigan's case the sentimental pull of home was stronger than the appeal of tax relief. Then yesterday the rest of the world heard the news that Terence Rattigan must have known for many weeks: that he was being knighted in the Birthday Honours. Now, it may well be that the knighthood had no connection whatsoever with his return to Britain. But ought he not to have waited for the official announcement before giving us all that guff about the joys of friends, cricket and home?'[1] Rattigan objected strongly, and the paper published a retraction, saying that they had not meant in any way to impugn his motives for returning and accepted that his decision had been made months before he had received any indication that he was to be honoured.

The truth, as so often, probably lay somewhere between the two statements. The news of the honour may well have reinforced an already strong desire. His interest in returning cannot have been unconnected with his mother's worsening health. It is, however, curious that the actual announcement of his intention to return permanently did not occur until immediately after her death, at the age of eighty-two. She had in the last few years become a rather difficult and self-centred old lady. Relations between her and Rattigan had worsened, although remaining outwardly unchanged. He had probably begun a reassessment of his attitude towards her before her death, but it only came to the surface in his work immediately before his own death, in his last completed play.

Plans to celebrate Rattigan's sixtieth birthday with revivals of his work suggested the possibility of the rehabilitation of his critical reputation. He moved into Claridges while he looked for a London flat and a country home near a golf course. He was to lecture at the National Film Theatre in connection with a season of his films. A London revival of *The Browning Version* was in preparation, as well as numerous provincial productions. No less than four of his plays were to be produced on television. The most curious announcement was that Thames Television were to produce a Rattigan play which had been lost for twenty-five years. This turned out to be none other than the third of the plays written for John Gielgud in 1947 to go with *Harlequinade* and *The Browning Version*, an insubstantial piece, lasting just over an hour, called *High Summer*.

John Kershaw, the Story Editor of a series called *Armchair Theatre*, had written to all the agents of well-known playwrights asking for rejected or little-known plays. From Rattigan's agent, Dr Jan Van Loewen, he had received *High Summer*. Peter Duguid, a television director working at Thames TV, was sent the script, but when he read it he was convinced that they had finally 'gone mad'. However, he agreed to do it if Rattigan could be persuaded to make some alterations. Being used to 'the blood, sweat and tears' of Stratford, rather than the rarefied atmosphere of Binkie Beaumont's West End, which Rattigan personified, Duguid was extremely nervous before their meeting, which had

286

been arranged in Rattigan's suite at Claridges. But Rattigan put him at his ease immediately when he said, after the introductions: 'I've been looking at this piece—it's awful, isn't it?' They parted with Rattigan promising that he would look at it again and do some rewriting.

Rattigan suggested Margaret Leighton for the principal role and she agreed to do it. But when the script came back from Rattigan and she read it, she said to Duguid: 'I don't know what he's doing letting this go on.' Duguid, still unhappy with the script himself, sent it back yet again to Rattigan, who by this time had returned to Bermuda. Duguid heard nothing for a month and was getting worried, when it came back with a note from Rattigan agreeing that indeed the scene which most worried Duguid was bad and he had rewritten it, incorporating his suggestions. Duguid called a meeting with Margaret Leighton and Christopher Gable (playing the other lead) and together they decided there was enough to make it a reasonable production. Despite the strong cast, which also included Roland Culver, Thames gave it a cardboard production (it was finally transmitted on 12 September 1972) which did nothing to disguise its essential weaknesses.

The plot of *High Summer* concerns the black sheep of an aristocratic family, who has run away to Paris to become a painter, having disgraced himself in the Diplomatic Service. He comes home to reclaim the family house, symbolically called Manly. Finally realizing his actions are motivated by an unnatural and possessive love of his mother, he leaves. The play contains many familiar pieces of Rattigan's symbolic luggage, but it works neither as a drama nor as a comedy. The characters are unconvincing, the symbolism uncompelling. If Gielgud's original rejection of the *Playbill* idea as 'second rate' stuff had been applied only to this play, it would have been fully justified.

Even after the birthday year was over, the honours and the revivals continued. In January 1972 there was a midnight matinée in Rattigan's honour at the Theatre Royal, Haymarket, at which he broke his rule of not appearing on stage for the first time since the opening of *French Without Tears*, by acknowledging the cheers at the end. In May he spoke at a Gallery First Nighters' Club dinner in his honour at the Criterion, attacking those modern playwrights who 'despise their audiences', and confessing that although he had tried to move with the times he recognized that he was now really 'an old square'.

He was now being looked upon as if he were an old master whom people had suddenly discovered was still alive. The impression had been heightened perhaps by the fact that he had moved back into the Albany, taking over the only set of double chambers. There he had started to surround himself with all his old furniture, the padded board on which he had written all his plays, and some additional antique furniture collected by his father and left him by his mother. It was there, early in 1972, that he met James Cellan Jones, who was to direct the film of *Bequest to the Nation* for the autocratic Hollywood independent producer, Hal Wallis. Rattigan was receiving £70,000 for the script, but by this time he regarded Hollywood money simply as 'fairy-gold', and he hardly bothered to adapt the play at all. There was just under three months to the start of shooting and Cellan Jones was apprehensive about meeting the 'great man', especially as he knew he was going to have to let Rattigan know that the script wouldn't do as it stood. Rattigan, who had not been very well, was sitting up in bed. That first meeting was conducted as though they were playing a stock scene themselves: 'naïve young director meets famous author'. Fortunately, Cellan Jones is a modest man and was quite prepared to play his part. Unfortunately, some of the others involved in the production turned out to be not quite so unassuming.

In fact, Rattigan and Cellan Jones soon became great allies. Rattigan nurse-maided Cellan Jones and offered him moral support from then on, remaining calm and amenable in the face of Hal Wallis's dictatorial insistence on script changes.

When the film was eventually released, the critics savaged it. Although most of the attacks were levelled against Rattigan himself, he still found time to sympathize with Cellan Jones. At the première, which was attended by Princess Alexandra and Lord Mountbatten, Rattigan and Cellan Jones arrived without the paper invitations and were barred from the cinema by the commissionaire, who would not accept that they had anything to do with the film. Rattigan eventually managed to sneak into the back of the auditorium, but Cellan Jones spent the entire performance in the manager's office.

Glenda Jackson, who starred in the film, was conspicuous by

her absence at the Royal Première and in a television appearance made no secret of the fact that she thought she had given a poor performance in a part for which she had been badly miscast. Rattigan, who had so far maintained a dignified silence on the subject, now responded to the inevitable press questions. He did not think she had behaved very well, he said. Pressed further, he added gently that although he might be old-fashioned, in the old days 'one's leading lady didn't feel it necessary to say such things, even if they were true. A film is, after all, a team effort. Perhaps it is the new fashion to knock the film you're in. But she has not, so far as I know, returned her cheque.' Saying that he was trying hard not to damage the film's chances any more than Miss Jackson had already done, he claimed that she was very good, but added mischievously, 'In saying she's miscast I'm afraid she's right. It's a pity we didn't cast Liz Taylor, who would have loved to do it and would have done it for practically nothing.' (Miss Jackson was reputed to have received £70,000 for her efforts.) Finally Rattigan demolished her, proving he could be just as waspish when he thought the occasion merited it, as any of the new generation had been about him: 'Of course Miss Jackson did leave rather a lot out—Emma Hamilton's love for Nelson, for one thing, which is quite important. She played her as a mean-spirited bitch, instead of a great-hearted whore, but I suppose that is her range. And she could not possibly look fat enough.'[2]

In April 1973, Rattigan announced that he had written a new double-bill of plays called *In Praise of Love*, which he hoped would open in London that autumn. In view of the hostile reception accorded to his new work since 1960, it would have been understandable if he had decided to rest on his laurels. Yet Rattigan had always regarded himself as first and foremost a playwright, and his ambition was still to write a great play. His health continued to be suspect, and there is a good deal of evidence for supposing that *In Praise of Love* represented a decision to write a theatrical testament. With the exception of *Heart to Heart*, written for television, all his plays since 1958 had been period pieces. In the more substantial of the two plays in *In Praise of Love* he returned to a modern setting and subject, while making no concessions to changes in theatrical taste since the 1950s. The genesis of *In Praise of Love* is complex, but the initial impulse and the necessary self-confidence seem to have come from

289

the spate of revivals and the renewed interest in Rattigan's work which began in 1971.

It will be recalled that in that year Stephen Mitchell had announced a revival of *The Browning Version* starring John Mills. To accompany this, a lighter piece was needed to replace *Harlequinade*, which was now thought to be dated. At first Rattigan thought of writing a play set before the opening of *The Browning Version*, showing Millie Crocker Harris before she married the classics master. This was quickly abandoned in favour of a lighter piece featuring an amateur company rehearsing *The Browning Version*. Rattigan had been very amused by a group of local nurses who had been rehearsing *French Without Tears* when he arrived in Freetown after the hair-raising wartime flight when he had nearly lost his manuscript of *Flare Path*. He had remembered that incident and other amateur productions, and decided to set his play among a group of present-day amateurs in a British colony, possibly Bermuda. A potentially disastrous notion, it was fortunately dropped. The important point that emerges from both ideas is the temptation to spoof the play which he had always regarded as his most accomplished work. 'If today I had to justify my choice of career before a heavenly jury, this is the play I would want to represent me,' he had said in 1957.[3]

The idea of doing a completely new double-bill of short plays seems to have grown out of the talk of reviving *The Browning Version*. He still had the comedy about a successful Marxist painter confronted by a conformist son, which he had completed for Rex Harrison in 1961. This had never been used, because the play with which it was to have been paired had been shaped into *Heart to Heart* in response to the BBC commission. Rattigan re-examined it. While keeping much of the surface form of a comedy, he decided to change and deepen it. In one of his most audacious dramatic strokes, he made comedy dialogue carry a deeply serious personal story. The painter was turned into a writer and the son into a Liberal, about to have his first play done on television. Most important of all, the wife and mother was dying of cancer, which the husband was trying to conceal from her. Rattigan also said that an ingredient in the final choice of subject had been Binkie Beaumont's suggestion that he should try a comedy about death.

From the time of Kay Kendall's death Rattigan had mulled

over the idea of writing a play about her and the way Harrison had fought to preserve her happiness by keeping the truth about her illness from her until the end. There were, too, the obvious autobiographical elements from his own confrontation with the mistakenly diagnosed leukaemia in 1963, and the time he had been given up for dead in the Naples hospital in 1968. Finally, and perhaps decisively in triggering off the completion of this long-contemplated project, the impresario who had been planning to present the revival of *The Browning Version*, his friend Stephen Mitchell, had recently gone through a similar ordeal, watching his wife die of leukaemia and trying to conceal the truth from her until the last possible moment. At a deeper level, the death of his own mother may have played a part in the play that finally emerged, especially in the discussion of how both son and husband will face the world without her.

The play is so packed with personal references and allusions as to make it unique in Rattigan's career. Perhaps because the play first began to take shape in his mind twelve or thirteen years earlier, and had never been long absent from his thoughts over the intervening years, his distinctive process of absorption and distillation had rarely worked more effectively. Inside a simple plot and a light texture is condensed a depth of feeling and a degree of perception equalled in its economy and richness only by *The Browning Version*. Inevitably, the play operates on a number of different levels. As a piece of elliptical, condensed autobiography, which would only have been understood at the time by a handful of people who knew him very well, and by them only incompletely, it is truly astonishing. Without dissecting almost every line, it is impossible to convey the concentrated richness of its autobiographical texture, but a brief outline of the plot and some of the strands running through it may indicate some of its qualities.

The setting is the fourth-floor London flat of Sebastian and Lydia Cruttwell. At the start, Sebastian is struggling to meet his deadline for an article about Shakespeare for the *New Statesman*. He is a Marxist who twenty-five years ago wrote a novel which was hailed as a minor masterpiece, but he gave up and became a critic ('joined the enemy') when the reviews of his second book were unfavourable: 'They all turned on you for not writing the original novel all over again.' He is, however, diffidently contemplating a new book. With the passing years his Marxism has become more rhetorical than real: 'He only spouts Marxist revolution as a spell to prevent its ever happening.' His son, Joey, a budding playwright, incenses his father by campaigning for the Liberal Party, portrayed by Rattigan as the new generation of idealists. Joey's mother, Lydia, is an Estonian refugee who married Sebastian after he found her in a Berlin brothel at the end of the war, where she had been working to save herself from death in a Nazi concentration camp. He married her to rescue her from the fate that would have befallen her at the hands of the Russians if she had been returned to her native country. She has incurable leukaemia, but is determined to keep the knowledge of it from Sebastian and to devote the rest of her time to finding someone to take her place as mother, wife and servant.

The fourth character is Mark, their mutual friend and confidant. He is a best-selling popular novelist, whose books are snapped up by Hollywood for huge sums before they have even appeared. His work no longer gets reviews, the critics simply dismissing each new book as a carbon-copy of the last. Sebastian envies Mark, but sneers at his success and makes a show of boorish ingratitude for his lavish presents and hospitality. Mark's writing is not literature, he claims, but a sell-out, a calculated manipulation to maximize sales.

All four characters owe something to real-life models among Rattigan's acquaintances, yet are fully realized fictional people. Simultaneously, however, all four are facets of himself: Mark, the free-spending and publicly popular self; Joey, the youthful idealist clashing with his father and worshipping his mother, naïvely setting out to be a playwright; Sebastian, the literary idealist who, behind a bantering façade, hides both diffidence and strong emotions; Lydia, the refugee dying in the country of her choice, with so much love to give but no one with whom to share it, trying to face her own end without whimpering—as Rattigan himself was determined to do. Their clash is the clash within himself; and, in a more intense way than in any other play, the stage becomes the symbolic arena in which Rattigan works through the central conflicts of his own life. Yet there is no disguised striptease about this play. Nothing masquerades as what it is not; the charge that 'its real subject is something other than its ostensible subject' cannot be levelled at the play. Sex is subsumed to emotion; the conflicts centre on the revelation of feeling. It is a play about the nature and expression of love.

It takes the form of a psychological suspense story. The initial veneer of comedy is slowly peeled away as the audience is allowed to perceive the depth of emotion that each character hides behind jokes or boorish behaviour.

By two-thirds of the way through, an almost unbearable tension has been created. The inevitable crisis is precipitated when Sebastian, who has that afternoon received final proof that his wife's condition is incurable, fails to come home in time for the transmission of his son's first television play. He has tried to keep the fact of his wife's illness from her and still believes he has succeeded, but knowledge of the certainty of her impending death has made him forget his son's play. When he returns, Lydia lashes out at him. Then, left alone with Mark, he breaks down and weeps. Cursing himself for his show of weakness, he questions whether, despite all their years of marriage, he has only really loved Lydia since he knew he was losing her:

> ... Did I feel about her like this from the beginning? It's possible. And wouldn't allow myself to? Yes, possible. *(Angrily)* Do you know what 'Le vice Anglais?'—the English vice—really is? Not flagellation, not pederasty—whatever the French believe it to be. It's our refusal to admit to our emotions. We think they demean us, I suppose. *(He covers his face)* Well I'm being punished now, all right—for a lifetime of vice. Very moral endings to a Victorian novel. I'm becoming maudlin. But, oh Mark, life without Lydia will be such endless misery.

Yet, confronted with Lydia, Sebastian still cannot reveal his true feelings for her. So Mark allows her to find out that Sebastian knows the truth about her illness by revealing where he has hidden the papers with her monthly blood counts.

The audience now expects a tearful reconciliation and an open declaration of their true feelings. In a stroke of heart-breaking skill, which is symbolically and emotionally consistent, Rattigan denies them the sentimental ending. The pretence is maintained between the two, their love remains unspoken. Lydia, now aware that Sebastian's boorishness and unfeeling jokes are a cover for his feelings, has no immediate need to shatter his illusions. Now that she knows the truth it is easier for all three of them—husband, wife and son—to endure their situation so long as they continue to avoid too overt a confrontation with the pain which has been an integral part of the discovery of their love. For them, and for Rattigan, there is an eternal conflict between love and pain, between revelation and concealment. No element can be banished; all that can be hoped for is temporary equilibrium. The last ten minutes of the play are among the most perfectly crafted and economically effective passages anywhere in British drama.

The play is as fine a statement about the loss of illusions which has beset the 1970s as any so far written by younger and more obviously idealistic dramatists. It condemns both the easy permissiveness and the blind extremism to which disillusioned idealists have turned in desperation. It reminds them of the stern disciplines of rational moderation and true humanism. Joey attacks his mother for putting up with Sebastian's callousness, claiming that her concern for other people's feelings sounds like 'a gooey sort of ultra-Christianity'.

LYDIA: There isn't any sort of *ultra*-Christianity. There's just Christianity. And if it's gooey—well, it's gooey.
JOEY: I didn't know you were religious.
LYDIA: It's wonderful how that word today is made to sound like some curious perversion—permissible of course, like all things, but rather unmentionable ...

But Lydia is not a Christian. She maintains the discipline of love and consideration not out of blind belief, but out of self-awareness and rational choice, born of the hardest of experience: Catholic upbringing, Nazi and Stalinist terror.

On another level, Rattigan brings out many of his beliefs about writing in the exchanges between Sebastian, the critic, and Mark, the popular novelist. Sebastian calls Shakespeare: 'That complacent old burgher of Stratford-on-Avon. God, he's so maddening. With his worship of the Establishment, he makes nonsense of everything we write ... Well Shakespeare *must* infuriate people like us who passionately believe that no man can write well whose heart isn't in the right place.' (By which, as Mark points out, he means 'the left place'.) He was both Royal Court and Shaftesbury Avenue, in fact—inconsistent. At the climax, when he breaks down, Sebastian quotes Shakespeare:

No Lydia—

'She'll come no more.

Never, never, never, never, never.'

Oh damn! I'll never review that bloody man again. I won't review anyone after all they all make you blub somewhere—if they're good.

The extent of Rattigan's self-identification in this play is easy to trace, but it is much more difficult to detect in the second play in the double-bill. As with *The Browning Version* and *Harlequinade*, and the two plays in *Separate Tables*, Rattigan wanted plays which would meld by being the converse of each other. So if the first play was about real love unspoken, the second would have to be about unreal love spoken. In the first play there was plenty of love but too little said about it; in the second there would be no love, but too much would be said about it.

Before Dawn is a crude burlesque on *Tosca*. Baron Scarpia, the wicked head of the secret police, gives Tosca a choice, as in the play and the opera: either she shares his bed, or her lover Mario is shot as a spy. Reluctantly Tosca consents, but then Rattigan invents a new ending. Scarpia proves impotent, and is so embarrassed by the damage his failure will do to his reputation as a villain that he will either have to make good his failure or have Tosca shot too before the night is out. The play is unaccountably feeble, depending for its laughs on obvious *double entendres*. It is difficult to understand why Rattigan should write such a piece, or, having done so, consent to having it put on in a double-bill with one of his finest plays. Holly Hill has pointed out that not only is it a play unworthy of him but in it he appears to deride both his own playwriting tradition and himself. First, by burlesquing Sardou's most famous play, he is burlesquing the founder of the tradition of the well-made play which he himself had carried on and defended even when it fell out of favour. Second, he pokes fun at one of his own recurring themes—the conflict between physical and spiritual love—the Baron representing the former and Tosca's lover the latter. Rattigan actually makes a cheap joke about Tosca's lover being able to offer her only spiritual love because he is a homosexual.

It is probably kindest to dismiss *Before Dawn* as an aberration. Yet one begins to suspect, in a dramatist as aware of his theatrical antecedents and his own dramatic intentions as Rattigan, a degree of deliberation. Is it not too complete to be an accident? We have already noticed two elements in the genesis of this double-bill that might support this thesis: the way in which the serious play reads like a testament, a final drawing together of the personal strands of Rattigan's drama; and that even when the plan was only to find a *divertimento* to go with a revival of *The Browning Version*, the play on which he was prepared to let his reputation stand, he was actively considering a send-up of it. May it not be, then, that *Before Dawn*, which was intended to be played after the serious play, was meant as a final cynical pay-off to his whole career? A kind of pulling the building down on top of himself at the end?

Whatever Rattigan's intentions, the effect of *Before Dawn*, as it affected the reception of the double-bill, was disastrous. It was found during the try-out tour that the audience would not accept it after the serious play (which in England was called *After Lydia*). So *Before Dawn* was played first. But it created such antipathy in the audience and critics alike, that many were unready to accept *Before Lydia* and became unduly intolerant of its minor faults. When *In Praise of Love* opened at the Duchess Theatre on 27 September 1973, directed by John Dexter and starring Donald Sinden and Joan Greenwood, it did not enjoy the success it deserved.

Further proof of the way in which *Before Dawn* damaged the appreciation of *After Lydia* was provided by the New York production. There *After Lydia* was performed on its own, under the title, *In Praise of Love*. The play, already over-long in exposition, was lengthened to make a full evening in the theatre. This was achieved mainly by restoring cuts from an earlier version which gave more detail about Lydia's wartime experiences. The British production had done little to maximize the play's chances, but the New York production did even less. Although nominally better cast, with Rex Harrison at last playing the part which he had done so much to inspire, and Julie Harris as Lydia, much of it was played in a way which went against the author's intentions, and new lines and business were introduced which Rattigan did not initiate or approve—although he failed to take effective steps to have them removed. Yet the play got better reviews in New York, and ran for 199 performances, as against 131 in London.

While the play was in rehearsal in London, Rattigan had written a long letter to Rex Harrison saying that he hoped he wouldn't mind that he had used Kay Kendall's illness as the basis for the plot of his new play; he apologized for doing it, but said that he had changed so many details and introduced so many other elements that he didn't think anyone would recognize its origins. He added that he was anxious for Harrison to see it and approve. When Harrison went to see the play in London, Rattigan waited for him in the foyer and then sat through the performance with him. Afterwards, when he took Harrison out to dinner, he was still anxious in case it had upset him. Shortly afterwards Harrison was told that there was to be a New York production. Rattigan was very anxious that he should play Sebastian and flew down to Harrison's house in Portofino to go over the play with him. The bulk of the extra dialogue went in at that stage, but the most damaging changes were made later, during rehearsal, when Rattigan was not able to be present.

Rehearsals for the New York production began in October 1974. Rattigan had pneumonia, which he had caught while campaigning for the Liberal Party in the second of the 1974 General Elections. Rattigan had been a member of the party ever since Puffin Asquith had signed him up after the war. In 1974 Rattigan, like so many other people, found his dormant political idealism rekindled by the fundamental issues raised by the clash between Prime Minister Edward Heath and the miners. In October, he put up one of his manuscript copies of *The Deep Blue Sea* for auction to raise money in support of the campaign by the Liberal candidate in Richmond, Alan Watson, who was standing against the left-wing Labour Minister for the Arts, Hugh Jenkins. He also went out on the stump for Watson, making public appearances with him. The pneumonia prevented him from seeing the American production of *In Praise of Love* until just before the New York opening. What he saw worried him greatly. Harrison was playing Sebastian for sympathy from the moment he came on, thus destroying Rattigan's careful build-up of tension and the dramatic revelation that Sebastian's callousness is a cover for feelings he can hardly bear. He even sneaked a look at Lydia's latest medical report shortly after the rise of the curtain, thus betraying his concern about her condition from the start. Rattigan was also unhappy about the way in

297

which Julie Harris was playing the ending. In the text Rattigan directs that she should smile radiantly at Sebastian, revealing her happiness at the knowledge that her love is returned. Julie Harris seemed unwilling to smile. Rattigan kept telling her that this smile was her 'most important line, it's the most important line in the play'.

Rattigan was very angry, and there seems to have been a stand-up row between him and Harrison, followed by an angry exchange of letters. However, the play opened on Broadway substantially as Rattigan had seen it on tour, and the text, as published in America, contains the new lines and the additional business put in by Harrison and Dexter. Almost the only American critic to spot what had been done to the play was Holly Hill. Writing in the *Educational Theatre Journal*, she began by declaring that the production illustrated an artistic and critical failure: 'Rex Harrison's performance distorts the character which Rattigan created, and the critics' praise for this distortion exposes their inability to distinguish between acting and writing.' She concluded that the Broadway presentation was a 'misrepresentation of Rattigan's work'.

The full power of the play was not realized in production until Anglia Television televised it in 1977. Superbly directed by Alvin Rakoff, who had worked with Rattigan on *Heart to Heart* and who understood the full implication of the play, it was done in a version based on the original English script, which was tactfully cut down a little so that it fitted a television slot. This cutting was generally of benefit, tightening the play and increasing the tension in the first and second scenes. The production benefited too from superb performances by Claire Bloom, ideally cast as Lydia, and Kenneth More giving perhaps the best performance of his career in a part that might have been written for him, as Sebastian. When the recording of the play was complete, Rakoff ran it for Rattigan and one or two other people connected with the production. At the end all the people in the room sat in tears, unable to speak for a moment. The one with most tears running down his face was Rattigan himself.

Notes

1 *Sunday Express*, 20 June 1971.
2 *Daily Mail*, 4 April 1973.
3 Introductory talk to a season of his plays on BBC Radio — recorded 17 September 1957.

18
Justice

Rattigan may have regarded *In Praise of Love* as a final summation of his life in the theatre, but he was now more active than at any time in the previous ten years, when he had virtually given up the theatre in favour of making money from films. Of course the film work still rolled in and he did not turn it away—there were commissions to adapt a stage success, *Conduct Unbecoming*, and a French novel called *The Film of Memory* for Liza Minnelli. Work on the latter, however, was held up by his participation in a strike. Rattigan was a member of the Writers Guild of America, which had called a stoppage against the Hollywood film companies, and even though he was living in England he was not the man to break ranks.

As his involvement in the Liberal campaign in the 1974 Election showed, he was more active in outside causes than at any time since he was a young man. In October 1974, he was one of eleven leading authors—others included John Betjeman, J. B. Priestley, Veronica Wedgwood and Rebecca West—who signed a letter to *The Times* in support of the campaign for a Public Lending Right, a long-overdue scheme to compensate authors for the loss of royalties resulting from the drop in their sales because of the increased availability of books on loan through public libraries. He was letter-writing as never before. He was particularly prone to sound off at critics whose opinions he disagreed with. His letters to Bernard Levin developed into a full-scale correspondence but a critic in any medium might suddenly receive a salvo from H5-6 The Albany, often written late at night, and apparently under the influence of brandy. Typical, and very revealing of his current mood, was one received by Elkan Allan of the *Sunday Times*, who had previewed a television programme about the McCarthy hearings called 'Hollywood on Trial'. Rattigan's letter consisted of six increasingly wildly scrawled postcards. (It should be said that Mr Allan was not aware of ever having had a letter from Rattigan before.) Across the top of the first card was a postscript: 'Answer please, for once, personally ... *We don't want 'ed.s', and 'pub'* (doubly underlined by Rattigan).

Dear Mr Allan,
I don't think you are wont to answer my letters, but please answer this, for I write with a real grievance.
'The Hollywood Ten' (Omnibus Rpt) ... Why *disappointing*? You nearly stopped me seeing what is surely a really brilliant statement of an ethical—not political—problem: do you betray a friend to The Special Branch when you happen to know he's joined General Walker's private army—in whose aims you once misguidedly believed, and which aims you now consider dangerous to the State? ... Your career is at stake. *Do* you, or don't you?
Best, T.R.
P.S. I can't remember the occasion, but I believe that you *do* owe me a letter. Possibly, before I was pleading against your fixed determination to dismiss any film directed by Anthony Asquith (Liberal) written by me (Lib-Lab) and produced by Anatole de Grunwald (Anti-Stalin, pro-Kruschev) as Fascist propaganda ... Something of the kind, anyway ... Of no importance, of course ... Except that 'fascist' doesn't and never did, fit. But *don't* stop your readers watching what we *should* watch—And don't let your political slip show more than it need. An inch is enough. 'King Street' [address of the British Communist Party] would approve this advice—as I *very well know*.
P.P.S. I repeat: no publication, please. Someday later, perhaps. Not now.

P.P.P.S. If I'd been in Hollywood during those years, instead of being happily employed by Liberals at Shepperton (and I include Alex Korda) it would have been the 'Hollywood Eleven' (which makes a better title than 'Ten' doesn't it?).

But I realize now, that the title of the programme in question was 'Hollywood on Trial'. 'The Hollywood Ten' would have been better (except that it's been used). 'The Hollywood Eleven' best of all. Nudge, nudge, nudge!—make of it what you will. I care no more. T.R. and I don't think King Street does, either.'

In fact there had always been more consistency in Rattigan's political attitudes than in his public statement of them in his published work. For instance, in the mid 1950s, when he seemed most out of step with the young, anti-militarist generation, he had raised heated private objections to the jingoistic sentiments and glorification of German civilian deaths in the most popular British film of the period, *The Dam Busters*. Once again it seems a pity he never gave vent to his feelings in public.

In 1973 BBC Television commissioned a script on Nijinsky from Rattigan. But no sooner had news of the commission got out than he ran into furious opposition from Romola Nijinska, Nijinsky's widow, who wrote to him insisting that he stop. A few years earlier, there had been talk of Rattigan scripting a film based on Romola Nijinska's own biography of her husband, who had died in 1950 after years of mental disorder. This time, however, Rattigan was taking Richard Buckle's biography of the dancer as his starting point. Rattigan was at first willing to accede to Madam Nijinska's demands and was ready to stop work. However, the BBC said she had no case and told him to proceed with the commission, for which he had agreed a contract. The parties are still rather coy about the correspondence which continued while Rattigan wrote, but it seems that allegations and counter-allegations mounted, calling into question not only Nijinsky's sexual relations but Rattigan's 'bestial proclivities' too. In this atmosphere Rattigan proceeded to write one of the most sensitive scripts of his career.

He traced Nijinsky's life from his childhood examination for a place in the St Petersburg Imperial Ballet on to his stardom and through into irrevocable madness. In the script Rattigan squarely confronted the subject he had so often shied away from or

302

concealed in the past: homosexuality. Because one can accept Nijinsky as other-worldly throughout and does not have to believe in him as a man of action, as in the case of Alexander, Lawrence or Nelson, the play works in a way that the previous episodic portraits of real-life heroes do not. There is very little dialogue, much of the significant action being contained in minutely detailed camera instructions. The relationship between Nijinsky and Diaghilev is spelt out with delicacy and precision. There is none of the sexual hypertension in the writing which mars *Bequest to the Nation,* nor the evasiveness that flaws some other plays. Yet the play is not about homosexuality, but about love. After Romola's successful pursuit of Nijinsky and marriage to him, Diaghilev withdraws his love—possessively jealous, he cannot share Nijinsky with anyone. The play ends with Nijinsky locked in madness. Bereft of Diaghilev's love, for which Romola's is an inadequate substitute, Nijinsky becomes trapped in himself, unable to communicate with the real world. During her pursuit of Nijinsky Romola tells Diaghilev that Nijinsky has no gender. There follows a line which goes far beyond the immediate situation of the play in its significance for Rattigan. Nijinsky says: 'But an artist should have no gender ... Art comes directly from God. Has God a gender? Is he male or female? Isn't he both?'

The rows over *Nijinsky* dragged on after it was completed. Rattigan was unwilling to risk having to appear in court to defend his interpretation of Nijinsky's emotional life and so, tragically, asked the BBC not to proceed with the production until after Romola's death. Rattigan regretted this for the rest of his life. (As this book goes to press, it is reported that, following the death of Romola, the BBC will now produce the play.)

Revivals of Rattigan's early work had increased rather than decreased in number since the end of his sixtieth birthday celebrations in 1971. Two had been particularly influential in helping a proper reappraisal of his achievement and had a great effect on him personally. The first, *While the Sun Shines,* opened at the Hampstead Theatre Club in December 1972. When he heard about the revival, Rattigan thoughtfully provided some rewrites for the director Alec McCowen, a distinguished actor directing his first play. Rattigan thought he might want to explain bits of the action and dialogue which would seem unintelligible or dated to a modern audience with no first-hand knowledge of the war. McCowen tactfully accepted but didn't use them. He recognized that *While the Sun Shines* was now a period piece and one of the interests of a revival lay in playing it as that.

When Rattigan arrived for the previews, having agreed to sit up on the stage after the performance and answer questions from the audience, he found the theatre had been adorned with pictures of Churchill, the youthful de Gaulle, and old programmes which reminded their readers that 'tube trains don't run during air-raid alerts'. The foyer loudspeakers blared out Tommy Dorsey's 'I'll be seeing you'. Although some of the parts were stupendously miscast, Rattigan was excited to find the predominantly young audience rocking in their seats with laughter. 'Oh, the whole thing is utterly reprehensible, and yet I thoroughly enjoyed it,' commented John Crosby in *Plays and Players*.[1] The same thing happened again when Frank Dunlop, in spite of opposition from the Arts Council (touched on in the Introduction to this book), staged *French Without Tears* at the Young Vic the following year. The majority of the critics, although in some cases rather shocked or surprised at themselves, found that they too were laughing. 'So we were not wrong, those of us who remember *French Without Tears* as delicious, and somehow something more than a mere frolic,' began John Barber, a critic of the older generation and a contemporary of Rattigan's at Oxford, in his review in the *Daily Telegraph*.[2] His conclusion, that it was 'a beguiling classic of its kind', was echoed by the younger critics. 'The one great theme that runs through all our comedy and farce is the nervous fluster to which the average Englishman is reduced by sex, and Rattigan's play demonstrates this to perfection ... Far from being a tenuous divertissement the play in fact mocks certain durable aspects of the English character with affectionate skill,' commented Michael Billington in the *Guardian*,[3] adding, 'And it's interesting to reflect that much of Rattigan's later, serious work ... is likewise concerned with the paralyzing emotional reticence of the English male.'

Rattigan was, in his own words, 'terribly encouraged'. Not least because as well as laughing, new young audiences had found some substance in the comedy. They were more enthralled by the serious passage about the young man's pacifism in *French Without Tears* on the hard wooden benches at the Young Vic in the 1970s than they had been in the gilt and velvet of the Criterion in the 1930s.

But although young audiences seemed once again to be in touch with him, he knew that he was, in a sense, out of touch with them. He confessed more than once to finding it increasingly difficult to write about modern young people. Frank Marcus had congratulated him on getting the son Joey just right in *In Praise of Love*, which had gratified him, but he knew that if he wanted to write about young people in future it would be safer to make them young people of his own generation or earlier. This was exactly what he did when, in the summer of 1974, the BBC commissioned a radio play from him. It was an arrangement somewhat similar to the international television agreement which had produced *Heart to Heart*. Normally meagre radio fees were bumped up to something like £6,000 for a ninety-minute play by the prospect of foreign transmissions. Rattigan went back to an idea he had had thirty-nine years earlier, during the summer of 1935 when he had been busy working with Gielgud on the fated adaptation of *A Tale of Two Cities*—the Rattenbury murder case.

The case had obvious appeal to him. The events had actually occurred in Bournemouth, an archetypal Rattigan setting. Alma Rattenbury, a small-time composer of popular songs, herself middle-aged, was the wife of an older man who could not satisfy her sexually. She had taken as her lover her eighteen-year-old chauffeur-gardener. After taking the young man away with her for a few days of high life in a London hotel she found that he had become jealous of her husband on their return home. When he suspected that Mr and Mrs Rattenbury were having sexual intercourse together, he murdered Mr Rattenbury by beating him over the head with a mallet. Alma Rattenbury and her young lover were jointly charged with the murder. At the time of the trial Alma Rattenbury was the victim of massive popular prejudice. Whether she was really guilty or not, she was held to be guilty for what had happened, because she was the older partner in the affair, a fact which spelt domination in the public mind; having taken a boy for her lover, she was assumed to have led him into a life of depravity, of which murder was the outcome. There was no pity for her, no willingness to try to understand that, 'out of this unpromising material she had created something that to her was beautiful and made her happy.'[4] In the event, only he was found guilty, with a strong appeal for clemency. Although she had been acquitted, Alma Rattenbury committed suicide. She left a note, in which she spoke of what a beautiful world we live in—'If only we could let ourselves see it'.

Rattigan does not tell the story in simple chronological narrative but starts, as so often before, at a point of crisis and explores what has led up to it during the course of the working-out of the crisis itself. In this case the play opens at the beginning of the trial and, as it proceeds, uses a complex series of flashbacks to build up a composite picture of what has happened. Thus Rattigan shows the way public prejudice places different values on the same events. He heightens this by means of a sub-plot, centred around a sexually repressed lady juror, whose frigidity has driven her husband into the arms of other women, and her adolescent public schoolboy son. This amounts to a separate play. It is as though instead of creating two separate items to counterpoint each other in a double-bill, as with *The Browning Version* and *Harlequinade* or the two plays in *Separate Tables*, he had interlaced the two together and allowed them to develop side by side in a form of continuous musical counterpoint in which they sometimes touch and affect each other.

The sub-plot comes closer to literal autobiography than anything in Rattigan's work. The idea of writing an autobiography had cropped up a number of times in the previous twenty years, but it was only in the last three years of his life that he talked about it in a way that suggested a real determination to get down to it. Whether thinking about the autobiography determined the shape of the sub-plot of *Cause Célèbre*, or whether writing the sub-plot sharpened his interest in an autobiography, is not clear. Although he agreed with his publishers to write an autobiography, it seems unlikely that he would have actually written it, even had he lived longer. It was an essentially alien form for him, a man whose life had been devoted to forms of concealment and role-playing. In any case, each play had contained autobiographical elements, and he seemed to thrive on the disciplined restrictions imposed by playwriting. Even so, the autobiographical elements in the sub-plot were explicit and he made no attempt to conceal them. He told the director of the later stage version, Robin Midgley, that the woman, Edith Davenport, was not an exact portrait of his mother because she was more understanding

306

towards him than Mrs Davenport is to her son in the play, but at the same time he made it clear that most of the things that happen to the boy, Tony, had happened to him.

Even the incidental details are correct: she comes from a family of distinguished lawyers who served in India, and now lives not simply in a West Kensington hotel like Aunt Edna, but in Cornwall Gardens, Rattigan's own birthplace. Herself sexually repressed, she finds Alma's willingness to gratify her sexual needs with an adolescent particularly shocking. She loves her son excessively as the only thing she has left from her failed marriage, but will not countenance his adolescent interest in sex. She refuses to have the subject discussed. His only sexual experience so far has been with other boys at his boarding school, but he is avid to 'try it' with a woman. With money from his father he experiments with a prostitute, but it is a humiliating failure. After this he goes back to an attractive younger boy. During the course of the play he discovers that the picture his mother has painted of his father, who is living apart from the family, is unduly harsh. His flagrant affairs with other women in fact add up to no more than occasional 'medicinal' sexual encounters, without any emotional content, and are the result of his wife's inability to provide sexual satisfaction. The myth of the affairs has been perpetuated principally to save his mother's self-esteem as a 'wronged' woman. This last element in the story may represent Rattigan's re-evaluation of his parents' relationship, but it had only become possible for him to incorporate such a re-evaluation in a play after his mother's death.

By the time *Cause Célèbre* was broadcast in October 1975, Rattigan had become ill again. Once more he underwent a long series of painful and exhausting tests. Then, while he was in Bermuda for Christmas, the news that everyone had dreaded came through. He had cancer. This time there seemed no room for doubt about the diagnosis. The prognosis was not good. It was in his bones, was spreading and, although it might be slowed down, seemed irreversible. One of those staying with him in Bermuda when the confirmation came through was his editor at Hamish Hamilton, Roger Machell, a friend since prep school days at Sandroyd: '... he took the whole thing outwardly very much more lightly than the characters in *In Praise of Love* and with the most extraordinary courage and cheerfulness,' Machell said.[5]

When he returned to London and more tests and treatment in January 1976, he refused to stay in hospital when there was no absolute need. Instead, he moved himself into a suite at Claridges. This time he made no attempt to conceal the truth about his condition. Inviting David Lewin of the *Daily Mail* to share a bottle of champagne with him, he said: 'When this happens you suddenly stop counting the cost of anything. So in the time that's left I shall work harder and indulge myself more.' He was resolutely determined not to be sorry for himself. The earlier leukaemia and burst appendix scares had prepared him for the idea of death. Even so, he couldn't fail to be moved by the viewing of Alvin Rakoff's television production of *In Praise of Love.* Later that evening, talking to the journalist Philip Oakes back in his suite at Claridges, he said: 'I seemed to spend a great deal of time mopping tears from my face. Not surprising in the circumstances, perhaps, it was not the most ideal entertainment.' It was a question of identification with the heroine dying of leukaemia, he explained. Oakes had a slipped disc and it was typical of Rattigan that, although his own cancer was in his back, he showed more concern about his guest's comfort than his own. 'Don't move,' Rattigan said, getting up to pour drinks. 'Frightful things, backs. Are you sure you're seeing the right man? Is your bed hard enough? I really do sympathize. You must be having an awful time.' Oakes felt a surge of guilt as he remembered the location of Rattigan's cancer. Perhaps Rattigan sensed it, for he pressed on: 'The other thing is not to dwell on it. It's so easy to become a back bore. People don't like it.'[6] The potential embarrassment of the situation was removed by Rattigan's matter-of-fact approach to his illness: 'There's no doubt about the diagnosis. I have to accept it. And, of course, the question arises: how much time do I have left? I would like to complete a couple more plays and write my autobiography. Five years would do it. But there's no guarantee about these things. I'm pushing on as best I can. I actually did some work this morning and I felt rather proud of myself.' All the old discipline had returned, but already it was beginning to become more difficult physically: 'But I still try to do four hours' work a day. If a scene isn't finished I go back to it at night. The excuse of not feeling like it isn't good enough. It's much too obvious.'

He now had two projects in hand: a stage version of *Cause*

Célèbre which he had been asked to do by the impresario John Gale, and a play about the Asquiths. More than a year previously, while he was in New York for the Broadway opening of *In Praise of Love*, he had told Holly Hill that he was full of the Asquith play. She asked him how conscious was his repeated use of understatement and emotionally repressed characters in his plays. He told her he found it difficult to know how conscious his choice of subject and style were. To illustrate what he meant he gave her a very complete description of the play he was planning:

It's about the father of a great friend of mine, a Prime Minister called Herbert Asquith. I always wanted to write a play of 1916 because I believe the Battle of the Somme saw the end of a form of Western Civilisation, and life was never the same after that. [It will be remembered that the Battle of the Somme had a special significance for the Rattigan family because of the death of Frank's younger brother, Cyril, on the first day.] Until that moment, life could have gone on—perhaps it wasn't right that it should have gone on in that way, but it could have gone on. And it was in Asquith's power to stop the war ... If peace had been settled with Germany—we were not dealing with Nazi Germany—on the basis not of unconditional surrender but a negotiated peace, the holocaust could have been stopped in 1916—if Asquith were not a sick man.

He was made sicker than he need have been by the death of his favourite son Raymond, who was one of the great leading lights of that generation, the Rupert Brooke generation. He was a brilliant scholar, he had a marvellous future, probably in politics, but quite possibly as a writer. He was killed in the Battle of the Somme, and he chose deliberately to go as a second-lieutenant in the front line when, of course, he could have had what they called 'a cushy job' as the Prime Minister's son.

I found out that during Asquith's visit to General Haig in his headquarters, six weeks after the battle opened, Haig allowed Raymond, this paragon, to come and see his father. A week later Asquith learned the boy had been killed.

Now, two months later, Lloyd George shoved Asquith out. Lloyd George was a 'La Guerre' figure, like Clemenceau—the war has to be won, to the last drop of blood, as it were. And so to 1918, so to Versailles, so to the next war. It's one of the fascinating 'ifs' of history: what would have happened if Raymond hadn't been killed—and Raymond didn't have to be killed. First of all, he was slightly suicidally inclined himself. Secondly, of course, his father could have saved him. He didn't—with the repressions of the period it wasn't possible. It might have been possible that Margot Asquith, who's a good character to write about, said 'Henry, your duty is plain. You must save that boy. He's wasted in the front line. Get him into Headquarters or somewhere.' But, by chance, I found out that the Asquiths never touched each other. It used to madden Margot. She said: 'They're unfeeling brutes, these Asquiths. They never even shake hands.' But they loved each other. Of course, Asquith loved his son passionately and the son loved his father. But I, of course, was instantly thinking of the scene with the son and father at opposite ends of the stage, when he's come back from the front line. And from that oddly enough, from just that fact, plus the lucky coincidence really that it should have been right in the middle of the battle that Asquith went to the front, possibly to stop it. Raymond was killed in the second phase of the battle a week later. Asquith didn't stop it—and the emotional link with Raymond; I think there's something to write about there.

We were talking about emotional repression. It's so right for this play, because I think that could be so very deeply moving that they never touched each other at all. And when he decides to go back, say he's given the choice of going to Headquarters—the 'cushy job'—or going back to the front line; say he decides to go back, which I think is possibly what happened, it could well be, and he says 'goodbye' to his father and they're at opposite sides of the stage. That is the last we see of him before the special telegram arrives.

Early in 1976 he was still full of the Asquith play. He told Anthony Curtis, who did the first full-scale radio appreciation of his work, that this was the play he was 'engaged in at the moment' and he thought that 1916 was a period he could probably write about better than some of the younger playwrights.[7]

At the time of Rattigan's return to London early in 1976, a

310

revival opened which did even more than other revivals of recent years to jog those who had long since dismissed him into a reassessment of his distinctive genius. At the King's Head, a pub theatre in Islington, normally the home of young radicals and the avant-garde, that seemingly most alien and middle-class of Rattigan characters, the emotionally repressed public school-master, Crocker Harris, was holding a new and unlikely audience spellbound. Unrecognized among a predominantly young and unkempt audience for *The Browning Version*, Rattigan himself went to a performance in the crowded small back room in Upper Street, Islington. If any of the hundred or so people squashed on to hard wooden chairs or sitting at small tables noticed the immaculately blue-suited elderly man who sat among them, they didn't remark on him. His hair was now greying slightly at the edges and receding a little. The chin sagged a little. His face was already puffed, not by old age so much as by cortisone treatment. He would have passed more readily as a successful stockbroker or barrister from near-by Canonbury or newly gentrified Barnsbury than as the author of the evening's entertainment at North London's leading fringe theatre.

The audience was crammed into the hot little room wherever they could find space or a vantage point, separated from the actors by nothing more than the tacit agreement that creates an invisible boundary between the acting area and the auditorium. It was a very different setting from the one for which Rattigan had created the play almost thirty years earlier. Yet when the lights went down, the effect of the play on the 1976 audience was the same as it had been on the smartly dressed stalls and galleryites of 1948. At the opening they laughed when Taplow surreptitiously took the chocolate from the Crock's box and practised his cruel schoolboy imitation of him for the popular science master. By the end they were frozen, close to tears as the full tragedy of the Crock's lifelong emotional repression lay revealed in a magisterial performance by Nigel Stock.

Stewart Trotter's King's Head production of *The Browning Version* received the annual H. M. Tennent award for the best production outside the West End. In the *Daily Telegraph* John Barber referred to Rattigan as 'an old master', saying that the young audience's laughter and appalled silences were a new generation's tribute, 'not only to Rattigan's delicate craftsmanship but to his penetration into the hearts of men and women'.[8] John Elsom in the *Listener* pointed out that Rattigan had always championed the individual against the system—all systems—and thereby expressed 'certain liberal, humane values which we are in danger of forgetting'.[9]

Most of the remainder of Rattigan's life was a race against death, increasing pain and infirmity, to complete the stage version of *Cause Célèbre*. By April 1976, the doctors gave him only about another year to live. He had completed an adaptation of the play by the summer, and might have been able to return to his Asquith project, but getting *Cause Célèbre* staged turned out to be fraught with difficulties. The first problem arose when he met Robert Chetwyn, the director, in Bermuda. Rattigan was still unsure about how to stage the play. He hoped that Chetwyn would have been able to do some work on it by the time they met and would come up with some solutions. He was disappointed. Chetwyn had apparently been busy with other projects. Rattigan, aware that his time was running out, asked for another director. Rattigan's agent then suggested Peter Coe, a man with a long record of successes with complex, episodic productions, the most notable being the musical *Oliver*. Coe liked the idea, but favoured the documentary elements in the play at the expense of the sub-plot. He was one of a succession of people involved in the production who thought that the sub-plot should be scrapped. Rattigan was now in no doubt that this was his last play—he habitually referred to it as such to those he worked with—and was therefore even more determined than usual that what appeared should be *his* creation rather than someone else's. He said that various strands represented each of the main preoccupations of his writing, and that by combining them all in one play he was in a sense trying finally to tie them all together. The autobiographical sub-plot was therefore not only very important in his overall design, it was the thing which made the play his own.

Rattigan felt in an increasingly awkward position. The more he worked with Coe, the more convinced he became that he was the wrong director. But he had been suggested by his agent after he had himself asked for a new director, and he was diffident about going to John Gale and asking for yet another change. By the time he had plucked up the courage to have Peter Coe taken off the production and another director had been found, it was the end of the year and Rattigan was back in Bermuda for the winter. It seemed doubtful that he would ever be strong enough to make the journey to Britain again. As so often with cancer, the disease seemed to progress through alternating ups and downs. Though the pain and the quantities of pain-killing drugs progressively increased, there were still days, even weeks, when he was up on the terrace enjoying the winter sun. But the ups were interspersed with longer stays in bed, increasing weakness and continual tiredness. Even the physical act of writing was sometimes difficult. His constant companion was Peggy French. She added to the self-imposed duties of secretary and housekeeper those of nurse. As well as comforting and protecting him, she learnt how to give him his injections. Harold French, a close friend now for forty years, since the first production of *French Without Tears*, was also with him that last winter. Now more or less retired, French had written two volumes of chatty memoirs, one with an affectionate introduction by Rattigan himself. There were occasional visitors from England too: old friends flown out for a week or two, to bring the latest gossip, reminisce and play chess. To the old enthusiasms for cricket and golf, new and seemingly alien obsessions had been added: baseball and American football, which he followed avidly from the radio and the newspapers. Still, people brought him projects for new work; two Americans had a scheme for a film about British and American airmen holed up with a woman in a French château during the war. Rattigan himself, after all these years, continued to turn over ideas for a play that would star John Gielgud. The latest was to adapt *The Warden* by Anthony Trollope. But he knew there was no chance of being able to complete it on his own, so he asked the new director of *Cause Célèbre*, Robin Midgley, if he would work on it with him.

Midgley was the Artistic Director of the Haymarket Theatre in Leicester, one of the leading provincial repertory theatres. From there he had launched a number of productions which had gone on to become successes in the West End. Although associated with the new wave in the theatre—he had produced at the Royal Court—he was a long-standing admirer of Rattigan's work. When first approached, Midgley had been keen to do a new Rattigan play, but after reading the version Rattigan had worked on with Peter Coe, he turned it down. It seemed a hybrid—not a play, not a thorough-going documentary. But he was interested enough to read both the original radio script and Rattigan's own first stage version. These he liked, and he wrote to Rattigan in Bermuda telling him that the play he would like to do already existed inside those two scripts. This was the news Rattigan had wanted. He cabled Midgley, asking him to compile his own version from the three scripts he had read, and inviting him to fly out to Bermuda for discussions. Midgley found the compilation more difficult than he had expected, as Rattigan had evidently rewritten each script as though from scratch. A lot of scenes were common to each, but the dialogue of these scenes had clearly been rewritten without reference to the earlier versions. Glueing them together into one smooth whole turned out to be a very complex job. Midgley arrived in Bermuda late in January 1977, a very nervous man. When the two men met, Rattigan was also very shy; this was, after all, the third director with whom he had attempted to work on the play. Time was running out, and if this didn't work then the chances of the play being done in his lifetime were slim. Rattigan asked Midgley to read him his version aloud. This was a shrewd move; not only would it preserve his own dwindling reserves of energy, it would break the ice between the two men.

At the end of the reading it was clear that they had a basis for collaboration. Then began two weeks during which they substantially rewrote the play for the final time, and Midgley gained a unique insight into Rattigan's mind and method of working. They worked for two hours each morning and two hours each afternoon. This was now about all that Rattigan had energy for. The additional exertion of actually writing down what they had discussed was too much for him, and this fell almost entirely to Midgley. During the first week they built up Act One scene by scene. When they were satisfied with that, they moved on to Act Two. The importance attached by Rattigan to the sub-plot can be gauged by the fact that he was now using a new title for the play—*A Woman of Principle*. Although this title could just conceivably apply to Alma Rattenbury, albeit ironically, the character it most obviously fitted was the repressed mother-figure, Mrs Davenport.

As the fortnight progressed, two of the most exciting weeks in Midgley's life, Rattigan seemed to gain strength. He reminisced

314

about his early life, his mistakes, his intentions as a writer and his regrets. His greatest single regret seemed to be that his creation of Aunt Edna had been so misunderstood, and that he had failed, by the joke-trial scene he had written for the third volume of his *Collected Plays*, to get through to people that what he had meant was not that he had written specifically for the popular audience, but that like Shakespeare he knew he had to write what was acceptable to the groundlings before he stood any chance of getting beyond them to make contact with the more discerning audience. It was that audience who mattered to him. His two other regrets were the failure of *Adventure Story* and that *Nijinsky* had not been produced. But not all their talk was serious. Midgley found that Rattigan was still a great giggler and an inveterate gossip.

Rattigan was determined to get to England for the production, which was to open a three-week season in Leicester in mid-May, before transferring to London. It remained doubtful if he would make it. But, he told medical advisers and friends alike, he would rather die in the stalls of a draughty theatre at a rehearsal of his play than in the comfort of his own bed. He set out on 28 April, arriving in the early morning at Heathrow, and was taken, exhausted from the long flight, to a private room in the King Edward VII Hospital, close to London's theatreland.

By then the play was already in rehearsal, but things were not going well. Rumours of the production's problems were beginning to leak out to the theatre world, but Midgley and Gale were determined to do all they could to shield Rattigan from what was going on. Rattigan was by now living on borrowed time. The year of life proffered by the doctors was up. In London he was due to have an operation. Although he told people it gave him a slender chance of some sort of recovery in return for a high degree of risk, our information, which was fairly generally accepted by those around him at the time, suggests that the operation's primary function was to reduce the extreme pain in which he now lived. He wished to delay the operation until he had at least seen the play in performance at Leicester. The problem of getting him to Leicester for a performance necessitated at least six hours away from the hospital—a two hours' dash up the motorway, followed by the performance and a further two hours for the return journey. The only feasible performance was a matinée. The first was on Saturday 21 May.

A week before the opening, a further crisis broke: Glynis Johns had to leave the cast. When that happened, Charles Gray, who was holding the production together with a virtuoso performance that wrung every piece of available drama and humour from the pivotal role of Alma Rattenbury's defence lawyer, announced that since his contract specified his appearance opposite Glynis Johns, he was going too. In the event, his contract covered his appearances in Leicester and he agreed to stay until the end of the run there. Heather Sears, hardly ideal casting for the sex-starved Alma Rattenbury, courageously stepped into the breach to take over from Glynis Johns for the Leicester run.

The packed Leicester first night was an edgy occasion. The cast and the audience contained a number of Rattigan's friends, notably Harold French, who would probably report back to him in his London hospital bed. But no one could honestly say it was a success. The set, although minimal, seemed cumbersome and unattractive, the playing was understandably slow and in places uncertain. Gallantly though Heather Sears tried with Alma Rattenbury, Charles Gray's performance was the highlight of the evening. Without him the prospects for the London production looked grim. Yet Robin Midgley, like Harold French more than forty years previously, kept his nerve. On the Saturday, Rattigan made the journey from London and attended the matinée. Both he and Midgley remained coolly professional, discussing changes to the script and replacements for Glynis Johns and Charles Gray. Returning to London, Rattigan set the date for his operation—1 June. At the same time he used his veto to prevent the imminent appearance in the West End of a revival from another provincial theatre of *The Deep Blue Sea*. *Separate Tables*, starring John Mills, was already enjoying a successful revival at the Apollo Theatre, and the immediate revival of another of his earlier and most powerful plays might jeopardize the chances of *Cause Célèbre*.

One week before his operation, the authors of this book showed him his television obituary. He was not told that it was his obituary, but he must have guessed that was what it would turn out to be. Although it had been impossible to disguise from him that the BBC were working on a programme about him, most of the work had had to be done while he was in Bermuda and without direct access to him, since throughout that winter his death had been thought imminent. Shortly after his arrival in London he had expressed a desire to see the programme. So, late on a fine early-summer afternoon, a television engineer, followed by the director and producer and Rattigan's agent, went up to his airy corner room in the King Edward VII Hospital with a colour television set and video playback machine to show him the tape, which included not only an outline of his life and extracts from his work, but also the statements of friends, foes and critics, some of whom he had not spoken to in years. All had spoken candidly on film in the belief that he himself would never hear their posthumous assessment. Fortunately most of them were favourable, or we would have been more reluctant to agree to his request. John Osborne compared him with Jane Austen and said there had never been any personal animosity between them; Rex Harrison gave no hint of their disagreement over *In Praise of Love* and recalled Rattigan's kindness to him and the first night of *French Without Tears*; critics as varied as Sir Harold Hobson, Michael Billington and E. A. Whitehead were united in recognizing distinctive and unique qualities in his writing. Yet it was an oddly tense cluster of people who surrounded him as he sat up in bed in the small room watching the screen at the foot of his bed. Throughout the hour that the programme ran nurses bustled in and out, seemingly oblivious of what was going on. Rattigan himself, sipping continuously from a glass of brandy and water—a dozen more bottles were packed in a cardboard box on the floor—made almost no comment, except occasionally to laugh, to say 'That's true, I'd forgotten', or to sigh nostalgically at the sight of some long-unseen friend, sometimes an actor, sometimes a wartime colleague. The programme reached *Adventure Story*, and Peggy French visibly stiffened. When the dismissive comment came—recalling that '*Adventure Story* was an expensive and tasteless flop'—there was a sharp intake of breath from her, but Rattigan's face didn't change. At the end he seemed drained but pleased. He had laughed, not loudly, but a lot; he had cried silently too. He was shy in his thanks. His agent asked him if we could write this book, and he agreed.

On 4 July, five weeks after his operation, he attended the first night of *Cause Célèbre* at Her Majesty's Theatre in London. This time he was in no doubt that this was his last first night; nor were the people in the audience, who recognized the figure propped up, but as always immaculately dressed, next to and slightly behind Michael Franklin in the Royal Box. He had been delivered in a limousine in good time for the performance, so there was no awkward last-minute scramble to get him into his seat, nor any ovation as he made his entrance. Glynis Johns was now recovered and back in the cast. Charles Gray's place had been taken by Kenneth Griffith. Griffith, although an equally idiosyncratic actor, was the very opposite of Gray; where Gray was slow-moving and suave, dropping his barbs of wit with effortless aplomb, Griffith promised quicksilver theatricality, giving the play much-needed speed. In the event it turned out a wise choice, because although less subtle than Gray, he served the play better. Nevertheless as the end of the first act approached, the audience seemed to be getting restless. The scene where Alma is confronted with her child who pleads with her to try to save herself by incriminating her lover in court was the only one left before the interval. It was a dangerous moment. The success of the evening seemed suddenly to hang on a child actor called Matthew Ryan. In the event, he gave the most composed and truthful performance of the evening, raising the emotional temperature of the theatre and providing the springboard for Glynis Johns' anguished playing of Alma Rattenbury's decision to give evidence on her own behalf at the trial. The evening was saved.

The final curtain was not the storming success of *French Without Tears*; nor was it the anticlimax of *Man and Boy*. The prolonged clapping and the solid but not over-excited cheers from the back of the Circle were in gratitude for a pleasant evening in the theatre, and for a long and distinguished career. Although it was by no means his best play, the most important thing at that moment was probably that he had made it—he had survived not only to see it on to the stage, but to see himself fully accepted back into the West End. For the next few months he had two successes—the other was *Separate Tables*, still running after six months—playing simultaneously in London. It was the first time in more than thirty years.

Next day, the reviews were almost uniformly good, the only dose of cold water coming from Milton Shulman in the *Evening Standard,* who found not only the sub-plot contrived but the whole evening lacking in suspense and insight. Bernard Levin summed up the evening best in the *Sunday Times*; 'Rattigan's act of defiance' was the headline to his column. It began: 'A critic has a duty to ignore anything happening off stage, and to make no allowances for any shortcomings that may result ... All the same, I am at any rate partly human, and it would be absurd, as well as impossible, for me to persuade myself that I do not know that Terence Rattigan has for the last couple of years been staring into the eyes of the old gentleman with the scythe ... So I am doubly delighted to say that *Cause Célèbre* (Her Majesty's) betrays no sign of failing powers; on the contrary it could almost herald a new direction for Sir Terence, and a most interesting one, too.' He concluded: '*Cause Célèbre* is by a man who knows that in every human being there is a capacity to reflect the divine, and that it is love in all its forms, from the noblest to the most tawdry, that is most likely to show the gleam of that reflection. His play is theatrical in the best sense of the word, and I hope he will be spared to write many more such.'[10]

As though buoyed up by such words of praise, two days later Rattigan threw the hospital staff into confusion by getting up and taking himself for a walk round the block without telling anyone. Once outside, he scared himself by finding out how weak he really was. Even so, when we arrived later in the afternoon to talk to him, he was still very pleased with himself; twinkling like a small boy who has played truant and got away with it. The staff told us we were not to stay too long and overtire him, but each time we got up to leave he insisted that we sit down and have another drink and another story. At one point a doctor arrived but, as we were leaving, Rattigan told us on no account to go away, there was more he wanted to say. But even that day, when he seemed so bright, he was still in almost continuous pain. Lying fully dressed on his bed, he could only stay in one position for a few minutes at a time. Every few minutes he would apologize and then laboriously haul himself on to his other side. It was, he said, as if he had two elephants sitting on him alternately. 'I have either Jumbo sitting on my hips, or it's Dumbo. It's very rarely nothing.'

Earlier that morning he had given a final radio interview to an old friend, Sheridan Morley. In it, he looked back over his whole career. At only one moment did his voice become bitter—when he recalled the early 1960s: 'I discovered that any play I wrote would get smashed. I just didn't have a chance with anything. But,' he added reflectively, 'perhaps I should have stayed and fought it out.

I don't know.' Nevertheless, to be acclaimed again in his own lifetime was very, very gratifying. 'I didn't think it would happen to me. I had hoped, though, that it might. I always thought they had been a bit unfair to me—and at a particular time they *were* being a bit unfair to me. It's all very well to dislike one's plays, but they ought to be disliked for a better reason than that they're out of fashion. Out of fashion isn't enough, I think. I always thought that justice would one day be done to me, but whether in my lifetime or not I didn't know. But it is very gratifying that it's happened in my lifetime.'[11]

Two weeks later, having made arrangements to have all his plays specially bound and sent as a gift to the Queen, he ordered a car to drive him for a last time through London's theatreland. Down Shaftesbury Avenue past the Apollo, where *Separate Tables* was still playing in the theatre once occupied by *Follow My Leader* and *Flare Path*; past the Globe, the Lyric and the Queen's—the scenes of triumphs and disasters; down the Haymarket, passing Her Majesty's, where the posters for *Cause Célèbre* looked across to the Theatre Royal, once the home of *Ross* and *Bequest to the Nation*; and finally, on the way home, round Piccadilly Circus and past the Criterion, where it had all really started on an inauspicious night just over forty years earlier. He had come a long way since he had queued for the galleries of those same theatres and lain on his hard school bed at Harrow dreaming of saving England in a Test Match and being kissed simultaneously by Marie Tempest and Gladys Cooper after making speeches to wildly cheering first-night audiences.

In August, a week after arriving back in Bermuda, he collapsed again and was taken to hospital. This time he was reported to have meningitis. Everyone assumed that he could not survive. Yet he did, for another three months. He even came out of hospital again. The end came on Wednesday, 30 November 1977. The first news of his death was reported to the British public on 'News at Ten' on ITV that evening. By 11.30 BBC 2's Late News was carrying a full report of his death and an assessment of his achievements. The eclipse of his reputation seemed finally over. He died a national figure.

Rattigan would have turned eagerly to see what sort of press he got next morning. He would doubtless have been glad to find that he had been promoted from the Arts page to the front page in many of the newspapers, while on the inside pages the space allotted to the obituaries was generous. Whether, however, he would have been quite so pleased by what they said is another matter. True, *The Times* headlined him an 'Enduring influence on the English Theatre', but the familiar, slightly deprecating, emphasis on 'craftsmanship' still predominated in the assessments. 'A prolific writer in the sleek tradition of Pinero, Maugham and Coward,' his old friend John Barber called him in the *Daily Telegraph*. Rattigan would doubtless have bowed his head a fraction and, smiling slightly, thanked Barber for the compliment, but secretly he would have been disappointed. He had wanted to be so much more; and in our view, while he did not fully realize his ambitions, he undoubtedly was. Why, then, has his achievement still not been generally recognized?

It is perplexing that common assessments fail to come to grips with the evidence of the plays themselves. Harold Hobson started his uniquely perceptive obituary in the *Sunday Times* by saying that Rattigan 'had the greatest natural talent for the stage of any man this century'. He thereby asked the question which he set out to answer in the rest of his article—how well had Rattigan put that talent to use in his career? 'Natural talent' would seem the very opposite of the quality with which he was generally credited, craftsmanship, which is essentially something learned and deliberately applied, rather than natural. The implication, therefore, of most critics' assessments was that he had not made good use of his natural talent. At the end of the 1950s, Kenneth Tynan had expressed a widely-held sense of disappointment in Rattigan, which rapidly escalated into a feeling of betrayal. If Rattigan was, in Tynan's widely reiterated phrase, 'the Formosa of the British Theatre', possessed of the geographical potential to become part of the revolution, then he betrayed those who believed in revolution by remaining obstinately occupied by the 'old guard'. The sense of betrayal perhaps accounts for the sustained virulence of the attacks on him and the persistent refusal to look beyond the stereotyped image of the calculating craftsman to the actual plays themselves. Earlier in this book we suggested that Rattigan was like a resistance fighter whose rebellious cast of mind makes it impossible for him to join the new administration after the liberation. The fact is that he regarded the 1956 Royal Court revolution as only a partial liberation. His most deeply cherished values were neither those of the old guard nor those of the new revolutionary dictatorship. It is perhaps only now, in the polarized and disillusioned late 1970s, that we can begin to appreciate those values, which remained essentially those of his boyhood at Harrow when he subversively circulated the works of Huxley and Russell.

John Osborne, himself a victim of the twin evils of excessive early praise and later critical disappointment, said this to us about critical reaction to Rattigan:

'The critics do talk a lot of rubbish about craftsmanship because it's something they don't understand at all ... The fact is that Terence Rattigan's craftsmanship is like a carriage clock. They can see the insides and the workings of it, so it makes them feel more comfortable. They think: "Oh, yes, I see, that's what he's going to do next—very good!" And so he gets ten out of ten all the time, quite rightly.'

The important point about what Osborne says is that he does not find craftsmanship Rattigan's most praiseworthy quality. In this he is joined by another of the younger generation of dramatists whom we quoted at the beginning of the book, David Rudkin. He said that it was Rattigan's rigid craftsmanship that led him into structural clumsiness. For him Rattigan was not at all 'the commercial, middlebrow dramatist his image suggests, but someone peculiarly haunting and oblique, who certainly speaks to me with resonances of existential bleakness and irresoluble carnal solitude'.

In addition to the reasons given by Osborne, the critics' persistent over-emphasis of Rattigan's craftsmanship owed a lot to his unprecedented run of successes. To be so consistently successful over the twenty years between 1936 and 1956 implied a degree of calculating workmanship which could only be put down to exceptional craftsmanship. But the image ignored his failures, both as craftsman and popular entertainer. Two crucial plays, so to speak, disappeared from Rattigan's canon: *Follow My Leader* and *After the Dance*. Rattigan sealed this disappearance by excluding them from his *Collected Plays*. *After the Dance* is his best serious play before *The Browning Version*, and is in no way the work of a boulevard dramatist. Its commercial failure was, at least in part, due to the accident of timing by which it opened on the eve of the Second World War. The failure of *Follow My Leader* was likewise due to circumstances beyond Rattigan's control. Had it opened in the autumn of 1938, so coinciding with the Munich crisis, *Follow My Leader* must have had an impact on Rattigan's reputation, even if it had failed commercially. The failure of those two plays bit deep with Rattigan and he banished them from memory, along with *First Episode*, until late in his life. It was a weakness that he allowed himself, throughout his life, to be so much affected by public disapproval.

By the time of *Flare Path* there was, as Keith Newman suggested, evidence of his writing sometimes being too much influenced during conception by glances at the box office, with the result that some of his dramatic babies were born with more than a hint of theatrical squint.

Yet if Rattigan bent to the wind of popular expectation, he still did not deviate far from his own chosen course. At the core of most of the plays the values still remained consistently his own. Three of his most philosophically uncompromising plays were written at the height of his popularity and were among his most commercially successful: *The Browning Version, The Deep Blue Sea* and *Separate Tables*. There is a comment, by an unknown critic, in one of Rattigan's scrapbooks dated about 1954. It says: 'He chooses lost and confused people who are afraid of life. And in the last act he reclaims them triumphantly through the sympathy of their neighbours. He makes them feel they belong to the human race.' The important thing about Rattigan's plays, despite changing fashions, is their unvarying humanism. His characters, no matter how much they are driven by their feelings, their circumstances, their instincts or their backgrounds, are in the end masters of their own fates. The climaxes of the plays, while often depending on a self-revelation, always involve a decision, a conscious choice on the part of the principal characters. The much-criticized 'happy endings' are never the result of fate; they are the result of a deliberate and hard-come-by decision. They are not really happy endings because while they may lift the heart of the audience through some small act which reasserts human dignity, they nevertheless leave the characters with a lifetime of further, unresolved decisions ahead of them. Their future is in their own hands and depends upon the triumph of the rational over the irrational, courage over cowardice, imagination over pig-headedness, liberalism over prejudice. In the plays that end tragically the cause is the result of a deliberate choice and the defeat of the same rational and liberal virtues. Rattigan's values are the values of the rational humanist philosophers of his youth, men like Huxley and Russell, who so outraged his parents' generation.

When the theatrical revolution came in the mid fifties, Rattigan's image ensured that he would not be recognized for what he was. When he tried to move with the times, he failed. The removal of theatrical taboos coincided with an increased preoccupation in his plays with sex, rather than sex subsumed in love. When he tried to write openly about sex, he found he could not. This was not so much from fear or lingering doubts about the acceptability of homosexuality on the stage, but because his whole personality and quality as a writer was geared to the oblique and the implicit. In any case a lifetime of concealment and regret of one's own homosexuality is hardly the best preparation for successful uninhibited writing about it. The result was plays which, in the atmosphere of exuberant taboo-smashing that characterized the decade after *Look Back in Anger,* seemed evasive. *Variation on a Theme* in particular seemed to be downright dishonest and the audience felt short-changed. But even in that play, and in *Ross, Man and Boy* and *Bequest to the Nation,* he kept faith with his own philosophical values. His emotionally- and sexually-driven characters are still the creations of their own choices and the victims of their own wills. In *Variation on a Theme,* Sam Duveen says that 'Feelings can't sometimes be helped—but the expression of them can.' *Bequest to the Nation, Ross* and even *Man and Boy* pose the question that had interested Rattigan in *Adventure Story*—whether a man is great because of what he is or what he does: an ethical question and, as Rattigan made clear in his letter to Elkan Allan, to him all political questions were fundamentally ethical questions.

Rattigan was, in fact, a descendant of that most ancient of all lines of dramatist, a moral dramatist. But although he came from a puritanical background and wrote about repressed characters, the morality of his plays was neither repressive nor puritanical. His philosophy was rational, his values anti-authoritarian and liberal. Writing of the difficulties of love and the inequality of passion, his moral was always affirmative, his plea was for sympathy and tolerance. At the end of *The Sound Barrier*, he depicted man as a child alone in a godless and uncaring universe, his fate in his own hands. This he refused to see as a depressing prospect, but as a challenge in which man has the advantage. He can conquer not only his environment but his pain and fear, if he uses the weapons he has been given—love, imagination, intelligence and courage. In the 1970s, disillusioned with extremes both of dogmatism and of permissiveness, we may be ready to re-examine the values of rational humanism. In his plays Rattigan set out to show that they offered no easy option, but that they are the only hope men and women have. If we are ready for a return to the judgement of politics through ethics; a re-statement of concern for the individual; opposition to prejudice and sympathy for the social, sexual or emotional misfit; acceptance of the need for the individual to recognize responsibility for his or her actions—then perhaps we may be ready to recognize the value and achievement of Terence Rattigan.

Notes

1 *Plays and Players*, February 1973.

2 *Daily Telegraph*, 28 July 1973.

3 *Guardian*, 28 July 1973.

4 *The Trial of Alma Victoria Rattenbury and George Percy Stoner*, edited by F. Tennyson Jesse, William Hodge and Co. One of Rattigan's sources.

5 'Rattigan's Theatre', BBC Radio, 30 March 1976.

6 Philip Oakes: 'Grace Before Going', *Sunday Times*, 4 December 1977.

7 BBC Radio Three, 30 March 1976.

8 *Daily Telegraph*, 9 January 1976.

9 *Listener*, 15 January 1976.

10 *Sunday Times*, 10 July 1977.

11 *Kaleidoscope*, BBC Radio 4, July 1977.

Bibliography

A. Rattigan's works

For the texts of Terence Rattigan's published plays we have used the following (except where otherwise noted in the text or notes):

The Collected Plays of Terence Rattigan (with Prefaces by the author):

I. *French Without Tears, Flare Path, While the Sun Shines, Love in Idleness, The Winslow Boy.* London, Hamish Hamilton, 1953.

II. *The Browning Version, Harlequinade, Adventure Story, Who Is Sylvia?, The Deep Blue Sea.* London, Hamish Hamilton, 1953.

III. *The Sleeping Prince, Separate Tables, Variation on a Theme, Ross, Heart to Heart.* London, Hamish Hamilton, 1964.

After the Dance. London, Hamish Hamilton, 1939.

The Prince and the Showgirl: the Script for the Film. New York, New American Library, 1957.

Man and Boy. London, Hamish Hamilton, 1964.

A Bequest to the Nation. London, Hamish Hamilton, 1970.

All on Her Own. Included in *The Best Short Plays 1970*, edited by Stanley Richards, Philadelphia, Chilton, 1970.

In Praise of Love (After Lydia, Before Dawn). London, Hamish Hamilton, 1973.

Cause Célèbre. London, Hamish Hamilton, 1978.

For unpublished plays, film, television and radio scripts we are indebted to the late Sir Terence Rattigan, to his agent Michael Imison of Dr Jan van Loewen Ltd, the British Broadcasting Corporation, Associated

Television, Thames Television and numerous of Sir Terence's friends and professional colleagues.

Rattigan's many contributions to newspapers, periodicals and radio are acknowledged in the text and endnotes, but the following of his contributions to other published works have proved especially useful:

'A Magnificent Pity for Camels' (included in *Diversion*, edited by John Sutro, London, Max Parrish, 1950).

Theatrical Companion to Noël Coward ('An Appreciation of his Work in the Theatre' by Terence Rattigan). By Raymond Mander and Joe Mitchenson, London, Rockliff, 1957.

I Swore I Never Would (Foreword by Terence Rattigan). By Harold French, London, Secker & Warburg, 1970.

Olivier (contribution by Sir Terence Rattigan). Edited by Logan Gourlay, London, Weidenfeld and Nicolson, 1973.

B. Works by other authors quoted or used in preparation of this book:

Agate, James, *The Contemporary Theatre 1944 and 1945*, London, George Harrap, 1946.

Baxter, Beverley, *First Nights and Noises Off*, London, Hutchinson, 1966.

Bolitho, Hector, *My Restless Years*, London, Parrish, 1962.

Dawnay, Jean, *Model Girl*, London, Weidenfeld and Nicolson, 1956.

— *How I Became a Fashion Model*, London, Thomas Nelson, 1960.

Denison, Michael, *Overture and Beginners*, London, Gollancz, 1973.

Driberg, Tom, *Ruling Passions*, London, Jonathan Cape, 1977.

Edwards, Anne, *Vivien Leigh—A Biography*, London, W. H. Allen, 1977.

Forbes, Bryan, *Ned's Girl—The Life of Edith Evans*, London, Hamish Hamilton, 1977.

French, Harold, *I Swore I Never Would*, London, Secker & Warburg, 1970.

— *I Thought I Never Could*, London, Secker & Warburg, 1973.

Gielgud, John, *Early Stages*, London, Macmillan, 1939.

Hamilton, J. R., *Alexander the Great*, London, Hutchinson University Library, 1973.

Harrison, Rex, *Rex—An Autobiography*, London, Macmillan, 1974.

Hart, Liddell, *T. E. Lawrence—In Arabia and After*, London, Jonathan Cape, 1948.

Hartnoll, Phylis (ed.), *The Oxford Companion to the Theatre*, Oxford, Oxford University Press, 1951.

Hayman, Ronald, *John Gielgud*, London, Heinemann, 1971.

Hickey, Dee and Smith, Gus, *The Prince—The Public and Private Life of Laurence Harvey*, London, Leslie Frewin, 1975.

Houston, Arthur H., *English Drama—Its Past History and Probable Future*, Dublin, Royal College of Science, 1863.

Hurren, Kenneth, *Theatre Inside Out*, London, W. H. Allen, 1977.

James, Robert Rhodes (ed.), *Chips—The Diaries of Sir Henry Channon*, London, Weidenfeld and Nicolson, 1967.

Jesse, F. Tennyson (ed.), *Rattenbury & Stoner* (Notable British Trials Series), London, William Hodge, 1946.

Kitchin, Laurence, *Mid-Century Drama*, London, Faber & Faber, 1960.

Lawrence, T. E., *The Seven Pillars of Wisdom*, London, Jonathan Cape, 1935.

Magee, Bryan, *One in Twenty—A Study of Homosexuality in Men and Women*, London, Secker & Warburg, 1966.

Minney, R. J., *Puffin Asquith—A Biography*, London, Leslie Frewin, 1973.

Montagu, Edwin, *The Archer Shee Case*, London, David and Charles, 1974.

More, Kenneth, *Happy Go Lucky—My Life*, London, Robert Hale, 1959.

Newman, K. O., *Mind; Sex and War—Blackouts, Fear of Air Raids and Propaganda*, Oxford, Pelago, 1941.

— *Two Hundred and Fifty Times I Saw a Play—or Authors, Actors and Audiences*, Oxford, Pelago, 1944.

Nicolson, Sir Harold, *Curzon. Volume 3: The Last Phase 1919-1925*, London, Benn, 1934.

Norwood, Dr Cyril, *The English Tradition in Education*, London, John Murray, 1929.

Oman, Carola, *Nelson*, London, Hodder & Stoughton, 1947.

Pratley, Gerald, *The Cinema of David Lean*, London, Tantivy, 1974.

Pudney, John, *Collected Poems*, London, Putnam, 1957.

Rattigan, Frank, *Diversions of a Diplomat*, London, Chapman and Hall, 1924.

Rattigan, Sir William Henry, *Events to be Remembered in the History of India from the Invasion of Alexander to the Latest Times*, Lahore, Punjabee Press, 1863.

Shaplen, Robert, *Kreuger, Genius and Swindler*, London, Deutsch, 1961.

Stone, Paulene, *One Tear is Enough—A Biography of Laurence Harvey*, London, Michael Joseph, 1975.

Storr, Anthony, *Sexual Deviation*, London, Penguin, 1964.

328

Taylor, A. J. P., *English History 1914-1945*, Oxford, Oxford University Press, 1965.

Tynan, Kenneth, *Curtains*, London, Longmans, 1961.

— *A View of the English Stage 1946-63*, London, Davis Poynter, 1975.

Wardle, Irving, *The Theatres of George Devine*, London, Jonathan Cape, 1978.

Zolotow, Maurice, *Stagestruck—Alfred Lunt and Lynn Fontanne*, London, Heinemann, 1965.

— *Marilyn Monroe*, London, W. H. Allen, 1961.

Quotations and assistance from newspapers, periodicals, radio and television are credited as appropriate in the text.

Appendix

Original Casts, Directors, Theatres, Opening Dates and Number of Performances of Principal Productions of Rattigan's Plays in Britain and the United States

Cast lists and directing credits have been compiled and cross-referenced from Rattigan's published plays, *Who's Who* and London and New York reviews.

First Episode (with Philip Heimann)

London: Q Theatre (opened 11 September 1933), transferred to Comedy Theatre
Opening: 26 January 1934
Performances: Approximately 80

ALBERT ARNOLD   Max Adrian
PHILIP KAHN   Angus L. MacLeod (Q Theatre: Owen Griffith)
JOHN TAYLOR   Meriel Forbes-Robertson
TONY WODEHOUSE   William Fox (Q Theatre: Noel Dryden)
DAVID LISTER   Patrick Waddington
MARGOT GRESHAM   Barbara Hoffe (Q Theatre: Rosalinde Fuller)
JAMES   Vincent King
A BULLER   Jack Allen (Q Theatre: Robert Syers)
Director: Muriel Pratt

New York: Ritz Theatre
Opening: 17 September 1934
Performances: Approximately 40

ALBERT ARNOLD   Max Adrian
PHILIP KAHN   Statts Cotsworth
JOAN TAYLOR   Gerrie Worthing
TONY WODEHOUSE   John Halloran
DAVID LISTER   Patrick Waddington
MARGOT GRESHAM   Leona Maricle
JAMES   Stanley Harrison
A BULLER   T. C. Dunham
Director: Haddon Mason

A Tale of Two Cities (with John Gielgud)

From the novel by Charles Dickens. Written in 1935 but unperformed
until 1950.

Britain: St Brendan's College Dramatic Society, Clifton
Opening: 23 January 1950
Performances: 6

JARVIS LORRY   Paul Vassalli
JERRY CRUNCHER   Brian Sweet
MADAME DEFARGE   Paul Casling
LUCIE MANETTE   Peter Evans
MISS PROSS   Michael Ryan
ERNEST DEFARGE   Michael Woodley
DR MANETTE   Murray Case
CHARLES DARNAY   Peter Pullin
BARSAD   Peter Hawkins
THE ATTORNEY GENERAL   Colin Culham
SYDNEY CARTON   Derek Crabtree
THE JUDGE   Paddy Love
MR STRYVER   Ralph Tozer
THE SOLICITOR GENERAL   Ronald Smith
GASPARD   John Blake
JACQUES—HIS CHILD   Robin Hallett
JULES   Michael Stewart
GABELLE   John MacDonald
THE MARQUIS DE ST EVREMONDE   Frank Pitt
A ROAD MENDER   Terence Ryan
A VALET   Robert Philpott
CLERK IN TEUSON'S OFFICE   Gordon Baker

AN EMIGRÉ   J. Tunnard Jackson
A GAOLER IN THE CONCIERGERIE   Peter Blake
A PATRIOT AT THE BARRIER   Terence Walsh
A REVOLUTIONARY   Clive Smith
Director: Hedley Goodall

(First professional production on BBC radio, 1950. Produced by Cleland Finn, with Eric Portman as Sydney Carton.)

Grey Farm (with Hector Bolitho)

(Written in 1935 but not performed until 1940)
New York: Hudson Theatre
Opening: 3 May 1940
Performances: Approximately 35

MRS IRON   Evelyn Varden
STEPHEN GRANTHAM   John Cromwell
JUDITH WEAVER   Jane Sterling
JAMES GRANTHAM   Oscar Homolka
MAVIS   Maria Temple
LADY WEAVER   Adrienna Morrison
ELLEN   Vera Mellish
Director: Berthold Viertel

French Without Tears

London: Criterion Theatre
Opening: 6 November 1936
Performances: 1,030

KENNETH LAKE   Trevor Howard
BRIAN CURTIS   Guy Middleton
HON. ALAN HOWARD   Rex Harrison
MARIANNE   Yvonne André
MONSIEUR MAINGOT   Percy Walsh
LT.-CMDR. ROGERS   Roland Culver
DIANA LAKE   Kay Hammond
KIT NEILAN   Robert Flemyng
JACQUELINE MAINGOT   Jessica Tandy
LORD HEYBROOK   William Dear
Director: Harold French

New York: Henry Miller Theatre
Opening: 28 September 1937
Performances: 111

KENNETH LAKE   Philip Friend
BRIAN CURTIS   Guy Middleton
HON. ALAN HOWARD   Frank Lawton
MARIANNE   Simone Petitjean
MONSIEUR MAINGOT   Marcel Valée
LT.-CMDR. ROGERS   Cyril Raymond
DIANA LAKE   Penelope Dudley Ward
JACQUELINE MAINGOT   Jacqueline Porel
LORD HEYBROOK   Edward Ryan, Jr.
Director: Harold French

After the Dance

London: St. James's Theatre
Opening: 21 June 1939
Performances: 60

JOHN REID   Martin Walker
PETER SCOTT-FOWLER   Hubert Gregg
WILLIAMS   Gordon Court
JOAN SCOTT-FOWLER   Catherine Lacey
HELEN BANNER   Anne Firth
DR GEORGE BANNER   Robert Kempson
JULIA BROWNE   Viola Lyel
CYRIL CARTER   Leonard Coppins
DAVID SCOTT-FOWLER   Robert Harris
MOYA LEXINGTON   Millicent Wolf
LAWRENCE WALTERS   Osmund Willson
ARTHUR POWER   Henry Caine
MISS POTTER   Lois Heatherley
Director: Michael Macowan

Follow My Leader

(Written 1938 but banned by Lord Chamberlain until 1940)
London: Apollo Theatre
Opening: 16 January 1940
Performances: Approximately 15

KARL SLIVOVITZ   Walter Hudd
QUETSCH   Frith Banbury

333

PAUL   Kenneth Morgan
RISZKI   Erik Chitty
MAJOR OTTO BARATSCH   Francis L. Sullivan
MARIE PILAWA   Eileen Peel
HANS ZEDESI   Reginald Beckwith
ANNOUNCER   Bush Bailey
FIRST PHOTOGRAPHER   Geoffrey Clarke
SECOND PHOTOGRAPHER   Raymond Leigh
CHILD   Odile de Chalus
POLICEMAN   Ronald Fortt
KING STEFAN OF NEURASTHENIA   Athole Stewart
SIR COSMO TATE-JOHNSON   Marcus Barron

Director: Athole Stewart

Flare Path

London: Apollo Theatre
Opening: 13 August 1942
Performances: 679

PETER KYLE   Martin Walker
COUNTESS SKRICZEVINSKY   Adrienne Allen
MRS OAKES   Dora Gregory
SERGEANT MILLER (DUSTY)   Leslie Dwyer
PERCY   George Cole
COUNT SKRICZEVINSKY   Gerard Heinz
FLIGHT-LIEUTENANT GRAHAM (TEDDY)   Jack Watling
PATRICIA GRAHAM   Phyllis Calvert
MRS MILLER (MAUDIE)   Kathleen Harrison
SQUADRON-LEADER SWANSON   Ivan Samson
CORPORAL JONES   John Bradley

Director: Anthony Asquith

New York: Henry Miller Theatre
Opening: 23 December 1942
Performances: 14

PETER KYLE   Arthur Margetson
COUNTESS SKRICZEVINSKY   Doris Patston
MRS OAKES   Cynthia Latham
SERGEANT MILLER (DUSTY)   Gerald Savory
PERCY   Bob White
COUNT SKRICZEVINSKY   Alexander Ivo
FLIGHT-LIEUTENANT GRAHAM (TEDDY)   Alec Guinness
PATRICIA GRAHAM   Nancy Kelly

MRS MILLER (MAUDIE)   Helena Pickard
SQUADRON-LEADER SWANSON   Reynolds Denniston
Director: Margaret Webster

While the Sun Shines

London: Globe Theatre
Opening: 24 December 1943
Performances: 1,154

HORTON   Douglas Jeffries
THE EARL OF HARPENDEN   Michael Wilding
LIEUTENANT MULVANEY   Hugh McDermott
LADY ELISABETH RANDALL   Jane Baxter
THE DUKE OF AYR AND STIRLING   Ronald Squire
LIEUTENANT COLBERT   Eugene Deckers
MABEL CRUM   Brenda Bruce
Director: Anthony Asquith

New York: Lyceum Theatre
Opening: 19 September 1944
Performances: 39

HORTON   J. P. Wilson
THE EARL OF HARPENDEN   Stanley Bell
LIEUTENANT MULVANEY   Lewis Howard
LADY ELISABETH RANDALL   Anne Burr
THE DUKE OF AYR AND STIRLING   Melville Cooper
LIEUTENANT COLBERT   Alexander Ivo
MABEL CRUM   Cathleen Cordell
Director: George S. Kaufman

Love in Idleness

London: Lyric Theatre
Opening: 20 December 1944
Performances: 213 (limited run)

OLIVIA BROWN   Lynn Fontanne
POLTON   Margaret Murray
MISS DELL   Peggy Dear
SIR JOHN FLETCHER   Alfred Lunt
MICHAEL BROWN   Brian Nissen
DIANA FLETCHER   Kathleen Kent
CELIA WENTWORTH   Mona Harrison

335

SIR THOMAS MARKHAM   Frank Forder
LADY MARKHAM   Antoinette Keith
Director: Alfred Lunt

Retitled *O Mistress Mine*

New York: Empire Theatre
Opening: 23 January 1946
Performances: 451

OLIVIA BROWN   Lynn Fontanne
POLTON   Margery Maude
MISS DELL   Esther Mitchell
SIR JOHN FLETCHER   Alfred Lunt
MICHAEL BROWN   Dick Van Patten
DIANA FLETCHER   Ann Lee
CELIA WENTWORTH   Marie Paxton
Director: Alfred Lunt

The Winslow Boy

London: Lyric Theatre
Opening: 23 May 1946
Performances: 476

RONNIE WINSLOW   Michael Newell
VIOLET   Kathleen Harrison
ARTHUR WINSLOW   Frank Cellier
GRACE WINSLOW   Madge Compton
DICKIE WINSLOW   Jack Watling
CATHERINE WINSLOW   Angela Baddeley
JOHN WATHERSTONE   Alastair Bannerman
DESMOND CURRY   Clive Morton
MISS BARNES   Mona Washbourne
FRED   Brian Harding
SIR ROBERT MORTON   Emlyn Williams
Director: Glen Byam Shaw

New York: Empire Theatre
Opening: 29 October 1947
Performances: 218

RONNIE WINSLOW   Michael Newell
VIOLET   Betty Sinclair
ARTHUR WINSLOW   Alan Webb

336

GRACE WINSLOW   Madge Compton
DICKIE WINSLOW   Owen Holder
CATHERINE WINSLOW   Valerie White
JOHN WATHERSTONE   Michael Kingsley
DESMOND CURRY   George Denson
MISS BARNES   Dorothy Hamilton
FRED   Leonard Michell
SIR ROBERT MORTON   Frank Allenby
Director: Glen Byam Shaw

Playbill

London: Phoenix Theatre
Opening: 8 September 1948
Performances: 245

The Browning Version
JOHN TAPLOW   Peter Scott
FRANK HUNTER   Hector Ross
MILLIE CROCKER-HARRIS   Mary Ellis
ANDREW CROCKER-HARRIS   Eric Portman
DR FROBISHER   Campbell Cotts
PETER GILBERT   Anthony Oliver
MRS GILBERT   Henryetta Edwards

Harlequinade
ARTHUR GOSPORT   Eric Portman
EDNA SELBY   Mary Ellis
DAME MAUD GOSPORT   Marie Lohr
JACK WAKEFIELD   Hector Ross
GEORGE CHUDLEIGH   Kenneth Edwards
FIRST HALBERDIER   Peter Scott
SECOND HALBERDIER   Basil Howes
MISS FISHLOCK   Noel Dyson
FRED INGRAM   Anthony Oliver
JOHNNY   Henry Bryce
MURIEL PALMER   Thelma Ruby
TOM PALMER   Patrick Jordan
MR BURTON   Campbell Cotts
JOYCE LANGLAND   Henryetta Edwards
POLICEMAN   Manville Tarrant
Director: Peter Glenville

337

New York: Coronet Theatre
Opening: 12 October 1949
Performances: 62

The Browning Version

JOHN TAPLOW   Peter Scott-Smith
FRANK HUNTER   Ron Randell
MILLIE CROCKER-HARRIS   Edna Best
ANDREW CROCKER-HARRIS   Maurice Evans
DR FROBISHER   Louis Hector
PETER GILBERT   Frederick Bradlee
MRS GILBERT   Patricia Wheel

Harlequinade

ARTHUR GOSPORT   Maurice Evans
EDNA SELBY   Edna Best
DAME MAUD GOSPORT   Bertha Belmore
JACK WAKEFIELD   Ron Randell
GEORGE CHUDLEIGH   Harry Sothern
FIRST HALBERDIER   Peter Scott-Smith
SECOND HALBERDIER   Tom Hughes Sand
MISS FISHLOCK   Olive Blakeney
FRED INGRAM   Frederick Bradlee
JOHNNY   Bertram Tanswell
MURIEL PALMER   Eileen Page
TOM PALMER   Peter Martyn
MR BURTON   Louis Hector
JOYCE LANGLAND   Patricia Wheel
Director: Peter Glenville

Adventure Story

London: St James's Theatre
Opening: 17 March 1949
Performances: 108

PTOLEMY   Raymond Westwell
PERDICCAS   Antony Baird
MAZARES   Marne Maitland
ALEXANDER   Paul Scofield
PYTHIA OF DELPHI   Veronica Turleigh
HEPHAESTION   Julian Dallas
PHILOTAS   Robert Flemyng
AN ATTENDANT   Natasha Wills

338

DARIUS, KING OF PERSIA   Noel Willman
BESSUS   William Devlin
QUEEN-MOTHER OF PERSIA   Gwen Ffrangcon-Davies
QUEEN STATIRA OF PERSIA   Hazel Terry
PRINCESS STATIRA OF PERSIA   June Rodney
CLEITUS   Cecil Trouncer
PARMENION   Nicholas Hannen
PALACE OFFICIAL   Walter Gotell
ROXANA   Joy Parker
GREEK SOLDIERS   Stanley Baker, John Van Eyssen
PERSIAN SOLDIERS   Terence Longdon, David Oxley, Frederick
    Treves

Director: Peter Glenville

Who Is Sylvia?

London: Criterion Theatre
Opening: 24 October 1950
Performances: 381

MARK   Robert Flemyng
WILLIAMS   Esmond Knight
DAPHNE   Diane Hart
SIDNEY   Alan Woolston
ETHEL   Diana Allen
OSCAR   Roland Culver
BUBBLES   Diana Hope
NORA   Diane Hart
DENIS   David Aylmer
WILBERFORCE   Roger Maxwell
DORIS   Diane Hart
CHLOE   Joan Benham
CAROLINE   Athene Seyler

Director: Anthony Quayle

The Deep Blue Sea

London: Duchess Theatre
Opening: 6 March 1952
Performances: 513

PHILIP WELCH   David Aylmer
MRS ELTON   Barbara Leake
ANN WELCH   Ann Walford
HESTER COLLYER   Peggy Ashcroft

MR MILLER   Peter Illing
WILLIAM COLLYER   Roland Culver
FREDDIE PAGE   Kenneth More
JACKIE JACKSON   Raymond Francis
Director: Frith Banbury

New York: Morosco Theatre
Opening: 5 November 1952
Performances: 132

PHILIP WELCH   John Merivale
MRS ELTON   Betty Sinclair
ANN WELCH   Stella Andrew
HESTER COLLYER   Margaret Sullavan
MR MILLER   Herbert Berghof
WILLIAM COLLYER   Alan Webb
FREDDIE PAGE   James Hanley
JACKIE JACKSON   Felix Deebank
Director: Frith Banbury

The Sleeping Prince

London: Phoenix Theatre
Opening: 5 November 1953
Performances: 274

PETER NORTHBROOK   Richard Wattis
MARY   Vivien Leigh
THE MAJOR-DOMO   Paul Hardwick
THE REGENT   Laurence Olivier
THE KING   Jeremy Spenser
THE GRAND DUCHESS   Martita Hunt
THE COUNTESS   Rosamund Greenwood
THE BARONESS   Daphne Newton
THE ARCHDUCHESS   Elaine Inescort
THE PRINCESS   Nicola Delman
FOOTMEN   Peter Barkworth, Angus Mackay, Terence Owen
Director: Laurence Olivier

New York: Coronet Theatre
Opening: 1 November 1956
Performances: 60

PETER NORTHBROOK   Rex O'Malley
MARY   Barbara Bel Geddes

THE MAJOR-DOMO   Ronald Dawson
THE REGENT   Michael Redgrave
THE KING   Johnny Stewart
THE GRAND DUCHESS   Cathleen Nesbitt
THE COUNTESS   Nydia Westman
THE BARONESS   Betty Sinclair
THE ARCHDUCHESS   Neff Jerome
THE PRINCESS   Elwin Stock
BUTLER   Sorrell Booke
FIRST FOOTMAN   William Major
SECOND FOOTMAN   Martin Waldron
Director: Michael Redgrave

Separate Tables

London: St James's Theatre
Opening: 22 September 1954
Performances: 726

Table by the Window
MABEL   Marion Fawcett
LADY MATHESON   Jane Eccles
MRS RAILTON-BELL   Phyllis Neilson-Terry
MISS MEACHAM   May Hallatt
DOREEN   Priscilla Morgan
MR FOWLER   Aubrey Mather
MRS SHANKLAND   Margaret Leighton
MISS COOPER   Beryl Measor
MR MALCOLM   Eric Portman
CHARLES STRATTON   Basil Henson
JEAN TANNER   Patricia Raine

Table Number Seven
JEAN STRATTON   Patricia Raine
CHARLES STRATTON   Basil Henson
MAJOR POLLOCK   Eric Portman
MR FOWLER   Aubrey Mather
MISS COOPER   Beryl Measor
MRS RAILTON-BELL   Phyllis Neilson-Terry
MISS RAILTON-BELL   Margaret Leighton
LADY MATHESON   Jane Eccles
MISS MEACHAM   May Hallatt
MABEL   Marion Fawcett
DOREEN   Priscilla Morgan

341

Director: Peter Glenville

New York: Music Box Theatre
Opening: 25 October 1956
Performances: 322

Table by the Window
MABEL   Georgia Harvey
LADY MATHESON   Jane Eccles
MRS RAILTON-BELL   Phyllis Neilson-Terry
MISS MEACHAM   May Hallatt
DOREEN   Helena Carroll
MR FOWLER   William Podmore
MRS SHANKLAND   Margaret Leighton
MISS COOPER   Beryl Measor
MR MALCOLM   Eric Portman
CHARLES STRATTON   Donald Harron
JEAN TANNER   Ann Hillary

Table Number Seven
JEAN STRATTON   Ann Hillary
CHARLES STRATTON   Donald Harron
MAJOR POLLOCK   Eric Portman
MR FOWLER   William Podmore
MISS COOPER   Beryl Measor
MRS RAILTON-BELL   Phyllis Neilson-Terry
MISS RAILTON-BELL   Margaret Leighton
LADY MATHESON   Jane Eccles
MISS MEACHAM   May Hallatt
MABEL   Georgia Harvey
DOREEN   Helena Carroll
Director: Peter Glenville

Variation on a Theme

London: Globe Theatre
Opening: 8 May 1958
Performances: 132

ROSE   Margaret Leighton
HETTIE   Jean Anderson
RON   Jeremy Brett
KURT   George Pravda
FIONA   Felicity Ross

342

MONA   Mavis Villiers
ADRIAN   Lawrence Dalzell
SAM   Michael Goodliffe
Director: John Gielgud

Ross

London: Theatre Royal, Haymarket
Opening: 12 May 1960
Performances: 762

FLIGHT-LIEUTENANT STOKER   Geoffrey Colvile
FLIGHT-SERGEANT THOMPSON   Dervis Ward
AIRCRAFTMAN PARSONS   Peter Bayliss
AIRCRAFTMAN EVANS   John Southworth
AIRCRAFTMAN DICKINSON   Gerald Harper
AIRCRAFTMAN ROSS   Alec Guinness
FRANKS (THE LECTURER)   James Grout
GENERAL ALLENBY   Harry Andrews
RONALD STORRS   Anthony Nicholls
COLONEL BARRINGTON   Leon Sinden
AUDA ABU TAYI   Mark Dignam
TURKISH MILITARY GOVERNOR   Geoffrey Keen
HAMED   Robert Arnold
RASHID   Charles Laurence
A TURKISH CAPTAIN   Basil Hoskins
A TURKISH SERGEANT   Raymond Adamson
A BRITISH CORPORAL   John Trenaman
A.D.C.   Ian Clark
A PHOTOGRAPHER   Antony Kenway
AN AUSTRALIAN SOLDIER   William Feltham
FLIGHT-LIEUTENANT HIGGINS   Peter Cellier
GROUP-CAPTAIN WOOD   John Stuart
Director: Glen Byam Shaw

Joie de Vivre

London: Queen's Theatre
Opening: 14 July 1960
Performances: 4

KENNETH LAKE   Brook Williams
BRIAN CURTIS   Donald Sinden
HON. ALAN HOWARD   Barry Ingham
MARIANNE   Anna Sharkey

343

MONSIEUR MAINGOT   Harold Kasket
LT.-CMDR. ROGERS   Terence Alexander
DIANA LAKE   Joanne Rigby
KIT NEILAN   Robin Hunter
JACQUELINE MAINGOT   Jill Martin
LORD HEYBROOK   James Land
CHI-CHI   Joan Heal
TERESE   Lilian Mowbray
PIERRE   John Leslie
GASTON   Glenn Wilcox
MAYOR   John Moore
Director: William Chapell
Music by: Robert Stolz
Lyrics by: Paul Dehn

Ross

New York: Eugene O'Neill Theatre
Opening: 26 December 1961
Performances: 159

FLIGHT-LIEUTENANT STOKER   Robert Milli
FLIGHT-SERGEANT THOMPSON   Ted Gunther
AIRCRAFTMAN PARSONS   Bill Glover
AIRCRAFTMAN DICKINSON   Francis Bethencourt
AIRCRAFTMAN ROSS   John Mills
FRANKS (the lecturer)   Kenneth Ruta
GENERAL ALLENBY   John Williams
RONALD STORRS   Anthony Nicholls
COLONEL BARRINGTON   Court Benson
AUDA ABU TAYI   Paul Sparer
TURKISH MILITARY GOVERNOR   Geoffrey Keen
HAMED   Cal Bellini
RASHID   Joseph Della Sorte
A TURKISH CAPTAIN   Eric Van Nuys
A TURKISH SERGEANT   Thomas Newman
A BRITISH CORPORAL   Del Tenney
A.D.C.   Nicolas Coster
A PHOTOGRAPHER   Scott Graham
AN AUSTRALIAN SOLDIER   John Hallow
FLIGHT-LIEUTENANT HIGGINS   John Valentine
GROUP-CAPTAIN WOOD   James Craven
Director: Glen Byam Shaw

344

Man and Boy

London: Queens Theatre
Opening: 4 September 1963
Performances: 69 (limited run)

CAROL PENN   Alice Kennedy Turney
BASIL ANTHONY   Barry Justice
GREGOR ANTONESCU   Charles Boyer
SVEN JOHNSON   Geoffrey Keen
MARK L. HERRIS   Austin Willis
DAVID BEESTON   William Smithers
COUNTESS ANTONESCU   Jane Downs
Director: Michael Benthall

New York: Brooks Atkinson Theatre
Opening: 12 November 1963
Performances: 54

CAROL PENN   Louise Sorel
BASIL ANTHONY   Barry Justice
GREGOR ANTONESCU   Charles Boyer
SVEN JOHNSON   Geoffrey Keen
MARK L. HERRIS   Austin Willis
DAVID BEESTON   William Smithers
COUNTESS ANTONESCU   Jane Downs
Director: Michael Benthall

A Bequest to the Nation

London: Theatre Royal, Haymarket
Opening: 23 September 1970
Performances: 124

GEORGE MATCHAM SNR   Ewan Roberts
KATHERINE MATCHAM   Jean Harvey
BETSY   Deborah Watling
GEORGE MATCHAM JNR   Michael Wardle
EMILY   Una Brandon Jones
FRANCES, LADY NELSON   Leueen MacGrath
NELSON   Ian Holm
LORD BARHAM   A. J. Broan
EMMA HAMILTON   Zöe Caldwell
FRANCESCA   Marisa Merlini
LORD MINTO   Michael Aldridge
CAPTAIN HARDY   Brian Glover

REV WILLIAM NELSON   Geoffrey Edwards
SARAH NELSON   Eira Griffiths
HORATIO   Stuart Knee
CAPTAIN BLACKWOOD   Geoffrey Deevers
MIDSHIPMAN   Stuart Knee
FOOTMEN, SAILORS, MAIDS   Stanley Lloyd, Conrad Asquith, Graham Edwards, Chris Carbis, Deborah Watling, Alison Coleridge
Director: Peter Glenville

In Praise of Love

London: Duchess Theatre
Opening: 27 September 1973
Performances: 131

Before Dawn

THE BARON   Donald Sinden
THE LACKEY   Don Fellows
THE CAPTAIN   Richard Warwick
THE DIVA   Joan Greenwood

After Lydia

LYDIA CRUTTWELL   Joan Greenwood
SEBASTIAN CRUTTWELL   Donald Sinden
MARK WALTERS   Don Fellows
JOEY CRUTTWELL   Richard Warwick
Director: John Dexter

New York: Morosco Theatre
Opening: 10 December 1974
Performances: 199

In Praise of Love

LYDIA CRUTTWELL   Julie Harris
SEBASTIAN CRUTTWELL   Rex Harrison
MARK WALTERS   Martin Gabel
JOEY CRUTTWELL   Peter Burnell
Director: Fred Coe

346

Duologue

Adapted from television play *All on Her Own*
London: King's Head Theatre
Opening: February 1976
Performances: unknown—approx. 15

ROSEMARY   Barbara Jefford
Director: Stewart Trotter

Cause Célèbre

London: Her Majesty's Theatre
Opening: 4 July 1977
Performances: 282

ALMA RATTENBURY   Glynis Johns
FRANCIS RATTENBURY   Anthony Pedley
CHRISTOPHER   Matthew Ryan
IRENE RIGGS   Sheila Grant
GEORGE WOOD   Neil Dalglish
EDITH DAVENPORT   Helen Lindsay
JOHN DAVENPORT   Jeremy Hawk
TONY DAVENPORT   Adam Richardson
STELLA MORRISON   Angela Browne
RANDOLPH BROWN   Kevin Hart
JUDGE   Patrick Barr
O'CONNOR   Kenneth Griffith
CROOM-JOHNSON   Bernard Archard
CASSWELL   Darryl Forbes-Dawson
MONTAGU   Philip Bowen
CLERK OF THE COURT   David Glover
JOAN WEBSTER   Peggy Aitchison
SERGEANT BAGWELL   Anthony Pedley
PORTER   Anthony Howard
WARDER   David Masterman
CORONER   David Glover
Director: Robin Midgley

Rattigan's Principal Films

Early in his career Rattigan contributed to numerous screenplays uncredited. The following are the principal films he scripted once he became well known.
French Without Tears, 1939. Director: Anthony Asquith.

347

Quiet Wedding (with Anatole de Grunwald), 1940. Director: Anthony Asquith.

The Day Will Dawn (US: *The Avengers*) (with Anatole de Grunwald and Patrick Kirwan), 1942. Director: Harold French.

Uncensored (with Wolfgang Wilhelm and Rodney Ackland), 1942. Director: Anthony Asquith.

English Without Tears (US: *Her Man Gilbey*) (with Anatole de Grunwald), 1944. Director: Anthony Asquith.

Journey Together, 1945. Director: John Boulting.

The Way to the Stars (US: *Johnny in the Clouds*) (with Anatole de Grunwald), 1945. Director: Anthony Asquith.

Brighton Rock (with Graham Greene), 1947. Director: John Boulting.

While the Sun Shines (with Anatole de Grunwald), 1947. Director: Anthony Asquith.

Bond Street (with Anatole de Grunwald and Rodney Ackland), 1948. Director: Gordon Parry.

The Winslow Boy (with Anatole de Grunwald), 1948. Director: Anthony Asquith.

The Browning Version, 1951, Director: Anthony Asquith. Rattigan won the 1951 Cannes Film Festival award for Best Screenplay.

The Sound Barrier (US: *Breaking the Sound Barrier*), 1952. Director: David Lean.

The Final Test, 1953. Director: Anthony Asquith.

The Man Who Loved Redheads, 1955. Director: Harold French.

The Deep Blue Sea, 1955. Director: Anatole Litvak.

The Prince and the Showgirl, 1957. Director: Laurence Olivier.

Separate Tables (with John Gay), 1958. Director: Delbert Mann.

The VIPs, 1963. Director: Anthony Asquith.

The Yellow Rolls Royce, 1965. Director: Anthony Asquith.

Goodbye Mr Chips, 1969. Director: Herbert Ross.

Bequest to the Nation, 1973. Director: James Cellan Jones.

Rattigan's Original Television Scripts

The Final Test First transmission, BBC, 29 July 1951. Director: Royston Morley.

Heart to Heart First transmission, BBC, 6 December 1962. Director: Alvin Rakoff.

Ninety Years On First transmission BBC, 29 November 1964. Producer: Michael Mills.

Nelson—A Portrait in Miniature. First transmission ATV, 21 March 1966. Director: Stuart Burge.

All on Her Own. First transmission, BBC 2, 25 September 1968. Director: Hal Burton.

High Summer (adapted from earlier, unperformed stage play). First transmission, Thames Television, 1972. Director: Peter Duguid.

Nijinsky Unproduced.

Radio

Cause Célèbre. First broadcast BBC Radio Four, 27 October 1975. Producer: Norman Wright.

Index

357

358